The *Nosferatu* Story

ALSO BY ROLF GIESEN

Nazi Propaganda Films: A History and Filmography
(2003; softcover 2008)

*Special Effects Artists: A Worldwide Biographical
Dictionary of the Pre-Digital Era with a Filmography*
(2008; softcover 2014)

*Chinese Animation: A History and Filmography,
1922–2012* (2015)

BY ROLF GIESEN AND J. P. STORM

*Animation Under the Swastika: A History
of Trickfilm in Nazi Germany, 1933–1945* (2012)

ALL FROM MCFARLAND

The *Nosferatu* Story

*The Seminal Horror Film,
Its Predecessors
and Its Enduring Legacy*

ROLF GIESEN

McFarland & Company, Inc., Publishers
Jefferson, North Carolina

ISBN (print) 978-1-4766-7298-4
ISBN (ebook) 978-1-4766-3533-0

LIBRARY OF CONGRESS AND BRITISH LIBRARY
CATALOGUING DATA ARE AVAILABLE

© 2019 Rolf Giesen. All rights reserved

No part of this book may be reproduced or transmitted in any form or by any means, electronic or mechanical, including photocopying or recording, or by any information storage and retrieval system, without permission in writing from the publisher.

Front cover: Max Schreck as Count Orlok the Nosferatu. Original watercolor allegedly made in 1922 from a film still and signed by Albin Grau (courtesy Gerd J. Pohl and Martin van Elten)

Manufactured in the United States of America

*McFarland & Company, Inc., Publishers
Box 611, Jefferson, North Carolina 28640
www.mcfarlandpub.com*

Table of Contents

Introduction: 100 Years After World War I	1
It Came from Max Reinhardt	5
Paul Wegener and Hanns Heinz Ewers: The Godfathers of German Film Fantasy	7
Conrad Veidt and *The Cabinet of Dr. Caligari*	21
Dr. Jekyll, Murnau and Dracula	31
Dracula in Germany: Henrik Galeen and the Screenplay for *Nosferatu*	35
The Storyline	41
Casting a Man Named "Shock"	62
Shooting *Nosferatu* in Kafka's Castle	71
Premiere and Contemporary Reviews	76
Frater Pacitius, Aleister Crowley's Berlin Disciple	80
Great Plans and Nightly Hallucinations: The Ill-Fated Prana Film Company	83
Fritz Lang Hits It Big—And Murnau Carries On	89
The Vampire Jew and the Curse of Anti-Semitism	103
How the Golem Came Into the World and Fought the Nazis	111
The Revival of *Nosferatu*	113
Christopher Lee vs. Klaus Kinski	119
Shadow of the Vampire: The Legacy	131
Appendix: Bios of the Crew and Cast of Nosferatu	137
The Nosferatu *Filmography*	155
Filmography II: The Silent Era of German Expressionist, Fantasy and Alchemical Films	169
Chapter Notes	211
Bibliography	215
Index	217

Introduction

> Nosferatu. Doesn't the name sound like the midnight call of the death bird?
> Beware of uttering it, or the pictures of life will turn to pale shadows, nightmares will rise up from the heart and feed on your blood.—Title Card of Act 1, *Nosferatu* (1922)

100 Years After World War I

More than half a century ago, I saw an eerie film clip on the small screen of a German TV set and was immediately bitten, fascinated by the supernatural quality of that horrifying specter. How could a 12-year-old kid in those days possibly escape that phantom? Back then, horror films on German television were as rare as pterodactyl's eggs. I was able to see the complete movie for the first time a few years later in Duisburg, where it had been brought back from the land of dead cinema and projected on its ancestral home, the Big Screen. Little did I know back then that every aspect of this mesmerizing movie, *Nosferatu: A Symphony of Horror*, was linked to the shadow world of the occult and would haunt and hunt me with mysteries and questions far more disturbing than I could have imagined.

In 2000, the movie *Shadow of the Vampire*, produced by Nicholas Cage and Jeff Levine, claimed to be an account of what happened when director Friedrich Wilhelm Murnau and cohorts filmed *Nosferatu*. At first glance, the background story of filmmaking seemed to have been depicted accurately, with the names of persons in front of and behind the camera properly recorded. John Malkovich played Murnau; the director, Cary Elwes was Fritz Arno Wagner, the cinematographer; John Aden was Henrik Galeen, the screenwriter; Udo Kier played the pivotal role of Albin Grau, producer and designer, although his part was not properly exploited by the filmmakers. At least all important characters turned up one way or another. The research being done, however, was merely superficial. Stephen Katz, the screenwriter, who died of prostate cancer five years later, resorted to the idea that the actor who portrayed the vampire must have been a vampire himself: Max Schreck, whose last name translates into English as "fear," "shock" or "terror." Willem Dafoe, a great actor with the shortcoming of being only 5'9" compared to the 6'3" of the original silent actor, was Oscar-nominated for Best Supporting Actor. (Benicio del Toro won.) But the imagination of both Katz as well as director E. Elias Merhige was rather restrained, considering all the quixotic facts that contributed to the actual production in 1921.

Nosferatu was born out of the meat grinder of death that was World War I. Like *Lucifer Rising*, a short film made by occultist Kenneth Anger, *Nosferatu* rose from the dying breaths of young soldiers murdered to protect the castles of the rich and wealthy, the descendants of Nosferatu the vampire. Screenwriter Henrik Galeen reflected in *Nosferatu* the stench of the naked truth that hung in the air in Europe after World War I. "The Great War," as it was called, the "War to End All Wars," was no more than a bloodsucking feast between empires of aristocrats and industrialists. It ended a hundred years ago in the armistice of November 1918. When *Nosferatu* was released, everybody tried to assume that such a war should never happen again and that vampires as well as arms and guns should rest in peace. Hitler was no more than local size. No big danger coming from him. Little did I know about the hidden anti–Semitic ingredients of what was one of my favorite horror films. When I became aware, I was ashamed that I was so bedazzled by the praise of other film historians that I liked it all the way through.

I am indebted to Hanns Eckelkamp, founder of Atlas Film Duisburg, who re-released that movie 60 years ago; to Horst Schäfer who let me see it for the first time, and to my former colleagues at Deutsche Kinemathek (German Cinematheque) who helped me with information and stills, notably Peter Mänz; to the late witnesses of German silents, cameraman H. O. Schulze and art director Fritz Maurischat; to the late Curt Siodmak, Forrest J Ackerman, Paul Hubschmid, Christopher Lee and Ferdy Mayne (who became Count Von Krolock in *Dance of the Vampires* after Roman Polanski had seen him with bloodshot eyes one evening at a party); to Polanski, whom I guided through the opening of Berlin's Film Museum; to Italian director Luigi Cozzi who worked with makeshift *Nosferatu* Klaus Kinski in Venice; and most of all to my dear wife Anna Khan for her advice and patience. I have to thank Mike Hankin and Robert Blalack, in the 1970s an Academy Award–winning VFX artist, who both took time to review my manuscript and suggest corrections and changes.

More grateful thanks are due to Christian Dörge, Jens Geutebrück, Caroline Hagen Hall, and Michael Skowronski (*Deutsche Kinemathek*), Hanns-Georg Rodek (*Die Welt*), Ivo Scheloske (*Anolis Entertainment*), Uwe Sommerlad and Philipp Stiasny, Wolfgang Klaue and Stefan Strauss for contributing stills and information.

Thanks to Holger Delfs who recreated the Nosferatu mask on himself, and to puppeteer Gerd J. Pohl, who granted us access to four yet unknown ultra-rare *Nosferatu* watercolors allegedly done in 1922 by the film's co-producer and designer, Albin Grau, based on film stills. Pohl also agreed to share his view on Werner Herzog's *Nosferatu* remake. I am still convinced that you cannot remake a film like that in the same style. You shouldn't. It was a different time period: the period of Expressionist cinema. But certainly Pohl is an honorary scholar. There is a noteworthy relationship between him and Murnau: When grave robbers invaded Murnau's crypt at the Stahnsdorf Cemetery near Berlin in July 2015, opened a metal coffin and made off with the head from Murnau's embalmed body, it was Pohl who put a bounty on them. The culprits are still on the loose.

While the structure of Expressionist theater consisted of static scenes, the antithesis of a well-made play, the characters bore many similarities to cartoon figures: They were stereotypes, grotesque caricatures, their inner psychological reality revealed by external means. This exaggerated style can be studied especially in German silent films like *The Cabinet of Dr. Caligari, The Golem* and *Nosferatu*. Sometimes, as in long shots, actors moved in patterns to correspond with the settings, almost dancing or gliding on tiptoe along a wall as Conrad Veidt as Cesare the somnambulist did in a famous *Caligari* scene. This type of filmmaking was deliberately copied in early American horror films such as *Dracula* and *Frankenstein* that owe a lot to German Expressionism. It was a deliberate departure from the realism of Stanislavski. Expressionist film stars endeavored to overact and adopt the stilted, mechanical movements of a puppet: a reversion to the world of animism and nature spirits. For Murnau, it was a balancing act because he would stylize not only the way his actors performed but nature itself.

Today, in the era of digital imagery, we have a different approach to acting which strives for utmost authenticity and less stylization. So you cannot repeat that 1922 Murnau touch. I felt lucky that it was Max Schreck giving me the shivers and not what followed after World War II although I enjoyed Hammer films since Christopher Lee and Peter Cushing, by today's standards, are fairy tale too.

Film critic Roger Ebert wrote in 2001 that *Nosferatu*'s eerie power only increases with age. We shouldn't forget that this is a movie that, by some legal machination, was ordered destroyed in the 1920s, the nitrate prints incinerated for all time. But it survived like the proverbial vampire despite being impaled. "Dracula *never ends*," Bela Lugosi said when interviewed by the Ship's Reporter, Jack Morgan, in 1951 on his return from Britain. "I don't know if I should call it a fortune or a curse but it never ends."

You cannot hold a good vampire down, and thanks to relentless scholars and film historians like Siegfried Kracauer and Lotte H. Eisner, it is even acknowledged by people who otherwise never care to go and see a "horror movie."

The shadow of Nosferatu approaching and threatening the unlucky Thomas Hutter (Gustav von Wangenheim) in F.W. Murnau's silent vampire film (courtesy Christian Dörge, Apex Verlag).

In the hands of a less inspired or visionary director, *Nosferatu* might have turned into some freak show that provoked giggles instead of dread, similar to *Abbott and Costello Meet Frankenstein, ... Meet the Invisible Man, ... Meet Dr. Jekyll and Mr. Hyde and ... Meet the Mummy.* But in the hands of a sensitive romanticist like F.W. Murnau, a perfectionist of orchestrating actors and visuals and one of Germany's great Silent Era directors, a true artist with extraordinary skills, it kept its eerie, uncanny quality (and hidden dangers).

Alas, when my generation became interested in *Nosferatu,* there was almost no firsthand account of the shooting of that milestone movie. In 1921, at the last shooting day, some Berlin reporters were invited to the studio, saw a scene with Schreck as the vampire filmed and talked to him. That's it. By the early '70s, most of the main participants had passed away: Murnau, Galeen, cameramen Krampf and Wagner, actors Schreck, Granach, Schnell and Gottowt (who was murdered by an SS man). We believed Greta Schröder, the actress who portrayed the heroine, dead but she was still alive and literally living round the corner. And her co-star, although round the corner too, might as well have been living on the Moon: He was in East Berlin. Nobody realized then the importance of a man named Albin Grau, who died in early spring 1971 somewhere in Bavaria. Max Nemetz, who played the ship's captain, passed away a few months later in a town in the Black Forest. The same year, in Düsseldorf, I was told by friends that they knew an old still photographer who was involved in the production. I eagerly wanted to meet him but I didn't insist strongly enough. To this day I don't know if the friends told the truth or just wanted to kid me. The only way to reconstruct the story was by way of documents. What other scholars thought or wrote about it was mostly their personal opinion. They remained unimpressed by thorough research and by horror, science fiction and fantasy, the "genres" that built German Cinema Expressionism.

Now this is the true account—or at least part of it—of the greatest vampire movie of them all, imbedded in a chronology of the German fantasy cinema of that time period. Come with me as I attempt to pry open the tombs of the real stories hidden in the darkness surrounding the birth and death of *the* most dangerously hypnotic vampire, a catalyst that propelled silent German fantasy cinema onto the world stage. I have personally translated excerpts from texts in German to English.

It Came from Max Reinhardt

When cinema left its infancy, producers everywhere went looking for name stars—actresses and actors who could only be found on the legitimate stage. But to many stage actors, the "nickelodeon" or "flickers" were just cheap entertainment, beneath their notice.

Some thespians, however, fell for the seductive persuasions of producers who offered good money, not only to comedians who came from vaudeville like Chaplin, but to proper, studied stage actors. In America, the lowbrow ban was broken in 1912 when Adolph Zukor's Famous Players Film Company, promising in its advertisements "Famous Players in Famous Plays," released the French *Les Amours de la Reine* starring Sarah Bernhardt.

Germany's fledgling movie industry found a passionate advocate in Max Reinhardt. He was born Maximilian Goldmann on September 9, 1873, in the spa town Baden, Lower Austria, to a Jewish merchant family. His family moved to Vienna where the boy frequently attended the Hofburg Theater. After landing his first job as a bank clerk, he took acting lessons in his spare time. He made his debut on a private stage in Vienna in 1890. In 1894, invited by Otto Brahm (1856–1912), theater manager, director and critic, he came to Berlin. Brahm, striving for realism in German theater, had become general manager of Deutsches Theater (German Theater). As Brahm's "discovery," Reinhardt was featured on the Berlin stage, usually playing an old man. In 1901, Reinhardt co-founded a cabaret, Schall und Rauch (Sound and Smoke), and became head of Kleines Theater (Little Theater) and Neues Theater (New Theater, today: Berliner Ensemble, Schiffbauerdamm). In 1905, he left his mark as Brahm's successor and general manager (intendant) of Deutsches Theater. He initiated plays of sometimes gargantuan scale, with hordes of extras populating elaborate sets, in what was called director's theater (Regietheater).

Influenced by the work of August Strindberg and others, his objective was a theatrical *Gesamtkunstwerk,* a whole unified work: a harmony of stage design, costumes, language, music and choreography. In 1919, as a crowning achievement, he opened *Grosses Schauspielhaus (Great Playhouse)* in the former Circus Schumann that became the Circus Reinhardt where he staged Shakespeare as well as Greek plays. Reinhardt cast the shadow of a titan across the theatrical world.

In 1910, two years before Zukor released the game-changing Sarah Bernhardt picture, Reinhardt directed a pantomime film titled *Sumurŭn* and subsequently established his own film company. On the eve of World War I, in 1913 and 1914 respectively, he directed two films for producer Paul Davidson, head of PAGU (Projektions-Aktiengesellschaft "Union") in Berlin Tempelhof: a fantasy play exploring an encounter with Greek gods on a remote Italian island, *Die Insel der Seligen (The Island of Bliss),* and *Eine Venezianische*

Nacht (*Venetian Nights*) with Alfred Abel, later to become Joh Fredersen, the mastermind of *Metropolis*. Among the *Island of Bliss* actresses was a young Greta Schröder (as Psyche), who later shot to fame as the woman who conquered Nosferatu. Cameraman Karl Freund would win adulation in Berlin and Neubabelsberg, where he photographed *Metropolis*, and in Hollywood, where he shot *Dracula* and directed Boris Karloff in *The Mummy*.

If Reinhardt, the master, was not ashamed to work for Davidson and the movies, neither were his performers, among them Emil Jannings and Ernst Lubitsch, who started as an actor before he made his way to the director's chair. Davidson's movie company was eventually devoured by the tentacles of UFA (Universum Film Aktiengesellschaft). The dynamic and then shattered Davidson, who had produced 39 movies directed by Lubitsch, committed suicide in 1927.

In 1933, Reinhardt left Germany. He first moved back to Austria and in 1934 arrived in the United States. After staging *A Midsummer Night's Dream* at the Hollywood Bowl, he once more turned to filmmaking. At Jack L. Warner's Burbank Studios he co-directed an expensive film version of the play with Wilhelm (William) Dieterle. Warner Bros. pronounced: "Three Centuries in The Making! An immortal literary classic becomes a triumph of the ages!"

After that Reinhardt reportedly toyed with the idea of casting Bela "Dracula" Lugosi as Mephistopheles in a version of *Faust*. (In Murnau's silent *Faust*, Emil Jannings played the Devil.) Alas, most of Reinhardt's films failed with reviewers and at the box office. Reinhardt, a great theater impresario and a disappointed movie director, died on October 31, 1943, at the age of 70, in New York City. Ironically, several of the directors who trained under him went on to become famous for their Hollywood movies: Dieterle, Lubitsch, Paul Leni, Otto Preminger—and Friedrich Wilhelm Murnau.

Reinhardt actors and actresses also triumphed on the screen: Conrad Veidt, Werner Krauss, Elisabeth Bergner, Heinrich George and Gustaf Gründgens. In Vienna there still is a Reinhardt Seminary founded by Max Reinhardt. Among those who trained there were Senta Berger, O.W. Fischer, Paul Hubschmid, Gertraud Jesserer, Klaus Löwitsch, Winnie Markus, Nadja Tiller, Elisabeth Trissenaar, Bernhard Wicki and Christoph Waltz.

The influence of Reinhardt's stage work permeated the silent German cinema generating what now looks like a "stagey" quality, perhaps because, as Reinhardt confessed, "I believe in the immortality of the theater, it is a most joyous place to hide, for all those who have secretly put their childhood in their pockets and run off and away with it, to play on to the end of their days."

Without Reinhardt's influence, there never would have been a *Nosferatu*, at least not made the way we admire it. The cast came from Reinhardt's actor stable: Schröder, Gustav von Wangenheim, Alexander Granach, John Gottowt and the luminous Max Schreck. Even the screenwriter, Henrik Galeen, was a devoted Reinhardt acolyte.

But still a mediator for the vision of *Nosferatu* was missing, someone who would recognize the value of speculative fiction on screen…

Paul Wegener and Hanns Heinz Ewers: The Godfathers of German Film Fantasy

Apart from some gruesome fairy tales recorded by the Brothers Grimm, the story of fantasy tradition in Germany began with Faust and all the Faustian characters that followed.

While still at grammar school, Paul Wegener attended a performance of Goethe's FAUST in Königsberg: "My decision to become an actor stood firm when I was at Obertertia [the fifth year of German secondary school]. After a FAUST performance I declared categorically that one day I would play the red guy with the feather on the head!"[1]

Wegener was born on December 11, 1874, in Arnoldsdorf, West Prussia, then part of the German Empire. (Today, under the name Jarantowice, it is part of Poland.) He began legal studies but dropped out to become an actor. In 1906, he joined Max Reinhardt's troupe.

He didn't join the movies just as an actor, Wegener explained, he was interested in the art of film in general. It was a time when many cinematic tricks were invented for the infant medium: partly adopted from photography, working with invisible wires and mirrors. Persons would disappear in false bottoms or melt into thin air by stopping the camera. The film was rewound, the camera cranked faster or slower, stop motion was created by shooting frame by frame. Georges Méliès and Segundo de Chomón became experts in the mindblowing field of cinematic make-believe.

Wegener became enthusiastic and tasted blood:

> The mysterious possibilities of the camera staggered my imagination. I invented the fable *Der Student von Prag* (*The Student of Prague*) because here was a chance to play opposite myself. I suggested the story to the Bioscop Company. They referred me to their dramaturge, and that was good because it was nobody else than Hanns Heinz Ewers.[2]

Paul Wegener's fantasy films wouldn't have been made without Ewers's input. It was Ewers, a novelist with dubious background, who got him into moving pictures.

From Ewers to Hitler

Siegfried Kracauer titled his well-known work about early German film art *From Caligari to Hitler* (Princeton University Press, 1947), yet one has to review this title with caution. However, if ever there was one author on German fantasy whose path led straight from Caligari to Hitler, it was Ewers (1871–1943):

> Already as a law student Ewers explored Berlin nightlife if he wasn't involved in bloody academic fencing. He attended spiritualist séances, researched in the entourage of social scientist Magnus Hirschfeld human bisexuality and, of course, the creative potential of drugs too. Many of his texts tell of psychedelic experiments, combined with sexual dissolutions, that often take place in exotic locations—like "Die Mamaloi," in which the first-person narrator—as pedophilic crook a true meanie—on Haiti gets mixed up with voodoo priests. [...]
>
> Allegedly Ewers himself once became a witness of a Haitian voodoo ceremony, where a child was sacrificed, although Ewers students aren't quite sure about the incident. [...] During his lifetime Ewers was famous and infamous equally. As a "German Edgar Allan Poe" he scored incredibly large editions of horror stories and novels...[3]

Ewers spent the early years of World War I in the United States. There, before the U.S. entered the war, he promoted propaganda for the German Empire and made the acquaintance of occultist Aleister Crowley, a soulmate, and Ernst Hanfstaengl, who later became a supporter of Hitler. After his return to Germany in 1920, he tried to get in touch with Walther Rathenau, the noted industrialist and statesman. After Rathenau was murdered in June 1922, Ewers turned his back on the Weimar Republic.

The Student of Prague

To please Wegener, Ewers compiled a *Doppelgänger* story. It contained elements of *Faust* and Adelbert von Chamisso's *Peter Schlemihl*.[4] Schlemihl was the man who sold his shadow to the devil for a bag of gold that never peters out, but the negative reaction of his fellow citizens to the missing shadow makes life miserable. Schlemihl becomes a homeless, outlawed traveler. Ewers's story also showed shades of E.T.A. Hoffmann, Germany's classic writer of spooky, fantastic yarn, and Edgar Allan Poe (*William Wilson*).

It's a story of Old Prague, around the year 1820. Balduin,[5] a poor student but the best fencer in town, sells his mirror image (and with it his soul) for the price of 100,000 guilders to an uncanny Jewish shylock (!) named Scapinelli, hoping for social advancement and prestige. Yet the mirror image hunts him like an evil demon. In a duel, the *Doppelgänger* kills Count Waldis, a rival for the hand of beautiful Countess Margit. To get rid of the mirror image, Balduin shoots it but only kills himself.

The Student of Prague was produced on a budget of 20,000 Reichsmark in the newly erected glass stage of the Bioscop Company in Neubabelsberg near Berlin, which had been dedicated the year before with the production of Asta Nielsen's *Der Totentanz* (*The Dance of*

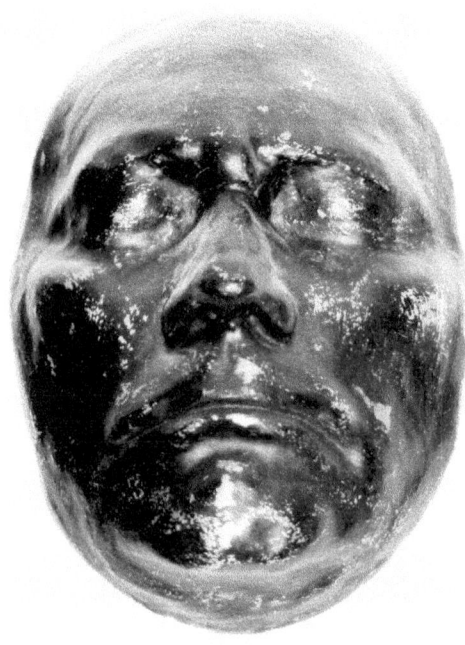

Life mask of actor Paul Wegener (courtesy Anna Khan).

Paul Wegener as *The Student of Prague* and his *Doppelgänger* (author's collection/Deutsche Kinemathek–Museum für Film und Fernsehen, Berlin).

Death, directed by Urban Gad). Featuring "original" locations in Prague, the film had opened—according to the gushing Wegener—"the way to fantastic art film in Germany."

Thanks to Guido Seeber's skilled cinematography, the *Doppelgänger* scenes turned out well enough to convince the audience. Seeber, Bioscop's chief cameraman, had to photograph Wegener twice on the same film strip for his dual role by putting a matte in front of the camera lens, then rewinding the film and using a counter-matte to create the split screen effect. According to Seeber, "For the first time I executed the split screen in the production of *Doppelgänger* shots well and truly, and as the technique proved flawless the impact of the film was incredible."[6]

German film director, producer and screenwriter Helmut Herbst provides a bit of trickfilm history.

> The term "*Doppelgänger*" shot was adopted from Romantic literature and defined a special photo technique that was already used in 19th century photography. The multiple exposure of a photographic plate by means of mattes and counter-mattes that were used either inside the camera in front of the plate or in the soft focus in front of the lens. The technique was described in the 1860s in photographic manuals. Méliès had transferred this field of "trick photography" onto the movies and executed mostly in front of black velvet. [...]
>
> There is no other field in the history of film where the dependence of aesthetic perception on technical inventions is so evident than in the history of special effects. The history of synthetic film is certainly the history of film technique.[7]

As Scandinavian films in those years were highly regarded, a Danish director, Stellan Rye, was hired to supervise the shooting of *The Student of Prague*. Ewers had read a screenplay written by Rye and invited him to Berlin. In World War I, Rye fought on the side of the Germans. He was wounded, resulting in French war imprisonment, and died on November 14, 1914. Rye's name isn't mentioned in the credits of the film. Instead we are told that the film was arranged in scenes by the author, Hanns Heinz Ewers. Author and actor are shown in a prologue "on the historical location of the story in Prague."

The premiere took place on August 22, 1913, in the Berlin *Mozart Lichtspiele* on Nollendorfplatz. Piano virtuoso Josef Weiss, a student of Franz Liszt, wrote the first specially composed film music for the premiere. *The Student of Prague* was advertised as the first attempt to portray "great, serious dramatic and literary art" on the screen.

Author Wolfgang Noa:

> The premiere was a rare success, the effect of the film, to which for the first time an individual score was composed, unprecedented. People yelled loudly, as Ludwig Gesek reported, and didn't dare to look to the screen because there appeared one and the same character twice. The impossible had become photographic truth in this movie. For the first time German film had acted in its own language. For the first time in the history of young cinematography, evidence was produced that moving images had their own artistic options and were able to do more than rather re-photograph scenes from the theatrical stage. *Der Student von Prag* was the first important art film in Germany that likewise picked up a motto that was typical for that time and for the art of those years: the split personality of a human who, driven by invisible powers, is not responsible for his deeds. It was a seminal work the world looked upon which engraved the name of its creator, Paul Wegener, forever in the history of film.[8]

This commentary is, of course, more than excessive but it became the founding stone of the legend of the so-called *Weltgeltung* (worldwide recognition) of German auteur films until today. Actually there were only a handful of German films that generated international attention. *Der Student von Prag* only belongs partly in that number. It was *too* German.

The original film was sold in 1915 by Deutsche Bioscop to Robert Glombeck Deutsche Filmindustrie KG. Ewers had been proud of producing a film with as few intertitles as possible. Glombeck, on the other hand, added for his 1926 "re-run," that was shown simultaneously in competition with a remake version starring Conrad Veidt in the dual role, 107 (!) new intertitles that were inserted right into the scenes.

For the restoration of the original film, alas, only this 1926 reissue was available as well as a shortened English-language export nitrate. Not until 1987 was the first reconstruction of the original version done under the supervision of Dr. Wilfried Kugel. The new digital reconstruction by the Film Museum Munich is based on the script by Ewers, the original piano score by Josef Weiss and contemporary reviews. The original length registered by German censors in 1913 was 1,548 meters, 85 minutes. Two minutes are still missing.

> *Der Student von Prag* introduced a topic to the screen that would become an obsession with German film: a pervasive and dreadful concern about the substratum of the self.[9]

Der Student von Prag wasn't the first *Doppelgänger* film and Wegener wasn't the first great actor in front of a film camera. That honor belongs to Albert Bassermann, who played a sort of poor man's Jekyll and Hyde in Max Mack's *Der Andere* (*The Other*) in late 1912: An attorney who denies the existence of split personality transforms into a criminal after a riding accident.

> Such *Doppelgänger* stories, which reflect basically phenomenological conditions, belong to the favorite topics of the romantics, particularly in the work of Jean Paul and E.T.A. Hoffmann. In them the notion—long before the systematic foundation of psychology—enunciated that the perception of a

subject as simple-identical is questionable, that psychic identity is endangered under contradictory social conditions.[10]

According to media scholar Michael Lommel, "The shadow is no time-transcending phenomenon. It has a history. It is the product of discourses and practices. In it meet systems of viewing, scientific and aesthetic forms of knowledge, ancient and new myths, ancient and new media."

An Actor and a Visionary

We are sure that it was Ewers who approached Paul Wegener. He already knew one of the actresses, Grete Berger. She was with Reinhardt and became Ewers's mistress. He supported her even after the end of their relationship. And *Der Student von Prag* was not Ewers and Wegener's first collaboration. This was, as we were told, *Der Verführte. Ein Soziales Drama in 2 Akten* (*The Seduced: A Social Drama in 2 Acts*. 1913; directors: Max Obal, Stellan Rye), but they were dissatisfied with the result and destroyed the film. Gerhard Lamprecht, film director and indefatigable chronicler of German silents,[11] disagreed and held the opinion that this film was indeed screened.

Like Wegener, Ewers had an affinity for the art of cinematography and opinions about its evolution, proclaiming, "Films of famous writers are the future of the cinema!" Ewers was lucky enough that the Deutsche Bioscop Company wanted to equal Nordische Films-Co. and Davidson's Projektions-AG "Union" and announced "Autorenfilme" (author's films), at a time when many productions didn't use elaborate screenplays.

In 1930, Ewers reflected:

In legendary film times, in 1913, one day a film man visited me. He had the outrageous idea to produce art films. His name was Erich Zeiske, he was the manager of the back-then largest production company, Deutsche Bioscop, which later transformed into Decla-Bioscop and merged with UFA. [...] Zeiske took me to his studio outside to Neubabelsberg, at that time one of the best in the world. Some small directors shot there with small actors and extras ten-minute films. The incredibly childish texts they wrote themselves. [...] The factory outside was in best order: two large stages, a laboratory, a large Oriental town under development, a crowd of regularly employed extras, splendid cameramen, among them Guido Seeber and his disciple Karl Hasselmann. Briefly speaking, there was everything needed; now, for the first time ever, a little wit and art should be brought into the film. A really lavish program was worked out and was realized as effectively as possible. Remember that back then no poet and no actor of reputation would step to the movies; they considered it as below their dignity. This egg was cracked by myself and Paul Wegener; after that, in a minimum amount of time, a number of first-class actors and writers signed with Bioscop. Within a few weeks I got: Wegener, [Alexander] Moissi, [Carl] Clewing, [Paul] Biensfeldt, [Lucie] Höflich, [Tilla] Durieux, [the sisters] Wiesenthal, besides that a number of superb artists of the Imperial Russian Ballet and of the Moscow Art Theater. Zeiske then got seriously ill and fell out for many months; so I took over overnight and managed the whole factory.[12]

According to the novelist and dramaturge Martin A. Bormann, who met Wegener on the occasion of his 50th birthday celebration on December 11, 1924, in the guildhall of Königsberg, Wegener's highly characteristic face wasn't formed Slavic, but Asiatic. Only the clear blue-gray eyes wouldn't fit in. Still a pupil, Wegener founded with some friends a drama club called Melpomene, and he wrote lyric poems and ballads. As an extra, although this was forbidden for pupils, he performed at the municipal theater. Pro forma, to oblige to the wishes of his father, a wealthy cloth manufacturer, he enrolled for law studies, philosophy and art history in Freiburg and Leipzig, but finally dropped out of university to fulfill his dream and become an actor.

His most important stations were the municipal theaters of Rostock (1895–96), Koblenz (1896–97), Bromberg (Elysium Theater, summer 1897), Aachen (1897–98), Lübeck (Wilhelm Theater, 1898), then back to the municipal theater of Aachen (1898–99), the Bernarts Theater of Aachen (summer 1899), municipal theater of Magdeburg (1899–1900), back to Bernarts Theater (summer 1900), Royal Court Theater Wiesbaden (1900–03) and the municipal theaters of Hamburg and Altona (1903–06). Eventually his colleague Rudolf Schildkraut would recommend him to Max Reinhardt, and so Wegener came to Deutsches Theater. In Berlin he played Richard III, Macbeth, Iago, Othello, Danton and Mephisto.

Wegener didn't participate in the production of *Nosferatu* but nevertheless he was close: *Nosferatu* screenwriter Henrik Galeen was an early associate of Wegener's (and Ewers's). John Gottowt, Scapinelli in Wegener's *The Student of Prague*, portrayed Prof. Bulwer, Max Schreck played a bit part in Wegener's *Ramper der Tiermensch* (*The Strange Case of Captain Ramper*), and above all Greta Schröder, *Nosferatu*'s female star, became Wegener's third wife.

In 1923, Wegener was persuaded to establish his own production company. Being a partisan of Buddhism, he decided the first production of his own to be *Lebende Buddhas* (*Living Buddhas*) and asked his friend, architect Hans Poelzig, who had transformed Circus Schumann into Reinhardt's Grosses Schauspielhaus, to build some lavish Tibetan sets in a dirigible hangar transformed into a film studio in Berlin Staaken. The story by Wegener and Hans Sturm, an actor who passed away in 1933, featured two British explorers who rescue a beautiful Tibetan girl (Danish actress Asta Nielsen) about to be sacrificed to a hideous goddess. But their attempt to escape to London is thwarted by a Buddha-like Lama priest (played by Wegener, who also directed). He commands the girl's return through his magical powers. In his 1927 book *Der Trickfilm in seinen grundsätzlichen Möglichkeiten* (*The Trickfilm in Its Fundamental Principles*), cinematographer Guido Seeber explained the technique employed to produce the movie's most impressive effects shot in which Wegener's Buddha head rises gigantically on the horizon and guides an ocean liner with the sheer power of his eyes:

> For the execution of this problem, a method was used which was already described in French literature as early as 1912. A person garbed in dark clothes is filmed against an entirely white background. From this shot a positive is printed which shows a dark person in front of an entirely transparent background. If this master positive is placed directly in front of a dupe negative—emulsion to emulsion with both strips running in bipack fashion through the camera—in addition to the objects of the now-filmed scene, the scene of the positive is also copied onto the dupe negative. In our case, the ship was filmed as it crossed against a cloudless sky. From this shot, as clear and as transparent as possible a negative was printed. Buddha's head was supposed to rise at the horizon line. To accomplish this, there was a white background which consisted of two parts. One was only as high as the horizon line of the previously shot sea picture, which was useful for hiding the body of the actor rising in the rear. About two and a half feet behind was the second white background which—as seen from the front—formed with the other part one big equally white plain. This white background was illuminated considerably from the front to achieve, by reflection of strong light, the printing of the bipack-run master positive. When the liner appeared in the positive, behind the lower white wall, the actor's head arose looking upon the crossing ship.

For a scene in which the Lama priest walked above the water, a traveling matte was employed.

Nosferatu (Max Schreck) aboard the doomed ship (courtesy Christian Dörge, Apex Verlag).

Despite its fantastic effects shots and sets, *Living Buddhas* was way too bizarre to become a success. It was rarely screened and turned out to be a costly failure. A broken Wegener, thinking that he had agonized the revengeful gods from the Far East, set out on a pilgrimage to Constantinople and Asia Minor, and after this hegira returned to a starring role in a Metro-Goldwyn picture *The Magician*, inspired by W. Somerset Maugham's eponymous 1908 novel. The film was produced and directed by Rex Ingram in his studios in Nice, France, assisted by a very young Michael Powell. Metro-Goldwyn's tagline for the film promised, "Bringing a Thousand Thrills and Mysteries Never Seen on the Screen!" The title character, portrayed by Paul Wegener with rolling eyes, could be nobody else than Aleister Crowley. Indeed, Crowley considered the idea of suing them. The unholy British occultist and big-mouthed charlatan also played an invisible part in the production of *Nosferatu*.

The Myth of the Man of Clay

The myth of the artificial man was a stimulus to many authors and filmmakers in the realm of the fantastic. Wegener became interested in the Talmudian legend of the Golem for his next screen entry.

Originally the word "golem" meant "earth seed," "unformed glob." In Talmud, it becomes a comprehensive term for all that is shapeless and incomplete. In the 12th century, however, the Golem transforms into a being that can be created by magic. German cabalists wrote about it, and we find comments in the Book Jezirah. The colossus of clay is brought to life and destroyed by the word, by the power of letters: "In the beginning was the Word…." By creating such a Golem, humans infringe the commandment "Thou shalt not make unto thee any graven image, or any likeness [of any thing that is] in heaven above, or that [is] in the earth beneath, or that [is] in the water under the earth" [Exodus 20.4–6].

In the 15th and 16th century, the legend infiltrated less educated social classes. Thus the Golem became a popular character: a real, distinct creature. The Word didn't become flesh and made his dwelling among us but became—so to speak—*clay*.

In literature, the Golem first appeared in the work of Jakob Grimm (*Zeitung für Einsiedler*, 1808), then Achim von Arnim (*Isabella von Ägypten*, 1812), E.T.A. Hoffmann (*Die Geheimnisse*, 1822) and Annette von Droste-Hülshoff (*The Golems*: Poems, 1844), all German authors.

The fable of the Golem allegedly created by the Maharal of Prague, Rabbi Judah Loew ben Bezalel (born between 1512 and 1526–1609), was conceived in early 19th century Prague, maybe as an answer to the age of enlightenment. There is no evidence that the real Rabbi Loew, a renowned Talmudic scholar and mystic, ever tinkered with giving life to a creature of clay. It's sort of a modern-day fairy tale that this colossus created to be a servant opposed its master and that there was no other chance than to destroy it.[13] There were later authors who simply imputed the Golem with the rabbi.

The earliest known text source for the accomplished but totally fictitious combination of Loew and Golem is found in an 1834 book, *The Jewish Gil Blas* by an anonymous writer.[14] In one paragraph, the author mentions relics left behind by a distinguished rabbi of an earlier time, including the *Golam* (which translates as "servant" in Hebrew and Persian) of Rabbi Liwa, the man whom people called *der hohe Rabbi Löw* (High Rabbi Löw):

> It goes on to mention his legendary relations with Emperor Rudolph II, and that he made this golem out of clay with his Kabbalistic knowledge. The rabbi Golem was animated by a special paper with God's name on it, and he had a different one for weekdays and Shabbos. At night he would remove it from his mouth. [...] One Friday night he forgot to remove it, and as soon as the 92nd Psalm was sung (when Shabbat begins) it began to cause a ruckus. The whole building swayed! So the prayer was halted, and the rabbi replaced the paper with the weekday name of God, and it calmed down, and then the prayer could be resumed.

Once there was a plague striking children in Prague. The rabbi finally found out that the case concerned two adulteresses:

> The solution posed by the Maharal was that a messenger should enter the cemetery adjacent to the synagogue at midnight, and some of the recently deceased children would emerge from their grave. His mission was to snatch one of their shrouds ("tachrichim") and bring it to the rabbi. And so it happened. So the ghost of the child missing its burial shroud came to the rabbi and begged him to return it, the Maharal said that he will, after he is told what is causing the plague. So the child told him that two couples in the Belelesgasse were, well, you can figure it out. With a little investigation, their identities were determined. The women were named Bella and Ella.[15]

The anonymous turned out to be Joseph Seligmann Kohn (1803–1850), a Jew who converted to Christianity.

Actually, the Golem is not the founding father of all the Frankensteins, robots and androids up to *Blade Runner* fame who oppose their servient fate but no more than a "contemporary." Mary Shelley's *Frankenstein, or the Modern Prometheus* was first published in 1818, 16 years before Kohn's version of the Golem.

In 1909, Jehuda Judel Rosenberg (1859–1935) published a chapbook devoted to Rabbi Loew and his Golem, *Wundertaten des Maharal von Prag*.[16] Rabbi Rosenberg was born in Skaryszew, Poland, where he became a follower of Hasidism, a mystical movement within Eastern European Judaism. It was this book that shaped the image of the Golem forever. In 22 chapters, Rosenberg outlined the miracles of Rabbi Loew and connected them with the man of clay. We learn of a ruthless priest named Thaddeus who accuses the Jews living in the Prague ghetto of ritual murder. A dream vision reveals to Rabbi Loew how to stop the villain. A Golem must be created. Although there are a number of mistakes in the book (Rudolph II was not emperor in 1573, names and places are misspelled), it became a huge success in the wake of Arthur Conan Doyle's detective stories and their central character Sherlock Holmes. Rosenberg's German translator, Rabbi Chajim Bloch (1881–1973), corrected some of Rosenberg's errata but didn't mention the author's name at all. This omission gave the impression that the text might be some old, rather authentic document. Bloch wrote:

> In front of me is a booklet written in Hebrew titled *Nifloet-Mhrl.: Miracle Deeds of Rabbi Loew*. It was composed three centuries ago, rich in tragic episodes and delightful legends. We don't know who the author is [*sic*!] nor do we know the year which would have given a clue of the age of the autograph that was kept in a library in Metz. According to some supposedly reliable information, it was written by R. Jizchak Cohn-Zedek, son-in-law of Rabbi Loew.[17]

As he acquired a taste for it, Bloch went so far as to edit his own collection of *Golem* stories which focused on the Golem of Rabbi Elijah, the Golem of Chelm rather than the Golem of Prague.

In 1913, when Rosenberg immigrated to Canada where he died in 1935, Paul Wegener was filming in Prague. It was there that Ewers got him interested in the legend of the Golem. At the same time as Wegener produced the first *Golem* of the movies, the famous *Golem* novel by Gustav Meyrink was published. The two handled the topic completely differently. In Meyrink's novel, the Golem is just a specter, a manifestation of the ghetto's inhabitants' collective psyche. In Wegener's film, the Golem became an outright, stalwart monster.

A Golem Runs Amok

Paul Wegener's first *Golem* film begins in the Jewish district in Prague: Three well builders unearth a clay statue and transport it on a horse cart to an antiques dealer named Aaron. Aaron seems to have an idea what they have found. He looks it up in an old folio:

> In Prague, in medieval times, there lived celeberrimous miracle rabbi Löw. He was a master of black art and of the kabbalah which won him fame in all worlds. He succeeded in making alive a strange clay figure, the "Golem," by sinking a mysterious charm, the "Schenn," into its chest cavity. As long as the Golem carried this Schenn, he was alive as a man, obedient to the will of his master, until the moment when the sorcerer removed the amulet from its breast. Then he was nothing more than deadly formed clay.[18]

Wegener's original intention was to film the original legend but Deutsche Bioscop wasn't willing to make an expensive period piece. So the actor was forced to content himself with a modern-day story of the Golem resurrected.

From a scholar, the Jewish antiques dealer purchases a Cabalist book which records the incantation, the so-called *shem*. (Note: Schenn, as erroneously called in the screenplay but: *Shem ha-Meforash* which according to cabbalistic belief consists of $6 \times 6 \times 6 = 216$ letters as the three verses Ex 14, 19–21 have each 72 letters, together likewise 216.) Aaron doesn't hesitate to push the actinoid capsule into the breast of the colossus: "This is the recorded magic spell which Rabbi Löw used to bring the Golem to life: rolled up in the capsule it causes the magic of life."

The eyes of the Golem open and we recognize the parallel to the presumptuous "creation scene" from the 1931 *Frankenstein*. We are almost certain that the writers of *The Golem* have read the novel by Mary W. Shelley, maybe even have seen the old Edison film version from 1910 in which Charles Ogle played the unfortunate creature. The script continues.

> The Golem doesn't move. The Jew smiles, shakes his head, raises the light to examine the Golem's face. In this moment the Golem slowly opens the eyes! Jew retreads terrified. Golem slowly twists his head like a child towards the light. Startled Jew retreads backwards. Golem follows him, heavy as if mechanical, staring at the light the whole time. The Jew backs towards next piece of furniture, staring at the phantom. Golem close to him, Jew holds the light towards him, falls down to his knees and slips away in the back of the Golem. Golem goes very slowly, with childlike smile, into the light which goes out. Jew has arrived at the other side, Golem turns around, perceives him now, strides heavily towards him. Jew has collapsed into a faint, Golem approaches. Jew screams out:
> "Back off!"
> Golem goes backwards like a colossal machine. Jew relieved:
> "Come here!"
> Golem slowly strides a few steps forward:
> "Stop!"
> Golem stands still. The Jew realizes that he keeps control over this creature; he stands up to examine it.

Having won control, Aaron decides to make the Golem his servant and he makes the giant the guardian of his beautiful daughter Jessica. In the arms of the mighty Golem, Jessica is like a puppet. The Old Man seems to suspect—and here begins the usual trashy story of those days—that his daughter hides a love story. Indeed, Jessica has fallen in love with a count.

In this moment, the scholar who sold the book to the antiques dealer returns. He senses something:

> Antique shop. Golem lies lifeless, scholar enters, sees the Golem, frozen amazement. He bows above him, palms him, laughs madly, examines the opening in the breast, suddenly sees the capsule, takes it, his thoughts tumbling. Injects the capsule into the breast of the Golem. Golem, faster than expected, flips up. Only one single thought moves him: "Where is the woman?" Pushes the scholar aside like an object. He falls against the wall. Golem looks around, exits through the door. The scholar wants to stop him. Golem throws him into the forge.

The early silent film, as this quote from the original film manuscript demonstrates, didn't care for extensive role profiles. Action was the quintessential topic of filmmaking. Avoid as many intertitles as possible, have less dialogue.

Suddenly the Golem isn't a servant any more. An unholy feeling of love, long before Philip K. Dick's androids with human feelings, has grasped him. The frightened girl tries to escape the uncanny wooer and flees to her lover, who is holding a reception. The rejection brings the colossus-turned-monster to the verge of sexual rage. The "Stalker" causes panic among the summer guests invited by the count to a masquerade ball:

> Golem's silhouette appears in the glass door. The music stops. Everybody pushes in confusion. Everybody runs to the door to see the bizarre stranger. Scared stiff. Retreading. Some flee already. Golem presses his face against the window, holds his hands against it, grinning. Suddenly he shakes the door. The door doesn't yield. So he strides recklessly around breaking glass and the framework with a grin through the door which falls partly into the room. Horrified panic. The count draws his pocket revolver, fires at the Golem. Golem proceeds with a smile. The servant rushes towards him, stubs a dagger into the breast. The dagger gets stuck inside the Golem. Golem proceeds smilingly. Pairs flee over the stairs. Golem follows the fleeing pairs.

The Golem pursues the girl and her aristocratic lover up to the tower of the castle:

A small round tower, ivy-covered. Count and daughter arrive. He opens the door with a key he had in the pocket. Slams the door behind him. Golem appears, approaches the door. Platform of the tower. View to the treetops. Sideways ahead a circular opening of the spiral staircase. Count and daughter appear, sink down exhausted on the cornice of the battlements. She lays her head onto his heart, he embraces and consoles her. Suddenly their faces distort fearfully, they hear the splintering of the door and the heavy step of the Golem. They rush to the rearmost battlement, pressed to each other.

Expecting the horrible.

Golem's head appears from the deep, he looks around searching, sees the group. Slowly he ascends and strides with a childlike smile towards the scared. Count plants himself protectively in front of the girl. Golem makes a step. The girl signals that she wants to talk to the Golem. She passes the Count and with a smile approaches the Golem. Hand and eye aim at the Schenn. Golem spreads his arms as if to lift her. Wants to embrace her. Count misconceives the gesture, sees his beloved in danger, leaps at Golem. Golem's smiling good-naturedness distorts into anger. He grabs the Count and lifts him up, strides with him towards the edge of the tower, desperate wrestling. Highest danger. Desperate resistance. Change of position. In the last moment the girl is able to rip the Schenn out of the Golem's breast. For a moment Golem stays with closed eyes at the rim of the tower, then he stumbles and falls into the deep. In this moment the head of the old Jew appears at the platform. He sees the couple, runs towards his daughter, daughter knees in front of him, pointing downwards.

At the bottom of the tower lies the figure of the Golem: smashed.

Platform of the tower. The silhouettes of those who bow over the rim. They look up shocked. The girl sinks into the arms of the Count, the Count extends his hand towards the Jew. The Jew takes it after some hesitation and blesses the couple.

The film ends with a note of poetry by Angelus Silesius:

> Nature always works deep,
> internally and externally,
> And all lives in death,
> And dead it is living.

Only a brief scene tinted red showing the Golem work at the bellows of the forge survived in Guido Seeber's collection of clips and a fragment of four minutes, tinted blue, of the film's showdown which you can view on YouTube. The rest is considered lost. (The claim that a complete print might have been once in the collection of Paul Sauerlaender is not true.)

According to the film script there was an epilogue, set in later days:

> Overgrown park, ivy-covered, masses of stones covered by weed and bellflowers. Birds fly, a child comes playing. Sits next to a block of stone. Bumps against it in play. Thrusts the ivy aside, the head of the Golem appears. The kid is startled, runs away. In the distance we see the girl and the Count as husband and wife.
>
> "Mother, look, the strange head!"
>
> Takes the mother by the hand and draws her. The father follows. They see the head of the Golem in silent emotion. The kid knees in the grass in front of the head, slow fade-out.

Gustav Meyrink

As already noted, there are no parallels between the *Golem* novel by Gustav Meyrink (Gustav Meyer, 1868–1932) and the *Golem* movie by Wegener.[19] In Meyrink's novel, the Golem appeared only as a nightmare, a representative of the ghetto's own spirit, awakened by the misery that its inhabitants had to endure over centuries. Kurt Wolff, the publisher, explained,

> The old motive of the Golem, that self-kneaded clay figure, that a Prague rabbi brought to a life of enigmatic servility by a magic spell and that haunted a long time the Jewish district of Prague, is reshaped

and deepened in Meyrink's book. Because the novel is basically a great dream, it is more sustainable than an ordinary novel. It turns away from reality and illuminates mysterious grounds and relationship between souls and the destinies of man. Thus those strange figures and adventures form in elaborate linkage to one of the most colorful, suspenseful and thoughtful works of German literature.[20]

Although Meyrink's *Golem* was published as a book not long before the premiere of Wegener's *Golem* film, it was serialized as early as December 1913 in *Weisse Blätter,* a periodical published in Leipzig by Erik-Ernst Schwabach. The creators of the *Golem* movie knew the novel for sure but they wouldn't refer to it.

It is important to mention the illustrations found in the novel. They were the work of Hugo Steiner-Prag. Born Hugo Steiner in Prague on December 12, 1880, he was the son of Hermann Steiner, a bookseller, and Berta Steiner (neé Knina) who claimed to be a descendent of Rabbi Judah Loew (1529–1609). Upon leaving secondary school, Steiner joined Jung-Prag, a group of young artists who tended strongly toward mysticism and the occult. He took private art lessons and in 1897 enrolled at the Prague Academy of Arts. In 1900, he moved to Munich. There, at the Royal Academy of Fine Arts, he became a student of Peter Halm and Franz von Stuck. In 1905, he converted from the Jewish religion to Catholicism and became a German citizen in 1907. He called himself after the city of his birth. He was a professor at the Royal Academy of Graphic Arts and Book Trade in Leipzig and art director of the renowned Propyläen Publishing House in Berlin. He illustrated Hans Christian Andersen's fairy tales, E.T.A. Hoffmann's *Elixiere des Teufels* (*The Devil's Elixirs*) and created 25 lithographs for Meyrink's *Golem*. His *Golem* illustrations were a great inspiration for a young Leipzig-born artist: Albin Grau, who became the creator of *Nosferatu*.

When the National Socialists rose, Steiner-Prag lost his professorship, returned to Prague and in 1941 immigrated to the United States. He became a member of the American Institute of Graphic Arts and worked for publishing houses, including Random. He died in New York City from a heart attack on September 10, 1945. His final project remained unrealized: a book devoted to the suffering of the Jews in the Prague Ghetto.

The Mask of Golem

But back to Wegener's first *Golem* movie: Hanns Heinz Ewers, a strong inspiration in creating the first *Golem*, wasn't involved in the actual production. Ewers had left the Germany of World War I. He was on a cruise to South America when he heard that Archduke Franz Ferdinand of Austria, heir presumptive to the Austro-Hungarian throne, was assassinated in Sarajevo. He preferred to pass the time in New York occupied with propaganda for the German Empire. Wegener chose Ewers' secretary to become his collaborator. That young man was born Heinrich Wiesenberg on January 7, 1881, in Stryj, Ukraine, near Lemberg, then Austria-Hungary. He worked as a journalist before he became an actor and joined Max Reinhardt as an assistant. In 1913, he began to work for Ewers, who introduced him to the movies.[21] His screen name is linked forever with *Nosferatu*: Henrik Galeen. After suffering a long time from cancer, he died on July 30, 1949, in American exile at Gifford Memorial Hospital, Randolph, Orange Co., Vermont.[22]

The role of the Golem's love interest, Jessica, was played by Lyda Salmonova. The dancer-actress was born in 1889 in Prague and debuted in 1910 on the stage of Deutsches Theater in Berlin. She belonged to Reinhardt's ensemble until 1918. Wegener fell in love with her and she became his third wife. Beginning with *Student von Prag*, she was Wegener's partner in most of his silent films until 1923 (*S.O.S. Die Insel der Tränen*). Later she founded the acting studio Lyda Wegener. After World War II, she returned to Prague where she died in 1968.

The Golem figure itself was a collaborative effort of Wegener and art director-costume designer Rochus Gliese (1891–1978). He is best remembered for F.W. Murnau's first American production *Sunrise* and worked on other Wegener films. Gliese said, "[Wegener] knew exactly what he wanted and he got it. The Golem figure for instance is a Wegener creation. The exterior was a sack, with a string, everything was padded, shoes with insoles. The head was heavily made-up and then there was a cap on top."[23]

The Golem mask was sculpted by artist Rudolf Belling (1886–1972). Starting in 1909, Belling was commissioned to a number of Max Reinhardt plays and got to know Ernst Stern, Hans Poelzig, Reinhardt and Wegener. After the Nazi uprising, he was denounced as *entartet* (degenerated) and left Germany. In 1935, he accepted a teaching assignment in New York. In 1937, he went to Istanbul where he spent the war years at the art academy. In 1966, he returned to Germany.

Whoever decided the basic look of Universal's Frankenstein Monster clearly had seen and studied Wegener's *Golem* approach, maybe not the 1915 version but the lavish *Der Golem wie er in die Welt kam* (*The Golem: How He Came Into theWorld*) that Wegener finally was able to realize as a period piece right after the war thanks to producer Paul Davidson, with the support of his architect friend Hans Poelzig who built parts of the 16th century Prague ghetto on the UFA Union backlot in Berlin Tempelhof. At the end, with the Golem wandering around the ghetto causing havoc, there is a scene in front of the gate with a little girl who shows no fear but removes the amulet, causing the Golem to collapse. (This is reminiscent of scenes with little girls from the Karloff *Frankenstein* [1931] and the Chaney Jr. *The Ghost of Frankenstein* [1942].) The girl, by the way, is played by Loni Nest, who also might have had a scene in *Nosferatu*.

In the 1920 version, Albert Steinrück (1872–1929) portrayed a rather Faustian Rabbi Loew opposite Wegener's Golem. Standing between the two is Lyda Salmonova as Loew's daughter Mirjam, standing between a father who is so much involved in his alchemical experiments that he overlooks Mirjam's sexual awakening, and Mighty Golem, the superhuman. Wegener's costume drama, flamboyant and clumsy at the same time, shows multiple aspects of racial, sexual and gender transgression as Cathy S. Gelbin writes:

> Like other artificial humanoids in Weimar film, the golem in Wegener's film represents an alternative type of masculinity, a "New Man" complementing the idea of the sexually empowered "New Woman" also presented in so many Weimar texts. This image is present in the figure of Mirjam, Rabbi Loew's daughter, as the Jewish *femme fatale* who had embodied the negative ideas about both women and Jews since the *fin de siècle*.
>
> In turn, Wegener's golem exemplifies the *fin du siècle* idea of the "Muscle Jew," a new Zionist warrior type who would till the soil and defend his people, which reimagined the anti–Semitic stereotype of the weak, effeminate ghetto Jew. This type is suggested in Rabbi Loew's Famulus, who has been unsuccessful in vying for Mirjam's attentions. Instead, Mirjam has entertained a liaison with the Christian Knight Florian, an act of transgression against the implied norms of a bounded female sexuality on the one hand, and the racial discourse against miscegenation on the other. Famulus thus calls on the golem to destroy the knight. This unleashes a violent desire in the golem, who overpowers Mirjam and drags her away. Mirjam will now succumb to Famulus's advances as he promises to forgive her wrongdoing and keep it a secret. The golem, therefore, functions as a narrative tool to restore the patriarchal order and its prescribed boundaries between Christians and Jews.[24]

There are anti–Semitic undertones in both *Golem* films. This is more than just mundane anti–Semitism and it's not even subliminal. The medieval ghetto reflects the fear of alien Jews who, with their waving robes and big bushy beards, look so different. Rabbi Loew would return in 1940 in a scene of Veit Harlan's *Jud Süss (Jew Suss)*. He, as well as other Jewish characters, was played by Werner Krauss. The silent period of German filmmaking is rather mundane but, on a closer view, even the few classics feed anti-Jewish prejudices.

An Actor's Vision of Optical Poetry

In a 1915 lecture, Paul Wegener showed that he was the first Berlin stage actor to dream of new developments in animation and an entirely new universe of synthetically created images. The fact that actors reflected synthetic images is unique. Georges Méliès found it easier to star himself in his films instead of hiring a comedian or an actor. These pictures appeared to be too tricky for actors. Wegener, on the other hand, became interested in trickfilm playing a key role in German silent cinematography and less interested in the acting, just in technique and aesthetics:

> You have all seen films in which suddenly a line appears, curves, and changes its form. Out of it grow faces and the line disappears. To me the impression seems highly remarkable. But such things are always shown as an intermezzo and nobody has ever thought of the colossal possibilities of this technique. I think the film as art should be based—as in the case of music—on tones, on rhythm. In these changeable planes, events unreel which are partly identified with natural pattern, yet partly beyond real lines and forms. Imagine one of [Arnold] Böcklin's sea paintings with all the fabulous tritons and nereids. And imagine an artist duplicating this work in hundreds of copies but with each copy having small displacements so that all copies revealed in succession would result in continuous movement. Suddenly we would see before our very eyes a world of pure fantasy come to life. Such effects can also be achieved with specially constructed little models animated like marionettes—in this field there are great achievements nowadays. One also can change the pace of different movements by shooting too slow or too fast, developing a fantastic vision which will produce entirely new associations of ideas. We are entering a new pictorial fantasy world as we would enter a magic forest. We are setting foot in the field of pure kinetics—or optical lyric as I call it. This field will perhaps be of major importance and will open new beautiful sights. This eventually is the final objective of each art, and so cinema would gain an autonomous aesthetic domain for itself. A movie could be created which would become an experience of art—an optical vision, a great symphonic fantasy! That it will happen one day, I am sure—and beyond that, I am certain, later generations will look upon our early efforts as upon childish stuttering.[25]

This is a vision of a true parallel world created by the manipulation of a sequence of moving images, an illusion put together by the dream machine and mechanics of the cinema projecting a light beam, perceived by the human eye and transferred to the brain. All this imagined, however, not by an engineering wizard or technical visionary but by an *actor* coming from the legitimate stage. Wegener understood that the movies were more than a novelty, more than an amusement attraction. It was a new art form and the manipulation of images was to be a part of it. With the end of the Great War, cinema hit puberty and was acknowledged as a new art. Cinematographer Guido Seeber's trick photography enabled Wegener to act with his own *Doppelgänger* on screen in *The Student of Prague* and transform into the Golem, but it was still Wegener's vision.

The *Doppelgänger* topic seems to be quite important for understanding acting in animation and trick photography. The character you are going to animate is not exactly *you*. It is like your *Doppelgänger*. Ray Harryhausen once explained how he mastered stop motion art technically: "It becomes your second nature." It is as if the animated character assimilates the animator.

Conrad Veidt and
The Cabinet of Dr. Caligari

The Love Tragedy of an Artificial Human

Homunculus was the first great fantasy serial produced in Germany. Since the successes French Gaumont Company had with *Judex* and *Fantomas* by Louis Feuillade (1873–1925), serials and sequels were demanded on screen as well as in newspapers where serialized novels became popular. *Homunculus*, like *Student of Prague* and *The Golem*, produced by Deutsche Bioscop, consisted of six episodes and was directed by Otto Rippert (who had played the captain of the doomed ship in the first *Titanic* film made in Berlin in 1912 under the title *In Nacht und Eis*): *Homunculus*; *Das geheimnisvolle Buch* (*The Mysterious Book*); *Die Liebeskomödie des Homunculus* (*The Love Comedy of Homunculus*); *Die Rache des Homunculus* (*The Revenge of Homunculus*); *Die Vernichtung der Menschheit* (*The Extermination of Mankind*); *Das Ende des Homunculus* (*The End of Homunculus*). Each episode was an hour long. In 1920, it was re-arranged for a re-release and cut down to three parts: *Der künstliche Mensch* (*The Artificial Man*), *Die Vernichtung der Menschheit* (*The Exertmination of Mankind*) and *Ein Titanenkampf* (*A Clash of Titans*).

A jealous Prof. Ortmann, after three years of vain experiments, is a witness when his student Hansen succeeds in creating what he, Ortmann, had in mind: a Homunculus, watching the first test-tube baby emerge, properly zapped, out of a bubble. When the artificial man is 25 years old and in his prime, he realizes he is unable to love. His core is hollow. He finds himself alienated from his carousing peers and therefore begins to hate his creator, like Frankenstein's creature did, and not only him but Hansen's daughter too. Although she loves him, he cannot love her. The *Übermensch* (superman), incapable of love, drives the girl into death and vows vengeance to all of mankind and its worthless world. Together with Edgar Rodin, an assistant of Hansen who had attended his birth, he makes a discovery which would enable him to destroy the world. Under the name Richard Ortmann, Homunculus becomes the head of a corporation of business people whom he leads with icy strategy towards his goal. At the same time he fuels the hate of the underground workers. He is uncovered and imprisoned but escapes. He kidnaps a female orphan and a shepherd on a remote island to breed a new human race. He plays God to a new Adam and Eve. As the attempt fails, Homunculus destroys the isle including the couple. Appalled about what happened, Edgar Rodin and Dr. Hansen decide to stop Homunculus by creating a second artificial man. Eventually the new Homunculus is old enough to challenge the first one in a showdown that anticipates a similar duel in David Cronenberg's *Scanners* (1981). But all the rest is not natural science, it is pure alchemy. The homunculus (Latin for *little man*) is referred to in alchemical documents of the 16th century. One of its advocates was Philip von Hohenheim, widely known as Paracelsus. In his work *De Natura Rerum,* he recommended using a horse as the surrogate mother of the homunculus. Then the semen of a man should be left inside the animal's womb to putrefy for 40 days, before the little man is born.

Alchemy became the fuel of German speculative fiction and films: creating artificial people, robots and soldiers by using magic, making gold.

A Danish Frankenstein

Screenwriter Robert Reinert had scrutinized Mary W. Shelley's *Frankenstein* novel very carefully and had it expanded, in the midst of World War I, to a length of 360 minutes.[1] It is a mix of megalomania, sexual impotence, superstition and science as the Germans understood it.

Olaf Holger Axel Fønss (1882–1949), who played the title part, made his stage debut in 1903 in Copenhagen. In 1912, he entered the movies and won fame in *Atlantis* (1913), from a novel by Gerhart Hauptmann. For *Homunculus* he was paid, according to *Lichtbild-Bühne* (May 6, 1916), the highest fee paid to a film actor in Germany up to that time. But his fame didn't last long. His final big starring part in a movie was in Joe May's monumental *Das indische Grabmal* (*The Indian Tomb*). In the early 1930s, he supported the Danish Social Democrats with two films. From 1933 until 1942 he was chairman of the Danish Actor's Union.

You Must Become Caligari!

In 1920, Deutsche Bioscop was absorbed by the Decla Company which had evolved out of Deutsche Éclair. By that time, Decla's most famous movie had already been completed: *Das Cabinet des Dr. Caligari* (*The Cabinet of Dr. Caligari*).

The movie became legendary thanks to a shrewd promotion campaign. Part of it was the following article that appeared in the trade press signed by one Claus Groth, but author and content belong into the realm of fantasy:

> A few weeks ago a new slogan emerged in Berlin: "Du musst Caligari werden." You must become Caligari. From the advertising pillars in the subway, in the big cafés, from everywhere it would yell at you in loud colors, and the call would propagate itself. In the nightclubs and bars, on the street friends and acquaintances would talk to us in the categorical imperative but no one knew the meaning of these words. When a brief time ago somebody claimed that I had become already Caligari, I decided to probe the causes of these words. One has to know the origin of such allegories. I tracked it down in the Decla Studios in Weissensee. The gray-bearded Cerberus at the gate explained to me the way to Caligari would lead only over his dead body. "Thou shalt not kill," I thought and stealed into the studio through the back door where I was received by director Robert Wiene a little warily at first but then amiably after I had identified myself as reporter. Encouraged and to hide my ignorance as best as possible I started my interview with the question: "Sind Sie auch schon Caligari? Are you already Caligari?" He hesitated and seemed to affirm but then he shook his head emphatically and said: "Thank God not yet but sure when the movie is finished, and Caligari?—Over there you hear him yell." At the

same moment an ear-shattering noise arose. Scared and curiously I followed director Robert Wiene who due to the noise had rushed back to his duties. I arrived at time to see to my astonishment how Werner Krauss in the splendid makeup of a scholar was put into a straitjacket while Fritz Fehér watched the procedure with an almost satanic grin. But he had laughed too soon because five minutes later I witnessed how Wiene let Werner Krauss—he was this Dr. Caligari—free to see Fehér in this garment that so favorably fits modern times. This all was so exciting and happened so lightning-fast that I became totally fascinated by this ominous imperative and felt that one simply had to become Caligari here. In the break following this scene Rudolf Meinert, supervisor of the Decla Production, introduced me to the rest of the staff. Conrad Veidt, made up as somnambulist (Cesare), I hadn't recognized at all, and Lil Dagover displayed such an other-worldly look that I recognized only her lovely smile with which she greeted me as an old friend. Finally it dawned on me: This must be the Expressionist movie she already raved about a few weeks ago. Expressionist film?—At your convenience, director Robert Wiene cut in and presented his artistic collaborators, painters Hermann Warm, Walter Reimann and Walter Röhrig who cleared their throat at the same time. I translated this cough immediately and begged for pardon and asked for an explanation. Each of the gentlemen began to lecture now about art in general, about expressionism in art and in movies in particular. [...]

The bottom line of these explanations that contained a lot of artistic truth I am going to repeat briefly. The "Expressionist film" is just a slogan, a sensationalist phrase, painter Reimann told me. There is no Expressionist film. Expressionism is—in terms of film technique—the rhythmic climax of the dramatic plot in the manuscript but not so far on a naturalist basis but built upon artistic perception. And this finds the valid and strongest expression necessarily in Expressionism.[2]

Claus Groth, the author, was, as film historian Ulrich Kasten speculates, not a reporter but an employee of the Decla Production, most likely Julius Sternheim, who was prominently involved in the press campaign that made *Caligari* famous at the first push.

Caligari's Zombie: Murder in Holstenwall

In the *Caligari* story, the filmmakers had found an ideal platform for their Expressionist design. So it became the first truly synthetic movie. It followed the Expressionists' outcry against the madness and consequences of war:

The garden walls of an asylum hide their mysteries. Franzis looks up to a Madonna: his fiancée. Together with her, he had experienced an incredible story that he tells his gray-haired conversational partner with whom he shares a bank. He explains about the funfair at the gates of Holstenwall and the cabinet.—A world of bizarrerie. Contrary to later claims, the frame story was there right from the beginning as we can see thanks to the only surviving, albeit incomplete original screenplay *Das Cabinett des Dr. Calligari*— the name allegedly derived from the Italian Cagliari, the capital of the island of Sardinia. It was left by Werner Krauss' widow to Deutsche Kinemathek. Yet it wasn't intended to play in the confines of an asylum, but told by Franzis at an evening party 20 years later. The change from a soirée to an asylum opened a chance for experimental design and Expressionist sets.

Franzis sees himself standing in front of the funfair with his friend Alan.

The title card reads, "Step rrrrright in! Presenting here for the first time Cesare the Somnambulist: The miraculous Cesare—twenty-three years old, he has slept for twenty-three years—continuously—Day and Night!

Right before your eyes Cesare will awaken from his death-like trance.

Step right in!"

Cesare, Caligari announces, is going to do things in sleep he never would do awakened. Franzis hears the old pitchman yell and lure the people under the tent roof. He feels how his friend, attracted by an invisible force, pulls him inside. Inside he sees a large box standing upright. Caligari the carny opens it. There he is, tall, dressed in black and like dead: the somnambulist. The tension rises. The horrifying creature inside the box opens its eyes jerkily. His look is empty.

> "Cesare—
> Can you hear me?
> Cesare—I am calling you—
> I—
> Dr. Caligari
> your master—
> Awaken for a moment
> from your
> Dark night—
> Cesare the Somnambulist will
> answer all your questions—
> Cesare knows every secret—
> Cesare knows the past
> and sees the future—
> Judge for yourselves.
> Don't hold back—
> Ask away!"

"Ask your question!" Caligari demands from Alan.

Alan closes his eyes: "How long will I live?"

"Till the break of dawn!" the Somnambulist yells. Alan and with him Francis shiver.

The next morning, Alan is dead, as predicted by the Somnambulist. He was stabbed with a dagger, right through his heart, his murderer unknown. A few days earlier, there was a similar murder: as the somnambulist had predicted. A stab with a dagger—right through the heart. No trace of the murderer. A few days earlier, a similar crime: The town clerk was murdered, a man who had offended Caligari.

Franzis suspects Caligari and his man-marionette. Together with a police commissioner he surveys Caligari, who is guarding the black box in his wagon.

At the same time, the murderer strikes again in Holstenwall but this time he cannot escape. He confesses that he wanted to kill an old woman but he denies having anything to do with the other murders. They don't believe him and put him in jail.

But then the true culprit strikes again. He kidnaps beautiful Jane, who was loved by Alan as well as Franzis. He drags her across the roofs but he doesn't come far. It's Cesare. He lies unconscious on the road. Police storm Caligari's wagon. They open the box. Inside isn't the real Cesare, just a wax puppet, a lookalike. In the confusion, old man Caligari disappears. His trail leads to the asylum. Franzis pursues him to the gate. His story finds the physicians shaking their heads. Then, in the office of the asylum director, they find an old chronicle, a collected edition devoted to somnambulism published by the University Upsala in 1726. The doctors knowing that this field is the specialty of their superior, read together:

> The Cabinet of Dr. Caligari.
> In the year 1703 a mystic by the name of Caligari toured the fairs of numerous villages in northern Italy, accompanied by a somnambulist named Cesare.... For months he sowed panic amongst village folk through a series of foul murders committed under almost identical circumstances.... He had entirely subjugated to his will the somnambulist whom he did compel to carry out his nefarious schemes.

> A puppet, the exact likeness of Cesare, and which took his place in the cabinet, allowed him to divert any suspicion that might fall on the Somnambulist.

The doctors search, skim, decipher. This Dr. Caligari is head of their asylum. The proof: They find his diary:

> 12 March
>   Finally … finally!
>   A somnambulist has been brought to the asylum for admission…
>   Afternoon—
>   My desire…. I shall be able to identify my life's unwavering wish…! Now I shall unravel the psychiatric secrets of this Caligari!
>   Now I shall discover if it's true that a somnambulist can be compelled to perform acts that—in a waking state—he would never commit and would be repugnant to him…. Whether it is true that a sleepwalker can be led to commit even murder…!
>   I must know everything
>   I must penetrate his secrets—
>   I Must Become Caligari!

Franzis has convinced them. But actually he is mentally ill, one of the patients, who tells one of his fellows the phantasms of his ill mind. He looks to the Madonna who does her rounds: "We queens are not free to answer the call of our heart." Jane too is a product of his vivid imagination, patterned after a patient. The director of the asylum, who, *sans* makeup, looks less demonic than the nightmare character of Caligari, learns about it and dismisses the cinema audience with an assurance: "At last I understand his delusion. He thinks I am that mystic Caligari. Now I know exactly how to cure him…"

Circle aperture on the physician's face that leaves, however, a last shadow of doubt.

Expressionist Sets to Cut Costs

The production manager responsible was Rudolf Meinert, born Rudolf Bürstein in 1882 in Vienna. He had come via the theaters of Budweis, Pilsen, Jena and Vienna to Berlin. Badly wounded in World War I, he was dismissed from military service in October 1915 and founded the Meinert Film Gesellschaft that merged in November 1919 with Erich Pommer's Decla Film Gesellschaft Holz & Co. At the same time, the *Caligari* film was in production with Meinert prominently involved. In 1933, Meinert, who was Jewish, immigrated to Prague, from there to Vienna and finally Paris. At the outbreak of World War II, he was interned in Camp de Gurs in the South of France, later confined to the Drancy Internment Camp. From there he was transported on March 6, 1943, to the concentration camp Majdanek where he died.

Reportedly Hans Janowitz, one of the two screenwriters, had suggested the Austrian graphic artist Alfred Kubin as set designer but instead the regular film architects of the Lixie Studios, a small glass stage outside Berlin in Weissensee, were commissioned. Hermann Warm was the supervising art director. Under the headline *Gegen die Caligari-Legende* [*Against the Caligari Legend*],[3] he wrote what he remembered:

> The screenplay conceived and written by Carl Mayer and Hans Janowitz was given to me by Rudolf Meinert in the presence of director Dr. Wiene whom I got to know at that occasion.
>   A brief conversation without any particular clue what the screenplay was about, only an appointment for the next day when I should make my suggestions considering design and sets. At the afternoon, after repeated lecture, making excerpts and working through this screenplay which was so completely

different with a nod to the settings I was fascinated more and more by the bizarre atmosphere. I recognized that one had to deviate in styling and design from the regular naturalist kind.

The movie images, turned away from the real, must receive a fantastic graphic styling. The images must be visionary, nightmarish. No real construction elements should be recognized. Instead a kind of bizarre painting that would serve the topic should dominate the screen.

If the film shouldn't be built with real or naturalist elements then painters should have the word, that is, hold the brush...

I informed my two painter friends Walter Reimann and Walter Röhrig who already had painted for various films backgrounds, images and tapestries for me. The time period was one year after World War I—no profitable time for freelance artists. Until night the three of us painters read and discussed the screenplay, talked about my opinion concerning the style which I have described and which should form the basis for the sets.

Reimann, who used in his art the technique of aggressive painting, cut through with his opinion that this topic must have an Expressionist concept for sets, costumes, actors and direction.

The same night we did some sketches.

The next morning I outlined to Rudolf Meinert and Dr. Wiene the result of the previous night. On the basis of the first art sketches I explained briefly that only a consequent execution all around, in short the Expressionist design would lend this film its absolute and strong effect.

Dr. Wiene recognized immediately the possibilities and agreed to adopt this style.

Production manager Meinert, thoughtfully contemplating, promised to let us know his decision the next day. It was positive and he explained it as follows:

He wanted to call the style and its execution mad, but one has to stick with it, everything as mad as possible. Then the film would become a sensational success, no matter if the press would write positive or negative comments, if the reviews are damning or acknowledging the artistic approach—in both cases the experiment would be worth it.

Thanks to this decision it happened that the *Caligari* film was made in the form that we had conceived, at least in the design that prevails in film. [...]

In one-and-a-half to two weeks we did all preproduction, designed sets and costumes, made lists of props and planned the construction work, selected from production designs, many of which existed in several versions.

There was a lot of work, layout planning and the classification for the studio plan, blue prints for the manufacture of individual components, furniture, props, etc.

Walter Reimann did additional sketches for costumes and makeup of the actors who had been hired in the meantime.

Director's meetings and presentation of the designs only in the presence of Dr. Wiene and Rudolf Meinert and cameraman [Willy] Hameister. [...]

With furor we went to work; even the stagehands enjoyed it. Us three painters worked always till night, as if in a frenzy. This was the new wave that washed around all participants and carried them away.[4]

All enthusiasm for Hermann Warm's formula aside, that the moving image must become graphic art, one shouldn't overlook that this demand most likely was caused by different, more materialistic circumstances outside the realm of art. Curt Siodmak, the German émigré author, who wrote *The Wolf Man, Frankenstein Meets the Wolf Man* and *House of Frankenstein* for Universal in the 1940s, knew Erich Pommer, the head of Decla-Bioscop. He claimed—and even this might be only half of the truth:

During production, a fire destroyed the sets. The producer of the film, Erich Pommer, didn't have enough money to rebuild the expensive sets. His inventive architects, Hermann Warm, Walter Reimann and Walter Röhrig, saved the movie by painting the backgrounds in the Expressionist style of those days on packing paper. Thus a legend was born.[5]

Siodmak added another legend to a legend. The fire is no more than a figment of the imagination. Contemporaries cannot recall such an event. Nevertheless, the Expressionist style helped to save electricity, which was rationed in postwar Berlin, while lighting the sets. Light and shadow were simply painted, and everything was erected in a hurry: a compromise that made film history.

According to Hans Feld, a film critic who worked for *Film-Kurier*, Robert Wiene said distinctly that the Expressionist style of Caligari could be simply explained with one reason—lack of money: "Film funding was difficult to find and Wiene was assigned to the project because they knew that he was an all-rounder. An art connoisseur and collector—he was the first to track down the expressive Benin sculptures, pride of his home, that are sought after today—he combined the know-how with a solid knowledge about the commercial substructure."

The previous Decla production was *Die Pest in Florenz* (*The Plague in Florence*), a mystery play set in the Italian renaissance, written by Fritz Lang and supervised by *Homunculus* director Otto Rippert. Its sets were so costly and took so much time to build that they jeopardized the productions scheduled to follow. This—and mainly this—was the reason for all experimenting. Expressionist sets were easy to build, didn't cost much money and were easy to light.

How the Story Was Developed

One of the two writers who conceived *Caligari* was Bohemia-born Hans Janowitz (1890–1954). He only wrote four films, two novels and lyric volumes. An officer of World War I, he had returned from the battlefields a pacifist. *Caligari* was an outcry against war and, so did Janowitz claim, was based on an experience he had had right before the war.

Olaf Brill has researched this claim in a doctoral thesis:

> Although much has been written about this film, its review in film literature was completely insufficient. There were smashing legends at every turn that were repeated and were firmly established. But everybody who tinkered a little with film history must have known that these legends were full of holes and contradictions. There was Fritz Lang telling one story, and Hermann Warm told another. And both couldn't be true at the same time. These contradictions were never solved so far. […]
>
> The first and foremost I did when I had decided to write a book about this film was to research a little story that Siegfried Kracauer had recorded in his book *From Caligari to Hitler*. Hans Janowitz, one of the two screenwriters, had told him about a personal experience he had in the year 1913 which allegedly became the core of the Caligari story that he wrote six years later with co-author Carl Mayer. The story dealt with the murder of a girl at Holstenwall in Hamburg that Janowitz claims to have witnessed. He believes to have watched the murderer and met him again at the funeral of the girl. This is only a little episode that formed the background of *Cabinet des Dr. Caligari*. But I was interested if this story was based on fact and if I could find out more details.
>
> So I looked up old newspapers. Kracauer had recorded the date of the murder relatively precisely and even told the first name of the victim: Gertrud. Therefore I could relatively fast hunt out the respective newspaper articles. The dating differed only about one week. The Hamburg newspapers were suddenly filled with the homicide case of little Gertrud Siefert and reported breathlessly each day about new horrifying details, progress in investigation, the funeral etc. The case gained some public attention at that time. With the exception that nobody had done some research about it. […][6]

This is the story that Kracauer had heard from Janowitz in his New York exile and that was reported by him in his book. He introduces us, rather poetically, to the Czech Hans Janowitz who was raised in Prague—the city where reality fuses with dreams, and dreams turn into visions of horror:

> One evening in October 1913 this young poet was strolling through a fair at Hamburg, trying to find a girl whose beauty and manner had attracted him. The tents of the fair covered the Reeperbahn, known to any sailor as one of the world's chief pleasure spots. Nearby, on the Holstenwall, [Hugo] Lederer's gigantic Bismarck monument stood sentinel over the ships in the harbor. In search of the girl, Janowitz followed the fragile trail of a laugh which he thought hers into a dim park bordering the Holstenwall. The laugh, which apparently served to lure a young man, vanished somewhere in the shrubbery. When, a short time later, the young man departed, another shadow, hidden until then in the bushes, suddenly emerged and moved along—as if on the scent of that laugh. Passing this uncanny shadow, Janowitz caught a glimpse of him: He looked like an average bourgeois. Darkness reabsorbed the man, and made further pursuit impossible. The following day, big headlines in the local press announced: "Horrible sex crime on the Holstenwall! Young Gertrude … murdered." An obscure feeling that Gertrude might have been the girl of the fair impelled Janowitz to attend the victim's funeral. During the ceremony he suddenly had the sensation of discovering the murderer, who had not yet been captured. The man he suspected seemed to recognize him, too. It was the bourgeois—the shadow in the bushes.[7]

Olaf Brill continues that the story as told by Janowitz, himself watching the murderer, "didn't correspond in important details with the facts.

Janowitz had simply read the story in the newspaper, had it poetically tidied up and told it from then on as a story he had experienced himself."[8]

Another inspiration was allegedly the carnival in Berlin's Kantstrasse where a showman introduced an attraction under the title "Man or Machine?" A man achieved miracles of strength in an apparent stupor and would break his chains under hypnosis while uttering words that sounded like predictions of the future. According to the writers, this sideshow experience was the initial spark for writing the story. In their script they had a scene with Cesare breaking his chains.

Olaf Brill is sure: The carnival wasn't in Kantstrasse. He places it at Luna Park: "The Expressionist settings of pleasure ground Luna Park in Berlin Halensee could have worked as an inspiration for the sets too…"[9]

The Luna Park had opened over the whole year and was within walking distance to Mayer's apartment. The Nazis considered it a *Schandfleck* (eyesore) and shut it down in 1934.

The main reason to write the story was, of course, to earn some money, but talking to Kracauer Janowitz pushed a pacifist reason to the fore:

> …as the radical critique of authority and control, of the ruthless tyrant who manipulates the unwary and vulnerable into committing horrific acts against their own will and better judgment, who dispatches unfortunate others to kill and be killed. Caligari stands for all the arrogant politicians and military leaders of Europe who, from the comfort of their ministerial offices and war rooms, sent so many thousands of young men, sleepwalking to patriotic anthems and jingoistic rhetoric, to their deaths.[10]

Janowitz claimed that, while the original story was an account of real horrors, Robert Wiene had transformed it into a chimera concocted by the mentally deranged Franzis.

Nevertheless, *Caligari* was one of the few German films that became a worldwide success, including the United States where it was released by the Goldwyn Pictures Corporation.

Later, in exile in London, Wiene hoped to be able to create a sound film remake starring Bela Lugosi, who had just filmed *The Mystery of the Mary Celeste* (U.S.: *Phantom Ship*, 1935; directed by Denison Clift) in Britain. In Paris he tried to convince Jean Cocteau, but death intervened. Wiene died on July 17, 1938. In 1962, Twentieth Century–Fox and Robert L. Lippert Productions used the popular title for a screenplay written by

Robert (*Psycho*) Bloch. In 2005, David Lee Fincher directed a "faithful" remake that was filmed entirely in front of a green screen. Thirteen years later, Fincher finished a *Nosferatu* remake along the same lines, funded by Kickstarter, with "Cesare" Doug Jones as vampire. Jones, a former contortionist, is one of director Guillermo del Toro's favorite actors, seen in *Pan's Labyrinth* and as Amphibian Man in *The Shape of Water*.

From Paul Wegener to Werner Krauss to Jew Suss

Bohemian-born actor Ernst Deutsch (who later had an important part in *The Third Man*) had introduced writers Janowitz and Mayer to each other. For Deutsch and Paul Wegener the authors had written their screenplay: for these two great Reinhardt actors and for their muse Gilda Langer. Carl Mayer (1894–1944), who later did some great work for F.W. Murnau (most notably *The Last Laugh* and *Tartuffe*), adored Gilda. He was dramaturge at the Residenz Theater where he could watch her closely. They planned to use the Holstenwall murder story as a vehicle for her to play the victim, Jane, with Ernst Deutsch as Cesare and Paul Wegener as the Caligari character. Langer signed with Decla and Fritz Lang, who used her in three of his movies. But then, tragically, she fell victim to the Spanish Flu and died, 23 years young (in the story, Cesare's age), on January 31, 1920. The part written for her was filled by Martha Marie Antonia Siegelinde Seubert (born on September 30, 1887—according to other sources in 1897—in Madioen, Oost Java, a province of Dutch East Indies, and passed away in 1980 in Grünwald near Munich). She had been married to actor Fritz Daghofer and had adopted the screen name Lil Dagover. In 1926, she married Georg Witt, who began in the press department of Decla-Bioscop and after World War II produced the popular *Spessart* films starring Liselotte Pulver, including the spooky *Das Spukschloss im Spessart* (*The Haunted Castle*) (1960). When Conrad Veidt, playing Cesare the tragic somnambulist, dragged her out of her bed and carried her away, she actually was so terrified by him that she pulled the duvet with her. The production company was not able to secure the services of Paul Wegener and Ernst Deutsch, as both of them were already scheduled to film *Der Golem, wie er in die Welt kam* in Berlin Tempelhof.

Veidt was born Hans Walter Conrad Veidt on January 22, 1893, in Berlin. In 1915, he was dispatched to the Eastern front and took part in the battle of Warsaw. He contracted jaundice and pneumonia and was evacuated to a military hospital at the Baltic Sea. As his condition did not improve, he was allowed to join a theater in Libau, today Liepaja, Latvia, not that far away, where he would be with his girlfriend Lucie Mannheim. He won fame on the stage of Max Reinhardt and made a hundred films, among those some prominent fantasy parts: *Unheimliche Geschichten* (*Eerie Tales*, 1919), a horror omnibus film similar to those later produced by Amicus in Britain, directed by Richard Oswald and co-starring Reinhold Schünzel and scandalous, drug-addicted dancer Anita Beber who died of tuberculosis at age 29, *Das Wachsfigurenkabinett* (*Waxworks*, 1924, directed by the exceptional Paul Leni) playing Ivan the Terrible, and *Orlacs Hände* (*The Hands of Orlac*, 1924; directed by Robert Wiene) in Vienna. In Hollywood, under contract to Carl Laemmle's Universal, he became *The Man Who Laughs* (1928; again directed by Paul Leni) and for Alexander Korda in London, at the beginning of World War II, the evil Grand Vizier Jaffar in the Technicolor fantasy *The Thief of Bagdad* (1940; directed by Ludwig Berger, Michael Powell and phony Tim Whelan). In 1934, Albert Whitlock, who had started as a runner in the British film industry, had seen him face to face while assisting German-born art director Alfred Junge on director Lothar Mendes's *Jew Suss*, the English version that was faithful to Lion Feuchtwanger's novel. Decades after the memorable meeting, the little man was still awed by the tall, gaunt, charismatic actor. Veidt became a memorable supporting player in *Casablanca* (1942) as Major Strasser of the Third Reich but was cut out—a final insult—in the postwar German edition of this film by Warners' German branch in order to avoid harming Teutonic sentiments. Veidt died at age 50 on April 3, 1943, of a massive heart attack while playing golf at the Riviera Country Club in Los Angeles.

While Veidt preferred not to return to Germany and stay in exile, Caligari himself accepted not one but four parts in Veit Harlan's anti–Semitic *Jud Süss* (*Jew Suss*, 1940): Werner Johannes Krauss (June 23, 1884, in Gestungshausen near Coburg–October 20, 1959, in Vienna) was an actor of great variety, seen as Hamlet and Wallenstein, Franz Moor and Shylock. "When Krauss entered the stage," Marcel Reich-Ranicki, a critic of Jewish birth, recalled, "the character he played was immediately present—without him saying or doing anything."[11] Gad Granach, the son of Alexander Granach, the real estate broker in *Nosferatu,* said in a TV interview that with Krauss, an avowed anti–Semite, playing Shylock, you became an anti–Semite yourself, on the spot. His career almost reflected the title of Kracauer's book *From Caligari to Hitler:*

From Caligari to Jew Suss.

Dr. Jekyll, Murnau and Dracula

Murnau or Wiene, Dreyer or Griffith?

Satanas was the title of another Robert Wiene production with Conrad Veidt, this time starring as The Devil himself: the Fallen Angel roaming through the ages, trying to find a way back to Heaven. It's considered a lost film except for a tinted three-minute fragment that was found in the Filmoteca de Zaragoza in Spain. It is not only important as a vehicle for Veidt but also marks F.W. Murnau's entry into the field of fantastic cinema.

Wiene had written the screenplay, designed the costumes, set up the schedule, cast the project but then was unavailable to direct it. He was urgently needed to prepare *The Cabinet of Dr. Caligari* in Weissensee and so Murnau became his substitute in the director's chair in Neubabelsberg where the movie was filmed in August and September 1919. The production was inspired by D.W. Griffith's monumental episode epic *Intolerance*. Carl Theodor Dreyer, the Danish director, had seen it too and planned a movie about the Devil who interfered unfavorably in world history. Dreyer based his almost three-hour-long *Blade af Satans Bog* properly on the 1895 book *The Sorrows of Satan* by British occultist Marie Corelli (1855–1924). Interestingly enough, Griffith would film that novel too, some years later, as *The Sorrows of Satan* for Paramount Studios. Dreyer's episodes would show Jesus Christ, the Holy Inquisition in Spain, the French Revolution in Paris and the Russian Revolution, with Satan scheming next to the Finnish border in Scandinavia. The *Satanas* production, on the other hand, is so similar in content and structure that Lotte H. Eisner asked herself in a book about Murnau[1] if the director might have visited his colleague Dreyer in Denmark. That's rather unlikely but certainly Wiene had read about Dreyer's ambitious project in the trade press and with only two months scheduled for production tried to outrun him. We don't know exactly why Murnau was chosen. At that time he had made just one or two films; he made *Der Knabe in Blau* (*The Blue Boy*, 1919) with Ernst Hofmann (1890–1946). So it might have been Hofmann who not only played in the first episode but also was the producer of *Satanas* who had hired Murnau. Hofmann's first film appearance, by the way, was in Max Reinhardt's *Die Insel der Seligen* (*The Island of the Blessed*). In 1917, Hofmann was cast as one of the actors in *Die Memoiren des Satans* (*Satan's Memoirs/The Memoirs of Beelzebub*), written and directed by Robert Heymann from a tale by Wilhelm Hauff. That four-episode big-budget movie is lost now but we know from a synopsis (and the literary source) that it had the Devil acting in a similar role.

How Plumpe Became Murnau

Wiene's film, that Murnau took over, consisted of three episodes. The first, *Der Tyrann: Eine Tragödie aus der Pharaonenzeit* (*The Tyrant: A Tragedy from the Time of the Pharaos*), was set in ancient Egypt and showed Fritz Kortner in the role of Pharaoh Amenhotep, who gives orders to execute his wife for adultery and makes the denouncer his new wife; the second, *Der Fürst. Lucrezia Borgias Tod* (*The Prince: Lucrezia Borgia's Death*), was an adaptation of Victor Hugo's 1833 novel *Lucrezia Borgia*; the third, *Der Diktator: Der Sturz eines Volkstribuns* (*The Dictator: The Fall of a Tribune*) told about Hans Conrad, a law student, who in a Zurich café comes upon a circle of Russian expatriates. Fascinated by their revolutionary agitation, he doesn't realize that Grodski, one of the Russian revolutionaries, is in fact Lucifer.

The premiere was scheduled in Marmorhaus at Kurfürstendamm in Berlin but had to be outhoused to Richard Oswald Lichtspiele because Marmorhaus was still occupied by the more successful *Caligari*.

Friedrich Wilhelm Murnau was originally Friedrich Wilhelm Plumpe. He was born in Bielefeld, the "city of linen" in Westphalia, on December 28, 1888. When Murnau was seven, the family moved to Kassel where the famous fairy tale writers and collectors Jacob and Wilhelm Grimm were born. Murnau's mother came from Flotho. Her father owned a big brewery. She was artistically minded, had an exquisite singing voice and supported the ambitions of her son Wilhelm. An avid reader from early childhood, Murnau read everything from Schopenhauer and Nietzsche to Shakespeare and Ibsen plays. He also became interested in puppet plays when still at elementary school. At high school he often went to the theater and at home, with his brothers Bernhard and Robert, restaged what he had seen. His father wanted him to become a teacher, but Wilhelm strived for the breadless profession of becoming an actor and director. When young Wilhelm decided to become an actor, he got into serious conflict with his father. In 1910, he changed his last name from Plumpe which in German means the same as in English: *plump* to Murnau. In Murnau, a small market town situated at the foothills of the Bavarian Alps, Wilhelm had spent his vacation.

To console his father, Plumpe studied philology at the University of Berlin and art history and literature in Heidelberg. There Max Reinhardt "discovered" him at a students' performance and invited him to his actor-school. Murnau appeared in many of Reinhardt's productions and toured with Reinhardt's ensemble.

During World War I, Murnau served in the First Regiment of the Guards and was stationed for quite a time in Lithuania. There he spent eight months straight in the trenches. Developing kidney disease which caused him a lot of trouble, he underwent surgery and was warned not to drink or smoke. He followed this advice throughout his life, although occasionally he did smoke. His friend Hans Behrenbaum was killed while Murnau, becoming a pilot, did an emergency landing in Switzerland where he was interned until the end of the war. During this time he began to write screenplays.

The Hunchback and the Dancer

Murnau's next movie was *Der Bucklige und die Tänzerin*. James Wilton, a hunchback who throughout his life had to suffer from women's disgust (Murnau was homosexual), discovers a diamond mine in Java and becomes a rich man. When he returns to his home country, he encounters a dancer named Gina and makes overtures to her. But when Gina reconciles with her former lover, a wealthy man named Smith, the jealous hunchback mixes a poisoned beauty tonic which kills everybody who comes near her. Only Gina is immune because of an antitoxin: a mix of Edgar Allan Poe and Hedwig Courths-Mahler (a famous German pulp romance writer) as the critic of the *Berlin Börsen-Courier* resumed in his review. Today we would say it sounds like something Jess Franco would have done, but not somebody of Murnau's stature. According to a July 9, 1920, article in *Film-Kurier*,

> Murnau's direction did the utmost for this work. There is good and bad direction, but I haven't experienced that cinema direction waves around the characters an atmosphere, something so inspired, almost the vapor that ascends from the Javanese perfume of the hunchback.[2]

This film was certainly inspired by the Oriental *Sumurun*, directed by and starring that great comedian, Ernst Lubitsch, as the hunchback.

Dr. Warren und Mr. O'Connor

Written by *Caligari* co-author Hans Janowitz, *Der Januskopf* (*The Head of Janus*) is a free adaptation of the Jekyll-Hyde plot by Robert Louis Stevenson,[3] although with changed role names. It marked F.W. Murnau's entry into the field of classic horror tales. Conrad Veidt plays the dual role of Dr. Warren (replacing Dr. Jekyll) and Mr. O'Connor (in place of Mr. Hyde). His co-star was future American screen *Dracula* Bela Lugosi (1882–1956) as Dr. Warren's servant, his name emblazoned in the credits of the first German edition of Lotte H. Eisner's *Murnau* biography.[4] The actor, a former functionary of the Hungarian Actors' Guild, had fled from Budapest when Béla Kun's government was overthrown. Before he left for America, he made a number of movies in Germany, including a two-part *Lederstrumpf* (*Leatherstocking*): *Der Wildtöter* (*The Deerslayer*) and *Der letzte Mohikaner* (*The Last of the Mohicans*, 1920) as Chingachgook, directed by Arthur Wellin and written by Robert Heymann, who had done *The Memoirs of Beelzebub*, as well as adaptations of novels by Karl May, the German counterpart of James Fenimore Cooper. Lugosi's German stay was like transit. From the late German-born Wendayne Ackerman, wife of collector Forrest Ackerman, I learned that upon his first (and final) visit to the Ackermansion shortly before his death, Lugosi, almost deaf, complained in loud German words about his fifth wife Hope.

A Big Loss for Film History

Walter Kaul, the author of *Schöpferische Filmarchitektur*, had seen *Januskopf* in 1920 and recalled it on the occasion of a retrospective of Berlin International Film Festival:

> A serious loss for film history as well as the art of the movies is the fact that all prints of the 1920 produced Conrad Veidt film *Der Januskopf* have vanished.... It was one of the most famous dual roles of the later global cinema: a film version of Robert Louis Stevenson's famous novel *Dr. Jekyll and Mr. Hyde*. The Janus character was named in the German film Dr. Warren and Mr. O'Connor respectively. By the way, in the same year Hollywood filmed *Dr. Jekyll and Mr. Hyde* too, with Veidt's later American

adversary John Barrymore.[5] I saw the American version some decades later but it couldn't extinguish the enormous impression that Murnau's film (and last not least Conrad Veidt) had on me in the beginning of the 1920s.

> One has hailed him [Veidt] justifiably as the film artist of Expressionism. His intensity is burning, incinerating. If we study his suggestive-drawing movements and gestures, we discover that the acting lines that occasionally protrude into the grotesque and draft awesome outlines also are unleashed by Jugendstil [art nouveau] that never really was removed by Expressionism.[6]

Maybe this is the film in which, even before Murnau's famous *Letzter Mann* (*The Last Laugh*, 1924), Karl Freund's camera was unleashed and became mobile. "The camera follows him across the stair," Janowitz wrote regarding a scene that has Warren stepping up to his laboratory.

With *The Hunchback and the Dancer* and *The Head of Janus*, most of the key persons and key elements were together that later would make *Nosferatu—Eine Symphonie des Grauens*:

1. F.W. Murnau had found his way to fantastic yarns and classic horror stories.

2. Considering the success of *Der Januskopf*, he was looking for another horror vehicle to star his friend Conrad Veidt.

3. *Hunchback*'s star John Gottowt, Paul Wegener's Scapinelli from *The Student of Prague*, brought in Henrik Galeen, who wrote what they considered a veritable follow-up to *The Head of Janus*: *Dracula*. Veidt playing Dracula, directed by F.W. Murnau promised a sensational success at the box office.

But still a producer was missing.

They might have approached producer Lipowetzki of Lipow Films who financed *Januskopf* but found him unwilling to take the risk.

Enter Albin Grau. At that time he wasn't a producer, but he was sure that he and his friends would be able to raise the necessary funds.

Dracula in Germany: Henrik Galeen and the Screenplay for *Nosferatu*

A Cosmic Vampire

Gustav Albin Grau, born on June 13, 1884, in Leipzig, was baptized evangelic Lutheran. His father Gustav Alwin Grau, born in 1851, was a factory worker. Three-year-old Gustav witnessed, together with one of his brothers, a deadly accident: A woman fell out of a window from the third floor. For Gustav, this developed into a lifelong trauma.

Grau had three brothers and three sisters. He began an apprenticeship as a baker but was not skilled enough. Then he was apprenticed to a master painter. Under Eugen Bracht, he enrolled in Dresden Art Academy and continued his studies in Berlin and Paris. Famous for his landscapes, Bracht (1842–1921) was a master not only in oil painting but also pastel.

During World War I, Grau served at the Russian front as paramedic and anesthetist. Allegedly, he had simulated rheumatism to be exempted from military service. Under Prof. Dr. Ferdinand Sauerbruch, he was trained as a medical orderly and learned how to perform amputations. Later a Bavarian officer asked Grau to portray him. Eventually he went on to design military maps for the officer corps.

To Albin Grau, the horrifying events of the Great War were like the roaring of a "cosmic vampire": the vampire of war. In one of the advertising articles that were published touting the release of *Nosferatu* Grau spun some fanciful story to describe the bloodlust he had experienced in this terrible war: In 1916, during the Serbian campaign, Grau said to have heard a tale from an old peasant farmer, who had actually seen an *Undead* in Romania. This was the Serb's own father, who had died without receiving the sacraments and rose from the grave as a *Nosferatu*. He haunted the village and claimed his victims. When he was exhumed, his body showed no signs of decomposition, but his teeth were strangely long and sharp, and protruded from the mouth. The villagers said the Lord's Prayer and laid him to final rest by hammering a stake through his heart, after which he gave a groan and died. Grau concluded, "It's here, where we're at in the Balkans, that one finds the cradle of those vampires."[1]

Like so many of his age-mates, Grau returned home a changed man. Film historian Philipp Stiasny is probably right when he compares the hero's tragic return in *Nosferatu* with the homecoming of war survivors: The veterans had death still in their field packs and carried it home like a disease. In this regard, Nosferatu is nothing else than Hutter's alter ego, which makes Murnau's movie another allegory of the Germans' favorite topic: split personality. According to Stiasny,

> Postwar cinema appears as a place where they try over and over again to re-enact the trauma of war, the shock, the physical and the mental injuries and, if possible, exorcise them. If we follow this interpretation the "undead" represent all the dead of the World War who wander about unburied and restlessly since, longing for a grave where they can be mourned; in the character of the vampire they emerge as a plague as well as lamentable creatures who must be redeemed from their nightly existence to finally pass away in the first light of the day.[2]

After the war, Grau connected with the Berlin film industry. He did a lot of promotional material, graphic art, advertisements and posters for several of the production and distribution companies that sometimes were no more than mayflies. In those days, the Berlin film community was mainly located at Friedrichstrasse. Grau worked for the following short-lived companies in the early 1920s.

Macht-Film Conrad Tietze: *Dämon Blut* (*Demon Blood*, 1920)

Filmverlag Bengen/Bengen Film Berlin Friedrichstr 5–6: *Das Gesicht im Mondschein* [*The Face in the Moonlight*]; *Der Leidensweg der Blanche Gordon* [*The Passion of Blanche Gordon*]; *Die Jagd nach dem Dollar* [*The Chase for Dollars*]

Justitz-Film G.mb.H./Emil Justitz & Co. released by Bengen Filmverlag: *Das Rote Plakat* [*The Red Poster*, 1920]; *Der Falschspieler* [*The Hustler*, 1920]

Centaur Film G.m.b.H.: *Die Rote Redoute* [*The Red Masquerade Ball*, 1920]; *Ewiger Strom* [*Eternal River*, 1920]

Grete Ly Film G.m.b.H.: *Sturm* [*Storm*, 1920]; *Menschen* [*People*, 1920]; *Dieb und Weib* [*Thief and Woman*, 1920]

Unitas Film Corporation: Five unnamed Italian films

Deutsch-Amerikanische Film-Union: *Hypnose und Suggestion* [*Hypnosis and Suggestion*, 1923]; *Der Berg des Schicksals* [*Mountain of Destiny*, 1924][3]

Humboldt Film G.m.b.H.: *Liebesleben der Natur* [*Love Life of Nature*, 1923]; *Litauische Nacht* [*Lithuanian Night*, 1923]

At Goron Films, Berlin, Friedrichstrasse 5–6, while working on advertisements for *Der Gang in die Nacht. Eine Tragödie in fünf Akten* (*The Walk Into the Night: A Tragedy in Five Acts*), written by Carl Mayer and starring "Homunculus" Olad Fønss, Erna Morena and Conrad Veidt, Grau met director Friedrich Wilhelm Murnau and learned about his ambition to direct a film version of the novel *Dracula*. For some reason, Grau felt he was the right person and saw a chance to become Murnau's legitimate producer.

To raise the necessary funds, Grau joined forces with a former partner from Filmverlag Bengen, Enrico Dieckmann. Bengen had distributed some minor American and a number of German films and Grau had become their graphic artist. Both decided to found their own production company, Prana. The offices were located at Berlin NW 87, Levetzowstrasse 15. Most of the investors remain unknown. Only one name surfaced: a Baron Grünau, aka Curt von Grünau (1871–1939).

The company was named after a theosophical magazine called *Prana*. There was also an occult catalogue distributor named Prana that handled literature, horoscopes, incense sticks, candles and so on. In Sanskrit, Prana means "the force of life."

Grau was deeply impressed by the way a great director like Murnau painted with the camera. In the summer of 1921, *Nosferatu* was in production and was hailed as Prana's first *Grossfilm* (big-budget movie).

The history of Prana Film turns out an infamous episode of the Weimar Republic and German occultism…

No Lecture for the Faint-Hearted

Henrik Galeen, whom we have met as the assistant of Hanns Heinz Ewers and Paul Wegener's assistant on the first *Golem,* was born to a Jewish family in Galicia. (According to Hans-Michael Bock, he was born Heinrich Galeen in Berlin, son of Adolph and Marie Galeen. This turned out to be a wrong guess.) From 1928 to 1931, Galeen lived and filmed in England, then returned to Germany. He tried to do a sound film remake of *The Golem* titled *Das Steinerne Phantom* (*Phantom of Stone*) but he couldn't get the project off the ground. With the Nazi Party's rise to power in 1933, he emigrated. His last registered directorial film assignment was *Salon Dora Green* starring Mady Christians, Paul Hartmann and Alfred Abel. Galeen went into exile in Sweden before moving to the United Kingdom and eventually the United States.

Subtitled *Ein Vampyr-Roman* (*A Vampire Novel*), Bram Stoker's *Dracula* was published for the first time in Germany in 1908, translated by Heinz Widtmann. The publishing house was M. Altmann in Leipzig, which also had theosophical books and Rudolf Steiner in its program. A second edition followed almost 20 years later in 1926. M. Altmann promised,

> The book is a sensation and will generate extraordinary attention because in Germany one knows very little about vampirism. It is no lecture for the faint-hearted, and even an indifferent, apathetic reader might be disequilibrated by the nerve-racking content of the book.

Dracula was a novel that could have made its author rich. But the Irish journalist, writer and theater critic Abraham "Bram" Stoker (1847–1912) died a poor man after a series of strokes. When *Dracula* was first published in 1897, it wasn't the sensation the author dreamed of.

Stoker was inspired by a novel that his countryman Joseph Sheridan Le Fanu had written, *Carmilla,* and most likely by the gruesome tale of the blood countess, Elizabeth Báthory (1560–1614). The name *Dracula* he found while doing research and translated it unprecisely with "devil." The original Dracula was a 14th-century Wallachian voivod with as bad a reputation as Báthory. He was a cruel ruler but some of the stories told about Vlad the Impaler are exaggerated, fake news and primitive political propaganda. According to one source,

> Once he lunched under the bodies of dead people put on stakes and there were many of them around his table, but he ate among them and enjoyed his meal. His servant who put the food before him could not stand the smell and held his nose and inclined his head, and Dracula asked him, "Why are you doing that?" and the servant responded, "Sire, I cannot bear the smell." So Dracula ordered him to be impaled too.[4]

For obvious reasons, Nicolae Ceaușescu, the megalomaniac Romanian dictator, declared this Dracula a national hero: "Those who know [Ceaușescu] personally insist that he cannot stand any Christian crosses or religious blessings of any kind. The incident in Venezuela, when he requested that the crucifix be removed from his room, was no accident. Nor was it a coincidence that, at a luncheon given in his honor by a group of New Orleans businessmen, he left the room because a pastor blessed the food."[5]

While Stoker borrowed Vlad Dracula's name, he had a different man in mind: Henry Irving (1838–1905), the first actor to be awarded a knighthood. He became Stoker's mentor and Stoker his business manager and agent. If one reads Stoker's description of Dracula he should think of Irving:

> His face was a strong—very strong—aquiline, with high bridge of the thin nose and particularly arched nostrils; with lofty domed forehead, and hair growing scantily round the temples, but profusely elsewhere. His eyebrows very massive, almost meeting over the nose, and with bushy hair that seemed to curl in its own profusion. The mouth, so far as I could see it under the heavy moustache, was fixed and rather cruel-looking, with particularly sharp white teeth; these protruded over the lips, whose remarkable ruddiness showed astonishing vitality in a man of his years.[6]

The Spanish Flu Takes Its Toll

Murnau's *Dracula* film came into the cinemas three and a half years after the surrender of the German armies: at the height of a wave of mystical and horror films. It was intended not only as a superficial answer to the blood loss on all fronts but also made under the influence of the Spanish flu, a deadly influenza pandemic that raged from January 1918 to December 1920 and hit an unprepared world like a tribunal, a judgment of God. It infected 500 million people and killed 50 to 100 million:

> Some researchers believe the story began on the morning of Mar. 11, 1918, when a soldier in Fort Riley, Kans., went to the camp infirmary with a fever. According to the PBS documentary *Influenza 1918*, more than 100 soldiers had reported to the infirmary by noon. Within a week, that number had quintupled. Several dozen soldiers died there that spring, before the contagion seemed to ebb; the official cause was pneumonia.
>
> As soldiers fanned out to fight World War I, however, the virus made its way around the globe, from European battlefields to remote areas of Russia and Greenland, spawning two more pandemic waves that were even deadlier than the first. (It became known as Spanish flu only because the Spanish news media was the first to widely report the pandemic, which had been hushed up by wartime censors elsewhere in Europe.)[7]

As Henrik Galeen saw it, the vampire was more than just a Transylvanian count sucking the blood of the living; he was a synonym of the pandemic, with rats all around him. This is completely innovative, including the idea that the vampire is killed by the rays of the early sun. No stakes are used, driven through the heart of the specter like in the Universal and Hammer *Dracula* series.

Nosferatu, by the way, was not the first film project to introduce the character of Dracula to the screen. Before Murnau's film was released, there was a nightmarish mix of *Caligari* and *Dracula* in Hungary that is now considered lost: *Drakula Halála* (*Dracula's Death*; 1921; directed by Károly Lajthay). The star, Austrian actor Paul Askonas (1872–1935), was to be seen in *Sodom und Gomorrha* and in Robert Wiene's *Orlacs Hände* alongside Conrad Veidt. *Drakula Halála* made use of Dracula only in name. The character had not much to do with Stoker's vampire. One of *Drakula's* writers was Kertész Mihály, who directed *Sodom und Gomorrha* before he went to Hollywood and won directorial fame as Michael Curtiz (*Casablanca*).

Contrary to the vampire's decapitation in Stoker's novel, Galeen and Murnau offer Lucifer a ritual sex victim and drive his vampire emissary into the sunlight. An angry power has sent out a demon manifesting itself in a plague, an incarnation of sexual repression that must be placated by a human sacrifice. This clearly is a reference to an occult background.

Back then, writers of both war parties, England (Algernon Blackwood, Sax Rohmer [the creator of Fu Manchu]) and Germany (Gustav Meyrink and all the others linked directly or indirectly to Paul Wegener and Hanns Heinz Ewers, with Galeen being a prominent candidate) outdid each other in presenting occult topics. Demonism and occultism found an ideal matrix in postwar Germany. Superstition and mysticism gave a seemingly comprehensive answer why so many precious lives were taken by war and plague. An allegorical figure straight out of a medieval mystery play, straight from the paintings by Hieronymus Bosch was the answer.

Not a November revolution is the answer but expiation, penance and reversal to calm that "cosmic vampire" that had drained so much blood out of Europe.

New Role Names

A single copy of *Nosferatu*'s screenplay survived and was found in Murnau's estate, marked with scribbles and annotations by the director, published in the reprint edition of Lotte H. Eisner's *Murnau* book of Deutsches Filmmuseum in Frankfurt/Main. Reading it, we learn that the original script didn't locate the climax of the story in Germany but, same as Stoker, has the vampire's ship land at the harbor of Whitby, the seaside town and port situated on the east coast of Yorkshire at the mouth of the River Esk. Here the ships for James Cook were built. Here resided Bram Stoker in 1890.

All the other names have been changed by Henrik Galeen following the example of what Hans Janowitz did with Robert Louis Stevenson's novel (although they remain English names). *Nosferatu* therefore is completely English, with Murnau transforming the locations from British to German. We don't know if the production company at an early stage tried to do some location shooting in England but found the venture too complicated.

Jonathan Harker becomes Thomas Hutter (*Hut* is German for protection and *Hüter* therefore means guardian), Mina turns into Ellen, Renfield changes to Knock the local real estate agent, Van Helsing to Bulwer. The latter was clearly a tribute to Edward Bulwer-Lytton, the author of *The Last Days of Pompeii, The Coming Race* and *Zanoni*, a novel that would be of importance to the producers.

Prof. Bulwer, by the way, is played by the same John Gottowt who was Paul Wegener's Jewish nemesis Scapinelli in *The Student of Prague* and Murnau's *Hunchback*. He was born Isidor Gesang in Lemberg, Austria-Hungary, on June 15, 1881, and joined Reinhardt and Deutsches Theater in 1905. He also appeared in Robert Wiene's Expressionist *Caligari* sequel *Genuine* and in *Algol* as an extraterrestrial who challenges the men of the Earth. Henrik Galeen was Gottowt's brother-in-law.

Last but not least, *Dracula* was to become *Nosferatu*. The term was used by Scottish travel book writer Emily Gerard in an 1885 magazine article, "Transylvanian Superstitions," and in her travelogue *The Land Beyond the Forest: Facts and Fancies from Transylvania*[8] that was used as a source reference by Stoker:

> More decidedly evil, however, is the vampire, or nosferatu, in which every Roumenian peasant believes as firmly as he does in heaven or hell. There are two sorts of vampires—living and dead. The living vampire is in general the illegitimate offspring of two illegitimate persons, but even a flawless pedigree will not ensure anyone against the intrusion of a vampire in his family vault, since every person killed by a nosferatu becomes likewise a vampire after death, and will continue to suck the blood of other innocent people till the spirit has been exorcised either by opening the grave of the person suspected and driving a stake through the corpse, or firing a pistol shot into the coffin. In very obstinate cases it is further recommended to cut off the head and replace it in the coffin with the mouth filled with garlic, or to extract the heart and burn it, strewing the ashes over the grave.[9]

But before her, it was one Wilhelm Schmidt who mentioned nosferatu in an article for an Austro-Hungarian magazine in 1865:

> At this point, I come to the vampire—*nosferatu*. It is this, the illegitimate offspring of two illegitimately begotten people or the unfortunate spirit of one killed by a vampire, who can appear in the form of dog, cat, toad, louse, flea, bug, in any form, in short, and plays his evil tricks on newly engaged couples as incubus or succubus—*zburatorul*—by name, just like the Old Slavonic or Bohemian *Blkodlak*, Vukodiak or Polish *Mora* and Russian *Kikimora*. That which was believed about this and used as a defense more than 100 years ago is still true today, and there can hardly dare to be a village which would not be in a position to present a personal experience or at least hearsay with firm conviction of the veracity.[10]

The term *nosferatu*, however, is not known in the Romanian language. The authors might have been mistaken etymologically. There is some evidence that they referred either to the Greek *nosophoros* (disease-bringing) or to the Romanian *nesuferitu* (the unclean, the insufferable one, the Devil).

Eventually the British locations were substituted by German-sounding ones. So Whitby by the sea became Wisborg by the sea. There is no Wisborg on the map. We might assume that the name was inspired by the City of Wismar where part of the filming took place.

Why Galeen changed the role names is not known because the filmmakers do not conceal that it is Stoker's novel that they used as a basis for their film. The credits read: "Freely adapted by Henrik Galeen from the book *Dracula* by Bram Stoker." They might have been misled by bad legal advice that they wouldn't have to pay the copyright owners for the film rights if they changed the story and names considerably. Indeed, nobody complained—until 1924.

The Storyline

Our story opens with the finding of a fictitious chronicle written down by an unnamed author, who signed with three crosses:

> Chronicle of the Great Death in Wisborg anno Domini 1838
> Nosferatu
> Does this word not sound to you like the midnight cry of the Deathbird
> Take care in saying it
> Lest life's images fade into shadows
> And ghostly dreams rise from
> Your heart and nourish themselves
> On your blood.
> Long have I contemplated the origin and recession
> Of the Great Death in my hometown of Wisborg.
> Here is its story.
> There lived in Wisborg
> Hutter and his young wife Ellen…

View over the roofs of an old-fashioned seaport in the 1840s. It's the time of Biedermeier that begins with the Congress of Vienna after the Napoleonic Wars when the Middle Classes began to grow.

The sun shines peacefully on the pointed gables and leafy squares of Wisborg, a harbor city.

Thomas Hutter is just married. His young wife, Ellen, is a woman of extrasensory perception.

While Hutter readies to leave for work, Ellen has opened the window, breathes in and greets the rays of the morning sun while the cat leaves the room. There are flowers in green window-boxes. On the window sill, the kitten is playing in the morning sun. With graceful movements she tries to catch a ball that dangles from a thread. Now the ball is being pulled in through the window. The cat jumps after it.

The morning sun casts the shadow of the window frame onto the floor. Ellen, by the window, is pulling in the thread with the ball. The cat follows it with a leap. Then she puts the little animal on her arm. Playing with it, she sits down on the window sill bathed in sunshine and looks out dreamily. She squats on the floor opposite the animal and plays with it. Her dressing gown moves in the breeze. Her big, childlike eyes are laughing.

Her chamber is poor-looking and tidy: a bed, a chair in period style.

Thomas Hutter, an early riser, is already downstairs picking some flowers.

Ellen comes over and begins to busy herself with knitting things towards her housewifely duties.

Hutter—white jabot, blue waistcoat—arrives back in the doorway, hiding a bouquet behind his back, laughing. Ellen sews. They kiss.

Hutter is holding a knife. For a moment, Ellen retreats. Then she realizes that it is a gardening knife he used to cut some flowers for her. Ellen smiles while Thomas produces the bouquet, hands it to her beaming all over his face. She is touched then, but suddenly saddening, she takes the flowers looking at the stems and stroking them. Hutter doesn't like her worried face: "What's biting you, Ellen...? It's such a lovely day."

Ellen: "It's only.... Why have you killed them.... Thomas ... the beautiful flowers?" Hutter sighs, lowers the knife and kisses her again. The intensity of the kiss makes her drop all ill feelings. Then they stand in an embrace. Hutter still holds the knife.

Although they are in love with each other, one can sense that something is darkening their relationship.

Ellen is sulking now and trying to placate him. Suddenly he pulls out his watch. He's late. He has to go to work. He kisses her goodbye and disappears.

Prof. Bulwer is walking vigorously, yet slowly along the road, enjoying the morning and the sunshine. His stick strikes the ground energetically. He greets young Hutter: "Not so fast, my young friend! No one outruns his destiny." Hutter overhears the admonishment and leaves. He is in great haste. Bulwer stands for a moment, shaking his head. Then he resumes the regular rhythm of his walk.

Hutter arrives at a building that looks rather daunting and spooky. Other pedestrians steer clear of the house that leaves an eerie feeling: a dusty, cramped, tight room, like a cage. Here resides Knock, the property agent, the subject of all sorts of rumors. They suspect him to be in league with everything that is dark and rotten. But anyway, he pays his employees well. Pale light is falling through tiny blind window-panes into the strange room which is eccentrically decorated with bits of old-fashioned furniture. Knock is sitting behind a high desk studying a letter.

Knock's spindly hunch-backed figure: Gray hair, half-bald, weather-beaten face full of wrinkles. Diminutive, stocky. Round his mouth throbs the ugly tic of the epileptic. In his

Thomas Hutter (Gustav von Wangenheim) and his wife Ellen (Greta Schröder) (from the stills collection of Deutsche Kinemathek-Museum für Film und Fernsehen, Berlin).

Alexander Granach as Knock. Watercolor made from a film still in 1922 (photograph prepared by Martin van Elten, courtesy Gerd J. Pohl).

eyes burns a somber fire. He doesn't take the blindest bit of notice when Hutter enters as he scans a letter.

On a sheet of paper decorated on the margin with grotesque, forbidden vignettes a medley of intricate and quite illegible, apparently occult signs. Knock, however, seems to be able to make sense of the strange writing, for his ugly mouth sets into an understanding smile that bursts into outrageous laughter.

Unobtrusively, Hutter has placed himself behind a nearby desk, working with another office clerk, and noisily blows off some dust.

Knock points to the letter with mysterious gestures:

"*Count Orlok—His Grace...*"

While he speaks out this name, he seems to be completely in awe.

"Count Orlok who lives in one of the wildest and least known parts of Central Europe ... wants to buy ... a house ... and come ... to our little town and bring some of his ancient wisdom."

For a moment, Knock, almost a Dickens character, becomes very friendly. Hutter watches the unexpected reaction: "If you would be so kind to volunteer and be the salesman you could earn a nice bit of money. Weren't you looking for a raise, by the way, my dear? You are newlywed. So you have a use for the money." Hutter forces a smile.

Knock says he is too old for the trip: "It will take some effort, of course ... a few drops of sweat and ... perhaps a little blood. You're young. You can afford some ... *blood.*"

In Hutter's face, expressions of mounting joy and strange apprehension are fighting each other.

Hutter's finger runs over a map at the wall pointing the route from Wisborg to Transylvania.

The region beyond the forest. *Ultra silvam*. The Germans call it *Siebenbürgen, Seven Fortresses*, after the seven Saxon cities in the region: Mediaş, Muhlenbach, Clausenburg (Cluj), Schässburg (Sighişoara), Reussmarkt (Miercuera Sibiului), Broos (Orăştie) and the capital, Hermannstadt (Sibiu).

They have some tasty and delicious gastronomic specialties over there, including *Siebenbürger Knoblauchsuppe* ... garlic soup. Knock: "Garlic—the natives claim—is a good protection against vampires." Hutter is not superstitious. He is a child of Enlightenment. He doesn't believe in specters.

The Orloks, Knock explains with a superimposed smile, belong to the oldest German-speaking families in the *Grossfürstentum*, the Grand Principality *Siebenbürgen*. Knock seems to be pleased as he turns back to the letter, now reading the back page. It is covered with the same illegible squiggles. But Knock seems to make sense of this page too.

For a moment, the old broker is lost in thought, but then he has an idea. He limps over to the window. There is a huge deserted house. The front is broken. The windows are black and hollow. No sign of life. Only shadows. Knock walks back from the window. Hutter seems to be a little taken aback by what he considers chutzpah: to offer a foreign nobleman such a rundown property. Knock hands him some money and readies the documents.

They shake hands: The deal is settled. They laugh in agreement. Knock pushes Hutter to the door and closes it behind him.

Ellen is sitting by the window. She sees Hutter coming. Her face lights up with joy. She hurries over to the door. Hutter enters. He has brought some food to celebrate. Moved and happy, he puts his arms around her and tells the news. Ellen eyes him quizzically. Excitedly he lifts her: "Knock sends me to sell a house, the old dark house across the street." He adds with a laugh: "To the country of thieves and specters. A nobleman from Transylvania is going to buy it."

Ellen is startled. A shadow passes over her forehead: "That monster of a house?! Thomas, you must be kidding." There is fear in her eyes. She is afraid to let him go. But Thomas is overly enthusiastic about what he considers a business challenge.

The next morning. Hutter, all ready for the journey, takes his leave from his friend Harding, a wealthy ship owner, and his sister Annie. Ellen, weeping, is supported by Annie, her best friend: "Be at ease."

Hutter takes both of Harding's hands and looks deep into his eyes. He entrusts Ellen to their care.

There is no escape from destiny. Everything is predetermined. Ellen gives him a medallion. The medallion contains her image. Hutter holds it, lost in thought for a while. For a moment he seems to hesitate. Then he pulls himself together and breaks away, mounting his horse. Another farewell, another wave of the hand and Hutter vanishes.

Young Hutter travels many dusty roads until the peaks of the Carpathian Mountains loom before him. Wild and rocky. The big mail coach drawn by four horses drives up and comes to a halt. The innkeeper, a little old man, comes out and sees the coach. Hutter jumps out first. He stands stretching his legs and looking around. The inn is one part brick-walled living area, the other coach house and open stables. In the meantime, the other passengers have alighted. Long-haired, black Huzules. All identically dressed and—

Max Schreck the uncanny coachman picks up Hutter (Gustav von Wangenheim) in the Carpathian Mountains (from the stills collection of Deutsche Kinemathek–Museum für Film und Fernsehen, Berlin).

so it seems—of identical appearance, almost like ghosts. They go into the house. The innkeeper comes up to Hutter and greets him with an inviting, servile gesture. The horses are now unharnessed and the coach is being pushed into the coach-house. Night is falling.

A large smoky room with an enormous tiled stove. A central hanging lamp throws out dazzling light. The passengers sit at tables in the background. Hutter looks around and sits down right in front. At once, an old woman, the innkeeper's wife, approaches with a mug of wine and puts a glass down in front of him. He overcomes a strange anxiety that was brought on by the evening mood in a strange country and puts on a sudden show of liveliness: "Give me something to eat. I'm in a hurry." He says that he must be off to—*Count Orlok's castle*!

For a moment it's so quiet, you could hear a pin drop. The woman recoils in horror and drops the mug of wine as he mentions the name. *"Orlok ... nu ... nu!"*

The strangely identical-looking passengers, sitting in the background, rise abruptly to stare at him. They whisper. The old innkeeper pricks up his ears. Hutter looks around in embarrassment, then takes up his glass resolutely and downs it in one gulp, giving himself liquid courage. The innkeeper's wife makes the sign of the cross.

Hutter stands alone, looking around. He is perplexed and wants to ask what is happening but he doesn't understand the native language. Suddenly, the innkeeper comes approaches him and whispers into his ear. He warns him, "You shouldn't go any further. The Werewolf roams the woods."

Hutter gets his bag and follows the innkeeper's wife, who is going to show him a room. The horses outside are nervous. There are wolves around. A tiny whitewashed room with sharp angles; a flickering light from the old woman's candle. She puts the candle down, goes out without a word. Her eyes express concern for him.

Hutter is alone. He goes over to the window, throws it open and looks into the starless night. For a moment, he shudders. In the light of the candle, Hutter, shivering, closes the window. His eyes spot a book on the nightstand. The innkeeper's wife must have left it for him.

He takes it, moves back to the candle, sits down on his bed and opens the small volume. He gets interested in it. The book's title page: *The Book of Vampires*. It's subtitled *Of Vampyres, Gastlie Spirits, Bewitchments and the Seven Deadly Sins*. Hutter reads:

Nosferatu
From Belial's seed sprang the vampire
Nosferatu
Who doth live and feed
On the blood of mankind.

Belial, the personified devil in the Hebrew bible!

Undying. From the bloody sins of mankind a creature will be born which will seek revenge for the sin committed by the parents and visited on their children and children's children. Whosoever lusts after blood without reason is under his spell, the spell of the vampyre NOSFERATU, grown up on his native soil—from which alone he draws his powers. Beyond deliverance he doth dwell in gastlie caves, sepulchers and coffins filled so with god-curst earth from the fields of the Black Death.

Hutter, shaking his head, shuts the book, having lost interest. It seems confused reading to him. He yawns and decides it's time to put out the candle, forgetting about the demons of the night.

The morning sun is flooding in from the window. Hutter wakes up. He sits up rubbing his eyes. They fall on the book on the bedside table. He spits on the floor in contempt of the confused rubbish but an inner voice tells him that he should take it with him. He puts it in his bag.

Noise outside. Hutter pauses to listen, then goes over to the window to open it. He takes a deep breath of the morning air. The grassy slope in the morning light. Coachman and grooms are rounding up the horses with long whips and lots of shouting. Hutter steps back from the window. He stretches himself happily; then he takes off his shirt, goes over to the washstand, pours water over his body and has a proper wash.

The innkeeper's wife, mother to all animals, throws corn to her chicken. There are sparrows too. Everything is bathed in bright sunlight.

The bustle of departure. The horses are in harness. The passengers are in the coach. Now, in the morning light, one can see their differences. They are much less uniform than they had seemed the previous nightfall. They are chattering noisily to the people who are staying behind and with the peasants and nosy children gathered around the coach. Hutter appears in an upstairs window, only half-dressed. He comes rushing out with his traveling bag and climbs to his seat on the coach-box. The horses start moving. The Huzules take off their hats. The children are waving. The innkeeper's wife has joined them: "God bless the travelers. May He guard them against evil spirits." They stretch out their hands as if warding them off.

The ride takes all day. In the distance, the coach steeply ascends through the wilderness. It is moving into the setting sun. Wisps of mist are rising and falling in the last rays of the setting sun. Patches of sun and shade.

A carved Madonna casts a long shadow across the road. The mail coach approaches, the horses pulling it with difficulty, breathing hard. Hutter gets off the coach-box. Now he stands at the crossroad. The passengers are anxious to move on, gesturing violently to him not to take the left fork. But Hutter disregards their shouting. He waves farewell with his hat. He pulls himself together and walks resolutely along the road on the left. The trees are casting long shadows on the forest path. To bolster himself, he whistles but the tune is absorbed by the dark trees that look like eerie specters.

Suddenly he balks. What's that? Animals? Rats? Something bigger? A wolf? Something comes racing up, as if moved by a hidden force, almost knocking him down. Hutter starts aside as the strange vehicle turns around and stops dead. So does Hutter.

It's a black carriage. No wheels? Two black horses—griffins? Their legs are invisible, covered by a black funeral cloth. Their eyes like pointed stars. Puffs of steam from their open mouths, revealing white teeth.

Like nearly every traveler into Hell, Hutter is met by a dark ferryman—or, in this case, a carriage driver. The coachman, wearing a feathered hat and hiding his face behind a scarf, looks like a skeleton wrapped up in black cloth. His face pale as death. His eyes are staring at Hutter, almost piercing him. He says no word. Raising his whip, he makes an inviting but also commanding gesture. He waits. Hutter cannot rally enough strength to follow the invitation. Yet those eyes assert their power. Step by step, as if pulled by invisible threads, Hutter approaches the uncanny creature and gets into the carriage.

Quick as lightning, the carriage reverses, dashes off and disappears. With mocking eyes, the raven follows the vehicle that disappears with top speed into a labyrinth of trees. The vehicle glistens eerily and iridescently in the darkness.

Somewhere out there—enshrined in the Carpathian Mountains—lies the dilapidated Castle Orlok.

The arch of a gate in the shade.

The silhouette of the carriage drives underneath it at a sharp angle. The carriage stops in front of the porch. Almost in a faint, Hutter slides down. He stands in front of the closed portal, holding his bag. Somewhere far back in the dark corridors, a figure can be seen. Reluctantly, Hutter bounds up the two steps and stands in the doorway. He would still like to go back. Yet it is too late now. The coach disappears.

Hesitantly he walks towards the stranger. Behind Hutter, the gates close with a noise. Now he is trapped, like the fly in the spider's web. Hutter faces a figure in front. Suddenly, while Hutter approaches, the strange character begins to move.

The other is a giant of a man: 6'4" tall, gaunt, very slim but with broad shoulders. The candle lights up his chalk-white, bloodless face. Is this pale, ghostly creature with hollow eyes and thin mouth embedded in a death skull the lord of the castle himself? Or is he a manservant as Hutter assumes first? The pale skin indicates anemia, lack of blood. His bald head is covered with a bonnet that masks his pointed ears. For a moment, elongated and sharp rat-like incisor teeth protrude over the lower lip. In a way, the slim, cadaverous figure looks like a mix of different nocturnal creatures: rat, bat, gray wolf, hyena, scorpion and spider. Nevertheless, the odd character is human. Or better: It was human.

Orlok smiles and motions for him to follow: "Mr. Hutter, aren't you? You have kept

Count Orlok (Max Schreck) welcomes Hutter (Gustav von Wangenheim) to his castle (from the stills collection of Deutsche Kinemathek–Museum für Film und Fernsehen, Berlin).

me waiting too long. Now it is nearly Midnight. The servants are sleeping!" He holds up the candle and walks ahead.

Hutter follows him to the dining hall. It is of gigantic dimensions. In the center, a massive Renaissance table. Somewhere in the distance, a fireplace. In olden times, this must have been used by knights for their drinking bouts.

Suddenly, Hutter notices that the count is waiting. For a moment he has forgotten his mission. Then he becomes businesslike: "Master Knock, my taskmaster, sends his best regards. He has commissioned me to deliver these documents and negotiate the sale of a house in Wisborg." Quickly he hands him Knock's letters. With a smile, Orlok takes them and gestures for Hutter to take a seat. A frugal meal is waiting for the traveler: "You must be hungry after so long a trip."

Orlok studies the papers. The back page of the letter shows a similar confusion of numbers, legible and illegible letters as Orlok's correspondence. The holy number seven is repeated several times. In between, there are cabbalistic signs. Hutter is spellbound, his eyes wide open. Everything here is so unreal.

Hutter (Gustav von Wangenheim) meets Count Orlok (Max Schreck). Watercolor made from film still in 1922 (photograph prepared by Martin van Elten, courtesy Gerd J. Pohl).

Over the top of the letter, Orlok's cold eyes watch his guest. He is looking over to Hutter like a snake about to hypnotize its prey (as is common belief). Hutter sits down and eats. While he puts a morsel into his mouth, he lifts up his eyes. His look turns into a stare. He is unable to swallow as the count looks daggers at him.

An antique clock with a pendulum. The skeleton's sense strikes the hour. The big hand points to 12 o'clock. Hutter holds a knife and stares into space as if transfixed. All of a sudden, he cuts his finger with the knife. Quick as lightning, the count rushes up to him, pretending to offer his help, arms outstretched: "You have hurt yourself! Your precious blood ... don't wipe it off! That sticky blood ... you see ... should be removed from the cut at once. You never know: The knife might have been poisoned." And before you know it, Orlok's lips are sucking at the hand.

Frightened, Hutter pulls his hand from the firm grip. He moves backwards towards the fireplace. The count utters some words of apology: "Never mind. Shouldn't we like to sit together a little while longer, dear friend. It is still quite a long time until sunrise—and I sleep by day, my dear fellow, I sleep the deepest of sleeps ... completely dead to the world." Then he joins him, wiping his blood-smeared mouth. He explains that one cannot be careful enough in this forbidding region: "Contagious blood poison is too dangerous to be trifled with."

The next morning, Hutter wakes in the large armchair near the fireplace. He has fallen asleep and can hardly remember the events of the night. The armchair opposite is empty. No sign of the lord of the castle. Hutter's gaze wanders across the hall, over to the window. It is very high and divided up into small panes. Morning light is streaming in. An old-fashioned window. An ancient hall, very dusty. But nothing strange about it.

Hutter yawns. His eyes fall on the cut in his hand and he remembers a few more things. But what has he got on his neck? He touches his throat. His bag is nearby on the floor. He takes out his mirror and examines his neck. The mirror shows two red spots on his neck, very close together. Hutter assumes mosquitoes and curses the damned little bloodsuckers. Everybody seems to like his blood here.

No manservant. No sign of life. He shakes his head, puts the mirror away, yawns once more. Suddenly he stops. What's this? He looks at the table, astonished. A still-life of food: fruit, a joint, all kinds of gastronomic delicacies. Hutter is overjoyed. He rushes over to the table and begins to eat as if he were starved. Still chewing, Hutter steps out into the sunlight. He looks around, seeming relaxed. He holds a sheet of paper and a pencil in his hands. Then he casts about for a suitable place and, leaning against the stone wall, he begins to write a letter: "My dear, my dearest, my only one…"

Hutter stands upright, pencil in mouth, looking at the clouds. Why does that stupid mosquito buzzing round his nose stop him from concentrating? Then he catches the insect quickly. And now he knows how to continue the letter. He puts pencil to paper again: "Grieve not that thy beloved is so far away."

He chases away the mosquito and then writes:

> There seems to be a mosquito plague around.
> I have been stung at the throat by two at once, very close together, one on each side. Big beasts they must have been…
> One dreams so heavily in this desolate castle.
> But fear not.

Hutter adds some loving word, then finishes the letter.

A man on horseback is approaching. He stops occasionally and peers over to the castle as if he were scared of it. Hutter stands outside the porch, waving with the letter. The rider comes up cautiously and takes the letter and some coins without dismounting. Then he dashes off at a gallop.

The spectral evening light seems to revive the shadows of the castle once more.

At dawn, Orlok is sitting by the fireplace bent over some plans. Hutter is standing behind him. Orlok shows more interest in the young man than in the papers. Looking over his shoulder, he asks for some more information. Suddenly the count discovers the medallion with the miniature portrait of Ellen. Hutter wants to hide it but Orlok preempts him with his talon-like fingers. He snatches the medallion and opens it heavy-handedly. Hutter says that this is his wife Ellen. Orlok's eyes open wide as he contemplates the picture. His lips look even thinner than before. He gently strokes the picture: "Your wife has a lovely neck." Hutter gasps.

Bitten by mosquitoes? Thomas Hutter still laughs at what he considers Transylvanian superstition (courtesy Christian Dörge, Apex Verlag).

This is too much admiration. Hutter is breathing hard. The fear which grips him in the count's presence is replaced by a sudden fear for his wife. Orlok decides to buy the house: "The handsome deserted dark house … opposite yours…" Quickly, he takes up the

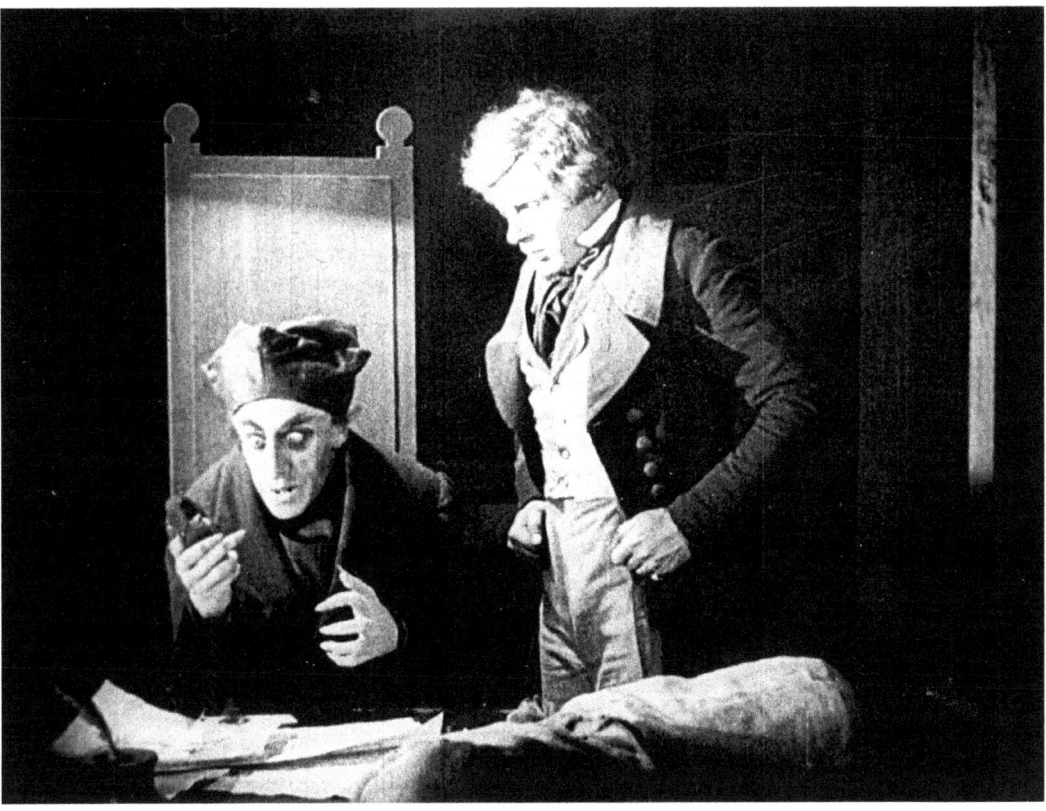

These actors came from Expressionist theater. Count Orlok (Max Schreck) is more fascinated by Ellen's portrait than her husband (Gustav von Wangenheim): "Your wife has a lovely neck…" (from the stills collection of Deutsche Kinemathek–Museum für Film und Fernsehen, Berlin).

contract and signs it. He hands it back to Hutter. Hutter bows uneasily. A satanic look comes into Orlok's snake eyes. His hands have turned into animal-like claws, which he extends like the talons of some monstrous vulture. Orlok: "A beautiful throat indeed. And her cheeks are so crimson." Then his fingers close possessively around the precious medallion. It takes Hutter some effort to get it back.

A candle is burning. Hutter is standing in the middle of the room, quite dazed. He shakes off his misgivings. He starts to undress and finds *The Book of Vampires* from the inn. Mechanically, he opens it to Chapter II. His lips form words:

> Night is the vampire's element.
>   NOSFERATU can see in the dark, which is a wonderful ability to have in this world, half of which is night.
>   We humans, however, are helpless and blind at night.
>   At night Nosferatu does clutch his victims.
>   And does suck like hellish life-potion its blood.
>   Take heed that his shadow not encumber thee like an incubus with gruesome dreams.

Hutter shuts the book. A horrible thought has occurred to him. He is feverish. Is it this book? These ancient walls—do they make him believe in the existence of ghosts? Doesn't the count seem to have claws like an animal and incisors that resemble those of rats?

It's midnight. Involuntarily, Hutter touches what he considered mosquito bites on his neck. He jumps up, first running, then sneaking to the door, opening it a tiny crack. By the fireplace, Count Orlok. No, not Orlok, but a gigantic vampire: Nosferatu, a motionless, somber watcher in the night. He looks to Hutter with a fixed gaze. He has lifted the bonnet to reveal his bulbous skull and bat ears: a sinister keeper of the night. A satyr's grin deforms his features. For a glimpse, he looks like a—*giant mosquito* bracing itself for sucking the unsuspecting sleeper's blood!

Hutter supports himself against the doorpost. A terrible realization has dawned on him. Once again, he peeks through the door. *Shut the door, shut it quickly!* There is no bolt. No lock. He looks around, puts the heavy oak-chair against the door.

Flee?! Hutter jumps to the window and opens it. Too dark, too deep. Hutter falls on his knees by the side of the bed. He holds the medallion, stares at the door behind. Somebody is at the door. Hutter jumps up and throws himself against it. Silence. Nothing. Through the open window, the chamber fills with fog that shapes into a vaguely human figure. Scared, Hutter covers his eyes with his arms. He mustn't see it! He mustn't look! He has been chosen to become the prey of the most horrible demon Hell has spit out. For self-protection he holds Ellen's medallion.

The same night, the same time that her husband is in danger, Ellen wakes up. She is dreaming. As if she has a vision. She has a premonition of danger.... Now she gets up, moves over to the window and steps out on the balcony. Harding, smoking a pipe, is sitting at his desk. He hears a noise and rushes out, storms into the room, finds Ellen's bed empty. He notices the open balcony door. Ellen is perched on the edge of the balcony. Harding doesn't know how to deal with a sleepwalker and begins to shout: "Ellen! Ellen!"

Woken by his yells, Ellen loses her balance and falls over. Harding runs up to her and gathers her in his arms. Annie has heard him yell. Harding carries Ellen over to the bed. Annie blankets her shivering friend. The servant appears. Harding orders him to call a doctor.

Hutter is in serious trouble. The foggy shadow of a huge, devilish creature creeps up on him. Opening his mouth, the uncanny undead reveals his fangs. Irresistibly, the creature bends over the terrified and helpless man, prepared to bury his fangs in his victim's throat. Hutter's only weapon is Ellen's medallion that he holds in front like a crucifix, as if saying: "Take her, not me."

Ellen back in bed ... in delirium. Annie is kneeling by her side. Dr. Sievers, the

Count Orlok needs a new house—and he certainly needs the blood of a woman. Watercolor made from film still (1922) (photograph prepared by Martin van Elten, courtesy Gerd J. Pohl).

town physician, is around. Ellen trembles like a wounded bird. The same moment the monstrous count wants to strike, Ellen screams, sensing the danger telepathically: *"Hutter!"*

Nosferatu turns his ugly head. He is listening intently as if he could feel—hear the terrified female voice from far away. Terror is what electrifies him. He virtually lives on fear. Nosferatu—blood on his lips—retreats from Hutter and disappears as if following the female's invisible voice.

Ellen is calming down slowly. Her terror turns into apathy. She is breathing weakly. Arms outstretched. She settles back listlessly into her pillows. Dr. Sievers' diagnosis: harmless congestions of the blood. Nothing serious. Nothing to worry. But her soul that night caught the cry of the deathbird. Nosferatu was already spreading his wings.

Behind a pointed gable of the castle, the sun is rising slowly. The light of dawn is falling through the window as through a skylight and moving along the wall until it reaches Hutter's face, looking half-fainting, half-asleep. Hutter starts up and clutches his throat. The wound seems larger now. He jumps out of bed, clenching his fists, runs over to the door. Carefully he looks out. The hall is empty. Hutter, pale and hollow-eyed, staggers in. He looks around ... nothing. Shaking his head, fists clenched with wild determination, willing to find the proof, he drags himself forward. Hutter is dragging himself along with difficulty. He goes down a few stairs. Orlok must be downstairs in the basement vault!

Downstairs he finds a door. He opens it. Stands in front of another door. Breaks it open. Inside it's dark and musty. Hutter takes a handkerchief and holds it in front of his nose. In the center of the darkness he finds a sarcophagus. Fear grips him. But he must make certain. He trembles heavily, and it takes some effort to shove away the heavy stone lid. Hutter recoils in fright. For inside the coffin he sees, black and long, the lifeless body of Nosferatu. Horror-stricken, Hutter almost collapses. He rushes out and slams the door behind him.

Hutter is crouched on the floor. His body is twisted with fear. His hair is standing on end ... his eyes staring. He is devastated.

Hours later. He starts up and listens. A noise from outside. Could it mean his salvation? Hope, at least for a brief moment. With difficulty, he drags his weakened body over to the window. He refuses to believe what he sees downstairs: a low-wheeled cart with the two fantastic horses harnessed to it. There are heavy black boxes piled up on the cart, into a gigantic pyramid. Hutter, staring with glazed eyes as the horses dash off with the cart at lightning speed. The big gate closes behind them with a bang. Hutter jumps back from the window.

The river flows majestically through the immense plain. The scenery is bathed in sunshine. All seems peaceful. Then a large raft appears round a bend in the river and floats slowly into view. Boatmen with long poles are pushing it with considerable effort. At the stern, a high pile of boxes. Black, coffin-like boxes stacked into a pyramid. The raft is coming closer and closer—like doom. Nature immediately reacts to the danger. Flowers are dying. Wind blowing. Trees losing their leaves. The sky suddenly darkens.

In the meantime: A long line of white beds. In one of the beds: Hutter in bandages, his eyes closed. The doctor questions the nurse. The nurse tells him that Hutter was brought in yesterday by Huzules. They said he must have fallen. He's still feverish. The doctor examines him. Hutter awakes. He is delirious: "Coffins! Coffins!"

Later, as the nurse reappears, she finds Hutter's bed—*empty*!

Nosferatu is on his way.

The Port of Vasna: At the quayside, ready for loading, and next to other cargo, the pile of black boxes. Customs officials are checking the lettering and bills of consignment. They are approaching the boxes.

One man searches among the papers and hands the freight letters over to the customs inspector. The customs inspector reads the bill of lading: "Mixed cargo, from Varna to Wisborg. Content: garden soil for experimental purposes."

"Open the boxes!" he demands.

Barefooted dock-workers drag up one of the very heavy boxes, heaving and swearing silently. They open the lid with difficulty. There is earth inside! The workers turn the content out. Sand is falling out … nothing but earth. With a shrug, the inspector turns to another pile of cargo. Yet in the sand … something moves inside … something is alive in the coffin's content … jumps out … horrible animals … *rats*! One of the dock workers, who is bending over to scoop the scattered sand back, strikes out violently. Did not one of the animals … reeling from the blow … bite his foot? The big hand pulley hauls up one of the boxes and drops it into the belly of the Russian sailing boat that is anchored at the quay. At the ship's stern, one can discern a name, underneath the baroque figure head of the Greek goddess of agriculture, fertility and marriage: *Demeter,* the name of the double-masted ship.

In Wisborg, Prof. Bulwer, the eminent natural scientist, is surrounded by listeners. He is studying the secrets of nature and their deepest unifying principles. Five of his students have gathered to listen in horror to his lecture on the nature of carnivorous plants. He points emphatically to a plant with a very strange shape: "See the flower, gentlemen. Its petals are reaching out like tentacles. Motionless. Until…. There…. Come closer, will you? Now watch that insect. Hovering, attracted by the scent…. See how it settles on the colorful calyx. Stupid fly. It is doomed." In the thrill of scientific anticipation, Bulwer rubs his hands. In a flash the tentacles have gripped the insect. It is trapped. Its struggling is in vain. With irresistible force, the flower has drawn it into the recesses of the calyx. Bulwer points to the flower: "Isn't it like a—vampire?"

Bulwer, in a quiet, scholarly manner, points to an aquarium: "Now look at that piece of rock." On a piece of rock inside the aquarium hangs a small polyp. As quick as lightning, it stretches out its tentacles, grabs a tiny fish and pulls it up to its mouth. It is almost transparent, colorless and of a jelly-like consistency. Bulwer is fascinated by the object of his studies: "A polyp … with tentacles … transparent … incorporeal … almost a—phantom."

The imminent arrival of Orlok so excites Knock that he has to be brought to the city sanitarium. One of the attendants seems worried: "The patient admitted yesterday is going mad." Dr. Sievers follows the attendant. Knock is catching flies, crying, "Blood is life! Blood is life!" They put him into a straitjacket. Greedily Knock watches a spider.

Ellen is often seen at the beach within the solitude of the dunes. Yearning for her beloved, her eyes scan waves and distance alike. The postman, a small old guy, rummages in his leather bag and produces a letter which he hands with an air of importance to Harding's gardener, who is also old and wizened. Before he leaves, the postman points to the stamp which seems to be of special value, lifting his eyebrows. Harding and Annie are playing cricket when they receive the letter.

Annie immediately takes it, runs to the beach and waves the letter. Ellen trembles. Quickly she takes the letter and tries to open it. But her hands are too weak. Does she foresee disaster? Looking pained, she gives the letter to her friend. Gladly and quickly,

Annie volunteers. She starts to read, gives a joyful laugh. With a cheerful heart, she returns the letter. But barely has she read the letter when Ellen's face assumes an expression of hurt certainty. Does she derive evil premonitions from these lines? Ellen takes Hutter's letter: "[T]here seems to be a mosquito plague around, A PLAGUE!" Annie isn't concerned: "But Ellen, these are only mozzie bites. Totally harmless."

Ellen's face, however, is distorted as if she were suffering physical pain. Annie is perplexed. It starts to get breezy.

Hutter is on the way by horse. Port of Constantinople. The *Demeter* at anchor. What's scuttling over there? A shadow from the ship to the land ... rats ... one ... four ... ten ... an endless stream ... they carry terror with them. Next morning, in a fresh breeze, the *Demeter* emerges from the confusion of mastheads and gains the open sea.

A newspaper report:

PLAGUE

A plague epidemic has broken out in Transylvania and in the Black Sea ports of Varna and Galaz. Young women in particular fall victim to it in large numbers. All victims exhibit the same peculiar stigmata on the neck, the origin of which still puzzles the doctors.

The Dardanelles were closed to all ships suspected of carrying the plague. It is, however, out of question that the epidemic will reach Western Europe very soon.

The ship's captain (Max Nemetz, left) and mate (Wolfgang Heinz) don't know what caused the illness of the delirious sailor (Albert Venohr) (courtesy Deutsche Kinemathek-Museum für Film und Fernsehen, Berlin).

In the distance, the *Demeter* sails through the waters gleaming in the evening night. The ship's mate is running up the companionway in great agitation and crosses the deck on his way to the captain's cabin. The captain is bent over maps, making entries in the log. The mate enters: "Below deck, captain, a sailor.... He has fallen sick. He's delirious, talking in a fever." The captain leaves his work and follows the mate. In the background, the ship's hold. Among other cargo in the deep darkness, the coffins. In the foreground, the crew's cabin with hammocks. In one of them rests the delirious sailor. Captain and mate go up to the sick man, who stares at them as if they were ghosts. He seems to listen intently. Every noise makes him start. Brooding, intense darkness. The lid of one of the coffins seems to open a little. The captain tries to comfort and console the ill sailor: "It's not that serious as you believe. You will be well again. A strong drink will make you rise from the dead." Promptly, the mate produces his bottle and gives it to the patient. The smell seems to wake the sick man up from his lethargy. He takes a long sip. The captain leaves with the mate. The sailor alone: His eyes are wandering. Suddenly they remain fixed, as if spellbound, on the open door leading to the hold. In horror the sailor sits up and remains in a crouching position as if turned to stone.

The illness spreads through the ship like an epidemic. The first stricken sailor pulls the entire crew after him into the dark grave of the waves. In the light of the sinking sun,

Max Schreck confronts the mate (Wolfgang Heinz) (from the stills collection of Deutsche Kinemathek–Museum für Film und Fernsehen, Berlin).

the captain and the mate bid farewell to the last of their comrades. They are about to push the shrouded corpse of the last sailor over the railing. The corpse is slid down into the water by ropes. For a moment the two last survivors pause in quiet contemplation of the horror of death. Suddenly, the mate's body stiffens: He has made a resolution. He shuts his eyes and tries to master the horror that is rising up inside him. Then he pulls himself together, tears the cloth off his face. He takes up an axe, brandishing it in the air. He's going down: "If I'm not back up in ten minutes..." With the courage of a desperate man, he hurries over to the companionway. In the darkness are the black boxes. They are the mate's target. He lifts his axe at the first one and shatters its lid. *Rats!* Round his ankles he feels the crawling of horrible creatures. Yet he pulls himself together. Another box, smashed by a second blow. And the same thing happens again: rats! He is wading through wriggling bodies which surround him from all sides. He withstands the horror. There, a third box. In despair, foaming at the lips, the mate prepares for the third blow. But suddenly the axe falls from his hand. His hair is standing on end. Covering his eyes with his hands the mate runs up the stairs, crazy with fear.

The captain is guarding the helm. From the hatch, the mate emerges ... his hair has turned gray ... his face looks crazed ... he is foaming at the mouth. Trying to escape ... he sways ... turns deliriously in a circle ... loses his sense of direction ... does not see the railing ... and overshoots it, falling head first: a victim of the storm waves.

The captain watches in horror. Now he is left all alone. But his face remains determined. He picks up a rope and ties himself to the helm, not to be tempted to leave it. Thus he awaits the horror. Out of the foam, a foggy character appears. The captain, lashed to his wheel. His face is contorted with terror but he stands firm at the wheel as a wave and a supernatural force engulf him. The ship of death has a new captain.

Nosferatu's deadly breath swells the sails of the death ship which flies on towards its destination with ghostly haste.

Back at Harding's mansion, Annie is asleep. The curtain is billowing and fluttering in the wind. Annie wakes up. Terrified, she jumps out of bed and tries to shut the window. She runs out of the room and finds Ellen's bed deserted. Immediately she realizes what's going on. Ellen, her clothes fluttering in the wind, her hair like a flag, is sleepwalking. She stretches out her arms defensively. A white figure against the black night sky: "I must go to him. He's coming!!!" In the distance, a sailing ship, the *Demeter*, at full sail.

The *Demeter* has come closer, reaching the harbor of Wisborg. A rope is dangling from the deck. Is it swaying in the wind? An endless number of rats climb down the swaying rope. With them, another messenger of death is leaving the ship. Under one strong arm he holds a coffin and heads toward the house he has purchased. Vampires can only draw their shadowy strength from the accursed earth in which they were buried.

At the same time, Hutter returns and embraces and kisses Ellen: "Thank God ... you're safe.... All's well now..." That takes a weight off his mind.

Nosferatu is around the corner. In a boat he passes the river, bearing his coffin, and enters the ruin of a house.

The next day.

Against the wheel, collapsed in death, is the body of the captain, slumped down to one side, supported only by the rope which is knotted about his wrists. Some men are climbing up on deck. They are aghast at the terrible sight. The dead captain, tied to the helm in discharge of his duty! One hand is still on the helm. The other clutches his chest in mortal agony. His head sunk back, face distorted. There are two red marks on his neck! His open eyes staring as if they have seen Hell. He must have died of fright. A man approaches the harbormaster: "Looked over everything. Not a living soul on board, Sir! A Ghost ship!" The harbormaster jots down some notes. Some men lift the dead captain and carry him off. Harding finds the log in the captain's cabin.

The large town hall. On the walls, a number of figureheads. Models of ships are suspended from the ceiling. A huge painting and a trident. The dead captain is lying in state. A physician notices the marks on his neck and turns to Harding. Harding opens the log and begins to skim. The harbormaster and the physician listen:

> Varna–July 12.
>   Crew—minus myself as captain - one helmsman, one ship's mate and five sailors.
>   Departing—for the Dardanelles.
>   Second day: July 13.
>   One sailor ill with fever.
>   Course: SSW, Wind: NE.
>   Third day: July 14
>   Ship's mate is babbling. He claims strange passenger is below deck.
>   Course: SE, Wind: NE

Harding flips pages:

> Tenth day: July 22.
>   Rats in the ship's hold. Danger of plague.

The physician understands: "Danger of plague! There was a report in the newspaper! Go home! All of you! Quick! Better shut all your doors and windows until we know for sure!" Deeply frightened, the bystanders move away. The women put the ends of their headscarves into their mouths.

The rodents set about seizing the town. In the center of the deserted square, a uniformed town drummer with his large drum appears. He beats a mighty roll. A closed window: The hatch opens and a woman's head appears. The drummer has produced a piece of paper and reads aloud:

> Proclamation. It is hereby decreed that the honorable Magistrate forbids the populace to transport the ill or plague-stricken to the hospital, lest the plague spread to the streets. All citizens of Wisborg are notified that the honorable magistrate of this town prohibits any movement of plague-suspects into hospitals to prevent the plague from spreading through the streets.

The drummer has finished reading, pockets the paper and goes off. The woman's face: emaciated, sunken cheeks, long disheveled hair. The disease has gripped her.

Sunset. A bend in a street. A man emerges from a front door and shuts it behind him. Quickly and with circumspection he chalks a white cross on the door. Then he goes on. The adjoining house. The man knocks hard on the door. From a window above, a head looks out. There are still people living here. The man moves on. The next house he knocks at remains quiet. He grabs the door handle; it is locked. Again he draws a cross on a deserted house.

The first house in the side street. A coffin is being carried out. The men carrying it have white bandages over their mouths. The man comes along and draws his white cross on this door. He walks on and on, following his horrible business…

Ellen is standing by the window watching the macabre scene downstairs. She tries to avoid looking down but some unknown power forces her. The old deserted house across the street. A window divided into four rectangular panes. Stuck to the window, almost completely covering it, something looking like a huge black four-legged spider with the face of an ugly rat.

The lamp-lighter comes down the darkening street and lights the street lamps. As every night, he fulfills his task routinely although tonight nobody else is around. Then he walks on.

Ellen knows that religion holds that repeated intercourse with an incubus will result in the deterioration of health, or even death. She feels doomed. Death is surely waiting for her. She gets up to open the window and breathe some fresh air.

The next day. In the distance, a strange procession is approaching: one coffin after another carried by solemn survivors. Ellen, on the point of fainting,

Nosferatu is in town (from the stills collection of Deutsche Kinemathek–Museum für Film und Fernsehen, Berlin).

turns away from the view. She cannot bear the sight of this wretchedness. She sinks into a chair, resting her head in her hands. She takes a book she has found among Hutter's things. Hutter has made her swear not to touch the small volume which frightened him with terrible visions, but she cannot resist. Hutter doesn't know that she is reading *The Book of Vampires*, reading about the Undead who appears at night to clutch his victim and suck his blood:

> Wherefore no other salvation is possible but that a maiden wholly without sin maketh the vampire forget the first crow of the cock. Would that she give freely of her blood...

Ellen lifts up her head, staring into space like a visionary.

When Hutter returns, she tries to hide the volume and shuts her eyes. But Hutter has seen: She knows everything. She points to the deserted house and its ghostly inhabitant: "This is what I see each evening." Hutter spots an ugly face: Nosferatu. There seems to be no escape, not for Ellen, not for him. But Ellen is determined to avenge the death of all these innocent people.

The horrified town needs a scapegoat. A man points at something opposite. People rush up to him; they all turn to face the same way, look up. They make threatening gestures. An old woman, a veritable hag, is the first one to throw a stone: That man has strangled the custodian and escaped from the asylum. His figure is crouching on the rooftop. It's Knock! *He* is the blood-sucking vampire! Knock is looking down with a sneer on his face and pokes out his tongue. A stone whizzes past Knock. He suddenly gets up and clambers off. Knock jumps down a wall and runs off. In the distance, some men appear, chasing him. Figures are running, no more than silhouettes. Knock is in front. His pursuers follow a long way behind. Evening mists. A cornfield. Between the ears of corn, a head with disheveled hair. Then a bony hunchback.

The landscape has grown dim in the evening light. The men chasing Knock are approaching but seem to have lost the trail. Suddenly, one of them sees something. He opens his eyes wide. "There!" One of the pursuers shouts: "Over there! There he is!!" They all look one way. All dash off in that direction. In the distance, one can still see the back and head. Is it Knock? He seems not to hear or see his pursuers. The men are coming near, rushing towards him across the field. They lift up their sticks and fists. But the thing they have seen is only a scarecrow. A black coat is dangling on a stick. The men fall on it in their disappointment. Suddenly they stop. There! What can that be? A hundred feet away, a head has appeared. Then the figure of a man. It is moving quickly, fleeing towards the moor.

Finally Knock, held by two men, is brought back to the mental asylum. Sievers comes in. Knock tries to break free. The men put him down brutally. "We got him—we got the vampire!"

In a stupor, Knock is perching on his bunk. He's gone mad. Something attracts his attention: A spider-web with a live spider in it which clutches, vampire-like, an insect and is sucking its blood. Knock is in exultation. To him, this is a tidbit. All of a sudden he jumps and gets himself the fat spider from the wall. Delicious.

Ellen wakes up. She gets up, walking as if pulled by invisible threads. She goes over to the window. She sees—*somebody* at the window. Slowly the shape raises what seem to be arms—waving as if saying: Come! Come to me! Gasping. Thirsting. Ellen is about to collapse by the window. Shaking with fear, she struggles violently with herself. Expecting the final battle, Ellen awakens Hutter. He promises to fetch Dr. Sievers but she sends him to Bulwer. She says he is the only one who can help.

The shadow character nears. Its claws open the door to her room. The creature knees besides her, sucking her blood: lost in thought.

Death of a vampire (courtesy Christian Dörge, Apex Verlag).

The long shadows of sunrise.

Knock alone in the sunlight, which is falling through the barred window. He is mumbling disconnected words. He hears the first crow of the cock. He fears for the "master."

The Undead, bowed over Ellen, hears it too. Slowly Nosferatu raises his fearsome head. Unbelieving, he rises and clutches at his heart. He turns at the window and—simply dissolves. A small heap of ashes is all that remains of the gruesome nightmare. Knock is fettered. "The master is dead. The master is dead," he agonizes.

When Hutter arrives with Bulwer, it's already too late. Ellen rises in her bed and calls for him: *Hutter!* It is fulfilled. Hutter runs over to her and holds her dead body in his arms.

Thus the Chronicle of the Great Dying ends:

> Witness the miracle on the heels of the truth. At that very hour the Great Death comes to an end, and as if confronted by the victorious radiance of the living sun, the Shadow of the Deathbird is dispersed.

Casting a Man Named "Shock"

A Skeletal Monster

We don't know how many revisions there had been, or what draft number was the one filmed. There was at least one revised script. The physician was named Stevens in Galeen's screenplay. In the film, he is Dr. Sievers. And the Russian ship—it was called the *Demeter* in Stoker's book—was to be renamed the *Empusa* (a demogoddess of Greek mythology who drank the blood of young men while they slept) when filming began. Murnau followed Galeen's final shooting script closely, but one should note that the final 12 pages that described Ellen's sacrificial death were written by Murnau and not by Galeen. It's interesting so far as neither Stoker nor Galeen saw a vampire dying at dawn. Daylight was a new means to kill a vampire, most likely invented by Murnau.

But once work was finished, Murnau would stick closely to the script. Film critic Béla Balázs wrote in 1923,

> Shivering fits and incubus, nightly shadows and premonition of death, lunacy, specters and ghosts are woven into images of gloomy mountain landscapes and stormy seas. Since *Caligari*, *Nosferatu* is the first film that is going to give us the creeps not with ridiculously intricate torture and murder machines. We are not frightened by the dangerous options of the technique but by the unknown mysteries of nature.[1]

Balázs concluded that the new and unsurpassed feature of the film was to make use of the latent poetry of nature.

David Pirie wrote that everybody who has seen *Nosferatu* will agree that the strength of the film radiates from the figure of the vampire. Nothing could deviate more from Stoker's trim vampire nobleman than this skeletal, crooked monster that shuffles over the screen. It was more dead body than any of those Hollywood zombies,

> In Murnau's film the vampire Nosferatu represents an apocalyptic affliction; an army of rats follows and with them comes the Black Death. Conquered is the vampire not by the ploy of a fanatic Dr. Van Helsing but by the courage of a young woman who, instead of flying from the creature, encounters him with open arms; by a sudden sun ray the vampire is destroyed.[2]

Conrad Veidt Is Not Available

To Murnau, it was clear that only one man could play Nosferatu: His friend and colleague Conrad Veidt, who had been Dr. Jekyll and Mr. Hyde. But for some reason Veidt was not available. He was still starring as the maharajah of Eshnapur in the monumental production *Das indische Grabmal* (*The Indian Tomb*) for director Joe May on May's film lot in Woltersdorf near Berlin. It may be that Murnau was deeply hurt by Veidt's rejection. Murnau would not work with Veidt again. They had made four movies together and were so close that at one time they had their own film company. And Veidt would never play the vampire, a role almost tailored for him. Universal was going to cast him as Dracula in 1930 but he turned them down because he felt that his English needed improvement. Bela Lugosi, who had English-language trouble too, had no qualms about accepting the role. To play Dracula on stage, he had learned the part phonetically.

There were a lot of rumors concerning the actor who became Veidt's substitute in *Nosferatu*. Edgar G. Ulmer, who assisted Murnau on *Sunrise* and *4 Devils*, later suggested that in some scenes a different actor played the vampire. Some say that in a few scenes, it was Murnau, who was quite tall and also an actor. That's certainly not true. Others said that the man who portrayed Nosferatu was a vaudeville performer. Ado Kyrou wrote, "The opening credits name Max Schreck in the part of the vampire but it is well-known that this is a deception. Who is hiding behind the Nosferatu character? Maybe a vampire in person?"[3] Some speculated that Max Schreck was a pseudonym for another actor, most likely Murnau's friend Hans Rameau. Well, Rameau was involved but in a different way.[4]

In the part of Nosferatu, Max Schreck became what they like to call "cult" today, not during lifetime but posthumously. He was a master of makeup and this was an asset for casting him as the monstrous vampire. According to Hanns-Georg Rodek,

> He appears to be half-decayed, with deep-set eyes, dried-up lips, fragmentary set of teeth. He is more insect than human, the scrawny fingers as long as the legs of a spider, the ears so distinctive like those of a bat. When he speaks one can imagine what he says—it's a silent—only as kind of a rattle in the throat.
> If the viewer overcomes the modern reflex of understanding the Expressionist play of the silent film basically as funny, involuntarily fright sets in. Even eight decades later the name stands worldwide representatively for the emotion that he describes. In *Batman Returns* Christopher Walken plays a villain named "Max Shreck," and the naming of the big, green, ugly swamp monster Shrek is a reference to the *Nosferatu* actor too.[5]

We have to add a character that Howard Vernon played in Jean-Luc Godard's Lemmy Caution dystopia *Alphaville* (1965, also known as *Dick Tracy on Mars*), a kind of forgotten *Blade Runner*: Prof. *Leonard* Nosferatu, who in the German dubbing became a Prof. von Braun!

Paul Wegener later cast Schreck, as we already mentioned, in a minor part in his horror drama *Ramper, der Tiermensch* (*The Strange Case of Captain Ramper*. 1927). But these two movies are all that connect actor Max Schreck with the so-called genre of horror films. And only one was needed to put him up there in the horror hall of fame, right beside Lon Chaney, Karloff, Lugosi, Lee, Cushing and Vincent Price. For a biography titled *Max Schreck. Gespenstertheater*, journalist Stefan Eickhoff meticulously researched Schreck's life and career but about his involvement in *Nosferatu* we don't learn that much.

The Miser

We guess that it was Hans Rameau who called Murnau's attention to Schreck when Conrad Veidt turned them down. At that time, Schreck appeared as Harpagon, Molière's

The Miser, who became an acting triumph on the Munich stage. Reviewers described him as the proverbial demon of miserliness.[6] Unlike Veidt who was a master of expression, Schreck was his own best makeup artist, but nobody got the idea to make him a star of a series of horror movies. In Hollywood he would have been immediately typecast, a fact, however, welcomed by Schreck. In Germany, Schreck was allowed to remain versatile. Schreck was too much a man of the stage and therefore did film work only when time allowed, mostly supporting roles and even bit parts. One has also to consider that tall actors were feared by those who were shorter and therefore had problems in getting the big parts of literature.

Anyway, Rameau, who played Cleanthe, Harpagon's son, convinced producer Albin Grau to travel to Munich and meet Schreck. In one afternoon, Grau and Schreck developed the mask of the Undead. Jens Geutebrück, a self-taught historian, has devoted a website to this actor, *Ein Grabstein für Max Schreck* (*A Tombstone for Max Schreck*):

> Max Schreck was delighted by the idea to prove his makeup artistry in a large, important movie part and began to experiment right on the spot during Grau's visit.
>
> Then they went to the costume stock of Munich Kammerspiele [Intimate Theater], and Max Schreck took an old frock coat. They tried some alternatives, and on the evening the shape of Nosferatu was almost perfect. The only feature that was changed later was the bald skull that wasn't planned in the beginning.
>
> Schreck pointed out that he only would be available in the theatrical break during summer because Grau indicated that the shooting schedule might include some work abroad.
>
> Two weeks later Grau sent Schreck a film contract.
>
> The character created by Schreck had a great impact on the script which was revised by Murnau and Galeen several times.
>
> The figure of Nosferatu was solely Max Schreck's very own creation. Photos during the shooting show that he didn't need a makeup artist, that he did everything by himself.[7]

Max Schreck in full makeup on stage in Munich in Molière's *The Miser* (author's collection).

The memorable meeting must have taken place around April or May 1921. Lon Chaney too was his own makeup artist when he did *The Hunchback of Notre Dame* and *The Phantom of the Opera* but those were after *Nosferatu*. *Nosferatu* was released before Chaney's big successes, and one might wonder if Chaney had heard about or even seen Murnau's movie.[8] The Nazis, however—they knew Chaney. They had not forgotten that he had starred in the anti–German Hollywood drama *The Kaiser, the Beast of Berlin* in 1918. *Völkischer Beobachter* raged at Carl Laemmle who became the *film Jew* par excellence having produced this movie and *All Quiet on the Western Front* in 1930. The Hitler paper complained that

Laemmle the Jew was still an honorary citizen of his so-called "home" village Laupheim in Swabia near Ulm.⁹ Anyway, the press was invited by Prana with exquisite invitation cards to attend the final scenes that Murnau shot with Max Schreck, who had returned for these interiors from Munich to Berlin:

> Camera! Action! Dr. [sic!] Murnau, the director, supervises the scene. When he calls the coffin lid springs open and slowly, slowly lifted by invisible hands, the figure of Nosferatu shoots up like an arrow: the vampyr, the typical two incisors in an otherwise toothless mouth. [...] The makeup of Nosferatu, portrayed by Max Schreck from Munich, is horrifying. Bloodshot eyes stare out of a bald skull, with the two pointed ears of a bat. The tall, slim actor is dressed in a black suit. Skinny arms, long curved fingernails.¹⁰

Schreck did create an artificial hook nose, heavy eyebrows, carved rat-like teeth held in place by his upper lip. He wore a bald cap that cut down near the actor's eyes and left little tufts covering the seam of the join between his pointed ear extensions, hiding the bald cap's edge, all covered with lots of greasepaint. Long, talon-like fingernails resembled those of Fu Manchu. Orthochromatic film made the blends easier. His shoulders were padded. "The slightly raised shoulder pads promote a vision of rigor mortis while the buttons down the front are reminiscent of spikes in a coffin."¹¹ The costume made him appear "gravedigger-esque." His body was built up to remain as stiff as possible.

> For the most part Count Orlack [sic] was shot in such a way as to make his head look bigger either by filming slightly above his height or by having the actor pull his chin in. This plus shooting with wide angle lenses will exaggerate the size of the head since it is nearest to the lens. This gives Count Orlack's head an even more unnatural look and a more skull-like appearance.¹²

Geutebrück studied the film frame by frame and saw that the makeup changed slightly from scene to scene: the nose, the bush of hair.

The press reported that Schreck "was happy that the part was finally finished. He tells us a lot about the serious artistic work that went into this film."¹³ Subcutaneously, Schreck also improvised a caricature of the Prussian official as part of his Nosferatu portrayal.

The mask, by the way, turned up again in 1979 when Austrian-born Reggie Nalder played Kurt Barlow, master vampire, in the TV version of Stephen King's *Salem's Lot:* he was made up to look like Schreck's Nosferatu. Jack H. Young, an old-timer who had made up Margaret Hamilton as the Wicked Witch in *The Wizard of Oz* (1939), was in charge of the special makeup.

Max Schreck was born Friedrich Gustav Max Schreck on September 6, 1879, in the fashionable Tiergarten district of Berlin, 75–76 Kaiserin Augusta Strasse. His father was Gustav Ferdinand Schreck, a Royal topographer in the Prussian military staff, a former artificer (*Oberfeuerwerker*). His mother was Pauline Schreck. Their neighbors were wealthy traders, high-ranked officers, bankers, privy counselors and artists. Six years later, his father purchased a house in Friedenau which at that time belonged to the administrative district of Teltow. Members of the educated classes, the Schrecks visited the theaters and took their son along. This was the seed for Max's future ambition: to become an actor. The father disliked Max's theatrical ambitions and asked him to finish business management training. The acting profession was still regarded as despicable. Comedians were compared with gypsies, tramps and molesters. Morally reprehensible persons pretend to be kings and men of science. Impossible! And actresses came next to prostitutes. But Max wouldn't give in. As a tall youth, he was used to being the center of attention, if not always favorably. As his family name Schreck meant fear, fright, shock or scare (not exactly terror as reported), he was also the butt of jokes and mockery. But his mother got him some money to secretly take acting lessons. He went to actor Max Winter from the Royal Playhouse and recited monologues which he had learned. Winter acknowledged the voice talent but told him what we already have observed: that he would be too slim and tall for certain leading parts such as Hamlet or Don Carlos. Schreck officially pursued his acting ambitions shortly after his father, who had been promoted Royal audit officer, died of a long illness at age 53 on June 17, 1898. Pauline Schreck sold the Friedenau villa but remained there as a leaseholder.

Max attended a regular acting school that was under the supervision of Marie Seebach. There the greats of the Berlin stage, actors like Adalbert Matkowsky and Rosa Poppe, educated free of charge. As most young actors would do, Max began to play the small theaters in the provinces. His debut took place in Meseritz in the West Prussian province Posen (Poznan); his first verifiable booking began in Speyer on October 6, 1901. He started out with touring companies, in German derogatorily called *Schmieren*, one of which was led by Demetrius Schrutz (1856–1938): Mühlhausen, Meseritz, Speyer, Rudolstadt, Erfurt, Weissenfels, next a longer stay in Gera. He became a member of Trummer's traveling troupe and appeared on stages in Wesel and Luzern where he played the Earth Spirit (and some minor parts) in Johann Wolfgang von Goethe's *Faust*. In this time, he met his future wife, actress Fanny Normann.

On October 14, 1904, Schreck entered a firm booking in the small town of Zittau in Upper Lusatia. Thanks to his height, he must have been an impressive Hagen von Tronje in the *Nibelungs*. He stayed in Zittau until April 1905. Then he went to the university city of Jena where he appeared on the stage of the Royal Theater. Another booking together with Fanny was at the Cure Theater in Freudenstadt.

Eventually better offers started to come in, leading Schreck to larger cities, Frankfurt included. From Frankfurt, he went straight to Max Reinhardt in Berlin (Deutsches Theater) and later to Otto Falckenberg in Munich (Kammerspiele/Intimate Theater).

In Munich and Berlin, Schreck was seen in Shakespeare plays: as Dr. Cajus in *The Merry Wives of Windsor*, as Tom Snout in *A Midsummer Night's Dream*, as Le Beau in *As You Like It*, as Pistol in *Pericles, Prince of Tyre*, Sir Colenso Ridgeon in George Bernard Shaw's *The Doctor's Dilemma*; as Old Ekdal in Henrik Ibsen's *The Wild Duck*, Anton Antonovich Skvosnik-Dmukhanovsky in Nikolai Gogol's *The Government Inspector*, the Angel of Death in Gerhart Hauptmann's *Hanneles Himmelfahrt*, Naryshkin in Shaw's *Great Catherine*, Liberty in Klabund's *Cromwell*, a lunger in Erwin Piscator's staging of *The Adventures of the Brave Soldier Svejk*, a man of letters in August Strindberg's *Comrades*, Father Ignotus in Erik Charell's production of Alexandre Dumas' *The Three Musketeers*, Bruchsal in Gotthold Ephraim Lessing's *Minna von Barnhelm*, Brander in Goethe's *Faust*, Escartefigne in Marcel Pagnol's *Fanny*—to name just a few of many plays. He enacted a variety of roles, the prerequisite for long-term engagements at theaters.

In between, he filmed in Berlin as well as in Munich, first in *Der Tanz in den Tod* (*The Dance Into Death*) which flopped. Then, under the direction of Fred Stranz, Schreck played an American newspaper publisher in the action film *Der unheimliche Chinese* (*The Uncanny Chinese*). In *Der Richter von Zalamea* (*The Judge of Zalamea*, 1920), he was Mendo, a young nobleman, a Junker. Only a fragment survives in the Bundesarchiv, the German Federal Archive, and it looks quite disappointing. There was also *Der Favorit der Königin* (*The Favorite of the Queen*, 1922; as Jack, a body snatcher), *Nathan der Weise* (*Nathan the Wise*, 1922; as Grandmaster of the Templars), *Der Kaufmann von Venedig*

(*The Merchant of Venice*, 1923; as Doge), *Die Strasse* (*The Street*, 1923; directed by Karl Grune, as the Blind One), *Die Finanzen des Grossherzogs* (*Finances of the Grand Duke*, 1924; as sinister conspirator in his second and final film with F. W. Murnau), *Am Rande der Welt* (*At the Edge of the World*, 1927; his second picture under director Karl Grune, as a peddler and enemy spy alongside Brigitte Helm who had just finished *Metropolis*), *Der Alte Fritz* (*The Old Fritz*, 1927–28; as Rietz the valet), *Waterloo* (1928, his third and last film with director Karl Grune; although we couldn't detect him on screen when we saw it, we know from a still that he was cast), the movie that turned out to be the Waterloo of the production company, *Emelka* (*Münchner Lichtspielkunst A.G.*), the forerunner of *Bavaria*, and *Der Kampf der Tertia* (*Fight of the Tertia*, 1929; directed by Max Mack, as Benno Biersack, a great supporting part). In talkies, his roles got smaller, and often producers and distributors didn't bother to mention him in the credits: He went unlisted in *Boykott/Primanerehre* (*Boykott*, 1930; as a scribe), *Die verkaufte Braut* (*The Bartered Bride*, 1932; directed by Max Ophüls, as Muff the Indian), *Fräulein Hoffmanns Erzählungen* (*Miss Hoffmann's Tales*, 1933; as Otto the valet), *Der Tunnel* (*The Tunnel*, 1933; directed by Curtis Bernhardt; as Chesterfield, an American investor in a scene with Gustaf Gründgens), *Das Stahltier* (*The Steel Animal*, 1934; as Cugnot) and *Peer Gynt* (1934; as the mayor). As dubbing artist, he might have been in Carl Theodor Dreyer's *Vampyr* voicing Maurice Schutz (we cannot tell for sure) and almost certainly was in the German release versions of *The Scarlet Pimpernel* (dubbing Ernest Milton, who played Robbespierre) and *The Count of Monte Cristo* (as Abbé Faria, in the original played by O.P. Heggie who still is remembered for the small part of a blind hermit in James Whale's *Bride of Frankenstein*).

As an actor, Schreck was a narcissist, always concerned about his exterior and semblance. In this regard, he was not different from most other actors whose conceitedness is part of their stability. He loved to entertain women including actress Anny Ondra, the wife of boxing champion Max Schmeling. His wife Fanny was aware of this friendship.

Schreck also appeared in literary, decidedly anti–Fascist cabaret performances organized by Erika Mann. He played the role of a cook who dictated to people what they had to eat and whatnot. The cabaret's name, Die Pfeffermühle (The Peppermill), was suggested by Erika's father, the famous novelist and Nobel Prize winner Thomas Mann. The show premiered on January 1, 1933, in the renowned "Bonbonniere" in the historic district of Munich, 29 days before Hitler was made Reich Chancellor. There Schreck's partners were Therese Giehse, Sybille Schloss and pianist Magnus Henning, all of whom would leave Germany soon after.

Schreck would stay and die. He passed away right before the premiere of his final UFA production *Die Letzten Vier von Santa Cruz* (*The Last Four of Santa Cruz*, directed by Werner Klingler on location in Teneriffa) in which he had a somewhat more prominent speaking part than in his previous movies. On February 19, 1936, he filled in for his colleague Will Dohm, who was on leave in *Don Carlos* as grand inquisitor. He then wanted to see a film but instead walked straight home. At night he felt unwell. A doctor sent him to the hospital immediately. On 8:30 on Friday, February 20, 1936, the actor who once was Nosferatu died. Otto Falckenberg, Fritz Reif and Hedwig Wangel spoke at his February 23 funeral. Falckenberg was the one to remind the mourners of Schreck's part as the eerie specter.

> In the night following Wednesday to Thursday unexpectedly actor Max Schreck died, one of the most loyal and oldest members of the Munich Kammerspiele in Schauspielhaus. Whoever saw the artist in his dotty, occasionally ghostly-grotesque parts will sense the acrimony of this loss.

Max Schreck without makeup (author's collection).

He was cremated at Munich East Cemetery (Ostfriedhof) and his urn was brought to Berlin by his older brother Augustin, a music teacher. On March 14, 1936, Max Schreck was buried at the gravesite of his mother Pauline in Wilmersdorf forest cemetery. Present was Schreck's niece, young actress Gisela Uhlen, who was born as Gisela Friedlinde Schreck and a few years later played in Nazi propaganda films: *Mann für Mann*, the anti–Semitic *Die Rothschilds* and *Ohm Krüger* (*Uncle Kruger*). After the war, she was seen in several West German Edgar Wallace films and in R.W. Fassbinder's *Die Ehe der Maria Braun* (*The Marriage of Maria Braun*). Gisela had a daughter with Wolfgang Kieling (Gromek in Hitchcock's *Torn Curtain*): Susanne Uhlen. So in a way, Schreck's acting legacy continued over the years.

From Hutter and Ellen to Knock

Gustav von Wangenheim, who played Thomas Hutter, the unintentional bringer of ill luck and vampiric disease, was born on February 18, 1895, in Wiesbaden, capital city of the federal state of Hesse. Ingo Clemens Gustav Adolf Freiherr von Wangenheim was the son of actor Eduard Clemens Franz Freiherr von Wangenheim, who entered the stage as Eduard von Winterstein, and his Jewish wife, actress Minna Mengers, who committed suicide when Gustav was four years old. Wangenheim attended Max Reinhardt's acting school. In 1915, after serving briefly on the Western Front, he was discharged due to an eye injury. He was seen on stages in Vienna, Darmstadt and Berlin. Under Reinhardt he was Laertes in *Hamlet*, Demetrius in *A Midsummer Night's Dream* and Donalbain in *Macbeth*. He was a member of USPD, the Independent Social Democratic Party of Germany, and in 1922 joined the Communist Party of Germany KPD: Kommunistische Partei Deutschlands. The Berlin press announced his death right before the premiere of *Nosferatu*: suicide by poison. One day later, the papers published a correction: It was not Gustav but his younger brother, who hadn't poisoned himself but had died from pneumonia. In 1933, Gustav and his wife Inge immigrated via Paris to the Soviet Union. The Nazis sentenced him to death in absentia. In 1935–36, at the Mezhrabpom Red Front Studio in Moscow, he directed *Kämpfer* (*Fighters*), a film about the 1933 Reichstag fire. (Joris Ivens was his assistant on the production, and Maxim Gorki was invited to act as consultant.) In September 1936, he was delegated to a four-day *chistka* (political purge) on behalf of the German section of the Soviet Writers' Union: "When I came here as a German party member, I saw during a purge [sitting] how comrades beat themselves on the breast and spoke voluntarily of what they had done, the terrible acts [*Schweinerei*] they had committed. I have to admit that I was aghast."[14]

In 1940, Wangenheim became a Soviet citizen. He was a founding member of the National Committee Free Germany. After the war, he returned to Berlin where he briefly became head of Deutsches Theater. "Be radical like Hamlet. Think things through the end. Act with decision! We are more fortunate than Shakespeare's Hamlet because we know the way out. We understand the purpose of our struggle."[15] He supported the release of fellow actor Gustaf Gründgens, who had been interned in Jamlitz. Wangenheim lived in East Berlin and was presented with the National Prize of GDR. Occasionally he directed films for DEFA, the state-owned film company: *Und wieder 48* (*'48 All Over Again*, 1948), *Du bist der Richtige* (*You Are the Right One*, 1950) and *Gefährliche Fracht* (*Dangerous Freight*, 1954). His final directorial effort in the movies, the unfinished *Lied über dem Tal* (*Song Over the Valley*, 1956), had to be shut down because of differences between the scriptwriters and the original director Helmut Brandis. Wangenheim died on August 5, 1975, in the capital of GDR.[16]

His bride is played by Mrs. Paul Wegener: Greta Schröder. Born Margarete Schröder on September 7, 1891, in Düsseldorf, she was educated for some time in Britain (she attended Oxford) and became a Reinhardt actress (and dancer). Her first husband, Hungarian-born Ernst Mátray, also a Reinhardt thespian, founded a company with Ernst Lubitsch, Malu Films (Mátray-Lubitsch). Greta wrote a script for them titled *Zucker und Zimt* (*Sugar and Cinnamon*, 1915). The next year she wrote for her husband the first film version of *Das Phantom der Oper* (*The Phantom of the Opera*) starring Nils Chrisander as Erik and Aud Egede-Nissen as Christine. She and Paul Wegener married in October 1926 (she was Wegener's fourth wife). The marriage was short-lived. (In 1931, Wegener married a fifth time. His last wife was Elisabeth Rohwer.) In the 1930s, when the Nazis came to power, Schröder was one of the select few who were allowed to film in foreign countries. In 1937 London, she had a supporting role as Baroness Lehzen in Herbert Wilcox's biopic *Victoria the Great*; in 1938 she was in the sequel *Sixty Glorious Years*. She was cast as Countess Voss in Veit Harlan's Agfacolor propaganda piece *Kolberg* (1944–45) as well as in two postwar Harlan films. On stage, she appeared until the late 1950s under the name Margarete Schröder-Wegener. Some sources claimed that Greta Schröder died on April 13, 1967, in Vienna but she actually passed away on June 8, 1980, in Berlin-Steglitz.

Unforgettable as Knock the real estate broker, was Alexander Granach. He was born Jessaja Gronach on April 18, 1890, in Werbowitz, East Galicia, the ninth child of a Jewish peasant family. In 1906, he came via Vienna to Berlin, joined a Yiddish amateur theater and in 1909 enrolled in Max Reinhardt's acting classes. In World War I, he fought at the Italian Front and spent time in Italian war captivity. After the war, he acted for directors Erwin Piscator and Leopold Jessner and also made some films. In 1933, he immigrated via Switzerland and Warsaw to the Soviet Union where he had a part in fellow actor Gustav von Wangenheim's production *Kämpfer* and almost fell victim to the Stalinist purge; author Lion Feuchtwanger took a stand for him and succeeded in getting him an exit permit. His stay in Hollywood from 1938 fueled his career. He played opposite Greta Garbo in Ernst Lubitsch's *Ninotchka* (1939), in the Hemingway adaptation *For Whom the Bell Tolls* (1943; director: Sam Wood) with Gary Cooper and Ingrid Bergman, the anti–Fascist *Hangmen Also Die!* (1943; director: Fritz Lang from an original story by Lang and Bertolt Brecht) and *The Seventh Cross* (director: Fred Zinnemann; from the novel by Anna Seghers). On March 14, 1945, Granach unexpectedly died after an appendicitis operation from a lung embolism in New York. His autobiography *There Goes an Actor* was published in 1945 by exile publishing house Neuer Verlag in Stockholm.

Georg Heinrich Schnell played Hutter's friend Harding, the ship owner. The son of a supplier of the Chinese army, he was born on April 11, 1878, in Chefoo, today Yantai. In 1900, he participated in the suppression of the Boxer Rebellion. In 1903, his German acting career started on the stage of the City Theater of Elbing before he arrived in Berlin where he worked for Max Reinhardt. Among his many films was Alfred Hitchcock's directorial debut *The Pleasure Garden* (1925). In 1934, he played Colonel Black in the anti–British colonial drama *Die Reiter von Deutsch-Ostafrika* (*The Riders of German East Africa*, director: Herbert Selpin). Some Germans remember him from his small role in *Die Feuerzangenbowle* (*The Brandy Punch*, 1944; director: Helmut Weiss), his last movie, as one of the old men who join Heinz Rühmann in his reminiscences. Schnell died on March 31, 1951, in Berlin.

For the part of Harding's sister Annie, Murnau was looking for some Kaulbach type[17] and found it in Ruth Landshoff (1904–1966), who was no trained actress but famous: According to a book by Sabine Rohlf,

> Even before she wrote her first article aged 23, newspapers published photos of her beautiful bob, well-known she was anyway. The niece of publisher Samuel Fischer played croquet as a child with Thomas Mann. She was portrayed by Oskar Kokoschka, acted in Murnau's *Nosferatu* and stood with Marlene Dietrich on the stage—acting-wise only moderately talented, as she conceded herself, she was quite decorative. She was one of the first women to drive a motorcycle, chauffeured Charlie Chaplin through Berlin and could be met everywhere where it was interesting and entertaining. In the evening she favorably wore smoking, some of her best friends were homosexual, there was always somebody to lie at her feet. A few years she was hooked up with playwright Karl Gustav Vollmoeller, later for a while with Friedrich-Heinrich Graf Yorck von Wartenburg, a handsome bank clerk. She loved during those relationships many others—male as well as female. Today we would call her polyamorous and queer.[18]

Shooting *Nosferatu* in Kafka's Castle

Exteriors

Murnau, Albin Grau and their film team found suitable locations in the Hanseatic City of Lübeck, Rostock and Wismar all doubling for the fictitious Wisborg. *Nosferatu* officially began with exterior shooting in Lübeck, the birthplace of novelists Heinrich and Thomas Mann as well as Willy Frahm, who changed his name in exile to Willy Brandt and became West Germany's fourth chancellor. In July 1920, one year before the shooting of *Nosferatu* started in Lübeck, philosopher Hans Blumenberg was born there. People had settled in this area after the last Ice Age ended. Around 1200, the port of Lübeck became the main point for colonists leaving for the Baltic territories conquered by the Livonian and later by the Teutonic Order. In the 14th century, Lübeck became the "Queen of the Hanseatic League," by far the most important member of the medieval trade organization until its decline.

The abandoned warehouses which Nosferatu chooses to make his quarters still exist in Lübeck. These are the former salt storehouses, historic warehouses where salt delivered from Lüneburg awaited shipment to Baltic ports. Since the 1920s, not much has changed there. Other buildings and streets in Lübeck, however, have changed considerably or don't exist any more. In World War II, Lübeck was heavily bombed by the RAF. The *Nosferatu* locations selected in Lübeck were close to each other, which made things quite easy for the filmmakers: Next to the salt storehouses is a street named Depenau (or Tiefe Au). A narrow passageway leads to Hutter's house, situated in a small square at the churchyard of St. Aegidien. The front of Hutter's house has changed little since.

An early scene where Hutter meets Prof. Bulwer was scheduled to be shot, according to Murnau's script, in Lauenburg, but actually they shot it in Lübeck, at Glockengassenstreet. Wisborg's harbor was located in a different city.

In the middle of July 1921, after wrapping the scenes in Lübeck, Murnau's film team headed 45 kilometers east and found more locations in Wismar, another Hanseatic City located adjacent to the Baltic Sea, full of brick Gothic constructions and patrician gable houses. Here Klaus Störtebeker, one of the Victual Brothers (a guild of privateers who later turned to piracy), was born circa 1360. On July 31, an ad appeared in *Mecklenburger Tagesblatt*, a local newspaper, that a film crew sought to buy 30 to 50 living rats. In early August, articles on the shooting of *Nosferatu* appeared. To shoot scenes on the open sea, the ferryboat *Juergen* was rented.

Exterior shooting in Wismar ended with the harbor shots. One early morning, Murnau filmed the arrival of the ship that doubled for the *Empusa*. At lunchtime, Nosferatu was filmed with a telephoto lens as he passes through the famed gate of Wismar. In the background, the sailing ship is visible. Finally, the rats were shot, although less rats than originally requested.

The establishing shot above Wismar-Wisborg shows a church tower and an empty marketplace which displays the waterworks fountain, a nice building for a drinking water supply created in 1563. Today all that's left is only the tower of St. Mary's Church, built in the first half of the thirteenth century. The large nave bombed in World War II was destroyed by the GDR government in 1960 against the protest of many Wismar citizens.

Other prominent Wismar locations were the south side of St. Nicholas Church and the inner court of the Holy Spirit Churchyard that became the marketplace. It was located just 200 meters from the harbor. The involuntarily funny scene in which *Nosferatu* passes carrying a casket was shot at two p.m. and later tinted blue (day-for-night). Hutter mounting a horse and leaving Ellen behind was filmed at the same spot.

There were a number of scenes that agitate horror film purists. According to *The Vampire in Legend, Fact and Art*:

> Stoker in his book describes the Count as moving quickly and jerkily; while this is impressive in print, Murnau, in his anxiety to be faithful to his source, has created moments which almost destroy the film. For these speeded-up sequences are ludicrous in the extreme, being more reminiscent of Mack Sennett than Gothic horror and they invariably have a hilarious effect on a modern audience. Murnau would have done better with slow motion, which would have conveyed the atmosphere of nightmare and terror much more impressively.[1]

The beach scenes with Ellen were shot on the Island of Sylt.

Murnau was particularly fascinated by working on the sailing ship *Jürgen* and dreamed of one day going to Java or Honolulu. Here the dream that ten years later became *Tabu*, had its origin. Walter Spies, a Russian-born primitivist painter, acted as Murnau's artistic consultant. He actually was the first to move to Java in 1923. In January 1942, he was arrested and deported. The ship that was carrying him to Ceylon was hit by a Japanese bomb and Spies was killed on the spot.

A Protagonist Named K.

"The location shots took place with enormous logistic expense in July and August 1921 in Lübeck, West Beach near List on Sylt and in the Western Tatras." Peter-André Alt wrote this in an article and found an interesting parallel to Franz Kafka's novel *The Castle* in which a protagonist named K. tries to gain access to the mysterious authorities who govern a village from a castle:

> Murnau's notes in the script record the shooting places and allow an exact reconstruction of the route the team took. If one follows the stations of the travel route to the final spot, one makes a surprising discovery that leads to Kafka.
>
> In the first half of August 1921, Murnau's staff traveled via Prague to the Western Tatras to shoot the Transylvanian locations of *Nosferatu*. Their destination is the little town of Dolný Kubín, with Castle Oravský nearby. There Murnau wants to shoot the scenes that play in the castle of Count Orlok, the vampire who was portrayed by Max Schreck. Only 90 kilometers distance from Oravský is the lung sanitarium of Matliary; here resides, while Murnau's team works in the castle, Kafka. In the late winter of 1922, shortly before Murnau's film is released abroad, he begins to write his final novel that, like *Nosferatu*, tells of a strange, eerie castle. The parallels between the locations are presumably anything but accidental. […]

If one looks up Kafka's novel, one recognizes intriguing similarities between the castle described here and the castle Oravský. About the castle we learn that it towers on a mountain and is formed of several individual buildings. In the centre the "battlements" of a tower jut into the sky...

Kafka's description reminds Alt of Oravský: "The search for traces that proceed from Murnau's shooting in the Western Tatras defines the symbolic function of a place that might have inspired cinema and literature as well."[2]

Oravský or Orava Castle was built in the Kingdom of Hungary in the thirteenth century, on the site of an old wooden fortification, built after the Mongol invasion of Hungary in 1241. Originally Romanesque and Gothic, it was later reconstructed as a Renaissance and Neo-Gothic structure.

Drumming up business, Albin Grau forwarded a report about the principal filming in Czechoslovakia to the trade press and talked about the manifold, mundane problems of making a movie:

Czech *Nosferatu* ad (author's collection).

> In Bodenbach[3] they took our camera and shipped it to the Central Customs Office in Prague. Together with our cameraman, we worried if the railway officials would handle the prized machine accurately. Thank God we found it safe and sound in a corner of the Central Customs Office at the Prague Masaryk railway station when we came to pick it up. But that was easier said than done. It [took] three days to get it. First all authorities involved had to give their permission.

Five thousand crowns customs duty, three sunny days lost. For equipment, props and costumes there were more officials to bribe and to convince that it was just—luggage. Finally they arrived in Poprad at the foot of the High Tatras. To get up to the Silesian lodge, 1700 meters high, they had to rent horse and cart and hire carters who would only work with the promise to get as much to drink up there as they wanted. As thanks, they volunteered as extras. The team got wonderful footage of the majestic mountains but had to do a lot of climbing.

From Poprad they went via Kraľovany to Dolný Kubin, for the scenes in and around the eerie castle:

> On the market we had changed one cart into the ghost coach. The people around looked amazed. The coachman (and owner) shuddered at each take the cart had to go uphill. He would bring each damage

to account and explain with wild gestures and in temperamental words how his mother would curse him if ever she would gain wind of the incredible tasks we were demanding from his horses and the cart. The simple-minded populace would eye the deathly pale figure of the Nosferatu actor with appalled gaze and shun him like the devil.[4]

Film historians vie with one another praising Murnau's sense for the photographic quality of nature. Grau's contribution is usually overlooked. So here is what Grau wrote about that topic: "Nature, seen with profane, secular eyes, will be equally profane and secular. This is the reason why there is nothing like it in this country. Germany, however, yes, all of Europe is richly blessed with natural settings of stylized grandeur. One only needs eyes to see them."[5] Many film historians call *Nosferatu* a masterpiece of Germany's Expressionist cinema. Grau saw it differently:

> Attempts undertaken lately with Expressionist sets, with only few exceptions (*Cabinet of Dr. Caligari*) didn't go well: The space is bent out of shape into impossible forms in such cases and as pathetic mutilation linked up like a stumbling block to the play's spirit.[6]

Interiors

To finish the film, Murnau and his team returned to Berlin. A number of interiors and the climax, the killing of the vampire, were left to be shot at Jofa Studios in Johannisthal. The studios were formerly a double hangar. As a consequence of the Versaille Armistice Treaty, that became such a heavy burden on Germany, the construction of airplanes was reduced. So Dr. Walther Huth, head of the Albatros Aircraft Factories located at the Airport Johannisthal, switched to movie production and on January 20, 1920, founded Jofa, short for Johannisthaler Filmanstalt G.m.b.H. Engineer Hackenberger was commissioned to change the factory buildings into the "largest film studio in the world." It opened on May 19, 1920. By the end of 1921, when *Nosferatu* was still in production, the studio business manager was engineer Hanns Otto.

> The Johannisthaler Filmanstalten basically consist of two fire-proof, glass-roofed stages of 137 × 21 meters floor space, a double stage linked by iron sliding gates. Stage A is reserved exclusively for shooting and is separated by plywood walls into three stages each 45 × 21. A working gallery 10 meters above leads through the complete stage. One can reach it by stairway from the adjoining hall. So the working personnel, for instance the electricians who have to work on the gallery, don't need to enter through the main hall and so do not disturb the shooting.
>
> Through all stages a track makes it possible to comfortably have a train enter the stage. A cart covered by plate and manned by the camera operator can be moved across the stage as well.
>
> To the Eastern side, the side of the airport, the stages can completely open by large sliding gates. Thus each stage is being enlarged double-length to the exterior. [...] Stage B consists of service rooms of each kind.[7]

Over the next ten years, approximately 400 movies were shot at Jofa, among them *Danton* (1921) with Emil Jannings as Danton and Werner Krauss as Robespierre and the four-part *Fridericus Rex* starring Otto Gebühr as the Prussian king as well as *Schinderhannes* and *Mutter Krausens Fahrt ins Glück* (*Mother Krause's Journey to Happiness*), produced by left-wing Prometheus Film that raised to prominence by distributing Sergei Eisenstein's *Battleship Potemkin* in Germany.

In 1929, the studios were equipped for sound film production and in 1931 adopted by Jofa Tonfilm-Atelier G.m.b.H., owned by Albatros Werke and Tobis Film that controlled the Klangfilm sound equipment. In 1933, Tobis Atelier G.m.b.H. took charge of the studios; in 1938, Tobis Filmkunst G.m.b.H.

Heavily damaged during the war, the studios in the Soviet zone of Berlin became part of DEFA. They were not only used for film production but also for dubbing purposes. The first film dubbed there was the first part of Eisenstein's *Ivan Grosny* (*Ivan the Terrible*). The dubbing director was Wolfgang Staudte. When Babelsberg again became East Germany's main production facility, only the smaller films of Group Johannisthal were produced in Johannisthal, and in the 1960s productions of GDR Television in nearby Adlershof.

The reviewer of *Der Film* magazine was invited to Jofa Studios to watch the final scenes being shot at the end of October 1921:

> On Thursday at Jofa Studios the final scenes of Prana film *Nosferatu* were shot. Among others on the backlot a part of the Port of Galatz was built. In picturesque assembly, ships that sailed the oceans lay at anchor. At the Quay lay bales and barrels, and longshoremen did their work—on all of them the pressure of something uncanny, horrifying seemed to rest—and plunged in eerie light, in piceous night, the scene left even on the expert who is used to have a look at the making of films—an excellent impression. Next to the sailing ships there was an airplane on the ground, the motor moved the propeller and—in the port the sails blow up mightily, and the banneretts and pennants wave in the wind.— As always every scene before judged ready for shooting by director Murnau is precisely worked out following psychological and picturesque principles by the art director of the company, Mr. Albin Grau, and drawn on paper before building the set. Every gesture, every costume (ca. year 1840), every step and every movement must be approved according to the laws of the psychological effect it will have on the viewer. Grau and Murnau achieve a noteworthy filigree work without neglecting the largesse of their work.[8]

During post-production, Murnau was already involved in another project, this time again for producer Sascha Goron and his Goron Films company: the melodrama *Der brennende Acker* (*The Burning Soil*), written by literary and film columnist Willy Haas, Arthur Rosen and Fritz Lang's wife Thea von Harbou. Fritz Arno Wagner, fresh from *Nosferatu*, began by photographing the first half of the movie and Murnau's favorite cinematographer Karl Freund finished it. Featured players were Werner Krauss, Eugen Klöpfer, Lya De Putti, Alfred Abel, Gustav von Wangenheim's father Eduard von Winterstein as Count Rudenburg, and, in a bit part, Gustav Botz, who had been a Martian scientist in Germany's first "extraterrestrial" movie, *Die Entdeckung Deutschlands* (1916), and had played the town physician in *Nosferatu*. Not much later, he would retire from acting due to the beginnings of blindness.

Premiere and Contemporary Reviews

The Feast of Nosferatu

On March 4, 1922, the Berlin premiere of *Nosferatu* took place enshrined by a great festive evening in the Marble Hall of Zoologischer Garten. Prana Company is promoting this event called "Das Fest des Nosferatu" (The Feast of Nosferatu) for days in imaginative advertisements made daily in Berlin news and trade papers. Max Schreck will travel from Munich to participate. It is announced that the audience will be filmed. Furthermore the guests are kindly asked to appear in Biedermeier costumes. Before the film, the overture to the opera "Der Vampyr" by Heinrich Marschner is played.[1]

Among the many people attending the premiere were Ernst Lubitsch, Johannes Riemann, Heinz Schall, who was Asta Nielsen's partner in a film version of Shakespeare's *Hamlet* the year before. Also Hanns Kräly, who wrote Lubitsch's first films. In Los Angeles in 1930, Kräly was awarded an Oscar for the screenplay of *The Patriot*. His career would end sadly with a cheap horror flick, Universal's 1943 *The Mad Ghoul*.

Hans Erdmann, the Composer

Dr. Hans Erdmann was in charge of *Nosferatu*'s score and the musical frame of the feast. The suite was published in 1926 in two parts. There were two versions published: one for large orchestra (Pantheon), the other for Salon orchestra (Valhalla). The suite, alas, has not survived in its complete form, just 40 minutes of it. Other parts were destroyed by a fire in the offices of the music publisher Bote & Bock in 1942.

> From reports by Erdmann and Giuseppe Becce we learn that Murnau discussed the score before completion of his film in detail with the composer. [...] The title of the original score for *Nosferatu* reveals a common misunderstanding. The production company Prana promoted it with the music title "Symphonie des Grauens" (Symphony of Horror), while Erdmann uses the term "Fantastisch-romantische Suite" (Fantastic Romantic Suite). While one connects the vampire plot ostensibly with horror, shiver, shock and thrill, Murnau interpreted it subtly as an artificial entanglement of the demonic possession with legend, fairy tale and nature.[2]

Fantastic Romantic Suite: A Musical Composition by Dr. Hans Erdmann

Part I

A. *Pastoral*. Idyll. Sleepy little town. Early Morning.—Pasturing herds. Jaunty plays. Cheerful-pastoral, playful.

B. *Lyric.* Longing. Submission. Forgotten pain. Resignation. Hope.

C. *Spooky.* Eerie. Spooky. Fantastic. Vision.—Uncanny, nightly tapping step (also comical).—Paranoia. Desperate fright. Uncanny nature mood. Dark lightning clouds.

D. *Stormy.* Wild hunting, fire conflagration, horror.

E. *Destroyed.* Plague. Funeral procession. Inescapable fate.—Approaching doom. Catastrophe. Easing.—Trembling horror.

PART II

A. All well. Magic. Vision.—Hunting. Happy exit.

B. Strange. Ghost steps in ghost castle. Uncanny surrounding.—Scottish Pipes. Melancholia-pastoral. Remember home.

C. Grotesque. Headless rush. Panic. Confusion. (Uncanny or grotesque.)

D. Unleashed. Night. Horror. (Growing.) A storm breaks.—Storms. Wave mountains (increasing and decreasing).

E. Perturbed. Spooky. Eerie vision. Fever dreams.

It sounds like a puzzle. Out of it, in 1984, Berndt Heller tried to reconstruct the original score. The art to form a suite out of a film score works reciprocally to the reconstruction of a film score from individual suite sentences.

Erdmann was born Hans Erdmann Timotheos Guckel on November 7, 1887, in Breslau (today Wrocław, Poland). In his home town he studied violin, music theory and composition and finished his studies with a thesis on Catholic church music in Silesia. During his studies he began his career as concert-master at the Playhouse of Breslau and as a répétiteur at the City Theater (in 1907 and '08). After finishing his studies in 1913, he staged the newly adapted (by him) *L'orfeo* by Monteverdi. Erdmann was drafted at the beginning of World War I. His career resumed at City Theater Riga. In the 1919–20 season, he became head of the Intimate Theater in Jena. There he staged his own dancing pantomime *Die Tänzerin* (*The Dancer*). From 1921 to '23, he was Prana Film Company's artistic head and developed film plans of his own. While he was scoring *Nosferatu* with Murnau's help, he also composed the score for Otto Suchland's monodrama *Pierrot*. In 1924, he became music referee for the Berlin *Reichsfilmblatt* and was busy at theaters in Potsdam and Brandenburg. In 1926, he became the editor-in-chief of the magazine *Film—Ton—Kunst* which focused on the theory of silent film music. In collaboration with Dr. Becce and Ludwig Brav, he edited *Allgemeines Handbuch für Filmmusik* (*General Manual for Film Music*) in 1927. In 1928, he became head of the Academy for Film Music at the Klindworth-Scharwenka Conservatory in Berlin. When sound came in he wrote scores for the documentary *Urwaldsymphonie* (*Jungle Symphony*, 1931), *Der tolle Bomberg* (*The Mad Bomberg*, 1932) and Fritz Lang's *Das Testament des Dr. Mabuse* (*The Testament of Dr. Mabuse*) which was banned by the Nazis in early 1933. His final film was *August der Starke* (*August the Strong*, 1935–36), directed by Paul Wegener. Dr. Hans Erdmann died on November 21, 1942, in Berlin.

> After the screening of the film [at the "Feast of Nosferatu"], Elisabeth Grube and Ines Mesina of the State Opera danced with the ballet the pantomime "The Serenade" by Hans Erdmann who has composed the score for *Nosferatu*. The Otto Kermbach orchestra played an overture. But the whole feast begins with an odd item on the programme: Kurt Alexander has written exclusively for this occasion

a prelude and an interlude that refers to the introduction of Goethe's "Faust." The persons: the theater director, the singer, the actor. Max Schreck as actor of modern days is selected to explain to an impresario of the past what the art of film means. At the prelude, "Herr Schreck claimed that he can do everything," notes the Film-Echo of Berlin Lokal-Anzeiger. Maybe Max Schreck even appeared as a kind of master of ceremonies who gave the signal to start the film. An interlude and a brief postlude followed in which the theater director bows appreciatively to the new art the actor has demonstrated to him. [...][3]

One assures that some ladies who on Saturday had attended the *Nosferatu* premiere had a bad night. And that doesn't seem unlikely. To pour such horror into art has been achieved in this perfection until now only by Hoffmann, Poe and Ewers in the field of literature. And the man who in Grimm's fairy tale went forth to learn what fear was would have got his money's worth watching this film. The *Nosferatu* film is a—sensation; for he leaves radically the well-trodden tracks of the hundredfold only slightly refurbished love stories and the mechanistic adventure. It scoops from presupposition-less speculative fiction whose source is the horrifying superstition of the vampire who drinks human blood. The story of the spectral vampire Nosferatu who spreads death, plague and terror is shaped into a moving picture with spellbinding intensity. Mood-creating elements were used wherever the camera lens found them. Gloomy high mountain cliffs, roaring sea, storm-beaten clouds, creepy ruins. A perfect example of how the film can make use of the atmosphere of landscape to its advantage.[4]

The Feast didn't turn out to be the glamorous event the heads of Prana had envisioned. It was too much, but it became less than the well-meaning organizer had intended. As they wanted to premiere their film play *Nosferatu* in the elongated frame of a feast (with ball gowns, tailcoats and smoking jackets, including some Biedermeier costumes), they had believed they should not eschew a prelude and an interlude.

Run like hell: Nosferatu is after you (courtesy Christian Dörge, Apex Verlag).

Kurt Alexander has done this comprehensive poetry which referred in its exterior structure to Goethe's Prelude on the theater. On a stage they were lucky to erect in the Marble Hall of the Zoo someone who called himself "the director" read off unintelligibly and inaptly verse after verse while "the actor" and "the singer" at least tried to memorize their parts. It was clumsy, tiring, superfluous, and evoked displeasure. Marschner's "Vampyre Overture" that an excellent working orchestra behind curtains played would have been a better, more faithful preparation. And it was wise that they decided to sacrifice the interlude and a prologue to the "serenade."

Although having at hand a masterpiece, for Prana Film Company and Albin Grau the "Feast of Nosferatu" was an act of desperation (and they messed it up) because they had problems of booking it into the leading cinema chains, notably the UFA cinemas. Since its inception suggested by Quartermaster general Erich Ludendorff in World War I, Universum Film Aktiengesellschaft (UFA) had become the leading German production and distribution company, with studios in Tempelhof and Neubabelsberg, and the largest chain of cinemas. What wasn't booked into UFA cinemas didn't exist. Prana tried to do anything to gain attention, create promotion and have the cinema goers demand that this movie simply must be played.

But why was UFA so reluctant to book *Nosferatu*...?

Frater Pacitius, Aleister Crowley's Berlin Disciple

A Letter from Nosferatu

Sylvain Exertier, a later reviewer, noticed in the first reel of *Nosferatu* two brief takes, close-ups of Nosferatu's letter to Knock, the real estate agent:

> Sure, the letter is fiction but it sticks to tradition. Murnau must have had—and with him most of Expressionist filmmakers—erudite occultists in his circle.
>
> Exertier reads the sign and asks, "A coquetry of the director or a wink for occultists? I will beware of giving an answer; only Murnau and his team can decide it. *Nosferatu—Eine Symphonie des Grauens*, this so idiosyncratic film is no work of magic but one of the greatest love stories of the twentieth century which amounts to the same.[1]

Nosferatu is indeed a film of occult symbols. In the harbor house, a trident looms prominently into the frame; letters are littered with cryptograms that only can be deciphered by adepts; reference to Dark Romance are created—the ghost ship reminds one of the *Flying Dutchman*—and foggy nature mysticism wafts through eerie forests with the negative image of a death coach rolling across, photographed by undercranking the camera and creating fast motion. All this seems to be inspired by artists like Caspar David Friedrich, Alfred Kubin and Hugo Steiner-Prag, the illustrator of Meyrink's *Golem* novel.

Ordo Templis Orientis

Grau got the idea to make a movie about the Undead, as he wrote in the promotional pressbooks, by observing a spider sucking an insect's blood. Stoker believed the same: that blood is life. Stoker transferred the fear of changes caused by modern times onto the fear of losing soul and blood:

> As some of the leading personalities of the Prana Film Company delved into occult studies, they got the idea to base a film script, for a change, on vampirism. The direct impulse for the idea was marginal: They watched a spider sucking its victim. But the idea was not enough. The point was not only to open a certain page of occultism but to make a real movie out of it. [...]
>
> A suitable source was found in a fantastic novel (the article doesn't mention Stoker and *Dracula*),

but it needed the painstaking work of Henrik Galeen to transform this novel into what the stimulators had imagined. On the other hand, Prana Film Company, as one of the few and first, had given the writer a free hand to a larger extent as is usual. Henrik Galeen not only wrote the manuscript but discussed it in preproduction with director F.W. Murnau. He was in great part present while the shooting took place and so most likely will be the first writer who won't be disappointed with the final result.

The actors, Grau remarks, were not cast for their name value but for their acting ability: "The role of fright and horror is played by Max Schreck who lives up to his name."[2]

But it was more than the speculative horror the filmmakers were striving for. Grau complained that the new film medium was a "wayward child," too primitive for intellectuals: "But strangely enough, just at a time when, for the eye of the unchurched, the film seemed to get tangled up with materialism of the crudest kind, the soul, the spiritual device and emotions of the film medium begin to stir."

All of a sudden there are films that contrast favorably with sensationalist American films: the occult film of the fantasists. Grau refers to *Homunculus* as one of the prime examples: "The specters of a Félicien Rops, of a Poe and E.T.A. Hoffmann might come live—spirited in their ghastly remoteness from real life." Films should not imitate, Grau said, and postulated a "film medium of the intellectuals" which to him is tantamount to the magic and occult.[3]

Félicien Rops (1833–1898) was an artist born in Namur, 65 kilometers to the southeast of Brussels, and a pioneer in Belgian comics, known for his Erotic-Satanic drawings:

> Rops, who had met Charles Baudelaire in Paris in 1864 and subsequently become a devoted disciple, thereafter commingled elements of death, prostitution and the Satanic in his work, particularly in his five-picture series *Les Sataniques*,1882. Pictures in this series such as "The Sacrifice" and "Cavalry" are clear and explicit representations of Black Mass and Satanism which still retain their original power to shock and disturb.[4]

The German artist was clearly influenced by him. It is no wonder that after the war, Albin Grau's path led him to a group of German occultists. The Ordo Templi Orientis, abbreviated OTO, the Order of the Eastern Temple, was founded as a Freemason Lodge in 1903 by a Vienna industrialist, Carl Kellner, Heinrich Klein and Dr. Franz Hartmann, a German theosopher and freemason. They hoped to be approved by the United Grand Lodge in England. The gnostic leader was Theodor Reuss, who focused on ritual magic. The occultists' intention was to equilibrate and unify the antagonist features of *thelema* (Greek, will) and *agape* (Greek, love) and thus perfect them. In 1904, Reuss became superior of the Order, naming himself Peregrinus.

Grau joined them and became known as "Frater Pacitius" thanks to numerous essays and esoteric works like *Visionen des Cheops II: Das Zeichen am ersten Tor* (*Visions of Cheops II: The Sign at the First Gate*), *Vom Untergrund der Welt* (*About the Underground World*), *Der Weg ins ewige Schweigen* (*The Way to Eternal Silence*) and *Liber I. Das Buch der Null Stunde* (*Liber I: The Book of Zero Hour*), a breviary for new acolytes of the Pansophical Lodge "Orient Berlin" which could be understood as a gnostic alternative draft to Aleister Crowley's *Liber Al Vel Legis*. "Men are searching for themselves beyond themselves," we read. "They are searching for the things beneath them—and God above them! But the inexhaustible treasure trove of Great PAN is the MAGICIAN MAN!!"

After Reuss' death in 1923, the organization split up. In 1925, Grau believed to have met this "magician man" in the controversial, dubious sex magician Crowley, during a conference in Thuringia (Weida Conference), where Crowley exposed his Law of Thelema. Here Crowley, universally cited as "the wickedest man in the world," proclaimed himself

"Redeemer of the World" (chief magus). Apparently Grau had a movie camera with him and shot some original footage of Crowley. Crowley's assumption, however, led to the schism of the Pansophic Society and to the foundation of Fraternitas Saturni. Grau, the temporary grandmaster of the new lodge, and the occult bookseller Eugen Grosche (alias Gregor A. Gregorius) were among those who cast their lot with Crowley. Some time later, however, Grau distanced himself from Crowley. He regretted that he had allowed himself to be used by a man who mixed esoterism with an expressive sex cult.

There is an interesting characterization in the foreword W. Somerset Maugham added to his 1908 black magic novel *The Magician*. Maugham had met Crowley, an adventurous, infamous man, and used him as a role model for his protagonist, Oliver Haddo—for some a gross misinterpretation:

> He was spending the winter in Paris. I took an immediate dislike to him, but he interested and amused me. He was a great talker and he talked uncommonly well. In early youth, I was told, he was extremely handsome, but when I knew him he had put on weight, and his hair was thinning. He had fine eyes and a way, whether natural or acquired I do not know, of so focusing them that, when he looked at you, he seemed to look behind you. He was a fake, but not entirely a fake. [...]
>
> At the time I knew him, he was dabbling in Satanism, magic and the occult. There was just then something of a vogue in Paris for that sort of thing, occasioned, I surmise, by the interest taken in a book by [Joris-Karl] Huysmans, *Là Bas*. Crowley told fantastic stories of his experiences, but it was hard to say whether he was telling the truth or merely pulling your leg. During that winter I saw him several times, but never after I left Paris to return to London. Once, long afterwards, I received a telegram from him which ran as follows: "Please send twenty-five pounds at once. Mother of God and I starving. Aleister Crowley." I did not do so, and he lived on for many disgraceful years.[5]

Maugham's novel was filmed, as we have mentioned, with Paul Wegener. Another film that used Crowley as an inspiration was made by a former assistant to F.W. Murnau, Edgar G. Ulmer: *The Black Cat* (1934) with Boris Karloff and Bela Lugosi.

> Karloff's Hjalmar Poelzig was based to no little extent on Aleister Crowley, a Peck's Bad Boy from Hell whose notoriety had captivated Edgar Ulmer for years. Known as a self-styled Satanic high priest who published graphic accounts of his depravity as well as pieces of "exotica" (pornography) when not in the throes of frequent opium dreams, the British Crowley, who claimed also to be an adept at magick (i.e., the real thing), was very much more of a sort of diabolical P.T. Barnum than the anti–Christ. Nevertheless, he made a very nice living, leading bizarre people in bizarre and degenerate games and espousing the kind of blasphemous folderol designed to outrage the moralistic tight-asses of his generation.[6]

Great Plans and Nightly Hallucinations: The Ill-Fated Prana Film Company

Saptaparna *and* Zanoni: *More Horror Films*

It was known among insiders that the people behind Prana Film Company and *Nosferatu—Eine Symphonie des Grauens* were occultists. The Prana Film-Gesellschaft m.b.H. was founded on January 31, 1921, in Berlin and traded under the Yin and Yang Logo. In big ads in the trade papers they announced a whole series of occult films, one of them titled *Saptaparna*. (Saptaparna is a bitter-astringent-tasting Ayurvedic herb used in skin diseases. To occultists it is known as the "Man-Plant," a seven-leaved plant that is sacred among Buddhists as it refers to the seven principles.) Others were *Nicolo Paganini, Gold, Der Sumpfteufel* (*The Swamp Devil*) and *Höllenträume* (*Dreams of Hell*, a four-part serial: *Echogespenster: Echo Specters; Die Tretmühle: The Tread Mill; Menschen im Eis: Men in Ice; Vril*).

Shortly before Christmas, on December 21, 1921, Enrico Dieckmann, Grau's partner, wrote Murnau a letter:

Dear Mr. Murnau:
 Considering our pleasant cooperation regarding the production and direction of our Grossfilm[1] *Nosferatu* we allow to thank you most respectfully and sincerely and extend our boundless appreciation for your direction.[2]

Dieckmann announced that Prana wanted to grant Murnau a share of two percent of the box office for the direction. *Nosferatu*, he stated, belongs to the best and most artistic works on the market, in their estimate Murnau's best achievement so far. Dieckmann hoped to negotiate with Murnau a contract for a new movie which might be along his lines. We don't know what was intended for Murnau. We wouldn't assume it was something like *The Swamp Devil*. Our guess: *Paganini*, as this project devoted to the Devil's Violinist who was resurrected from a state of apparent death, a vampire story in its own right, was clearly intended as a starring vehicle for Conrad Veidt. It was indeed produced in 1922 albeit not by Prana but by Conrad Veidt himself, along with Richard Oswald, and directed by Heinz Goldberg who had written the screenplay. It featured two members of the *Nosferatu* cast, Greta Schröder (in her last silent film part) and Alexander Granach. *Paganini*, by the way, marked the film debut of Gustav Fröhlich (as Franz Liszt), later to star in Fritz Lang's *Metropolis*. Otherwise none of Prana's announced titles entered production. (A later *Nosferatu* actor, Klaus Kinski, also became interested in Niccolò Paganini. He wrote, directed, played and cut his own *Kinski Paganini* in 1989.)

Right before the premiere of *Nosferatu*, a movie inspired by Edward Bulwer-Lytton's *Zanoni* was announced: *Non Mortuus*. Zanoni, the title hero, one Rosicrucian brother who has lived since the Chaldean civilization, was a soulmate of *Nosferatu*. He cannot fall in love and is damned to wander the face of the Earth until he meets a promising young opera singer from Naples. He marries her and thus loses the gift of immortality. He finally ends under the guillotine during the French Revolution. *Non Mortuus* was to be a musical–literary composition under the direction of Ernst Reschke and composer Dr. Hans Erdmann and touted as "Germany's most genius film creation." To please the audience, esoterism, spiritualism and a horror story were mixed into a film concept.

> Along with *The Coming Race*, a futuristic fantasy dating from along the latter part of his career, Edward Bulwer's *Zanoni* (1842) has enjoyed a certain following among fanciers of the occult, and some vigorous defenders among mainstream critics. Yet Bulwer's ultimate purpose in *Zanoni*, which draws on Gothic motifs, was to move beyond the Gothic to a revised definition of the spiritual life.[3]

The clear objective of Prana was to create something like an occult film company, but finally nothing of it was achieved. The scheme later became the pattern of the so-called Church of Scientology that tried to systematically undermine "Hollywood Babylon" to promote its ideas—and indeed there was a curious tie between the "Great Beast 666" Aleister Crowley and L. Ron Hubbard. I will go into that later.

What is nowadays common practice was new when *Nosferatu* was released: Inspired by the campaign that had made *Caligari* a success, half of the film's budget was reserved for marketing and promotion.

There were many reviews in the papers. Not all were favorable:

> The momentum and power of the movie lies not so much in its dramatic plot but in the spooky, unnerving. The plot is more of an epic process—without the inner compulsion of a victim by which the young Mrs. Hutter frees the world of Nosferatu. Nosferatu is a werewolf [*sic*!] who comes from Transbaikalia [*sic*!] as pest harbinger to Wisborg. The Great Death sets in, coffin by coffin is being carried in a long procession out through the desolating streets. And only if a pure woman sacrifices herself voluntarily to the vampire and keeps him until the first crow of the cock the curse can be averted. Here lies the mistake of the film that touches the psychological only loosely but doesn't comprehend it and takes the motivation of the soul too nonchalantly. Would Galeen not have stood still with volatile insinuations—this could have been an unusual film in every sense.
>
> Nosferatu was played by Max Schreck from Munich. He sought to express the demonic possession by stiff immutability which often appealed but wasn't always appropriate. Gustav v. Wangenheim had the feisty courage of youth, stormy, urging freshness, laughing live for this Hutter whose wife Miss Greta Schröder played with deep internalization.[4]

Other reviewers were more merciful and wondered why so many cinemas refused to play the film:

> This is film: ghostly coaches rush through forest ravines, terrifying specters hunt men, plague evokes, ships sail unmanned into ports, coffins with soil and mice dash from cellars onto cars, into ships, into house ruins. This is film: a being half ghost, half man, creeps across the screen—and in between as concession to the paying average audience: a love story with tragic ending. *Nosferatu* is the title of this film that in the tracks of *Dr. Caligari* for five acts evokes horror. Because no theater owner wants to let him in, they have presented it for the first time in a special screening in the Marble Hall at Zoologischer Garten with an inadequate prelude and before a gracious dancing play and ball. Henrik Galeen, the understanding writer, is a varlet from the school of Wegener. His vampyre "Nosferatu"

could have arisen from Wegener's workshop. [...] The castle of terror, the house of Nosferatu are thrilling achievements. A museum of themes. The part of Nosferatu was given to a novice on screen: Max Schreck. He brings him as bugbear, dark, as pale as death, with devil's claws. His henchman is Alexander Granach, deliberately grotesque. Refreshing in all this sad darkness: Gustav v. Wangenheim, the hero, the bright spot, the conqueror of the vampyre. And Greta Schröder, his wife, photogenic in big scenes. Hans Erdmann who composed the "Symphony of Terror" found a solution for the problem of film composition.[5]

This Prana film which was seen on Saturday evening only by a smaller circle must get out into the cinemas; one has not the right to keep such an interesting (if not sensational) work, such achievement away from the audience.[6]

Prana was not able to book *Nosferatu* into one of the prestigious first-run theaters on Berlin's Kurfürstendamm. It was like an unspoken boycott. Prana wasn't highly regarded, not so much because of its occult background but because of its dubious backers and business policy. When Prana run a Christmas ad in the trade papers in December 1921, they addressed it to "friend and foe." There seemed to be more foes than friends.

Instead of seeing it at the UFA Palace at Berlin Zoo or in the Marmorhaus where *Caligari* was premiered, viewers had to go to Berlin Neukölln, to the recently opened 960-seat Primus Palace located at Potsdamer Str. 19, at the corner of Margarethenstr. 9. The theater owners were Bruckmann & Co. In April 1939, following the plans for transforming Berlin into Hitler's intended megalomaniac World Capital Germania, the building and the cinema, at that time owned by Brandt & Deutsch, were destroyed.

Two Cinematographers: Krampf and Wagner

On March 23, 1922, three weeks after the gala premiere of *Nosferatu*, Prana issued stock in a total value of 42 million Reichsmark. The stock market launch was maybe fabricated by Dieckmann to deprive all liquid assets. Prana soon faced serious cash flow problems. The company had invested 1.7 million Reichsmark into the production of two films, approximately one million for *Nosferatu*, with the balance for a "science-oriented *Kulturfilm* documentary in three acts," an alpine mountaineer trip (Crowley, by the way, was an enthusiastic mountaineer too) titled *Hochtouren im Vorfrühling: Eine Frühlingswanderung im Dachstein- und Kaisergebirge* (*High Mountain Tour in Early Spring*, shot in spring 1922 at Dachstein Mountains and Kaiser Mountains) which according to contemporary trade ads was finished but never screened. Albin Grau had directed it by himself and just taken one of *Nosferatu*'s cameramen, Günther Krampf, to shoot it, with Paul W. Goritzke as second cameraman. In the silent days they used two cinematographers side by side, one cranking the domestic, the second the negative that was destined for export.

Günther Oskar Krampf was born on February 8, 1899, in Vienna. He studied at the Technische Hochschule (Technical University) in his home town and during the war, in 1916, began to assist on film productions in Vienna, Florence and Berlin. His name is found in the credits of Max Mack's two-part *Die Lieblingsfrau des Maharadscha*. Joe May hired Krampf in 1920 as second cameraman for *Die Legende von der Heiligen Simplicia* (*The Legend of Saint Simplicia*), written by Thea von Harbou and starring May's daughter Eva. (Eva, who also was in *Paganini*, committed suicide in 1924.) Following *Nosferatu*, Krampf became a much sought-after cinematographer. In 1923 he joined one of Germany's leading directors, Dr. Ludwig Berger (born Ludwig Bamberger), on *Der verlorene Schuh* (*The Lost Shoe*) and *Das Glas Wasser* (*One Glass of Water*) and eventually photographed

Conrad Veidt in Robert Wiene's *Orlacs Hände* (*The Hands of Orlac,* 1924), Henrik Galeen's remake of *Der Student von Prag* (*The Student of Prague,* 1926) and the early sound film *Die letzte Kompagnie* (*The Last Company,* 1930), with Alexander Granach in the supporting cast, as well as *Alraune* (1930) with Brigitte Helm and Albert Bassermann. With Slatan Dudow and Bertolt Brecht, he did the left-wing *Kuhle Wampe* that was banned in 1932 but re-released in a recut version. When *Kuhle Wampe* was released, Krampf already worked in London for Gaumont British where he made *The Ghoul* (1933) with Boris Karloff and later for Welwyn Studios, only to return once to Germany to photograph *Das Mädchen Johanna* (*Joan of Arc,* 1935, directed by Gustav Ucicky) with an all-star cast: Angela Salloker, Gustaf Gründgens, Heinrich George, René Deltgen, Erich Ponto, Willy Birgel, Theodor Loos, Aribert Wäscher, Paul Bildt, Bernhard Minetti, Fritz Genschow, Maria Koppenhöfer, Friedrich Gnass, Alexander Golling, Paul Dahlke, Albert Venohr, Fanny Schreck and Veit Harlan. Another commitment with an Austrian company didn't work out. It was said that Krampf was of Jewish heritage and therefore had to stay abroad. During the war, in 1944, Krampf collaborated with Alfred Hitchcock on two propaganda films: *Bon Voyage* and *Aventure Malgache*. He died on August 4, 1950, age 51, in London.

Yet Krampf wasn't mentioned in *Nosferatu*'s credits; Fritz Arno Wagner was. Wagner was ten years older than Krampf, born on December 5, 1884, in Schmiedefeld, Thuringia. Trained at the Ecole of Beaux Arts in Paris, he started as a cameraman for Pathé Frères in 1910. Within two years he was promoted to head Pathé's branch office in Vienna. In 1913, *Pathé Weekly* sent him to New York. During World War I, he served in the cavalry. After being invalided out, he was a combat cameraman. In 1919, he became a regular on some of the biggest German silent and sound films. On the strength of his work on *Schloss Vogelöd* (*The Haunted Castle,* 1921), Murnau chose him for first cameraman on *Nosferatu*. For Fritz Lang he lensed *Der müde Tod* (*Destiny*) in 1921, *Spione* (*Spies*) in 1928, *M* in 1931 and *Das Testament des Dr. Mabuse* (*The Testament of Dr. Mabuse*) in 1932. *Schatten* (*Wandering Shadows*) in 1923 and *Pietro der Korsar* (*The Love Pirate*) in 1925 reunited him with art director Albin Grau, and Karl Grune's *Am Rande der Welt* [*At the Edge of the World,* 1927] with Max Schreck who had a prominent part in that picture. With Alexander Korda, he shot *Eine Dubarry von Heute* (*A Modern Du Barry,* 1927) on the French Riviera with Korda's wife Maria, Alfred Abel and Marlene Dietrich in a bit part. He made some of his most acclaimed films with director G.W. Pabst: *Die Liebe der Jeanne Ney* (*The Loves of Jeanne Ney,* 1927), *Westfront 1918* (1930), *Kameradschaft* (*Comradeship,* 1931) and *Die 3 Groschenoper* (*The 3 Penny Opera,* 1931). With *Amphitryon—Aus den Wolken kommt das Glück* (*Amphitryon: Happiness from the Clouds,* 1935), he was involved in one of the most expensive films of the Third Reich. Emil Jannings acted in front of Wagner's camera in *Der zerbrochene Krug* (*The Broken Jug,* 1937), one of Hitler's personal favorites, *Robert Koch, der Bekämpfer des Todes* (*Robert Koch, the Death Fighter,* 1939), the anti–British *Ohm Krüger* (*Uncle Kruger,* 1941) and *Altes Herz wird wieder jung* (*Old Heart Gets Young Again,* 1943).

After the war, Wagner's talents were wasted. Like most of the old pros, he had to settle for mediocre stuff like the rare Austrian sci-fi state film *1. April 2000* (*April 1, 2000,* directed in 1952 by Goebbels favorite Wolfgang Liebeneiner), *Heideschulmeister Uwe Karsten* (*Eternal Love, 1954*) and Artur Brauner's CCC Central Cinema Company production *Der Czardas-König* (*The Csardas Princess,* 1958). On August 18, 1958, Wagner died in Göttingen having fallen from a camera truck during the shooting of another CCC production, *Ohne Mutter geht es nicht* (*It Doesn't Work Without Mother*); Karl Löb replaced him.

Waste of Money

When Prana's subdistributors, Excelsior Film Berlin (representing the territories East Germany, North Germany, Saxonia and Silesia) and Süddeutsche Film-Gesellschaft Karlsruhe (South Germany, Rhineland and Westphalia), also proved unreliable, Prana tried to release *Nosferatu* itself, with Willy Seibold acting as distribution expert. It didn't help. In the end, Enrico Dieckmann had spent all in all 2.4 million Reichsmark on production, promotion and business transactions. On January 21, 1922, he had bought, for even more investor money, the Bengen Filmverlag as a distribution company, with all its now justifiably forgotten film titles (such as *Aus den Akten einer anständigen Frau, Aus den Geheimnissen eines Frauenarztes, Der Dummkopf, Dokumentendiebstahl, Eiserne Acht* and *Taschendiebe*) and deferred money (money laundry and creative bookkeeping not excluded). Money Prana couldn't possibly recoup. According to Film-Kurier, "Mindless dissipation of loans, an overgrown organization of officials that cost hundreds of thousands and expensive promotion were the key features of a decline that happened quite soon to bankrupts that basically could have been viable."[7]

Grau's fellow mason Dieckmann turned out a money slider. *Prana* was liquidated on July 12, 1922.

Warning Shadows

The gullible Albin Grau remained faithful to his partner. He came up with a new name: Pan Film (*The Great God Pan* was written by occultist Arthur Machen). Under this name, Dieckmann and Willy Seibold founded a new company in 1923 that immediately produced the movie *Schatten*. Pan's trade register file doesn't tell much. There is a partnership agreement dated February 22, 1923. Original share capital: one million Reichsmark. Shareholders: merchant Enrico Dieckmann (200,000), Willy Seibold (200,000) and one Guillarmo Lorey (600,000).

Warning Shadows was developed, written and designed by Grau. Characters like Dieckmann and Seibold could and still can be found all over the world of movies and make-believe. Usually they are imaginative only when it comes to money and so have to exploit other people's talents, in this case the talent of a shy man like Grau who was never good at making deals and handling money. Similar to *Nosferatu* the theme of Grau's cinematic séance was a "Nocturnal Hallucination," so the subtitle: a phantasmagoria of fears and dreams which spread under the moonlight. A shadowplayer shows a wealthy but sadistically jealous husband what might happen if his guests, all bachelors, date the lusty lady of the house. The shadows reveal the consequences of the characters's desires and hatreds. "From the early days of mankind shadows seemed to men like magic. The spirits of the dead were called shadows, and the underworld was named the Kingdom of Shadows and was looked upon with awe and horror."[8]

Grau's original script was titled *Schatten der Nacht* (*Shadows of the Night*) and didn't need intertitles. It was based on the novel *Das unbewohnte Haus* (*The Uninhabited House*) by A.M. Frey. Grau also made a wish list for the cast: Ferdinand Marian or Ewald Balser as the rich man, Maria Rieber-Zimmermann as his wife, Franz Zimmermann as the young man who makes eyes at her, Aribert Wäscher, Hubert von Meyerinck and Boulanger as the three cavaliers, and Erich Ponto as shadowplayer. None of these artists were actually cast. Only the two servants Grau suggested were hired: Fritz Rasp and Karl Platen.[9] Fritz Kortner, the great Expressionist actor, played the husband and Ruth Weyher his wife. Two alumni of *Nosferatu* joined the cast: Gustav von Wangenheim as the young man and Alexander Granach as shadow player. Handling the camerawork was *Nosferatu*'s Fritz Arno Wagner.

As Murnau was working for better companies, namely UFA that produced a *Tartuffe* film that was similar in framework structure to Grau's film, Pan Film hired Arthur Robison as director. The son of a German-American, Robison was born on June 25, 1883, in Chicago. He studied medicine in Munich but decided to pursue an acting career. He wrote and directed his first films during World War I. In 1916, he directed Werner Krauss and Emil Jannings in what could be called a horror film, *Nächte des Grauens*, with Krauss donning an ape suit. In 1927, he made the first co-production between UFA and Paramount under the Parufamet contract, *Der letzte Walzer* (*The Last Waltz*), based on the Oscar Straus operetta. In 1929, six years before John Ford's U.S. version, he filmed Liam O'Flaherty's novel *The Informer* in London and went to Hollywood to supervise German-language versions for Metro-Goldwyn-Mayer. In 1933 he returned to Germany. Robison died two months after finishing the second remake of *The Student of Prague* (1935) with Anton Walbrook.

Robison got Grau an art director's contract with UFA in 1925 for a big-budget costume drama he was going to shoot, *Pietro, der Korsar* (U.S.: *The Love Pirate*, with Fritz Lang's *Nibelungen* stars Paul Richter and Rudolf Klein-Rogge). The same year, Grau designed the nest of the hornets for Waldemar Bonsels's nature drama *Die Biene Maja und ihre Abenteuer* (*Adventures of Maya*).

The Vampire Widow Asks for Money

Pan's distributor was to become Dafu, short for Deutsch-Amerikanische Film-Union A.G., another obscure venture of Dieckmann. Dafu took over *Nosferatu* too and received a letter from England written by a London lawyer on behalf of his client Florence Stoker, the widow of Bram. In early 1922, Florence had joined the British Incorporated Society of Authors hoping that this would help her receive a financial settlement for unauthorized use of her late husband's work that included *Nosferatu*. Florence had received an anonymous letter from Berlin that contained a program from the Marble Hall premiere. Managing director George Herbert Thring, an expert in copyright questions, consulted with Mrs. Stoker in person. He commissioned a Berlin lawyer, Dr. Wronker-Flatow. But Wronker-Flatow had to report that Prana was already bankrupt and that Dafu washed its hands of responsibility.

On February 9, 1925, the Pan Film Company was liquidated. Seibold had misappropriated money. The police hunted Seibold and Dieckmann. Dieckmann disappeared completely from public view, and spent some time in jail.

On July 20, 1925, a Berlin court decided that all negatives and prints of *Nosferatu* had to be destroyed. There still was a chance, but in August Dafu disclaimed the settlement of 5000 British Pound Sterling. That should have been *Nosferatu*'s end. It was not.

Florence Anne Lemon Balcombe Stoker was not immortal. She died in London on May 25, 1937, at the age of 78, having made some money from selling *Dracula* to Universal Pictures. Some prints of *Nosferatu*, however, survived.

Fritz Lang Hits It Big— And Murnau Carries On

Doctor Mabuse Meets Faust

After the departure of Ernst Lubitsch, there were three outstanding directors working for UFA at that time: Murnau, Dr. Ludwig Berger (Bamberger, 1892–1969) who had done *Ein Glas Wasser* (*A Glass of Water*) and a delightful Cinderella story titled *Der verlorene Schuh* (*The Lost Shoe*) in 1923, and Fritz Lang.

Fritz (Friedrich Christian Anton) Lang was born on December 5, 1890, in Vienna, the second son of Anton Lang, an architect and construction company worker. His mother, Pauline "Paula" Lang née Schlesinger, was Jewish, but had converted to Roman Catholicism and was baptized three weeks after Fritz's birth. She died in 1920, just when Lang's film career began to flourish. Lang had briefly studied civil engineering at the Technical University of Vienna before switching to art and painting. In 1910, he decided to travel around the world, throughout Europe and Africa, later Asia and the Pacific area. In 1913, he resumed his studies, this time in Paris. Wounded in World War I and confined to a military hospital, he wrote film scripts and sent them on spec to Erich Pommer's Decla Company. After the war, he went to Berlin and introduced himself to Pommer as his new director. The first film Lang directed for Pommer, *Halbblut* (*The Half-Caste*), starred Carl de Vogt, who later became an active member of NSDAP and SA. Lang's commercial breakthrough was the action film *Die Spinnen* (*The Spiders*). This time de Vogt played American adventurer Kay Hoog, on the track of a lost Incan civilization and a diamond ship. His adversaries, almost Bond-like, are the members of a crime syndicate calling themselves the Spiders. *The Spiders* was released in two parts in 1919 and 1920.

On the strength of his work, Lang was hired by producer-director Joe May to collaborate on the script for a serial that, like *The Spiders,* owed a lot to similar French entries: *Herrin der Welt* (*Mistress of the World*), originally announced as *The Countess of Monte Cristo* and starring Mia May, Joe's wife, on an adventurous trip searching for the lost treasure of the queen of Sheba. Lang also acted as assistant director on two of the eight parts and had high hopes that May's next production, the monumental *The Indian Tomb* (*Das indische Grabmal*), released in 1921, would turn out to be his next directorial assignment. He co-wrote the script with Thea von Harbou (1888–1954), a novelist married to actor Rudolf Klein-Rogge. She was more than the harmless German fairy tale aunt (*Märchentante*), as Paul Wegener once called her. Harbou's novels, for example *Der Krieg und die Frau* (*The War and the Woman*), published in 1913, were "patriotic and morale-boosting, urging women to sacrifice and duty while promoting the eternal glory of the fatherland.[1] This qualified Thea, who became a member of NSDAP, to dabble in Goebbels' propaganda films: *Der alte und der junge König* (*The Old and the Young King*) and *Der Herrscher* (*The Ruler*), both with Emil Jannings, as well as co-writing director Veit Harlan's *Kolberg*. In between, she became Lang's mistress and, after Lang's first wife was found shot, most probably an accident after a marital dispute rather than murder or homicide, the director's second wife. She had divorced Klein-Rogge in 1920. Her "ex" played the infamous master criminal in *Doktor Mabuse der Spieler* (*Doctor Mabuse, the Gambler*), Lang's great two-part silent film. Its success made Lang one of the highest-paid film directors of the Weimar Republic.

Dr. Mabuse, a contemporary reviewer wrote,

> is something like an ideal figure of our days. He isn't the crime king who works with plump means; it is not accidental that he is doctor. He has put all the mental powers of his academic education into the service of his enormous plans. He is an incredibly fine psychologist and knows how to use the mistakes and weaknesses of his fellow men for his means. He not only wants to collect big treasures, he is going as highest objective for the mental regimen of mankind."[2]

The depravity and anarchy of the Weimar Republic is reflected in that single character. In one scene we see Anita Berber, the well-known *femme fatale* and vamp of those days, dancing.

Fafnir, the Fire-Breathing Dragon

Before he began writing *Game of Thrones*, George R.R. Martin repeatedly came to Germany to kneel down in front of shattered castle ruins. Sure, he had seen Fritz Lang's celluloid version of Teutonic culture heritage: *Die Nibelungen* tells of the fair-headed Siegfried the Dragonslayer, who courted Kriemhild, the sister of the king of Burgundy. But Siegfried was killed by a traitor. Vengeful Kriemhild remarried and incited her new husband, the king of the Huns, to invite her relatives and extinguish them.

The technical highlight of Part I was Siegfried's encounter with Fafnir, the fire-breathing dragon. The master craftsmen behind the dragon were production designers Otto Hunte (who later became a Nazi), Erich Kettelhut and Karl Vollbrecht (who was to become the art director of Veit Harlan's *Jew Suss*). Kettelhut, the most inventive of the trio, proposed during a production meeting at Lang's home to put a living lizard into a miniature set and let it disappear into a miniature cave. A full-sized replica of the cave's entrance could then be built with a gigantic artificial lizard head setting upon the hero. But Lang ordered instead a full-scale mechanical dragon. So the three art directors went to work: Hunte prepared the basic sketch, Kettelhut contributed the technical designs to make the monster move, and Vollbrecht with his capable crew actually built it. The dragon's long neck was assembled with gradually enlarging iron rings, as was the tail. The neck's curve was created using stabilizing beechwood frames, which were fastened vertically into the ring forms. Wire tackles made it maneuverable. In all, the beast measured approximately 50 feet and was mounted on wheels. Inside its hollow body, a man was positioned to manipulate the eyes and mouth. Other grips, hidden beneath the dragon in a trench, provided the animation of the legs. Inside the monster's giant head was a petrol can with a hose leading to a pair of bellows concealed within the torso. On the other side of the can was a hole, and in front of that a small basin filled with acetylene fuel. Through the creature's open mouth, the can was filled with Lycopodium and the acetylene flame was lit. The bellows set the flammable Lycopodium powder in motion over the flame, which in turn produced a fiery burst 20 to 30 feet long and transformed the dragon into a flame-thrower.

In his memoirs, Kettelhut described the scene in detail:

> The dragon's first duty was to stand at the edge of a pond and sip some water. After this shot had gone well, Siegfried—played by Paul Richter—had to ride his splendid white horse through the giant trees of the dim forest until he spotted the dragon. Pushed uphill to the highest point of the canyon, the monster came down scouting left and right. Its eyes followed the movements of the approaching enemy and the mouth opened a little bit. Then it marched on until reaching the edge of the pond. This procedure was repeated several times. After each take, about 20 grips had to shove the monster uphill to its starting point. Naturally, that took a while. Lang used the time to photograph the approaching Siegfried from different angles in order to get enough footage for editing. Finally, Siegfried attacked the fire-breathing beast with his sword. Karl Vollbrecht and his men inside the dragon had their hands full executing the commands Lang was shouting by megaphone.
>
> For a few hours I experienced this myself when I had to replace Karl, who was needed elsewhere, inside the dragon. Though all I had to work was the movement of the beast, including the mouth and eyes, I felt the muscular exertion from it for days. Paul Richter's task wasn't enviable either. The head and the neck of the dragon were as hard as iron and moved around hastily and incalculably. An unfortunate stroke of this heavy mass could have broken a man's bones. First Siegfried had to get in under the monster's fiery breath and dig out one of its eyes. The dragon then craned its neck and stopped, as did the camera. At that point, Karl was able to replace the dragon's painted eye with a prepared pig's bladder. When the cameramen cranked again, a milky, glutinous mass flowed out. With the dragon now half-blinded and unable to fully defend itself, Siegfried drove his sword into the beast's left breast and then jumped out of the frame. The cameramen stopped again cranking while Vollbrecht provided a large rubber bag and disappeared with it inside the dragon's body. There he fixed it firmly at the reverse side of the point Siegfried had hit. Meanwhile, I stood outside with a pocketknife. As the cameramen started cranking, I cut the bag and disappeared quickly out of the frame. Meanwhile, Vollbrecht rhythmically pressed the bag from inside, causing the amber-colored blood of the mortally wounded monster to flow out into the pond. After some convulsive movements, it died.

Then Richter was supposed to take a bath in the dragon blood to make himself invincible. The blonde actor refused to appear nude in front of the camera. So Dr. Mabuse himself, Rudolf Klein-Rogge, volunteered as body double and went naked into the blood bath before he would marry Siegfried's widow Kriemhild and provide for blood spill among the Burgundians in the role of Etzel, better known as Attila, King of the Huns, in the second part of Lang's epic, *Kriemhild's Rache* (*Kriemhild's Revenge*).

A Shining Weapon of German Faith

The contemporary reviews were as bold as the movie itself:

> Like Volker von Alzey the bard once played his fiddle to spread the epic of the Nibelungs all over the world, Fritz Lang today grabs the silent chords of the film to present to the demanding eye what rested in the dark womb of an ominous past. He resurrects the Germanic heroic song and confesses himself to a deed whose audacity most Germans will not grasp. A defeated people poetizes its belligerent heroes in an epic of pictures like the world has never seen before—this is a powerful achievement! Fritz Lang accomplished it and a whole people remains steadfastly at his side. A whole people because he grabs its innermost heart. [...]
>
> This masterpiece will be carried in Germany by the national consciousness of our people, and so this achievement will bear fruit. [...]

This great, unique cinematic work shall bestow us hours of solemn emotion, it may make a contribution to awake the noble mind and to declare unrelenting war to evil! It may be a shining weapon of German faith which wields undauntedly and unconqueredly through the world with the bell ringing of pure, free humanity. It may be an enlightened symbol, the flaming torch of a new day, it may be like Balmung, Siegfried's sword, and prevail where it hits.[3]

Metropolis

After his national triumph with *Die Nibelungen* (*The Nibelungs*), Lang was convinced that in the future he had to deliver a size larger, nothing short of

A film of titanic dimension

*

A film about people of the future

*

An ancient biblical motive, the Tower of Babel,
Interwoven in a gigantic vision of the future

*

Man Machine and Machine Man

*

The greatest film ever made, one of the most memorable
achievements of art of all time

*

Catacombs and Eternal Gardens, the world of the workers
underground, below ground level, in the sunlight the city of wild orgies and cheerful lust for life

*

The Machine Woman who destroyed a city

*

Rebellion against the Machine in Year 2000

*

The metropolis of the future in all its fantastic glory,
the pounding of its gigantic machines—a symphony of mankind in roaring melodics and iron rhythm.[4]

The Golem was forgotten but the Robot, its legitimate successor, was more in demand than ever when Lang filmed *Metropolis*. Harry Piel, Germany's action film idol, had already been an Electric Man as early as 1915 when he produced, directed and starred as a walking automaton in the lost *Die grosse Wette* (*The Big Bet*) that can be termed Germany's first genuine science fiction movie, long before the term was brought up by Hugo Gernsback.

Lang would become master supreme of Germany's fantasy cinema of the 1920s and lived long enough to toot his own horn concerning his achievements: In *Metropolis*, Lang's wife Thea von Harbou combined ideas from Jules Verne (the little known novel *The Black Indies*, also called *The Child of the Cavern* or *The Underground City*) and H.G. Wells (the underground Morlocks from *The Time Machine*) and linked them with E.T.A. Hoffmann's idea of a female automaton, Olimpia. The term "robot" had been coined by Czech writer Karel Čapek in the play *R.U.R.*, that dealt with a rebellion of machine people, which Lang must have known. When he saw the result, Wells, the Utopian socialist, was appalled and threw his hands up in horror: "I have recently seen the silliest film. I do not believe it would be possible to make one sillier," he wrote in a review. He continued:

Metropolis: Tower of Babel (author's collection/Deutsche Kinemathek–Museum für Film und Fernsehen, Berlin).

> It is called *Metropolis*, it comes from the great UFA studios in Germany, and the public is given to understand that it has been produced at enormous cost.
>
> It gives in one eddying concentration almost every possible foolishness, cliché, platitude, and muddlement about mechanical progress and progress in general served up with a sauce of sentimentality that is all its own. [...]
>
> Possibly I dislike this soupy whirlpool none the less because I find decaying fragments of my own juvenile work of 30 years ago, *The Sleeper Awakes*, floating about in it.
>
> Čapek's Robots have been lifted without apology, and that soulless mechanical monster of Mary Shelley's, who has fathered so many German inventions, breeds once more in this confusion.
>
> Originality there is none. Independent thought, none.
>
> Where nobody has imagined for them the authors have simply fallen back on contemporary things.
>
> The aeroplanes that wander about above the great city show no advance on contemporary types, though all that stuff could have been livened up immensely with a few helicopters and vertical or unexpected movements.
>
> The motor cars are 1926 models or earlier. I do not think there is a single new idea, a single instance of artistic creation or even intelligent anticipation, from first to last in the whole pretentious stew; I may have missed some point of novelty, but I doubt it, and this, though it must bore the intelligent man in the audience, makes the film all the more convenient as a gauge of the circle of ideas, the mentality, from which it has proceeded.[5]

The skyscrapers that sum up to a new Tower of Babel in the center of the city were influenced by Lang's visit to New York and, being sort of an architect himself, by design concepts of Alpine Architecture.

The idea of "Alpine Architecture" was inspired by the work of German critic and Expressionist novelist Paul Scheerbart (1863–1915), particularly by his fantasy essay "Glass

Architecture." In this text, Scheerbart advocated the construction of buildings able to be completely invaded by natural light in all their interior spaces, a condition which, he believed, would have had huge positive consequences to the development of human environment.

Jewish Magic vs. Christian Saint

Like all megalomaniacs, Lang, who was said to have been a true dictator on the set of his films, dreamed of creating his own monument, in this case a cinematic monument of apocalyptic and eschatological elements, including Maria the Woman—"Hail Mary, full of Grace, the Lord is with thee"—and the Savior from the Skies. Their enemy—and here we get a classic German silent with anti–Semitic subtext—is a Jewish inventor, C.A. Rotwang, disguised in the monk's cowl of the alchemist. He abuses saintly Maria and—pure blasphemy, pure evil—transforms her into a robotic whore.

Lang was raised a Roman Catholic by his mother:

> Lang had learned about love and sex from Catholicism, and his outlook remained intrinsically Catholic throughout his life. There were Madonnas, like his own mother, pure and saintly (Kriemhild before the vengeful transformation; one-half of [actress] Brigitte Helm in *Metropolis*). And there were whores, who possessed the tempting inducements of sin. Sins could always be forgiven, and like Mary Magdalene, prostitutes could be uplifted. Prostitutes in the end were for Lang […] a shrine at which to prostrate and worship.[6]

Rotwang is nothing less than an evil version of Rabbi Loew holding a magic wand. He is killed by the Christian Savior on the roof of a cathedral:

> In the ultra-modern city of Metropolis, Rotwang is an anachronism, a figure out of an earlier time and age. He lives in a house of medieval design and dresses and acts like a figure out of earlier Expressionist films. His associations with medieval images of the Jew, which would be reinstitutionalized in Nazi propaganda—the scientist, the magician, the alchemist—bring forth associations of radicalized conflict, further impacted both by the use of the robot Maria and the Orientalism of the setting in which she first appears. […] The Robot Maria, Rotwang's most fearsome creation, is introduced to an intradiegetic audience in a nightclub of "Oriental splendour," the Yoshiwara (the name of the traditional pleasure quarter of Japan's Edo, now Tokyo). This association between an overly sexualized female and the decadence associated with the Orient also feature in anti–Semitic images of the Jew as "Oriental."[7]

The movie was butchered by the time of its American release. English-speaking trades ignored the ideological, racist background and just hailed the technology that was set in motion to produce it as the *Eighth Wonder of the Universe*:

> An ultramodern film spectacle set in the city of the future—Metropolis the awe-inspiring, machine-managed, machine-brained city of 100 years from now. Only a genius could conceive such a theme—only a master technician such as Fritz Lang, the great U.F.A. producer, could visualize the conception. There is no make-believe—the futurist city is there on the screen before your amazed eyes! Buildings towering thousands of feet into space, elevated railroads and roadways, aeroplanes whisking down those steel canyons in the heavens—and, marvel of marvels, the Robot Woman, the mechanical thing science dreams of—a living, walking, working being—minus a soul! Imagine A Great Dramatic Romance In Such A Setting! No Wonder This 10 Reel Marvel Has The Attention Of The Whole World To-Day![8]

City of the Future

This return of magic and alchemy is set in the year 2026, in the extraordinary Gothic skyscrapers of a corporate city-state, the Metropolis of the title. Society has been divided into two rigid groups: one of planners or thinkers, people of the mind, who live high above the earth in luxury, and another of workers who live underground toiling to sustain the lives of the privileged. The city is run by Johann "Joh" Fredersen, a man of mind and money, who took Hel, the woman that Rotwang loved. Subsequently, the American version names him Masterman. Hel died when she gave birth to Fredersen's son Freder Jr. Beautiful, altruistic and evangelical Samaritan Maria (or Mary) takes up the cause of the slave laborers. The peace-loving young woman advises the desperate men not to start a revolution but to continue suffering and pray for the advent of a Christ-like mediator who turns out to be Freder. Rotwang hates Freder, and he wants to destroy Fredersen.

As he saw that he had nothing more than a cheap novelette in his hands instead of true utopian content, Lang pushed just for form and visuals. He asked his *Nibelungen* art directors Hunte, Kettelhut and Vollbrecht to build the expensive sets and the scenery for a huge miniature of the city, complete with tiny airplanes flying above the skyscrapers, ground vehicles and even moving pedestrians to be animated frame by frame (all of which had nothing to do with future reality!). It took weeks to accomplish the task. According to Kettelhut:

> From our tests we knew that the aeroplanes had to be animated .6 inch after a single frame of film was exposed, the high-speed rail cars .4 inch, the automobiles about .3 inch and the pedestrians just minimally to get fluid movement in a believable tempo. An animation team was assembled by chief modelmaker Edmund Ziehfuss. Each man was assigned to a specific job. A blue light signaled the move. Cars, trains and pedestrians had to be animated conscientiously and for exactly the required distance. The aeroplanes were animated supported by wires. The work had to be done sometimes in uncomfortable positions since frontages and railway bridges and lamp sockets hindered our efforts considerably. When everybody had done his requested animation, the gaffer switched on full shooting light and another frame of film was exposed.

The Magic Mirror

One special technique that was used throughout *Metropolis* was the Schüfftan process. It was named after its inventor Eugen Schüfftan (1893–1977). He later worked as a cameraman in France and the United States, winning an Academy Award for his photography of *The Hustler* (1961) starring Paul Newman.

Essentially Schüfftan's technique entailed the employment of a mirror positioned in front of the camera lens at a 45-degree angle. After selectively scraping away the silvering, part of the mirror would be rendered transparent, allowing the photography of and compositing with a miniature, a photographic print or a different scene positioned behind the glass and a full-scale portion of the set complete with actors. Thus, both elements were combined simultaneously in the camera.

The Schüfftan process was not entirely new. In fact, some cinematographers expressed irritation upon learning that the technique had been patented by the Germans. But Schüfftan's method differed slightly—and significantly—from that of his predecessors. While earlier practitioners had attempted to conceal the outline of the mirror's selective silvering by aligning it *precisely* with that of the full-scale set—an approach which caused problems in blending—Schüfftan preferred broad zones with gradual crossings between the two elements, using an irregular zigzag line which also served to cover any dissimilarities

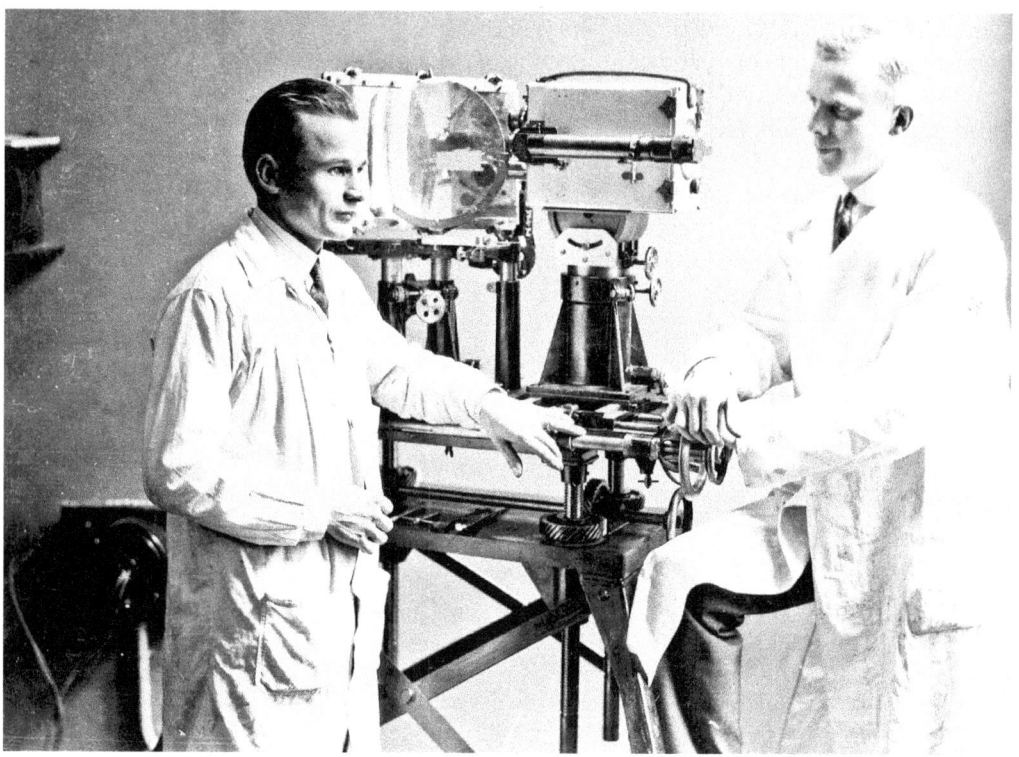

Technicians preparing a Schüfftan composite (author's collection/Deutsche Kinemathek–Museum für Film und Fernsehen, Berlin).

in the lighting. Although the patent was initially controlled solely by UFA and a joint-stock company (Deutsche Spiegeltechnik) specializing in the process, an American license was quickly purchased by Carl Laemmle's Universal Pictures Corporation. While it had been Schüfftan's aim to fully exploit the versatility of his process for fantasy films, UFA used it mainly for cutting costs in building sets by matching full-scale scenes with miniature buildings and models.

Schüfftan's dream project was *Gulliver's Travels*. He hoped to convince Laemmle's executives across the Big Pond to fund it. Together with his assistant Ernst Kunstmann, he left the Neubabelsberg lot for Universal City.

> In a projection room at Universal the other day I saw two reels of what is probably the queerest film ever made. They were comprised of a collection of random "shots" taken by the Schüfftan method.
>
> Certain views of the film version of *Gulliver's Travels*, which Universal plans to produce soon, will perhaps best illustrate the inner works of this clever Teutonic device.
>
> In one scene Gulliver is shown peering over a high wall into a courtyard. A Lilliputian regards him with awe from the court, while another appears in the second-story window of the building which serves as a background.
>
> Although he appears gazing at him on the screen, Gulliver didn't see the dwarfs when the scene was made. He was standing behind a wall that came up to his shoulders. The tiny man in the courtyard was situated on a vacant lot and his little friend in the window was off somewhere else in front of a black curtain. The building itself was merely a photograph several feet square which was placed in front of one of the mirrors.
>
> Here are four separate scenes, scuttered around without apparent regard for the location of the camera.

> Looking through the finder, all four scenes magically converge. The wall over which Gulliver leans fits perfectly into and becomes part of the building. The ground on which the dwarf is standing appears to be the site on which both building and wall rest.
> On the screen it was impossible to detect where the matching had taken place.
> To attempt a scene of this kind heretofore, it would have been necessary to make at least two exposures. [...]
> The all-important thing, of course, is the adjustment of the mirrors. This is accomplished by means of intricate gears, which permit adjustments to the thousandth part of an inch.
> Lenses which magnify or reduce are used to balance the perspective. Lighting of the various "sets" is a face that demands careful attention, particularly as regards matching.
> Through the use of curved mirrors distorted images are focused on the lens—a feat with great comedy possibilities...[9]

I do not know if the *Gulliver* test was shot on the Universal lot or in Germany. I guess it belonged to a test reel prepared by Schüfftan to arouse Universal's interest in the project.

While two mirror trick experts were in Hollywood—waiting to make a *Gulliver* that was *not* made—their Neubabelsberg colleagues struggled to finish *Metropolis*. For certain scenes featuring the New Tower of Babel located in the center of Metropolis, Erich Kettelhut employed what he would call *Maltrick*: painting trick. That was a technique similar to matte painting but no matte shot in the strict sense. Sweeping searchlight beams were laboriously animated using glycerin paint on a large sheet of glass positioned in front of the painted tower. Between each single-frame exposure, the glass surface was wiped clean and the beam repainted in its next sequential position. Günther Rittau, who along with first cinematographer Karl Freund and Freund's assistant Robert Baberske photographed the film and also served as effects cameraman, arranged the stop-motion equipment for Kettelhut's painted effects.

The Robotrix Comes to Life

To instigate the fire of revolution that brought the city to fall, Lang commissioned sculptor Walter Schulze-Mittendorf (1893–1976) to create the (wooden) armor of a robotic duplicate of Maria the Underground Preacher:

> Problems with the form? No!
> Expressionism was alive.
> The technical form had been discovered as a motif for painting and sculpture.

With this in mind, Schulze-Mittendorf began to build the prototype of the "Machine Man": "I didn't bother to make a figurine first. A plaster cast was made of B. Helm—and I worked on that directly—the figure, which could be dismantled into single parts, of course." He sculpted the design directly on the plaster cast.

> Priority in this case was: "Which material?" Thought of—at first, coppersheet—embossed—to have real metal. This meant = production of a model in natural size—looking for, and finding, a suitable metal chaser for the execution. "Cumbersome" I thought—when Fritz Lang got me interested in this work. But which material, really? Help came by chance.
> A shop of architectural models unwittingly provided the essential assistance. I was led there on account of a different task. A small cardboard box labeled "Plastic Wood"—"Sample Without Value"—a postal item, therefore—arrested my attention. This "sample without value"—of no interest to that shop—was placed at my disposal. A working specimen delivered instant proof—the material for the

production of the "Machine Man" had been found. "Plastic Wood" turned out to be a pliable wooden material—fast-hardening on exposure to air—with the possibility of being able to work on it—like naturally grown wood.[10]

The film's highlight was the duplication of the human, divine Maria into an evil automaton witch. The scene was quite challenging for trick cinematographer Günther Rittau. When Maria's flesh is transferred onto the metallic body of Schulze-Mittendorf's "Machine Man" as constructed per script by Rotwang, the mad Jewish scientist and alchemist played by Rudolf Klein-Rogge, the automaton is encircled by glittering light rings and electric flashes. Lap dissolves made it possible to change the robot's face into Maria's right there on the set (although a little incorrect even if you don't watch closely). The rings and flashes, however, were more complicated and needed to be done in post-production in a blackened barrack on UFA's Neubabelsberg backlot. Two Mitchell cameras were imported from the States for the production of *Metropolis,* one for Freund, one for Rittau. H.O. Schulze, Rittau's assistant who later photographed George Pal's first German trickfilms, did the tedious work but never saw Fritz Lang coming to the barrack where this work was done.

In front of Rittau and Schulze's rigidly mounted Mitchell camera, a plywood silhouette of the previously filmed Machine Maria—garbed in black velvet for matte purposes—was carefully positioned. Just over the silhouette, a simple lift was erected to maneuver two parallel rings attached to three fine wires. The rings themselves were made of a special grease-proof paper that dispersed light. To further diffuse the imagery, Rittau placed a sheet of glass smeared with thin layers of grease in front of the camera lens. After running some test footage, each ring was double-exposed six times onto the original negative, resulting in 12 glittering rings encircling the automaton. Electric flashes were superimposed to complete the effect. A clever trick shot in its day—but wherefore asked H.G. Wells in his devastating review:

> Then comes the crowning absurdity of the film, the conversion of the Robot into the likeness of Mary. Rotwang, you must understand, occupies a small old house, embedded in the modern city, richly adorned with pentagrams and other reminders of the antiquated German romances out of which its owner has been taken. A quaint smell of Mephistopheles is perceptible for a time. So even at UFA, Germany can still be dear old magic-loving Germany. Perhaps Germans will never get right away from the Brocken. Walpurgis Night is the name-day of the German poetic imagination, and the national fantasy capers insecurely for ever with a broomstick between its legs. By some no doubt abominable means Rotwang has squeezed a vast and well-equipped modern laboratory into this little house. It is ever so much bigger than the house, but no doubt he has fallen back on Einstein and other modern bedevilments. Mary has to be trapped, put into a machine like a translucent cocktail shaker, and undergo all sorts of pyrotechnic treatment in order that her likeness may be transferred to the Robot. The possibility of Rotwang just simply making a Robot like her, evidently never entered the gifted producer's head. The Robot is enveloped in wavering haloes, the premises seem to be struck by lightning repeatedly, the contents of a number of flasks and carboys are violently agitated, there are minor explosions and discharges. Rotwang conducts the operations with a manifest luck of assurance, and finally, to his evident relief, the likeness is taken and things calm down. The false Mary then winks darkly at the audience and sails off to raise the workers. And so forth and so on. There is some rather good swishing about in water, after the best film traditions, some violent and unconvincing machine-breaking and rioting and wreckage, and then, rather confusedly, one gathers that Masterman has learnt a lesson, and that workers and employees are now to be reconciled by "Love."
>
> Never for a moment does one believe any of this foolish story; for a moment is there anything amusing or convincing in its dreary series of strained events. It is immensely and strangely dull. It is not even to be laughed at. There is not one good-looking nor sympathetic nor funny personality in the

cast; there is, indeed, no scope at all for looking well or acting like a rational creature amid these mindless, imitative absurdities. The film's air of having something grave and wonderful to say is transparent pretence. [...]

The theatre when I visited it was crowded. All but the highest-priced seats were full, and the gaps in these filled up reluctantly but completely before the great film began. I suppose every one had come to see what the city of a hundred years hence will be like. It was, I thought, an unresponsive audience, and I heard no comments. I could not tell from their bearing whether they believed that *Metropolis* was really a possible forecast or no. I do not know whether they thought that the film was hopelessly silly or the future of mankind hopelessly silly. But it must have been one thing or the other.[11]

Wells would have been even more amazed if he would have known that Lang toyed with the project of launching a rocket to the stars with the loving couple, Maria and Freder, on board at the end of *Metropolis*. Then he decided to save the grand idea for a whole new movie that was titled *Frau im Mond* (*Woman in the Moon*/U.S.: *By Rocket to the Moon*, 1928–29) starring Gerda Maurus in the Maria part and Willy Fritsch in the Freder part, with *Nosferatu*'s Gustav von Wangenheim rounding off the *ménage à trois* on the Earth's moon. But behind the screen the *ménage à trois* was different: not Fritsch-Maurus-Wangenheim but Harbou-Lang-Maurus. Actually, Maurus (1903–1968) had become Fritz Lang's new Mistress of Mishap.

In making *Nibelungen* and *Metropolis*, Lang surrounded himself with some people who later became devoted Nazis. besides Thea von Harbou, chief designer Otto Hunte and actors Rudolf Klein-Rogge, Heinrich George, Theodor Loos and Siegfried's murderer Hans Adalbert (von) Schlettow, born Hans Adalbert Droescher, a feared denouncer who died in the battle of Berlin, the same day as Hitler, on April 30, 1945.

Fritz Lang, without knowing it, built on the screen what Hitler and the Nazis envisioned: a bizarre mix of heroic past and a "thousand year" future:

> Otto Hunte, Erich Kettelhut and Karl Vollbrecht's utopian structures created for the upper city in *Metropolis* became reality in the "regimented state architecture" of the Reich Chancellery and the Olympia Stadium; [Albert] Speer's artistry with lighting, based on the lighting techniques of the Nibelungs, made magically illuminated allegorical figures of the Führer and his vassals; Siegfried's tomb with its massive stone sarcophagus evolved in to a "dream image of Fascist necrophilia" and was imitated repeatedly in the tombs and memorial structures of the NSDAP.[12]

And the New Tower of Babel? Hitler redesigned it as the People's Hall, a monumental domed building in the center of Berlin-turned-Germania, the "capital of the world," over 200 meters (656 feet) high, 16 times larger than the dome of St. Peter's Basilica. It remained an insane idea and was never executed.

Later in his life, Lang disparaged *Metropolis*:

> I've often said I didn't like *Metropolis* because I can't accept the leitmotif of the message in the film. It is absurd to say that the heart is the intermediary between the hands and the brain, that is to say, the employer and the employee. The problem is social and not moral. Naturally, during the making of the film, I liked it, if not I wouldn't have continued to work.... But later, I began to understand what didn't work.... I thought, for example, that one of the faults was the way in which I showed the work of man and machine together. You remember the clocks and the man who worked in harmony with them? He should become, so to speak, part of the machine. Well, that seemed to be too symbolic, too simplistic in the evocation of what we call the evils of mechanization. As well, a few years ago, I had to revise my judgment again, at the spectacle of our astronauts walking around the earth. It was the experts, they were prisoners of their space capsule, nothing else—or almost, a part of the machine that carried them....[13]

Faust's Last Laugh

By 1931, Lang had left UFA in a rage and, having just finished his first talkie, *M*, starring Peter Lorre, performed the eulogy at Murnau's grave. Now that the great Friedrich Wilhelm was dead, there was no directorial rival on German screens any more. Lang had worked hard for that goal and it would last until he was able to do what Murnau already had achieved: directing in Hollywood. One Hitler was needed to make Lang want to leave the country. Initially he was flattered when Goebbels told him how much the Nazis thought of *Nibelungen* and his anti–Semitic *Metropolis* (we are sure that Lang wasn't that aware about the fact, the cuckoo's egg laid by Thea von Harbou) and that he considered *M* a plea for the death penalty. But then Lang's secretary, Lily Latté, whom he married decades later, convinced him that the Nazis would turn out evil partners and so he decided to leave. We also shouldn't forget that Lang's mother was Jewish. Catholic Lang had forgotten, for some time.

Back at the time, when both directors were working for UFA and Lang was preparing his big epics, Murnau did an Emil Jannings film that won him world fame: *Der letzte Mann* (1924), on American screens known as *The Last Laugh*, written by Carl Mayer and photographed by Karl Freund. Jannings played a proud hotel doorman who, due to his old age, is demoted to a less demanding (and important) job as a washroom attendant. As Grau did in his *Warning Shadows,* Murnau and Mayer managed to tell the story without intertitles.

In the meantime, UFA's third hot director, Dr. Ludwig Berger, planned a film version of *Faust,* the medieval scholar and alchemist who made a pact with Mephistopheles, the emissary of the Devil who is after his soul.

Berger's screenplay was titled *Das verlorene Paradies* (*The Lost Paradise*) and the great Conrad Veidt was cast as Mephistopheles. When Emil Jannings, now Germany's most prominent screen actor, learned that his colleague and rival Veidt was going to play that prominent part, he intervened and claimed the role for himself. The screenplay was rewritten by Hans Kyser to fit Jannings's size. But Jannings would refuse Berger's services and ask for Murnau, who had given him fame with *The Last Laugh* and another meaty part in *Tartuffe* (1925), based on Molière's play. Nothing was too expensive to be put into that production, that at least was downright medieval—while Fritz Lang, like the Nazis, undecidedly wavered between the Dark Ages and the future. While Lang only had a lesser writer in the politically naïve von Harbou, the great Jannings met the even greater Johann Wolfgang von Goethe, Germany's national poet and author of the definitive *Faust* play published in 1808, the whole event enshrined for posterity in a movie directed by Murnau.

Six months of shooting, a budget of two million marks, and Gerhard Hauptmann, Germany's most prominent playwright, signed to write the intertitles. However, Hauptmann's intertitles were hastily removed; as not even Hauptmann's long verses could do Goethe justice!

Screenwriter Hans Kyser had to fill in for Hauptmann, the idol of his youth, and volunteered to write brief intertitle prose. He washed his hands of responsibility by declaring, "We are going to lay the Faust film as a modest gift of homage at Goethe's feet."[14] Metro-Goldwyn-Mayer, the U.S. distributor, hailed the picture as "The Screen Sensation of Two Continents!":

> NEVER before has the screen revealed a spectacle of such size and impressiveness as in the epic production. The world-famous story of fate and temptation, renowned as an opera, has now been dramatically immortalized in a picture which can be truly called great.

> Emil Jannings, one of the world's most celebrated screen stars, reaches new heights of brilliance and power in this masterpiece, directed by Europe's greatest director. The storm scene alone will make it famous, but its magic blend of unforgettable beauty and dramatic power will make it the sensation of years.

Well roar'd, Lion!

But neither MGM nor Paramount would do much to support their temporary German partner UFA on American screens. Both *Metropolis* and *Faust* were partly destroyed in America by lukewarm distribution policy. While Paramount spoiled *Metropolis* and made its admittedly banal story unrecognizable, Metro-Goldwyn-Mayer ensured that *Faust* would only be screened in the big American cities and not in the countryside. This policy is continued to this day. Today American majors call it "local production," meaning their product is intended for the global market while everything else, from China to Germany, should remain local and enter American screens only in film festivals.

Returning to the unspoken rivalry between Lang and Murnau, we can declare that it was Murnau who won the competition. He was number one. America was hiring European talent, and after Lubitsch he became the second German director to be lured away by an American mogul. In 1926, Fox's Berlin representative Heinz J. Preuschhoff knocked at his door and approached him at the behest of his boss, William Fox. In June, Murnau signed a Fox contract and came to Hollywood to make *Sunrise* (1927) from a script by Carl Mayer, based on the novel *The Excursion to Tilsit* by Hermann Sudermann. Charles Rosher and Karl Struss were behind the camera and Janet Gaynor and George O'Brien in front.

Jannings (and Ludwig Berger) followed him but signed with Paramount. In 1929, Jannings was honored with the first Academy Award given to a male actor but then decided to return to Germany for his first talkie, which turned out to be *Der blaue Engel* (*The Blue Angel*), directed (at Jannings's request) by Paramount's Josef von Sternberg. The picture made Marlene Dietrich a world star. While she left for Hollywood, Jannings stayed and made a pact with the Nazis. Berger also returned to Germany, but the Nazis made his stay short, while Jannings became the highest-paid actor in Nazi Germany. Carl Zuckmayer, a writer sharp as a razor, portrayed him mercilessly in one of his OSS secret reports, but in the end he had to admit: "I love that old sow."[15]

In the meantime, Murnau's dead body returned from California. After three pictures, the director had left Fox and the American studio system to make a movie outdoors, as he had, at least partly done, with the production of *Nosferatu*. He joined forces with Robert J. Flaherty and set sail to the South Seas to film *Tabu*. Murnau finished the movie by himself (Flaherty had a different concept). Then, on the verge of signing with Paramount and one week prior to the opening of *Tabu*, Wednesday, March 11, 1931, on the way up the Pacific Coast Highway from Los Angeles to Monterey, Murnau's leased Packard vehicle crashed. John Freeland, the official chauffeur, was not at that time at the wheel, but a 14-year-old Filipino boy named Garcia Stevenson, very handsome and exotic-looking, most likely Murnau's "boy toy." Stevenson wanted to demonstrate his driving skills and drove at top speed and, shortly before Santa Barbara, near Rincon Beach, an oncoming truck caused him to lose control. The car tumbled down an embankment. Everyone—even Murnau's dog—was unhurt, but Murnau suffered a skull fracture that proved fatal. Rumors that both, Murnau and the boy were engaged in oral sex prior to the crash were made up by scandal-worshipping Crowley admirer Kenneth Anger of *Hollywood Babylon* fame.

Three years later, on board the *Ile De France* on the way to New York harbor in the summer of 1934, Fritz Lang signed his first Hollywood contract and became a naturalized citizen of the United States in 1939. He worked with Spencer Tracy, Henry Fonda, Ray Milland, Joan Bennett, Edward G. Robinson, Tyrone Power, Jean Gabin and Marlene Dietrich (who called him in a note "Sadist Incorporated"[16]), but remained largely a "hired hand," never finding his way back to the days of former glory. In 1956 he returned to Europe. West Berlin producer Artur Brauner offered him a remake of *Die Nibelungen* but Lang wouldn't touch it. Harald Reinl, a former Leni Riefenstahl assistant, remade the two-part epic for Brauner in 1966. Lang's final films were a two-part 1959 color version of the dusty *Indian Tomb* starring Debra Paget and Paul Christian Hubschmid and the first entry in a new series of *Dr. Mabuse* films (*The Thousand Eyes of Dr. Mabuse*, 1960). Apparently he had quit being innovative in the past three decades. He died, nearly blind, on August 2, 1976, in Beverly Hills.

The Vampire Jew and the Curse of Anti-Semitism

Nosferatu (Briefly) Returns from the Dead

While Murnau was still alive and filming abroad, *Nosferatu* turned up (briefly) but under a different title.

In her book on Murnau, Lotte H. Eisner called her find a riddle: The *Cinémathèque Francaise* had two prints of *Nosferatu* in its vaults, a French one and a German one. The German one was not only longer but contained two passages, which were not hinted at in the film script saved from Murnau's estate:

> As Hutter journeys in haste towards the enchanted castle, a German title says he "passes by merry feasts." And then come longwinded and commonplace sequences of peasants dancing and banqueting at a long table. There is no trace of Murnau's style in these scenes of would-be folklore of a kind that recurred so often in later UFA films.
>
> There are other puzzling scenes, too, like that of some young peasant girls roaring with laughter at a village conjuror whose hen lays a constant stream of eggs.
>
> Another strange sequence shows an interminably long mass said for a victim of the plague by a very handsome young priest assisted by some even more attractive choirboys [...] There is nothing of any of this either in Galeen's script or in Murnau's annotations.[1]

Eisner contacted Murnau's cinematographer, Fritz Arno Wagner, shortly before his death. He answered:

> The original was not very long, so it is quite possible that certain parts were added afterwards. Plenty of material was shot. But I don't know anything about the scene of the conjuror and the eggs. Nor did I ever shoot the mass for the dead; it must have been added ready-made. Moreover I've never seen this lengthened and changed copy, and I can vouch for the fact that Murnau himself never knew this second version.

This version clearly distorted Murnau's rhythm and narration:

> [O]ther variations appeared equally apocryphal. For instance, in the German version Ellen, instead of sacrificing herself and dying in order to save the city from the vampire, comes to life again. This surprising happy ending was achieved by simply transferring a sequence showing the couple living quietly and happily together from the beginning to the end of the film.[2]

The riddle was solved by film director-historian Gerhard Lamprecht, who presented a censor's certificate dated November 14, 1930. Murnau's movie was changed without his knowledge and retitled *Die zwölfte Stunde. Eine Nacht des Grauens* (*The Twelfth Hour:*

A Night of Horror) by a company called Deutsch Film Produktion. The role names were changed too: Orlok became Prince Wolkoff, Knock was renamed Karsten, Hutter Kundberg and Ellen Margitta. Murnau's name wasn't mentioned at all; a Dr. Waldemar Roger was credited as artistic supervisor. Two actors were hired to perform in some of the additional scenes: Hans Behal (the priest celebrating the mass for the dead) left Germany in 1933 and later went to Israel where he died in 1956. And Eugen Rex, a former construction draftsman, who began working on the stage in 1905 and was seen, mostly in supporting parts, in many silents and talkies. He became a member of the NSDAP in 1933.

The correct name of the compiler-adapter/reviser was not Roger but Ronger who, like Albin Grau, was a member of the Pansophic Society. The story goes that Grau waited until it was all water under the bridge. Then he sold all material and footage of *Nosferatu*, negative, prints and stills, to Ronger in 1928 for 15,000 Reichsmark. Ronger founded Deutsch Film Produktion and refurnished the property in 1930. He added new scenes as well as a musical score via a sound-on-disc system. *Die zwölfte Stunde* had a limited release and was screened in Berlin in the Kamera Cinema Unter den Linden, an early 300-seat arthouse theater. It was soon forgotten.

Vampires—Old and New

While *Nosferatu* was revived (even though Florence Stoker didn't notice), Carl Theodor Dreyer, whose film concept of *Blade af Satans Bog* Murnau had copied ten years ago in *Satanas*, created his own cinematic Undead called *Vampyr*, the first European sound film revenant. It was adapted (as in Murnau's case) very freely from a Gothic horror novel, this time by one of Bram Stoker's fellow countrymen and predecessors: Joseph Sheridan Le Fanu's *Carmilla* (1872). Dreyer was able to secure some funding from a private source, a true patron of the arts, Nicolas Louis Alexandre, Baron de Gunzburg, a nobleman of Russian, Polish and Portuguese descent. Gunzburg's only condition was that he would play the lead, under the pseudonym Julian West. In 1934, he left Europe; he died in 1981 in New York City.

Author and critic Kim Newman writes,

> I've always wondered whether Dreyer had seen Browning's *Dracula* (1931), released while *Vampyr* was in pre-production, or F.W. Murnau's *Nosferatu* (1922). All three feature a young, haunted-looking hero arriving at a remote location and falling under the sway of a malign vampire who dominates the region—but that could as easily be down to coincidence. [...] It's hard, somehow, to imagine the ascetic, spiritually inclined Dane buying a ticket for Browning's full-blooded Hollywood melodrama and shivering at the baleful glare of Bela Lugosi's Count Dracula. Obviously, he was closer in temperament to the German Murnau, who shot his film in real ruined castles rather than rely on elaborately Gothic studio sets.

Dreyer's *Vampyr* has a commercial title but indeed bears more resemblance to Luis Bunuel's early experimental films than to Le Fanu. Newman continues,

> The young, ethereal Carmilla is very unlike the aged, solid Marguerite Chopin (Henriette Gérard), though the two successive girl victims in the Le Fanu [story] might have transformed into the sisters Léone (Sybille Schmitz) and Gisèle (Rena Mandel). *Vampyr* seems more like a screen original that tries to feel like an oft-told tale, with silent-movie–style prose captions between scenes and characters who drift through the plot as if trapped in a recurring nightmare. Still, the evocation of Le Fanu's female vampire is significant—just as *Carmilla* established a counter tradition of the seductive female vampire. *Vampyr* is the first film to make much of such a figure, as incarnated by the dour crone Marguerite and the semi-transformed Léone. [...]

The character of Marguerite Chopin remains unusual, if not unique, in vampire literature and film. Vampires may be centuries old, but they tend not to look as ancient as Gérard's white-haired "woman from the graveyard," unless the light of day or a stake through the heart transforms them into a crone [...] Though Gérard's Marguerite is not as extravagantly repulsive as Max Schreck's Dracula stand-in Graf von Orlok in *Nosferatu* or Chaney's bogus vampire [in the lost *London After Midnight*], Dreyer makes her frightening simply by dwelling on her careworn face and blank eyes, which the audience invests with malevolence...[3]

Alraune

With the advent of sound films, Hanns Heinz Ewers also returned to the screen. His 1911 novel *Alraune* was filmed in 1927 by his former secretary Henrik Galeen, with Brigitte Helm as the *femme fatale* created by artificial insemination and Paul Wegener as her creator, and right away it became a talkie in 1929–30, directed by Richard Oswald, starring Helm again, and Albert Bassermann assuming the Wegener role. Wegener began to talk on screen in April 1930 in Ewers's story of a successful sex reversal, *Fundvogel*. It was produced from a screenplay written by Hans Steinhoff, an upcoming Nazi director, whom Billy Wilder once called a "man without any talent whatsoever." And Wegener talked in one of the first outspoken National Socialist films as a Soviet agitator: *Horst Wessel* was based on Ewers' eponymous novel. Wessel, son of a pastor, student, low-life bohemian, had joined the Nazi party and the SA in 1926. The same year he turned up as a corps student among the extras of the remake of Ewers's *Student von Prag*, directed by Henrik Galeen and starring Conrad Veidt! On January 14, 1930, he was killed by political enemies, most likely members of the Communist Party, in a brawl in his room.

Ewers claimed that Hitler himself had elected him to pen the *Horst Wessel* novel, but the man who had written about vampires, necromancy, artificial insemination and the occult was not welcomed with open arms by his fellow Nazis. Goebbels banned the first version of the *Wessel* film:

> As National Socialists we do not particularly value to watch our SA marching on stage or screen. Its sphere are the streets. Should however somebody try to solve national socialist problems in the realm of art, he must understand that also in this case the art does not come from ambition but ability. Even an ostantious display of a national socialist attitude is no substitute for an absence of true art. The national socialist government has never demanded the production of SA movies. On the contrary: we see a danger in this excess. [...] In no way does National Socialism justify artistic failure. The greater the idea that shall find a form the greater the aesthetic demands have to be.[4]

The *Horst Wessel* film had to be revised and retitled: not *Wessel* but *Westmar—Hans Westmar: One of Many*. And virtually all of Ewers's books were out of print in the Third Reich.

Siegfried Kracauer Meets Henrik Galeen

Henrik Galeen had immigrated to Sweden before moving on to the United Kingdom and eventually to the United States, where he died in 1949.

During the winter, Galeen lived in New York City, in summertime in Rochester, Vermont. In 1948, he married his second wife, "Baroness" Ilse von Schenk who worked in the manufacture of toys and dolls. The work was done by women in White River Valley, the results shipped to New York. Towards the end of his life, he talked to Siegfried Kracauer, who prepared his study *From Caligari to Hitler* and wrote an essay on film fantasy. So his name and *Nosferatu* were prominently featured in Kracauer's book:

> When speaking of *Nosferatu*, the critics, even more than in the case of *Caligari*, insisted on bringing in E.T.A. Hoffmann. However, this reference to the film's romantic antedecedents does not account for its specific meaning. The horrors *Nosferatu* spreads are caused by a vampire identified with pestilence. Does he embody the pestilence, or is its image evoked to characterize him? If he were simply the embodiment of destructive nature, Nina's [Ellen's][5] interference with his activities would be nothing more than magic, meaningless in this context. Like Attila, Nosferatu is a "scourge of God," and only as such identifiable with the pestilence. He is a bloodthirsty, blood-sucking tyrant figure looming in those regions where myths and fairy tales meet. It is highly significant that during this period German imagination, regardless of its starting-point, always gravitated towards such figures—as if under the compulsion of hate-love.[6]

Wherever Rats Appear...

And tyranny would indeed rear its ugly head a decade later, the fatal product of a lost war and of the Great Depression with the consequences of mass unemployment:

> The notion that *Nosferatu* contains anti–Semitic overtones is certainly not a new one. Critics and historians have debated the matter for decades. [...]

Contempt for Jews was certainly nothing new in Christian Europe. But by the 1920s, it had reached a modern high in Germany, where many blamed the Jews for sabotaging the war effort, even of secretly conspiring to use their supposed wealth and power to undermine Germany and hand it over to its enemies. In short, they were scapegoated, and it became more acceptable than ever to resent and mistrust them. This is the leverage that Hitler and his cronies would use to ascend to power, promising to rid the Fatherland of the vermin polluting it.[7]

In the Third Reich, not only Hanns Heinz Ewers, a declared advocate of the Nazi regime (albeit for many years with a ban on publication), but horror films in general had almost completely vanished from the screens (except *King Kong*, one of Hitler's favorites). There was the 1935 talkie remake of *The Student of Prague* written by Hans Kyser and directed by Arthur Robison, with Ewers reduced to an extra. Ewers died in Berlin on June 12, 1943, four months and ten days after the surrender of the 6th Army in Stalingrad. *Nosferatu* and *Dracula* were now replaced by *The Eternal Jew*. Such was the title of a "documentary" movie that symbolized the peak of anti–Semitism in Nazi Germany.

Announcing Veit Harlan's *Jud Süss (Jew Suss)* in 1940, posters showed a bearded, green-faced Ferdinand Marian with yellow eyes, similar to John Barrymore's portrayal of the title character in *Svengali* (1931). But the film itself was a naïve costume drama: a disgusting falsification of history that led to a miscarriage of justice and to the hanging of Joseph Süss Oppenheimer on February 4, 1738, cast with prominent actors who proverbially rolled their eyes. In one early draft of the screenplay found in the vaults of Deutsche Kinemathek in Berlin, there is a murder ballad that compares the Jew with a vampire: sort of a vampire Jew.

Der ewige Jude (The Eternal Jew), released the same year, is worse because it claims "authenticity." After the invasion of Poland, Dr. Fritz Hippler, then head of the German newsreel service Deutsche Wochenschau, ordered his camera crew to film a poverty-stricken Jewish community driven into degradation in the ghettos of Lodz, Warsaw, Lublin, and Cracow. In the Nazi press, Hippler stressed the "authenticity" of his work:

Orlok gets off the ship—and the rats do likewise (from the stills collection of Deutsche Kinemathek–Museum für Film und Fernsehen, Berlin).

> No Jew was forced into any kind of action or position during the shooting [of *The Eternal Jew*]. Moreover, we let the filmed Jews be undisturbed and tried to shoot in moments when they were unaware of the camera's presence. Subsequently, we have rendered the ghetto Jews in an unprejudiced manner, real to life as they react in their own surroundings. All who are growing to see this film will be convinced that there is never a forced or scared expression in the faces of the Jews who are filmed passing by, trading or attending ritual services.

But could these possibly be "their own surroundings" when those surroundings were created by the Nazi occupation forces? *The Eternal Jew* is a rather obscene, rotten, infamous propaganda compilation. This "cinematic contribution to the problem of world Jewry" was loosely based on a 1937 exhibition of the same title that was devoted to "degenerate art" and even contained a short "documentary" denouncing Jewish film actors of the Weimar Republic. The 1937 short, however, was rejected by Goebbels: "A bad propaganda film about Jews in films. Made despite my ban. I shall not pass it. Too pushy." By contrast, the 1940 *Eternal Jew* provokes the fear and hatred of the "Wandering Jew," of migration and superalienation effectively. The narrator is Harry Giese,[8] a well-known newsreel speaker and dubbing voice artist who delivered the commentary written by Dr. Eberhard Taubert:

> The war in Poland has given us the opportunity to get to know Jewry at its heart. Nearly four million Jews live here in Poland, although you would seek them in vain among the rural population. Nor have they suffered from the chaos of the war, as has the native population. They squatted indifferently, as non-participants, in the dark streets of the Polish ghetto—and within an hour of the German occupation they had resumed their money dealings.

The narrator promises that this "documentary" is going to show the Jewish migrants undisguised: without the "mask of civilized Europeans." According to Goebbels, Jews were not human beings: "Predators equipped with cold intellect that have to be rendered harmless." Giese says,

> These physiognomies refute conclusively the liberal theories of the equality of all men. Jews change their outward appearance when they leave their Polish haunts for the wider world. Hair, beard, skullcap and caftan make the Eastern Jew recognizable to all. If he appears without his trademarks, only the sharp-eyed can recognize his racial origins. It is an intrinsic trait of the Jew that he always tries to hide his origin when he is among non–Jews.

Hippler then shows a "bunch of Polish Jews—now wearing caftans—ready to steal into Western civilization." As these "assimilated" Jews look a little bit awkward in front of the camera, the commentary has to concede that "these ghetto Jews do not yet know how to look at ease in fine European suits." Berlin Jews, however, we are told,

> are more adept. Their fathers and forefathers lived in ghettos, but that's not apparent now. Here in the second and third generation, Aryanization has reached its zenith. Outwardly they try to imitate their hosts. People lacking in intuition let themselves be deceived by this mimicry and think of Jews as just the same as they are. This is a dreadful danger. These assimilated Jews remain forever foreign bodies in the organism of their hosts, no matter how they seem to appear outwardly.

This story sounds like a record of demonic possession or, in the language of science fiction, like the seed of an alien Fifth Column: a whole bunch of extraterrestrial horror stories that ranged from *It Came from Outer Space* and *Invasion of the Body Snatchers* to *Alien*. According to Giese, "We recognize the pestherd [center of pestilence] which threatens the Aryan race. The Jews are a race without farmers and without natural laborers, a race of parasites." To the followers of Nazi ideology, the lesson is clear: Jews are *Untermenschen*, they belong to a subhuman species and are spread by migration like an epidemic.

But what about *Nosferatu*? Why do we think that a masterpiece by "Europe's leading director" belongs in that category?

> As many have pointed out, Murnau's version of "Dracula," a.k.a. the repulsive Count Orlok, possesses many physical features commonly found in stereotypical caricatures of Jews at the time: A long hooked nose, long claw-like fingernails, bushy eyebrows, a large forehead with bald head, and a general feminization of his appearance which was also common. His appearance is not only comparable to anti–Semitic imagery, but he is also made to look something like a rat, in accordance with the disgusting rodents he brings with him. This, in turn, ties back into the Jewish stereotype, as Jews were often equated with rats as well.[9]

Let us return to *The Eternal Jew*, to its most disgusting sequence. All of a sudden, Hippler interjects images of rats:

> Comparable with the Jewish wanderings through history are the mass migrations of an equally restless animal, the rat…. Wherever rats appear they bring ruin, they ravage human property and foodstuffs. In this way they spread disease: plague, leprosy, typhoid, cholera, dysentery, etc. They are cunning, cowardly and cruel and are found mostly in packs. In the animal world they represent the element of craftiness and subterranean destruction—no different from the Jews among mankind!

The Jew as disease-causing agent, louse, germ, poison, abscess, ulcer, parasite and flagellum: The Jew as incarnation of an apocalyptic plague. This basic image is what *Nosferatu* and *The Eternal Jew* have in common.

> The parallels between vampirism and European anti–Semitism go back much further than *Nosferatu*, and were in fact part of the continental zeitgeist for centuries. Jews—as well as gypsies, another popular scapegoat target of post–World War I Germany—were often depicted as bloodsuckers, and some have

even traced the vampire's aversion to Christian imagery to this parallel. There was also a popular myth that circulated for centuries regarding the alleged Jewish practice of drinking the blood of Christian children.[10]

Nosferatu is no explicit anti–Semitic movie, but it is a piece of a jigsaw that is a sad part of Teutonic culture and xenophobia.[11]

What then about *Nosferatu*'s original source: *Dracula*? Yes, the seed is already to be found there. If we read more precisely we find a few noticeable clues of Stoker's conception of man:

> Though it only explicitly expresses so once, Bram Stoker's *Dracula* is an anti–Semitic text. When meeting [Immanuel] Hildesheim [Dracula's Jewish attorney], Stoker describes him as "a Hebrew of rather the Adelphi Theatre type, with a nose like a sheep, and a fez" (Stoker 302). By describing the man this way, as well as noting how easy it was to bribe him, Stoker relies on age-old Jewish stereotypes.
>
> As well as this blatant anti–Semitic remark, Stoker integrates much contempt for Jews in his novel. First, he compares Dracula to Hildesheim (and all stereotypical Jews) by describing his large nose, pointed ears, and prominent eyebrows. He uses the word "aquiline" to describe Dracula's nose, which is a very clear reference to the Jewish stereotype of hooked noses. Stoker writes of Dracula's "hair growing scantily around the temples, but profusely elsewhere. His eyebrows were very massive, almost meeting over the nose, and with bushy hair that seemed to curl in its own profusion" (Stoker 23). Dracula is repeatedly portrayed as an alien presence, whose ultimate intent is to undermine the way of life of the British characters. In writing this invasion narrative, Stoker echoes many contemporary worries about Jews at this time. As written in the footnotes, "Jewish emigration swelled" in the 1890s, leading to much fear about disruption of the Western status quo.[12]

In a way, Stoker's depiction of *Dracula* exploited widespread anxieties concerning Yiddish-speaking immigrants to Great Britain. In Stoker's first surviving note (scrawled maybe in March 1890), by the way, Dracula's lawyer is named Abraham Aaronson. So it's certainly not a Jewish screenwriter's mistake: It's right there in the source, in Stoker's novel. That's how *Nosferatu*'s mad real estate broker Knock, as played by Jewish actor Alexander Granach, becomes a close relative of this Aaronson-Hildesheim.

> [T]he way Nosferatu reveals and exploits the prejudices and stereotypes is unmistakable. The first sign we get of this is in the character of Knock, a real estate broker and Hutter's boss. Knock is never identified as Jewish—nor is Orlok—but an interesting intertitle informs us that he was a figure "about whom all sorts of rumors circulated," and that "the only thing for certain was that he paid his people well."
>
> As Orlok will later, Knock personifies nearly every negative stereotype of Jews that was prevalent at the time, from his ratlike physical appearance—the bushy eyebrows, the hook nose, the gnomelike physiognomy—to his greedy, money-mad demeanor and his willingness to aid the enemies of Germany. (There was a widespread conspiracy theory at the time that Germany's defeat and surrender in 1918 was the result of internal subversion by "liberals, Socialists and Jews.")[13]

The idea of the Jewish bloodsucker goes way back:

> The metaphor of the vampire Jew was not forged in a cultural vacuum, but rather was derived from a new anti–Semitic genre, the hateful and terribly efficient trope of the blood libel. In these two-dimensional portrayals the story went that on Passover eve the body of a Christian child was found, resulting in the inevitable conclusion that the Jews had killed the child and used his blood to bake their matzos. After all, as every good baker knows, in a pinch, you can substitute flour with children's blood! [...]
>
> 1922 saw the first cinematic meeting of the concepts of the vampire and the Jew. [...] Count Orlok, the film's main character, had the face of a mouse with a curved nose and greedy little eyes that lusted hungrily after young, fair-haired Aryan women.
>
> Seated in the audience at the film's premiere was Julius Streicher, who would become chief editor

of *Der Stürmer*, Hitler's anti-Semitic newspaper. Streicher was immediately infatuated with *Nosferatu*. So aroused was he by the blood gushing from the young woman's fair flesh that he returned to watch the film day after day. As chief editor of *Der Stürmer* he was inspired by the film's vampire image, and soon dozens of caricatures began to appear of vampire-like Jews. For Streicher, the vampire represented the Other—the deformed, ugly, un-German, disease-ridden well-poisoner. In other words, the Jew.

Vampire experts (yes, that's a thing) say that the vampire represents the darkest, most repressed urges of the human mind—the lust, violence and sexual urges that cultural and societal conventions tend to oppress. These experts claim that the vampire is a projection of our desires, and this is the key to the vampire's phenomenal success in 20th century popular culture. In 1920s Germany there was one primary group upon whom those dark characteristics were naturally projected: the Jews.

Interestingly enough, in recent years the vampire has undergone a dramatic visual transformation. Today's vampire tends to be white, tall, blue-eyed and handsome. The vampires depicted in *True Blood*, *Twilight* or *Buffy the Vampire Slayer* could easily pass for members of the Hitler Youth. Does this mean that in modernity the white man has become the bad guy? Not necessarily. But if Hitler knew that the vile image of the Jewish vampire had morphed into his own beloved Aryan, he'd be rolling over in his grave.[14]

How the Golem Came into the World and Fought the Nazis

The Stone Guerrilla Strikes Back

On July 30, 1949, two years after Siegfried Kracauer's book was published, Henrik Galeen succumbed to cancer at Gifford Memorial Hospital, Randolph, Vermont. In the States, he never worked in films again. Only once, with Fritz Lang's old collaborator Paul Falkenberg, who was also involved in the German version of Dreyer's *Vampyr,* would he try his hand on another scenario that updated the *Golem* in December 1943 and would use his power against the brutal savageness of the Nazis. Alas, it remained unfilmed:

> Did Hitler know what he was doing when he deported a helpless crowd of Jews, of all walks of life, from all European nations to Chelm in the district of Lublin?
> Did he know at this very spot 350 years ago the holy Rabbi Baalschem had brought to life an image of clay, called the Golem, in order to save his people from ruthless persecution?
> Did Hitler know that the now lifeless clay figure of this Golem was underneath the narrow streets where modern Jews were thronging this new Ghetto?

With these questions the treatment opened.
The Synagogue is half in ruins. Rabbi Jonah wanders around and prays over the dead, spending comfort to the wounded, listening the living pleading for help. The old man promises the suffering:

> God will help. He will strike the enemy with His Own weapon. He has helped his children in the past ... 350 years ago it happened.... The Emperor ordered the Jews from his place to exile. Pleading was of no avail. It seemed that the end had come. At this time Rabbi Baalschem, after a long and fervent prayer, created the Golem. The Rabbi was a man of such holiness that God gave him the strength for this task.

According to the magic book Jezirah and following the secrets of the Cabala, the Rabbi formed the image of a man out of rough clay. Then he put the Shem, written on parchment, into the breast of the clay image.
So the Golem came to life, as Rabbi Jonah explained: "Neither walls nor moats could keep off this superhuman monster. Bullets could not hurt it. Swords were powerless against Baalschem's magic.... The enemies were smitten by the sign of God and the community was saved.... Baalschem took the Schem from the Golem and buried the lifeless figure of clay ... here..."
Rabbi Jonah taps the floor with his cane. The crowd demands that he should bring the

Golem to life again to save their community. The Rabbi raises his hand and tells them that the time has not come yet. He is going to see Steinhardt, the German district governor. Steinhardt's belief in his Fuehrer is unlimited but otherwise he is dissatisfied with his life, far away from Paris, Brussels or even Warsaw. Life in this Polish town enervates him. His boredom is not likely to be dispelled by the Rabbi's plea for mercy. Steinhardt declares bluntly that all food is to go to the German army. Rabbi Jonah is a broken man as he leaves the governor.

In the meantime, more Jews, from Norway this time, are deported to the already overcrowded ghetto. One, Elna, catches Steinhardt's eye. To him, she looks pretty Aryan. He invites her into his car. In a narrow street, a bomb hits the automobile. The driver is killed, Steinhardt is unhurt. Elna escapes and is saved by Sholem, a young member of the underground.

Sholem goes to see the Rabbi and learns that the governor has issued an ultimatum: If Elna, kidnapped by the Jews, is not brought to him within 24 hours, the Ghetto will become another Lidice. Elna is devastated: "Hundreds of human lives against one ... can there be any choice?"

German guns are pointing towards the Ghetto. Rabbi Jonah has no choice but to enter an arched cellar beneath the synagogue and revive the Golem. Horrified, the old man recedes, leaning against the wall. The brickwork gives way and crumbles, burying the Rabbi.

Elna, back at Steinhardt's, is treated like a queen. Steinhardt sees in her a prototype of the "Nordic race." In the meantime, the Golem haunts the district.

In the midst of a feast, a telegram is handed to the governor: "Immediate retreat ... after destruction of all commodities that might be of value to the enemy." Before Steinhardt's orders can be carried out, a gigantic shadow appears on the wall of his castle, illuminated by the moonlight. In the distance, they hear shots. "What is this? The Russians?" Elna asks. Steinhardt follows Elna to the window: "Not yet.... Those are German guns! Their aim ... the Ghetto! But before I leave here, you will be mine..."

> Triumphantly he walks towards her.... The girl stares at him wide eyed, silent ... no tears left.... A gust of wind rushes into the room ... the door has opened.... Steinhardt turns around.... In the door stands the Golem.... Steinhardt raises his revolver ... shoots. But the Golem walks into the room.... Steinhardt draws back to the wall ... speechless. The Golem, relentless hunter, stalks his quarry ... but as he walks on he leaves a trail of blood...
>
> Elna covers her face in her hands ... a body thuds to the floor.... Elna looks up ... the Golem turns...
>
> The Germans are in full retreat. The Ghetto has fought off the attack. The guerrillas have led the thrust, now they follow the fleeing Nazis.
>
> Elna bends over Sholem whose head rests on her lap. She dresses his wounded arm.... On the floor lies a mask ... slanted eyes over mongolic cheekbones, lips frozen in a grin...
>
> The drone of many planes is heard in a distance...
>
> Elna smiles...
>
> "The Russians!" Sholem says.

Fritz Lang was interested in producing this film but the project remained unmade.

The Revival of *Nosferatu*

A Forgotten Survivor

While Henrik Galeen was interviewed by Kracauer for his book, and while Lotte H. Eisner prepared her *Haunted Screen* and *Murnau, Nosferatu* was finally rediscovered by the public. Albin Grau was believed dead at that time but he was actually still around. He was nearby, but nobody took the time or the interest to find out to interview him.

In the time between 1933 and 1945, Grau was not, as sometimes suggested, pursued by the National Socialists, nor was he forced to immigrate to Switzerland. On the contrary, the opportunist became a small part of the Nazi system: a fellow traveler. For his doctoral thesis *Albin Grau—Biografie und Œuvre*,[1] Stefan Strauss researched Grau's life and career and unearthed hitherto unknown facts: During World War II, Grau worked as technical draftsman and was linked to the Motor Transport Authority of the German Wehrmacht. After the war, he faced financial problems. In Bayrischzell where he ran a guesthouse with his wife Annamaria, he would "pay" his bills occasionally with paintings. He died on March 27, 1971, in Hausham, two years after the death of his wife, six years after the reissue of *Nosferatu*.

Grau's stepdaughter Laura, who was disabled, was taken with Grau's artistic estate to Switzerland, to the Crowley-related Ordo Templi Orientis (OTO) that Grau had joined shortly before his death. All in all there were 1250 graphic, architectural and scenic items as well as six film scripts that were not filmed. Laura succumbed to a "malignant tumor" in 1972.

Today Grau's artwork and scripts are part of the Collectio Magica et Occulta of the Canton Library Appenzell Ausserrhoden which consists of the archive of the Swiss Psychosophical Society. Here Strauss located poster and scenic designs for *Nosferatu* as well as unpublished stills that were taken during the shooting.

The objective to make Prana something like an occult film corporation was not fulfilled back then. But one will recognize in the activities of Scientology a pattern to try and infiltrate *Hollywood Babylon*. Grau might have liked this. There is a strange link: the story of a scientist-turned-alchemist. Lafayette Ron Hubbard was acquainted for some time with John "Jack" Whiteside Parsons (1914–1952), the James Dean of the occult, who was a rocket engineer and, after a brief flirt with Marxism, became interested in witchcraft and voodoo and converted to Crowley's *Thelema* movement:

> It's hard to find as weird and tragic a tale in the annals of science as that of John Whiteside Parsons. […]

> When he died in a mysterious explosion at his home laboratory, the tabloids weren't the only ones to label him a mad scientist. So too did the scientific establishment. [...]
> By the late 1930s, he had begun frequenting nightly meetings of the Ordo Templi Orientis, an occult society that met in nearby Los Angeles. The OTO, as it is known, was created by the English occultist Aleister Crowley [...]
> His fortunes were not helped by the arrival at his house of a hugely charismatic young science fiction writer named L. Ron Hubbard.[2]

Ultimately Hubbard ran off with Parsons's girlfriend and $20,000 of his money. For Parsons it was a rude awakening and a long drop down. The FBI had him on its list for consorting with communists in the pre-war years and, as if this wasn't enough, for being involved with a "love cult." In the end he had to make his knowledge available and provide explosive squibs for Hollywood movies:

> On June 17, 1952, a huge explosion ripped through his home laboratory. Arriving police found Parsons still alive, although half his face had been ripped off, exposing the skull beneath. His right arm was missing. Surrounding him were rocketry papers and pentagrams, occult drawings and chemical formulae. He died shortly afterwards. He was just 37 years old.[3]

Interview with a Vampire

Although a Berlin court had decided that all negatives and prints of *Nosferatu* had to be destroyed, there were film societies and archives that kept the memory alive and even some prints. André Gide, 1947 winner of the Nobel Prize in Literature, agreed *Nosferatu* should be salvaged, but he personally didn't like the film, which he saw on February 26, 1928. He found it nevertheless mind-provoking. He called that German film relatively mediocre, a mediocrity however that forces one to think and inspires to make it better. Fright as well as empathy is evoked in the viewer (at least of his kind) only if you don't realize the director's intent to create horror and empathy not too clearly.

If he, Gide writes, was to remake this film, he would introduce Nosferatu whom you identify right from the beginning as a vampire in horrifying and fantastic shape on the contrary, with the features of a benign, courteous, charming young man. Only very faint evidence might disturb in the beginning, first the viewer, then the hero. Wouldn't it be scarier if Orlok would present himself to the woman in a seductive mask? A kiss would transform into a bite.... If he shows his teeth right from the beginning, he isn't any better than a bugbear. He would, Gide continues, begin to show Nosferatu's true nature on board the ship.

Gide, a homosexual, might have liked some of the modern vampire films such as *Interview with the Vampire: The Vampire Chronicles* (1994) with Brad Pitt and Tom Cruise. He was way ahead of his time and even in his condemnation of that film ploughed a lonely furrow.

Georges Sadoul, the great French film historian who saw *Nosferatu* at the same time as Gide, said that even at a time when they didn't know about Murnau, they were devotees of this picture. The film had already vanished from the repertoire of the cinemas but there was a small cinema, much beloved by intellectuals, the Carillon, that would dig up a print and made a dupe. All the surrealists went there to see it.

American experimental filmmaker Stan Brakhage had a different view. He considered Murnau's decision to film on location perverse. A fantasy like *Nosferatu* would have been better done in a regular studio under controlled conditions. To him, *Nosferatu* was a tourist travel film, just the opposite of the Expressionist sets of *Caligari* (an assumption that hits the nail on the head).

Three Grave Crosses

Henri Langlois had preserved a print of the French version from 1927. This was the version that fascinated André Breton and the Surrealists. A print of this version came to the Museum of Modern Art in New York. The French titles were translated into English.

The French version named the writer of the diary that reports the Nosferatu story in the film: Johann Carvallius, an old city counselor and experienced chronicler of his home town. In the German original, the writer had remained anonymous and signed the document with three grave crosses. But while the French version still had the German role names, the English titles changed these and used the ones Stoker had created for his novel. Finally Orlok became Dracula, Hutter: Jonathan Harker, Knock: Renfield, and Bulwer: Van Helsing.

In New York the print with English titles was seen, among others, by Jack Kerouac, the poet of the beat generation. He called it in his review a masterpiece of nightmarish horror, fantastically photographed in the old corny brownish black-and-white tones. He wrote a detailed, ravish synopsis,[4] saying at the beginning that Nosferatu is an evil name— its uncanny components, "fer" and "eratu" and "nos" having a red sinister something like the film itself. Nosferatu's castle, he observes, has tiled floors which let him assume that there is more evil in tiled floors than later in the dripping dust of the Bela Lugosi castle where women, with spiders on their shoulders, drag dead muslin cloths over the stone floor. He then speculates about different bat species. Nosferatu, he claims, has the long hook nose of a Greater spear-nosed bat, the large eyes of a Horseshoe bat, incisor teeth as Desmodontinae bats, common vampire bats, have, the hideous harelip-like sight of the Noctilio, little guillotines in its mouth, his hands like the giant claws of a Greater bulldog bat.

He concludes that Murnau must not only have known about bats but must have studied the vampire theses by Michael Ranft (1700–1774) and Augustin Calmet (1672–1757). Vampires, he tells us, are blood-sucking ghosts, presumably representing the souls of deceased sorcerers, witches, suicides, homicide victims and persons banned by family or church. But there is a species of vampires that represents the souls of common living people who leave their bodies during sleep and come over other sleepers in the shape of pillow feathers ... so don't sleep in sleeping bags in Transylvania (or even California).

The Haunted Screen

From New York the movie returned to Europe, first to London, to the National Film Archive, and from London it found its way back to Germany, to Atlas Film, a distribution company in Duisburg, a city located in the western part of the Ruhr Area. The company had specialized in art films and reissues. Until Atlas got hold of it, *Nosferatu* was more an insiders' tip among cineasts; now it would become a household name.

For a number of decades, Hanns Eckelkamp was a household name too in the German film business. Born in 1927 in Münster, Westphalia, he was active in exhibition since 1946. Having seen Ewald Balser as *Rembrandt* in 1942, he convinced his father, a restaurateur, to transform their Gertrudenhof, a large beer hall, into a cinema. He told Hanns Eckelkamp, Sr., "I do not want to make people drunk." After the war, both father and son controlled a cinema chain in their home town and in Duisburg. In 1959, Eckelkamp, Jr., turned to releasing. He had purchased 25 percent of the re-release rights to *High Noon* starring Gary Cooper and developed a creative advertisement concept with modern poster art. In 1960 he founded Atlas Film, which introduced a great number of classic as well as recent films to a young generation of German cinephiles: the works of Akira Kurosawa, Ingmar Bergman (*The Silence* in 1964 became Eckelkamp's greatest success as a distributor), Chaplin, Buster Keaton (Keaton came to Germany to kick off the revival of *The General* in 13 cities, arriving in a 100-year-old locomotive), Jacques Tati, Truffaut, Hitchcock, Ford, Eisenstein, Polanski et al.

As a producer, Eckelkamp supported from the outset the New German Cinema including Rainer Werner Fassbinder and helped to make *Maria Braun* (1979) an international success.

Under the headline of Lotte Eisner's book *Dämonische Leinwand* (*The Haunted Screen*) and with Erwin Leiser, who had compiled the documentary *Mein Kampf* in 1960, curating the program and selecting the films, Atlas tried to restore the memory of early German film history and in 1964, with 24 frames per second, re-released silent films with new soundtracks composed by Konrad Elfers and Peter Schirmann: *Caligari, Destiny, Dr. Mabuse, The Last Laugh* as well as Murnau's undying vampire classic. The running time of the Atlas *Nosferatu*, due to the projection rate of 24 fps, was 77 minutes. The music score was composed by Schirmann, who used parts of his new *Nosferatu* soundtrack also for scenes of the Atlas re-release of Laurel and Hardy's *Way Out West* (in Germany *Zwei ritten nach Texas: Two Rode to Texas*) in 1965.

Peter Schirmann was born on July 31, 1935, in Berlin. He enrolled at the former Stern'sche Conservatory in Berlin-West and *the Hochschule für Musik* (today Hanns Eisler) in Berlin-East, studied violoncello and oboe, theory, musical composition and music history. From the end of 1959 until 1965, he was musical director of the West Berlin cabaret Die Stachelschweine (The Porcupines). In 1966, he attended Deutsche Film- und Fernsehakademie (German Film and Television Academy), at that time supervised by Erwin Leiser, and entered the directing classes of Egon Monk, a former collaborator of Bertolt Brecht. Later he arranged and conducted chansons for Marianne Rosenberg, Peter Maffay, Udo Jürgens, Graham Bonney and Roland Kaiser.

Another composer who stepped in later was Berndt Heller. He tried to re-arrange the original Erdmann *Nosferatu* score. Heller had studied at the Mozarteum in Salzburg, at Hochschule der Künste in Berlin and at Yale University. From 1975 to 2002 he lectured on film music at Hochschule der Künste and achieved some fame adapting Gottfried Huppertz's film music for *Die Nibelungen* and *Metropolis*.

The original titles were calligraphed by Albin Grau. Some of these were preserved in the version in the files of the GDR Film Archives. Enno Patalas, Film Museum Munich, proceeded to reconstruct *Nosferatu* (as he did with *Metropolis*—until an almost complete print was found in Rio de Janeiro).

From the 525 scenes that are in the reconstruction of Film Museum Munich, 27 were found in other versions. Much of it came from the needle-sound print of *The Twelfth Hour* that was secured at the Cinémathèque Française. All this footage was black-and-white, so for a screening at the Berlin International Film Festival in 1984 they tried to reconstruct a tinted version: day scenes brown, night exterior scenes blue, night interior yellow.

Since then, thanks to the research of Luciano Berriatúa, who was assigned by the *Filmoteca Española*, they found another print at the Cinémathèque: a *tinted* print of the first French release of 1922. Although large parts were missing and the colors had changed, one could still determine the colors.

Nosferatu *in Thuringia?*

A collector living in Gotha, the fifth-largest city of Thuringia, 12 miles west of Erfurt and 16 miles east of Eisenach, claims on the Internet that he has purchased all *Nosferatu* material from the heirs of Dr. Waldemar Ronger, the mastermind behind the 1930 reissue *Die zwölfte Stunde. Eine Nacht des Grauens*. The total price, he said, amounted to 5000 Mark in 1999, for a complete nitrate release print from 1922, Ronger's *The Twelfth Hour* version, stills, all you could wish for.

We have mentioned the collector's name in connection with his website *Grabstein für Max Schreck* that is worth reading. But his astonishing claim couldn't be verified. Film archivists tried repeatedly to get in touch with him, but he refused steadfastly to let them check, let alone have the footage. Some experts like Stefan Drössler, Film Museum Munich, consider him a phony. Why should Ronger's heirs have sold a much sought-after print and what else to a totally unknown collector and not to film companies and archives that were hunting for years for every snippet of the production? In a letter to this writer, Christina Schnieber wrote on behalf of the board of Friedrich Wilhelm Murnau Stiftung:

> Since the nitrate print from French distribution seems heretofore the only surviving original footage, another genuine source as Mr. Geutebrück insists to have would be a sensation. Therefore we have exercised a lot of patience and have postponed the high-def digitization again and again in the hope of getting access to this footage. After several unsuccessful attempts to check the footage and to verify the authenticity of the source we had decided, due to inquiries of license partners and due to funding possibilities, to renounce a new digital restoration and to digitize the previous master.[5]

I talked to Jens Geutebrück on the phone and found him, despite all rumors, true or false, passionate, competent and affable. A resident of former GDR, he told me that his interest was aroused when he got hold of two old 35mm reels of *Nosferatu*, running about ten minutes each, right before reunification in early 1989. When he checked the footage, he found that there were slight differences to other prints. From then on, he was hooked. His guess is that there was more *Nosferatu* footage than the two prints officially recorded by the State Film Archive. Wolfgang Klaue, the former head of the State Film Archive of GDR, regretted that he was asked to ship a print to DEFA Laboratories that cut condensed Super 8 versions in the early 1970s. (The home movies, by the way, were hard to come by in East Germany.) I got one such print but didn't realize what Geutebrück had discovered: Even the substandard film contained a scene with Max Schreck and Gustav von Wangenheim in the castle yard that was a tiny bit longer.[6]

Right now I cannot confirm Geutebrück's claims. So far any meeting was postponed. But we are in touch by mail and phone. He unearthed some biographical information about producer Enrico (Heinrich) Dieckmann that was up to this point unknown. Dieckmann was not that interested in the production of *Nosferatu*. He was a wheeler-dealer, a friend of the equally dubious producer-actor Erich Claudius and the son-in-law of famed American bass-baritone Clarence Whitehill (1871–1932), who is best remembered for his association with the work of Richard Wagner. So Dieckmann travelled regularly to the United States. In 1932 he remarried and changed his name and identity: From then on he was known as Heinrich Holk but was still interested in bookkeeping. He died in 1958. There seems to be a parallel story that film historians didn't notice yet.

In spite of its anti–Semitic background, *Nosferatu* is the only horror film that made it into the film canon of Bundeszentrale für politische Bildung (Federal Centre for Political Education).

Christopher Lee vs. Klaus Kinski

Bela Lugosi

No vampire filmography would be complete without mentioning Bela Lugosi, born as Blaskó Béla in Lugoj, Austria-Hungary, today Romania. When Universal planned its sound film *Dracula,* Carl Laemmle, Jr., got hold of a print of *Nosferatu* but then would do the exact opposite of what Murnau had done. The Universal version became (except for the opening scenes) a stagy vampire play in three acts written by Hamilton Deane and rewritten for American theaters by John L. Balderston. One month after the premiere of Universal's *Dracula* on Valentine's Day, February 14, 1931, Friedrich Wilhelm Murnau was dead. He certainly didn't go to see *Dracula* before his untimely death.

Universal's inventive publicity department added the flair of mystery to its new acquisition and faked interviews, reminiscent of Albin Grau's close encounter with a Serbian peasant whose father was said to have been a vampire:

> The strangest creature in America is living today in Hollywood, surrounded by a brooding atmosphere of horror and madness. A tall, straight figure of a man, he goes among his fellows with a strange aloofness that marks him as a man apart. Unfathomable thoughts gleam behind his deep-set eyes, and on his throat he bears two tiny wounds that prove a terrible attack by a human vampire.
>
> Bela Lugosi is the name of this strangest of men, a Hungarian born amid the black mysterious mountains where vampires take a heavy toll among the natives, and the whole countryside lives in terror of the night. For it is only after sunset that these strange undead creatures rise from their graves.
>
> Lugosi is loathe to discuss his terrifying experience in his native land. "It is all a terrible nightmare which I am destined never to forget," he says, "until a certain woman in Hungary shall go to a peaceful and lasting death. She is an actress with no more than usual amount of feminine charm, but many men are her abject slaves, because within her smolders the burning flame of the vampires.
>
> "It was her sharply pointed teeth which made these wounds in my throat, and it was her unspoken but irresistible commands which caused me to visit her again and again. At length my mother noticed that I was rapidly losing weight, and she soon divined the cause. I had fallen under the influence of a vampire. Shortly afterward, at my mother's insistence, I fled the country and I shall probably never go back."[1]

Not only did the publicity people invent all kind of mysterious stories. Lugosi, too, lied in those days for publicity's sake and claimed to be the son of one Baron Lugosi (actually he was the son of a baker and banker and had no higher education). One like him wouldn't have played a monster like Max Schreck. No, his image was that of a fallen but suave Continental aristocrat: the Rudolph Valentino of Vampires, so to speak.

He wanted to get out of horror pictures as soon as possible:

> One of the most famous of all actors on stage or screen would like to forget the character that made him famous! Audiences on Broadway were thrilled for more than two years by his artistry; millions of picture fans throughout the country are being fascinated by the startling impersonation he gives on the screen. But the character haunts him, and he never wants to play it again.[2]

After a lukewarm attempt at creature makeup and a screen test, Lugosi turned Universal down on *Frankenstein* and let Boris Karloff, then virtually an unknown, have the part of the man-made Monster:

> Something has got to be done for Bela Lugosi. Lugosi has been trying for a week to make a screen test for *Frankenstein*. He has to wear a weird makeup, with two or three different colors, stripes, streaks and striations.
> But after a few blasts of hot air, the makeup all fuses together, making him a clown instead of a menace.[3]

"I was a star in my own country and I will not be a scarecrow here!" Lugosi didn't want to be typecast, but that's exactly what happened. When he needed money badly, he had to eat crow and even play the Monster in 1943's *Frankenstein Meets the Wolf Man*, a role he unwisely turned down a decade before. It didn't do him any good. He died a wreck of his former self, drug-addicted (he took morphine for medical reasons), an alcoholic, finding work only in the cheapest of pictures, with the posthumously released *Plan 9 from Outer Space* becoming his memorial. Lugosi died on August 16, 1956, at age 73, but he looked older. As a "horror" star he never came near an Academy Award like Fredric March did when he starred in *Dr. Jekyll & Mr. Hyde* in 1931, but when Martin Landau portrayed Lugosi the Wreck in Tim Burton's *Ed Wood* (1994), *he* would be given an Oscar for Best Supporting Actor.

Horror of Dracula

A year after Lugosi's funeral, a small London film company, Hammer Films, produced a no-nonsense horror flick, not a spoof like the ones Abbott and Costello had done but an X-rated *Frankenstein* with all the gore in color and Peter Cushing as the baron patching together a creature. This Cushing was no alchemist, no Rotwang. The role profile had changed. Now he was indeed a natural scientist who just had no scruples. *The Curse of Frankenstein* became an international hit.

To Carroll Borland, his co-star in Tod Browning's *Mark of the Vampire* (1935), Béla Lugosi remarked that his rival Karloff could never play the vampire. Nonetheless Richard Gordon (1925–2011), an American-British film producer, planned exactly that after Hammer's incredible success: a *Dracula* starring Karloff in a part that wouldn't have been Lugosi's East European aristocrat but more something like Max Schreck in *Nosferatu*. But he had to give up the project when he learned that Hammer was already after *Dracula*. James Carreras (1927–1994), Hammer's chief executive, struck a deal with Universal in order to make the picture, because the American company still owned the film rights to Stoker's novel.

Hammer director Terence Fisher (1904–1980) once remarked that British audiences prefer ghosts while Americans love monsters.[4] This meant that there would be no Karloff monster and not a second Max Schreck, but Lugosi's acting style was out of the question too. It was too slow, too dignified, his gestures too Expressionist to be "authentic"—and authenticity was what a young generation was asking for.

The chill of the tomb won't leave your blood for hours…
   after you come face-to-face with DRACULA!
   The terrifying lover who died—yet lived!
   Who Will Be His Bride Tonight?

Peter Cushing, the official star of Hammer's *Dracula*, was great again, not in the role of Dracula but as Van Helsing, a supporting part in the Lugosi *Dracula* (back then played by Edward Van Sloan, a minor actor). His co-star, who had been cast as the mute creature in *Curse of Frankenstein*, was only fourth-billed but would take the audience by storm. He was a believable aristocrat, but at the same time he was as fast as a predator. His play had a brutish, animal-like, even wolfish quality and fit in with the expectations of a postwar audience that wanted to see the vampire's fangs that shed women's blood in full color.

The name of this "definitive Dracula" was Christopher Lee. He was born on May 27, 1922, in London. After the war, he became one of Rank's up-and-coming actors but remained in the background for being too tall, a little taller even than Conrad Veidt.

> Dracula was a part which has had a suitable effect on my career … but at the same time, which has also been very much of a mixed blessing to me. Because if one becomes too much associated with a certain character in the cinema, or television, or in the entertainment medium, people are inclined to think either that you can't do anything else, that you don't want to do anything else, or that you never do anything else.

Lee thought of *Dracula* and the sequels rather as fairy tales of the harmless sort: "[T]he Grimms' fairy stories and others are far more gruesome and alarming and frightening than anything I've ever done on the screen. People of course can differentiate between reality and unreality, particularly children, and they know that *Dracula* is not real…"[5]

Lee didn't even like the term *horror*. When I met him in 1982 in Berlin, we talked about the changing horror film business, from Gothic horror down to zombies—and I still hear the ring of his deep, agitated, mighty voice in my ear. While Lee was active in horror films and made a number of *Dracula*s; it was *Sex and Blood*. Two decades later, thanks to Lucio Fulci [*Zombi 2*], Joe D'Amato [*Man Eater*], Umberto Lenzi [*Eaten Alive!*] et al., it had become *Sex, Blood and Mutilation*.

> The films I have made were real fantasies. Today's films are only real: vicious right down to the last detail. *Everything* is shown: how people are being eaten, how their stomach is being ripped open, how heads are rolling and eyes are being scratched out. Disgusting!
> **BLOOD! BLOOD! BLOOD!**
> **BLOOD ALL OVER THE SCREEN!**

According to Lee,

Today they don't make films any more like they used to do. In the Golden Age, in the 1930s, 1940s, 1950s, they made each type of film. With actors who could play everything: comedy, western, history, thriller, horror, adventure—anything. There was an enormous variety.

Christopher Lee as Dracula. The German Blu-ray version of the 1958 *Dracula* released by Anolis in 2017 is the best available (courtesy Anolis Entertainment GmbH & Co. KG).

But what are they making today? Special effects pictures and films for the 15- to 20-year-olds. The actors are between 15 and 20 too. They call themselves stars. But how can these people be stars? How can they act at all in this age?

Sir Christopher Frank Carandini Lee was lucky enough to play in front of the camera right up until his demise on June 7, 2015, at the age of 93. He had an exceptionally long career that spanned seven decades and finally made peace with SFX blockbusters that proved to offer a better income than Hammer's neat-looking but cheap horror flicks. Long after the old Hammer had gone down the swanny, Lee entered the greener pastures of George Lucas's *Star Wars* saga and J.R.R. Tolkien's *Lord of the Rings* with director Peter Jackson.

When it came to *Dracula,* Lee always took great pains to entirely concentrate on Stoker's conception of the character:

> I try to portray him physically, even though incorrectly from the point of view of my appearance—not as an old man with a white mustache growing younger, although you may know I did this in a Spanish film [*El Conde Dracula*, 1970]—I've always tried to portray the character that Stoker defined in his writing. The character of aloof majesty, ferocity of dignity, and of somber mystery, or irresistibility that the women find marvelous and the men unstoppable. The character that veered from the tigerish to the still, in the physical sense.[6]

Dracula's (Christopher Lee) demise is filmed on the back lot of Bray Studios in 1965 for *Dracula, Prince of Darkness*. Anolis released the title in an outstanding Hammer Film series (courtesy Anolis Entertainment GmbH & Co. KG).

Lee mentioned his appearance in what was sometimes called a faithful approach to Stoker's novel but actually was another cheap affair by bustling, penny-conscious British producer Harry Alan Towers and his Spanish director Jess Franco (a.k.a. Jesús Franco Manera, 1930–2013): *El Conde Drácula* (*Count Dracula*). In this film, he had an interesting German sidekick: Klaus Kinski. When I saw the movie for the first time in 1970, I found it tedious (a consequence of low budget) but at the same time liked Kinski's portrayal (if he acted at all). But I never would have anticipated that one day Kinski would become Dracula or even Nosferatu.

New German Cinema: Werner Herzog *and* Nosferatu

It was Hanns Eckelkamp of Atlas Film who claimed to have inspired Werner Herzog to remake *Nosferatu*. Murnau's film, Eckelkamp enthused in Cannes in front of Herzog, is a cathedral.

Herzog liked the idea and studied the film books written by German émigré Lotte H. Eisner. A friendship with the grande dame of film history was built and Herzog was reminded that, before the Third Reich and before Federal German postwar cinema, there was a thing called Expressionist Cinema that was lost but artistically worthwhile enough to dig out. He left Eisner an illuminated man: "*Nosferatu* in my opinion is the most important film ever made in Germany. So this is some sort of a challenge. And it establishes some sort of a link between the great Expressionist Cinema that we had in Germany and our film renaissance now. It is a film that is beyond my own private person."

He was born Werner Herzog Stipetić in Munich on September 5, 1942. He grew up in a remote mountain village in Bavaria and studied History and German Literature in Munich and Pittsburgh. He made his first short film, *Herakles*, in 1961 at the age of 19 and became what might be called a filmmaker who liked to work under extreme, sometimes *very extreme* conditions.

From November 23 until December 14, 1974, when his new mentor Lotte Eisner was quite ill and near death, Herzog walked from Munich to Paris in the middle of the winter. He kept a diary that was published afterwards: *On Walking in Ice*, walking himself into intoxication.

The diary began with the words "Only if this would be a movie I would believe it." He stylized himself into the role of the Suffering Savior: "It was clear to me that if I did it, Eisner wouldn't die. It wasn't superstition, however, but something the Catholic Church calls assurance of salvation—an expression one should treat with great caution. I wasn't surprised that Lotte Eisner had already been released from the hospital when I arrived in Paris."[7] Eisner lived another ten years and died on November 25, 1983, in Paris. So she was able to consult, see and applaud her Savior's *Nosferatu* remake.

In 1984, by the way, when West Germany began to "distance" itself from the goal of reunification, Herzog walked around Germany, "always carefully following the border, because it was clear now that only poets could provide unity."

Filming in Wismar/German Democratic Republic was not possible. So Herzog chose Delft in the Province of South Holland as the location for his *Nosferatu* remake and called it a very stylized and idyllic place. For the first time, Herzog said, he made a genre film (the term had become popular since the French used it): "I follow the laws of the genre, and that of course is a difficulty and a challenge for me. But more than anything it is a question of establishing a link to the great of German Cinema of the '20s."[8]

Filmmaking, Herzog knew, "is not too easy and it causes pain." To make sure that it would really and truly cause pain, he hired a gifted but extremely awkward actor for the title role: Klaus Kinski, who was said to have abused his own daughters. Kinski was born Nikolaus Günther Nakszynski on October 18, 1926, in Zoppot, Free City of Danzig, now Sopot, Poland, the son of Bruno Nakszynski, a pharmacist, and his wife Susanne *née* Lutze, a nurse. On the cinema screen he was typecast very often in eye-rolling villain roles. Step by step he had sold his talent and temper for money to a sheer endless series of German Edgar Wallace films produced by Horst Wendlandt: *Der Rächer* (*The Avenger*), *Die toten Augen von London* (*The Dead Eyes of London*), *Die Tür mit den sieben Schlössern* (*The Door with Seven Locks*), *Das Geheimnis der gelben Narzissen* (*The Devil's Daffodil*), *Das Verrätertor* (*Traitor's Gate*), *Die seltsame Gräfin* (*The Strange Countess*, with Lil Dagover of *Caligari* fame), *Das Gasthaus an der Themse* (*The Inn on the River*), *Der Zinker* (*The Squeaker*), *Der schwarze Abt* (*The Black Abbot*), *Das indische Tuch* (*The Indian Scarf*), *Die Gruft mit dem Rätselschloss* (*The Curse of the Hidden Vault*), *Neues Vom Hexer* (*Again the Ringer*). He wavered between genius and psychopath and filled both parts 100 percent. Indeed, he had stayed in a psychiatric hospital in 1950.

> [H]is volatile personality—the anger, the passion that fueled his performances—caused him to be labeled as too difficult. To compensate, and keep a roof over his head, he performed one-man shows reciting Shakespeare, Oscar Wilde and François Villon. […]
> In 1971 Kinski hired the Deutschlandhalle [in Berlin West] to perform his own 30-page interpretation of the life of Jesus Christ—*Jesus Christ Erlöser* (*Jesus Christ Savior*). It was no ordinary show. […] A production about Jesus Christ by one of Germany's most notorious actors was bound to cause confusion and controversy. Some of the audience seemed to think Kinski was evangelizing, rather than interpreting a role. This led to constant heckling from the spectators. The Christians thought he was blaspheming. Those on the Left thought he was a snake oil salesman for Christianity. Kinski was doing none of this. His Christ was part Kinski, part revolutionary, and part troubled soul. As the audience heckled, Kinski responded to the abuse, as Twitch Film notes:
> "[A]fter someone stated that shouting down people who disagreed with him was unlike Christ, Kinski responded with a different take on how Christ might respond: 'No, he didn't say "shut your mouths," he took a whip and beat them. That's what he did, you stupid sow!'"
> "He challenged the audience: 'Can't you see when someone lectures 30 typewritten pages of text in this way, that you must shut your mouths? If you can't see that, please let someone bang it into your brain with a hammer!' The evening's festivities also turned physical as an audience member is shown getting bounced from the stage by a bodyguard. Someone responds that 'Kinski just let his bodyguard push a peaceful guy, who only wanted to have a discussion, down the stairs! That is a fascist statement, Kinski is a fascist, a psychopath!'"[9]

In the meantime, Kinski, like many other actors, had gone to Italy and achieved some success in the Spaghetti Western productions directed by Sergio Leone (*For a Few Dollars More*) and Sergio Corbucci (*The Great Silence*). He also had a bit part in David Lean's *Doctor Zhivago* (1965), one of the few prestige films he was involved with. When nobody else was willing to work with him, Werner Herzog appeared. Today it is mainly the Herzog films that Kinski is remembered for. Besides *Nosferatu*, these are *Aguirre, der Zorn Gottes* (1972), *Woyzeck* (1979), *Fitzcarraldo* (1982) and *Cobra Verde* (1987).

Kinski at 5'8" was a nasty little runt against Max Schreck, Lugosi or Christopher Lee. Like Dwight Frye in Tod Browning's 1931 *Dracula*, he was a perfect Renfield opposite Lee in *El Conde Drácula*. But as Nosferatu he wasn't the slim, towering danger. He was more like the dwarfish murderer in Nicolas Roeg's spooky *Don't Look Now*.

Kinski about his part in *Nosferatu*,

> It's me. It's me because I am Nosferatu in a Nosferatu picture. So my answer is: Nosferatu is me. It's real. If you are something, you…. I mean, of course, you automatically believe in it. You haven't to point it out so much that you believe in it. I would have never accepted it if it wouldn't be in me, if I couldn't feel the metamorphosis. I look as I have to look.[10]

Kinski described his work a bit more coherently in another interview,

> In Holland and Czechoslovakia and all the way to the Mountains on the Czech-Polish border. The departure point is Munich. Four weeks before shooting starts, I have to fly there for costuming. And this is where I shave my skull for the first time. I feel exposed, vulnerable, defenseless. Not just physically (my bare head becomes as hypersensitive as an open wound) but chiefly in my emotions and my nerves. I feel as if I have no scalp, as if my protective envelope has been removed and my soul can't live without it. As if my soul had been flayed.
>
> At first I go outdoors only when it's dark (I've been through that with *The Idiot*, but this is much, much worse). Besides, I wear a wool cap all the time even though it's spring. You may think, "So what? Some guys are bald." But the two have absolutely nothing to do with one another. What I mean is the simultaneous metamorphosis into a vampire. That non-human, non-animal being. That undead thing. That unspeakable creature, which suffers in full awareness of its existence. […]
>
> There must be some significance (even though I don't give a fuck) in the fact that I play parts involving what I have to experience myself but can barely endure. Or do I have to experience it personally after playing the part? Is it a warning or a repetition? Is it a chain reaction? Does one detonate the other? Or do both happen simultaneously—my life, and the part I have to play? Do I transfer other people's bells to my own life, or do I transfer my own life to the character I have to play? Does the event in question occur in my own life through mystical force, so that I may suffer more deeply when I have to play the part? No one can answer these questions. In any case, it's part of the curse of being—as they put it—"the ultimate actor." Which, however, has nothing to do with this hammy bullshit.

As always, Kinski behaved extravagantly and revealed himself as the eccentric everybody expected: "When we move from Holland to Czechoslovakia […] I demand a trailer that I pick myself so I can live in it, sleep in it, cook, and do my laundry. I don't want to be billeted in some shitty Czech hotel, where you run into the whole motley crew after shooting."[11]

While he was performing in *Nosferatu*, Kinski's third wife Minhoi (Loanic), a Vietnamese, was about to divorce him. She also was going to take their son Nanhoi, better known as Nikolai. So he felt even more vulnerable.

There were some reviewers who felt that Kinski's portrayal of the Undead had a lot to offer.

> [K]inski and Herzog were successful for a number of reasons, the first being that Kinski was physically scarier than Schreck. The end result shows echoes of Schreck's version, but there's also a touch of Captain Howdy from *The Exorcist* layered in, with the help of expert costuming, set design and lighting. Certain shots completely isolate Kinski's white head and hands amidst a void of black. A Japanese artist named Reiko Kruk was hired to do the makeup,[12] and Kinski had to sit for four hours every day for her to shave his head, pale his skin, affix rat-like teeth, sculpt pointy ears, and attach long sharp nails to his fingers. You would think all of this would make a volatile actor like Kinski furious, but Herzog attests that he was totally docile during these makeup sessions because Kruk had "something magic about her—which I didn't have." Of course, once Kinski was released from makeup, "he would immediately start destroying the set." Herzog made it his mission to capture this pent-up intensity into a great performance on film rather than have it "evaporate [sic] in wild tension and mayhem." You can sense this rage in Kinski, and it's amazing that Herzog managed to direct him towards such controlled body language and terrifying stillness.
>
> The second and seemingly counter-intuitive reason Kinski's vampire in Nosferatu succeeds is because it is funny. That very same controlled body language also contains humor as well as terror, because it

disrupts the natural rhythms of human interaction that we are used to. The whole film, in fact, has an offbeat sense of humor mixed with horror that only few classics such as *Rosemary's Baby* manage to balance successfully. [...]

In closing with a final thought on just what made *Nosferatu* so memorable, Herzog said it's because Kinski played "a vampire with a soul," not simply a monster."[13]

For Herzog, it didn't count when they called Kinski a "pain in the ass": "You should not count the difficulties. You should not count the money. You should not count the extras. What counts is what you see from the screen. Nothing else.... All my films—maybe you have seen any—come out from pains. That's the source where they come from. Not from pleasure." This kind of deceased displeasure of working in caves and deserts, he liked to transfer onto the actors.

Others called Herzog "the world's most gonzo filmmaker and centerpiece of some of the most spectacular and extreme making-of-a-movie stories ever heard.... [A]lthough Klaus Kinski, the lead, was not a real vampire, he was a very real nut. This made him the perfect foil for Herzog, who, unable to get the right shade of rat he wanted for filming, simply painted thousands of white rats gray."[14]

> His signature touch is on display from the start of the film's sad and haunting opening credits. The documentary-style footage shows mummified bodies, chronicled from infants to old age as the sequence progresses, propped against a cave wall. The expressions and contortions of the corpses are so vivid that it seems the agony and terror they felt at the moment of death has stayed imprinted on their bodies for hundreds of years. It's easy to imagine that someone killed by a vampire would look this way.[15]

Klaus Kinski's Nosferatu mask and claws manufactured by Don Post Studios (purchased from Forrest J Ackerman by author's collection and Deutsche Kinemathek–Museum für Film und Fernsehen, Berlin).

The footage was shot at the Mummies of Guanajuado museum in Mexico, where dozens of victims of an 1833 cholera epidemic are preserved.

Werner Herzog's *Nosferatu* is an example of what the Germans called amphibian film: cinema and TV in one, with the television part represented by Zweites Deutsches Fernsehen.

Kinski's Nosferatu mask was later distributed in a limited edition by the Don Post Studios of Los Angeles and has become a collector's item.

I am not the biggest fan of Herzog's version of *Nosferatu*. So I talked about it with a friend, puppeteer and actor Gerd Josef Pohl, who has done a lot of research over the years.

What ranking do you think Herzog's Nosferatu *will have in film history?*

I must admit that for a long time I didn't have any use for Herzog's film. Today I love it and consider it a milestone of German postwar cinema.

Herzog's Nosferatu *was an international production. Only minor portions were actually shot in Germany.*

Yes, but the main roles were cast with Kinski, [Bruno] Ganz and [Walter] Ladengast, with a German director at the helm and the music of Popol Vuh as Krautrock Band, typically German. And it is a film that pursues profoundly a very Teutonic intention, bridging the gap between German film culture pre–Hitler and the 1970s. In between, due to the Nazi regime, there was a void that was deepened through the incredible mentality of suppression of the 1950s and 1960s. In those days, they produced some good and watchable movies, but they didn't want to really go into the depth—and in the Eastern part of Germany they weren't allowed to do so. And when somebody appeared who would bring up the painful subject like Peter Lorre in his excellent *Der Verlorene* [*The Lost One*], they hounded him out of the country. This gap Herzog wanted to close with his *Nosferatu*. Insofar it is more than just a literary film or an entry into genre cinema, it is a political picture.

But why do you consider it a milestone?
　　Because I think that everything is right in this film. It is excellently cast, down to the smallest bit part, there are wonderful landscape photography and great locations and perhaps the best score ever in a Dracula film. Of course it's all a question of personal taste, and the tardiness of the picture is not everybody's cup of tea. But personally I like it and think that Herzog has really created a masterpiece. And Kinski surprises us as Dracula with his quiet, reduced performance.

If you had to cast a Nosferatu *film or play, whom would you cast?*
　　In any case I would select an actor who is not well known to audiences. Under no circumstances would I choose a famous movie star. A familiar face would spoil the part of the remote and mystic and disenchant it. That's, by the way, my only criticism concerning Herzog's film: casting the main part with a well-known star. I like Kinski very much and he did his thing as Dracula extremely well, but I wouldn't have him cast in that part. This should be a part for an actor, who would fill the role physically and physiognomically, an actor who has body control and talent as a dancer. Nosferatu's movements are very redeemed. But you can redeem only what you once had. This is in acting the same as it is in art or music. One would have to look out for such an artist in theater troupes.

A Puppet Nosferatu

　　Pohl did create a *Nosferatu* of his own. He and his co-author Gisbert Franken decided not to settle on a *Nosferatu* play with live actors but with live marionettes.

> We take the character out of his previous context and pursue the question where this ancient vampire is coming from. We are researching his origins in pre–Biblical times and accompany him in several episodes through the centuries. We encounter him in the Roman catacombs where he is facing problems with Christians for the first time and into the northern part of Europe at the time of the Great Plague. We meet him in Venice at the time of the Renaissance and in the destroyed Berlin and ask ourselves where he might hide today and when and in which shape he might return. This has nothing to do with Bram Stoker's novel. The name Dracula isn't mentioned in the whole play, not a single time.

I asked Pohl if he sees Count Orlok and Dracula as characters on the same level:
　　We don't use these names in our play but use the term "Nosferatu" which is just the name of the species. The difference is that Dracula is embedded in the context of a certain

Top: Nosferatu marionette (photograph prepared by Martin van Elten, courtesy Gerd J. Pohl). *Bottom:* Nosferatu marionette and German puppeteer Gerd Josef Pohl (photograph prepared by Martin van Elten, courtesy Gerd J. Pohl).

period: The plot of the novel and the film versions unfold within weeks or months. Dracula himself is not older than 500 years. Nosferatu, however, inheres something eternal. Time-wise, he eludes any classification which renders him a demon, something that is unfathomable. This demonic quality that is literally not of this world shines through the portrayal of Max Schreck: a vampire from the outset. Nobody has accomplished this since. I never believed in those other vampire actors in their tailor-made suits, patent leather shoes and velvet capes. They were children of their respective time.

I guess Nosferatu doesn't perceive himself as evil but as sort of a "liberator."

I see him differently. I believe that Nosferatu doesn't possess any kind of feeling. He doesn't reckon with the effects of his deeds just as little as a hyena reflects while mangling its prey. There are no emotions and above all there is no altruism. Nosferatu doesn't want to free his victims, he doesn't want to save. He is more or less an anti–Savior who demands his victims but would never make a martyr of himself for the benefit of all.

Nosferatu in Venice

Kinski returned to the role (and more money) in the Italian *Nosferatu a Venezia* (*Vampire in Venice*), produced by Augusto Caminito in 1988. But the actor this time refused to have his head shaved, refused to don the troublesome makeup again. Instead, when he arrived on the set, he sported long blond hair. So Kinski looked like, well, Kinski, who, as some line says, has longed for death for 1000 years and needs the love of a woman to conquer him.

Kinski's behavior on the set caused many delays. All the action on the set, as Hitchcock once put it, nothing on the screen. Originally, Maurizio Lucidi was chosen to direct. He did shoot a few crowd scenes in Venice but then the producer paid him off. Caminito then hired Pasquale Squitieri, but his script and ideas proved too expensive. On the first day of shooting, Kinski got into a violent argument with B-movie director Mario Caiano (1933–2015), a specialist in pirate films, Hercules, Perseus, Maciste and the inevitable Spaghetti Westerns. The director preferred to leave the set taking full salary. In big trouble, Caminito decided to tackle the directorial chores himself and finish the movie. In his autobiography, Kinski claimed that he directed some scenes too. *Starcrash* director Luigi Cozzi, a colleague of Dario Argento, was involved in the production. He confirmed the rumor,

> At a certain point, [Kinski] convinced the producer, who was also the director having taken over from the first director, to let him do some scenes at dawn. But the producer-director wanted to go to sleep, so he said to me: "Luigi, you take care of Kinski." So for nearly two months, every morning at four o'clock I had to get up and go around Venice with Kinski and just two or three cameras, just five or six of us shooting what Kinski told was worth shooting. But the silly thing was that Kinski just wanted beautiful scenes with the sun starting. So I said okay, you walk from here to there, so beautiful scene with the sun again. And again. Okay, walk from here to there, so okay, we shot for two months beautiful light, beautiful scenes, but absolutely meaningless scenes. The mess was perfect: The picture was not what was written. It was re-edited completely and scenes like these were put in the film. I did all this material with Kinski but not directing. You cannot direct Kinski. Kinski directed himself. I was trying to limit the damage because he was shooting, shooting: "Let's shoot, let's shoot, let's shoot…"[16]

Kinski's actions off-camera led to the actor being arrested as he violently sexually assaulted two of the actresses.

The role of heroine Maria Canins was originally played by Amanda Sandrelli, but Kinski forced the producer to fire her. He suggested the casting of Anne Knecht, who visited her friend Yorgo Voyagis on the set and deeply impressed Kinski, who had a sex scene with her.

Christopher Plummer played Prof. Paris Catalano, a Van Helsing character who visits Venice to investigate Nosferatu's last known appearance during the carnival in 1786 and faces a madman. Kinski, however, was pleased not only to play the madman but to become one. He died on November 23, 1991, of a sudden heart attack at his home in Lagunitas, California. His ashes were scattered into the Pacific Ocean.

Gerd Pohl called my attention to the fact that Kinski's son Nikolai, born in 1976, did *Nosferatu* in New York City in 2000:

> In the immortal words of Tim Rice, "like father, like son." Nikolai Kinski, son of actor Klaus Kinski, grew up watching Dad play Dracula on screen in his most famous movie, the 1979 remake of F.W. Murnau's silent movie classic *Nosferatu*. Now Nikolai is carrying on the grand old family tradition, donning a cape and false teeth for *Nosferatu*, the Telluride Repertory Theatre Company's new Off-Off-Broadway production [...]
>
> Also based on the Murnau film, *Nosferatu* is adapted for the stage by French-Italian director Rene Migliaccio, who will employ a cast of 24. The production is described as having an "expressionistic-realism" acting style and a scenic design made up of "shadow and light" and works by 18th and 19th century painters.[17]

In the part, in full makeup, Nikolai looked exactly like his dad.

In 1995, New Line Cinema released a low-budget horror thriller titled *Embrace of the Vampire* that had nothing to do with *Nosferatu* but, as a tribute to the late Kinski, was titled that way when it came to Germany: *Nosferatu—Vampirische Leidenschaft* (*Nosferatu: Vampiric Passion*).

In between both Kinskis, father and son, another "icon," the "King of Pop" himself, was said to have worn a *Nosferatu* mask. At least this was what the late Forrest J Ackerman, for many years the editor of *Famous Monsters of Filmland* magazine, claimed. In 1995, at one of Forry's conventions, a guy showed up who might have been Jackson as Nosferatu, because this "Neverland Monster Kid" was in the company of a man recognized as Jackson's bodyguard.

Shadow of the Vampire: The Legacy

Max Schreck, Vampire

Was Max Schreck a real vampire? Did the star of *Nosferatu*, the 1922 horror classic, strike a bargain with its director F.W. Murnau—to appear in his movie in return for being allowed to drain the entire cast and crew of their blood afterwards? E. Elias Merhige's semi-serious comedy *Shadow of the Vampire*, starring Willem Dafoe as Schreck, takes this fantasy and runs with it to remarkably silly effect. […]

John Malkovich plays Murnau as a Teutonic professor running amok in a lab coat and goggles. Ready to sacrifice life, limb and cast members to get "the shot," he's a stereotypical director-as-dictator, convinced that since art (and movies) last more or less forever and people don't, then one is expendable in the service of the other.[1]

Shadow of the Vampire bears not much truth, neither to the background of the original production nor to the characters involved: a huge team, more people than Murnau had seen on his original production, sets, costumes and makeup perfect, a great cast with Willem Dafoe even nominated for an Academy Award, but a hopeless screenplay that was based on a single idea: that Herr Schreck was a real vampire, built on no or only superficial research.

Steven Katz, in fact, had written [the screenplay] more than a decade ago, and it circulated widely before winding up with actor Nicolas Cage, who had established a production company in 1996 to bankroll independent pictures. And it was Cage, who had seen and loved [director] Merhige's debut *Begotten*, who contacted him about doing *Vampire*. […]

One of the reasons [for Merhige's involvement] was his admiration for Murnau and the 1922 *Nosferatu*. "It is one of my favorite films," Merhige said. "It's a film I saw first when I was 11 years old, and it scared the hell out of me, and it still terrifies me. The way that Schreck moves, he seems deliberate and yet dangerous, he's almost like a shadow." […]

Merhige's enthusiasm for Katz's screenplay was tempered, however, and so he worked with the writer to refine it. "The script was like an unfinished sculpture," he observed. "I just worked to hone it and bring certain things out and diminish certain other things. There was a certain danger of campiness in the script that I wanted to sort of extinguish and move into a more serious direction with it, and at the same time maintain the humor as a vehicle to express those serious ideas." One of the notions that he was at pains to include in the script was an analogy between filmmaking and vampirism: "I wanted to establish the motion picture camera itself as a vampire…. As the camera fixes its gaze on the subject, it drains it of its flesh and blood and reduces it to a sort of shadow. And the shadow outlives the subject. It's a pretty creepy idea, [but it was] stylistically imperative and important and critical that that was shown and expressed."[2]

The budget was roughly $8 million, the box office receipts in the United States not much more. The movie entered lots of festivals but turned out a dismal failure. Yet it helped to revive interest in this old silent film at a time when youngsters weren't fascinated by anything pre–*Star Wars*.

More Nosferatu *Incarnations*

Apparently a new generation of film freaks was taking an interest in the old "property," even before the release of *Shadow of the Vampire*:

The American rock band Blue Öyster devoted a song in its 1977 album "Spectres" to *Nosferatu*.

An English rock band called itself Nosferatu and has become one of the commercially most successful Second Wave Gothic Rock Bands.

Bernard J. Taylor adapted the story into a musical: *Nosferatu The Vampire* (1995), opening with "Wild Talk of Vampires." An opera version composed by Alva Henderson in 2004, with libretto by Dana Gioia, was released on CD in 2005.

Nosferatu (DJ) is the pseudonym of Dutch Hardcore Techno DJ and producer Erwin van Kan and of a species of cichlids.

BBC Radio 3 used it as the basis for a radio play, "Midnight City of the Deathbird" with Malcolm Raeburn as Count Orlok.

A *Nosferatu* comic book was published by Viper Comics in November 2010: "The most obvious shift in dynamic for this modern-day version of the story is that married couple Thomas and Ellen Hutter turn into goth-chick lesbian couple Tommy and Elle. Tommy is an up-and-coming photographer, with Elle his model muse."[3] Christoph Howard Wolf was the writer, Justin Wayne the artist.

Nosferatu: The Wrath of Malachi was a horror first person shooter game, developed by Idol FX (Sweden) and released in 2003 by iGames Publishing:

> This is a creepy and fun game featuring a well-realised spooky old castle and a host of classic horror monsters. Standard FPS game-play and a good overall atmosphere are let down slightly by the obvious low-budget nature of the title and some nasty design flaws.
>
> You play as James Patterson, a British sabre fencer on your way to Carpathia to attend your sister's wedding. However your new brother-in-law is a nasty vampire and he has been tormenting your family in his huge castle. You have to rescue them and see them safely to the sanctuary, slaying a lot of ghosts, vampires, demon dogs and other assorted nasties along the way. There is also a time limit to consider, and as the clock ticks down to the witching hour family members you have been unable to save will die. The story is the usual clichéd horror tale and the game is really focused on exploration and battle.[4]

Back to the movies: Tony "Tex" Watt, a Canadian multimedia artist, didn't rack himself. He hadn't ideas of his own but simply and sacrilegiously incorporated the footage from the original *Nosferatu* into one of his own dubious film ventures and added something of a new plot. He titled it *Nosferatu vs. Father Pipecock & Sister Funk*:

> Tony Watt may lay claim to being possibly the worst director currently at work in the world. A former organiser of Toronto's Twisted Sinema exploitation festival, Watt first appeared with the mind-boggling *Frankenpimp* (2009), an excruciating film dragged out to three plus hours that may well be one of the most agonizing watching experiences I have ever had—all deliberately bad acting, racial caricatures, cartoonish sound effects and fart noises run together with a mishmash of exploitation genre elements in a near-incoherent plot. [...]

> *Nosferatu vs. Father Pipecock & Sister Funk* is different than most of Tony Watt's films. Where these others are films that quote classic exploitation cinema and set out be as mind-numbingly bad as possible in every way, here Watt has sourced another entire film and simply laid voice and joke tracks over the top. This is something that horror hosts of the 1970s and '80s would habitually do—insert themselves into or interrupt horror films with corny jokes. […]
>
> There are a few additional scenes that have been filmed but essentially what we have on screen is a *Mystery Science Theater 3000* version of *Nosferatu*. […]
>
> In the handful of original scenes shot for the film, Watt turns up as Father Pipecock, which seems something like a classic Hammer-styled vampire-hunting priest conducted as a horrendous Black and White Minstrel Show version of blaxploitation hood where Watt plays the part with ridiculous stovepipe hat, thick glasses and a girly falsetto.

Father Pipecock is a Vatican monster hunter who, aided by the gun-toting Sister Funk, invades the castle to eliminate Orlok's vampire wives.

> Even though these scenes only comprise a matter of minutes, Watt's agonizing bad acting, silly voices and cartoon sound effects manage to go on and on and on. There is the occasionally amusing line like when Ellen greets Orlock's [*sic*!] classic death scene in the sunlight: "You idiot—vampires don't sparkle."[5]

Don't believe the IMDb-estimated budget of $ 2,000,000. Movies such as this miserable affair are being made on a shoestring. In the "Thanks" section of the credits, Watts names all of his movie heroes, half of whom are dead and cannot defend themselves: Pedro Almodóvar, Michelangelo Antonioni, Hal Ashby, Ingmar Bergman, Mel Blanc, Tod Browning, Luis Bunuel, Claude Chabrol, Brian De Palma, Rainer Werner Fassbinder, Abel Ferrera, Jean-Luc Godard, Werner Herzog, Terry Jones, Akira Kurosawa, Sidney Lumet, Radley Metzger, Ted V. Mikels, Sam Peckinpah, Nicholas Ray, George A. Romero, Ernest B. Schoedsack, Preston Sturges, Jan Švankmajer, Tom Tykwer, Roger Vadim, Peter Weir, Wim Wenders, Amy Winehouse. Where is Ed Wood?

Dracula vs. Nosferatu: What About the Legal Situation?

How does one pin down the rights to a movie that by court's order simply shouldn't exist any more? There are almost no rights concerning *Nosferatu*. *Nosferatu* is something like an orphaned picture.

This uncertain situation didn't let Hanns Eckelkamp, who gave Herzog the basic idea, rest. Thanks to a scout, he was able to locate Henrik Galeen's Swedish heirs and sign a contract with them. He therefore owned, as he claimed, the only rights available: the screenplay rights. Acting through an agency, he immediately proceeded to sue Werner Herzog. But Herzog's lawyer gave him the cold shoulder. What had been a problem for Prana, Grau and Galeen, is no more: *Dracula*, the novel written by Bram Stoker, is in the public domain. Herzog was clever enough to refer to Stoker when he made the Kinski *Nosferatu*. He used the role names of Stoker's novel and not those of Murnau's film. The lawyer claimed that Murnau's *Nosferatu* was no original work. Ideas which seemed to be original were derived from folklore. And anyway, Herzog's *Nosferatu* was no remake, the lawyer wrote, but a homage. Period. Since then, it has become Herzog's official version: "I should caution you, it's not a remake."

> When Werner Herzog gives a warning, it is advisable to heed it. So do not call his 1979 film *Nosferatu the Vampyre* a remake of the 1922 film *Nosferatu* by F.W. Murnau. Rather consider it an interpretation or tribute. […]

"Let me say one thing about Kinski," Herzog added. "No matter what we have seen about vampires so far, no matter what's going to come at us in the next half-century, there won't be another vampire of the caliber of Kinski again. When you see him you know he's the best, you'll never see anyone like him again."[6]

In desperation, Eckelkamp sold the screenplay rights via his agency to Friedrich Wilhelm Murnau Foundation, which didn't own anything of *Nosferatu* before and to this day doesn't even know the salesman, just the agency's name. The remake rights, however, Hanns Eckelkamp kept for himself or better: for one of his sons. The screenplay rights are going to expire in July 2019, 70 years after Henrik Galeen's death.

Nothing, alas, came out of a story idea that would have placed Dracula against the undead Orlok: the image of vampires vs. rats. This was an attempt by Eckelkamp's son to make use of the Galeen script rights. He signed a contract with this author, who went ahead and conceived the premise of a film script:

> The conflict *Nosferatu vs. Dracula* deals with is sized like Greek mythology.
> **A FIGHT FOR SUPREMACY BETWEEN IMMORTALS**
> Kronos, the all-devouring son of heaven and earth, the ancient leader of the titans who castrated his father Ouranus, was defeated by Zeus, the lightning god, who condemned the "original" into Tartarus.
> In our story, Nosferatu, the ancient Lord of the Vampires, is like Kronos: a monstrous creature of destruction born from Hell, leading an army of death-bringing rats and a pandemonium of other creatures from the depths of the abyss to the surface of earth. His strongest weapon against mankind is the plague. His objective: Extinguish humans and their environment and make the surface of earth uninhabitable, make it like hell—no sun, no water, no hope, no life.
> Dracula, the skyborn vampire, represented by the wings of the bats, suave, seductive and erudite, uses modern tactics to defeat his gruesome ancestor and conceal his identity, his equally gruesome origin and past.
> Unlike Nosferatu, Dracula is a creature of light: a fallen angel condemned to live in darkness which he loathes and abhors. His main mistake: He wanted to become like God himself. His main goal is to overcome his shortfall and return into light—as new god and ruler of all heaven.
> Dracula wants to destroy in order to rebuild. Nosferatu wants total destruction and chaos.
> The struggle for power and world domination is staged as final war between bats and rats.

A treatment was written—and that was it. Never heard of it again.

The dream of a new German *Nosferatu* was over, at least for this writer.

The Americans seemed to be faster.

The Witch

Robert Eggers is a director said to have been offered a *Nosferatu* remake. He is a hot choice. His directorial debut *The Witch* premiered at the 2015 Sundance Film Festival.

First the director denounced the rumors. He told the press that he is fascinated by Murnau's picture but that *Nosferatu* is too much a masterpiece to touch it carelessly. Do not forget, he added, that Peter Jackson was obsessed by *King Kong* and you know how that came out.[7]

It seemed that Eggers was back-burnering a *Nosferatu* remake in favor of a *Rasputin* miniseries or a fantasy yarn called *The Knight*. But finally the rumors grew stronger:

> The remake has been a project Eggers has wanted to make since childhood, though he's just as shocked as everyone else that it will be his follow-up to his breakout debut *The Witch*. "It feels ugly and blas-

Nosferatu makeup test by Berlin-based FX technician Holger Delfs (courtesy H. Delfs and M. Schmidt).

phemous and egomaniacal and disgusting for a filmmaker in my place to do *Nosferatu* next," he told IndieWire's Filmmaker Toolkit Podcast last fall. "I was really planning on waiting a while, but that's how fate shook out."

Eggers also teased that his version of *Nosferatu* will have a similar tone as *The Witch*. "This is going to be the same approach as *The Witch*, he said, "where 1830s Biedermeier Baltic Germany needs to be articulated in a way that seems real."[8]

Eggers' version is set to be produced by Jay Van Hoy and Lars Knudsen for Jeffrey Robinov's Studio 8. American-born Argentine-British actress Anya Taylor-Joy is said to take Greta Schröder's part as Ellen Hutter.

Having a new take on an original is incredibly important when remaking a film or there wouldn't be any reason to remake it. However, that shouldn't mean abandoning the very aspect that fans love about the first film. As Herzog did with his rendition of *Nosferatu*, including the aspect the original is known for and building upon them with his own style, is how you remake a famous film. […]

It is unclear yet how Eggers will approach his version of *Nosferatu*, but looking at his work in *The Witch* makes his involvement feel promising. His attention to nature […] is exactly what a story like *Dracula* needs. The atmosphere is everything when it comes to building the tension of that story and Eggers did that tremendously with *The Witch*. Not only has he proved he can create something of a similar tone. Eggers is a huge fan of Murnau's original version, which hopefully means he will honor it as Herzog did.[9]

There are still doubts, however, as expressed by Pamela Hutchinson in *The Guardian*:

Following the gruesome news that Murnau's grave has been ransacked, now his most famous film has been exhumed—neither for the first time. Thirty-six years after Werner Herzog channeled the ghost of F.W. Murnau's *Dracula* adaptation into his *Nosferatu the Vampyre*, starring Klaus Kinski, former Warner Bros. executive Jeff Robinov is itching for another go.

Although producers and director have excellent credentials Hutchinson expresses unease about the project:

Nosferatu's influence over cinema is so significant that something as reductive as a remake seems unnecessary. The 1922 film was not the earliest exponent of German expressionism, but a crucial one. Murnau's killer move was to take expressionist design and render it truly disturbing by extricating it from the painted sets of a film such as *The Cabinet of Dr. Caligari* (1919) and applying to the exterior world. From expressionism, via the influx of European émigré directors in Hollywood, we have film noir. And from *Nosferatu* itself we have a library of horror images that crop up time and again [...]

Nosferatu has become a shorthand for horror, its presence is felt everywhere from *Buffy the Vampire Slayer* to video games to *SpongeBob SquarePants* to the name of Dreamworks' cuddly green ogre franchise. [...] Even if Eggers were to film an original vampire story, I'll bet he'd find it hard to resist the influence of Murnau and Schreck at some point.

But what really gives me the heebie-jeebies about this proposed remake is the implicit idea that silent films are lacking, so they need to be remade with sound to have any currency today. Deadline calls this project a "visceral adaptation of F.W. Murnau's 1922 silent film masterpiece" as if the original were weedy and needed fattening up. That's simply not true. *Nosferatu* is the perfect example of a film that is all the stronger for being silent [...]

Robinov's studio has reportedly been trying to pin down the rights for this film for months, so this film is at least legit.[10]

Appendix: Bios of the Crew and Cast of *Nosferatu*

Behind the Camera

Paul Wegener

Spiritus Rector
Born on December 11, 1874, in Arnoldsdorf, West Prussia; died on September 13, 1948, in Berlin

No official filmography lists Wegener's involvement but he seemed to have inspired, behind the curtain, at least a number of cast and crew members such as Henrik Galeen, Greta Schröder (who later became his wife) and John Gottowt. Max Schreck had a bit part in Wegener's *Ramper, der Tiermensch*. Wegener and Alexander Granach were not only to be seen on screen in *Svengali* but on stage in the play *Rasputin*, directed by Erwin Piscator (with Wegener as Rasputin and Granach as Lenin). Cinematographer Fritz Arno Wagner photographed the 1934 propaganda picture *Ein Mann will nach Deutschland* directed by Wegener. And composer Hans Erdmann wrote his final film score for a movie directed by Wegener (*August der Starke*) in 1936.

Silents: 1913: *Der Verführte* (*The Seduced*); *Der Student von Prag* (*The Student of Prague*); *Die Augen der Ole Brandis* (*The Eyes of Ole Brandis*); 1914: *Evinrude*; 1914–15: *Der Golem* (U.S.: *The Monster of Fate*); 1915: *Die Rache des Blutes* (*Blood Revenge*); 1917: *Der Yoghi* (*The Yogi*); *Der Golem und die Tänzerin* (*The Golem and the Dancer*); *Hans Trutz im Schlaraffenland* (*Hans Trutz in Schlauraffen Land*); 1918: *Apokalypse* (*Apocalypse*, short); *Der Rattenfänger* (*The Pied Piper*); *Der fremde Fürst* (*The Unknown Prince*); 1919: *Madame DuBarry*; *Der Galeerensträfling* (*The Galley Slave*, two parts); 1920: *Der Golem, wie er in die Welt kam* (*The Golem: How He Came Into the World*); *Nachtgestalten* (*Figures in the Night*); *Sumurun*; *Steuermann Holk* (*Steersman Holk*); 1921: *Der verlorene Schatten* (*The Lost Shadow*); *Die Geliebte Roswolskys* (*Roswolsky's Mistress*); 1922: *Das Weib des Pharao* (*Loves of Pharao*); *Vanina Vanini*; *Lucrezia Borgia*; *Herzog Ferrantes Ende* (*Duke Ferrante's End*); *Sterbende Völker* (*Dying Peoples*, 2 parts); *Monna Vanna*; *Das Liebesnest 1* (*The Love Nest 1*); 1923: *Der Schatz der Gesine Jakobsen* (*The Treasure of Gesine Jacobsen*); *S.O.S. Die Insel der Tränen* (*SOS: The Island of Tears*); 1925: *Lebende Buddhas* (*Living Buddhas*); *Der Film im Film* (himself, documentary); 1926: *Der Mann aus dem Jenseits* (*The Man from Beyond*); *The Magician*; *Dagfin*; 1927: *Die Weber* (*The Weavers*); *Glanz und Elend der Kurtisanen* (*Queen of the Boulevards*); *Arme kleine Sif* (*Poor Little Sif*); *Svengali*; *Die Welt ohne Waffen* (*World Without Arms*); *Ramper, der Tiermensch* (U.S.: *The Strange Case of Captain Ramper*); 1928: *Alraune*.

Talkies: 1930: *Fundvogel*; 1932: *Unheimliche Geschichten* (*Eerie Stories/Tales of Horror*); *Ein Liebesroman im Hause Habsburg* (*The Secret of Johann Orth*); 1932: *Marschall Vorwärts* (*Marshal Forwards*); 1933: *Hans Westmar*; *Inge und die Millionen* (*Inge and the Millions*); 1935: *...nur ein Komödiant* (*...only a Comedian*); *Der Mann mit der Pranke* (*The Man with the Paw*); 1938: *Stärker als die Liebe* (*Stronger Than Love*); *In geheimer Mission* (*In Secret Mission*); 1939: *Das unsterbliche Herz* (*The Immortal Heart*); 1941: *Zwielicht* (*Twilight*); *Das Mädchen von*

Farnö (*The Girl from Fano*); *Mein Leben für Irland* (*My Life for Ireland*); 1942: *Der grosse König* (*The Great King*); *Hochzeit auf Bärenhof* (*Wedding in Bärenhof*); *Diesel*; 1943: *Der Flachsacker* (*The Flax Acre*); 1944: *Seinerzeit zu meiner Zeit* (*Back Then in My Days*); *Tierarzt Dr. Vlimmen* (*Dr. Vlimmen, Veterinarian*); 1944–45: *Kolberg*; 1945: *Shiva und die Galgenblume* (*Shiva and the Gallows Flower*, not finished); *Dr. phil. Doederlein*; *Der Fall Molander* (*The Case Mollander*); 1948–49: *Der grosse Mandarin* (*The Great Mandarin*); 1951: *Augen der Liebe* (*Eyes of Love*, originally made in 1942–43, released posthumously).

Director only: 1919: *Gegen den Bruderkrieg* (*Against the War of Brothers*, short); 1934: *Die Freundin eines großen Mannes* (*The Girlfriend of a Great Man*); *Ein Mann will nach Deutschland* (*A Man Wants to Get to Germany*); *Der rote Tod von Riga* (*The Red Death of Riga*, not finished); 1936: *August der Starke* (*Augustus the Strong*); *Die Stunde der Versuchung* (*The Hour of Temptation*); *Der Weg nach Shanghai* (*The Road to Shanghai*); 1937: *Krach und Glück um Künnemann* (*Row and Joy About Künnemann*); *Unter Ausschluss der Öffentlichkeit* (*Private Hearing*).

Friedrich Wilhelm Murnau

Director
Born on December 28, 1888, as Friedrich Wilhelm Plumpe in Bielefeld; died on March 11, 1931, in Santa Monica, in a car accident
Silents: 1919: *Der Knabe in Blau* (*The Boy in Blue/Emerald of Death*); 1920: *Satanas*; *Der Bucklige und die Tänzerin* (*The Hunchback and the Dancer*); *Der Januskopf* (*The Head of Janus*); *Abend—Nacht—Morgen* (*Evening—Night—Morning*); 1921: *Sehnsucht* (*Desire: The Tragedy of a Dancer*); *Der Gang in die Nacht* (*Journey Into the Night*); *Schloss Vogelöd* (The Haunted Castle); **1921–22: *Nosferatu*;** 1922: *Marizza, genannt die Schmuggler-Madonna* (*Marizza, Called the Smuggler Madonna*); *Der brennende Acker* (*The Burning Soil*); *Phantom*; 1923: *Die Austreibung* (*Expulsion*); 1924: *Komödie des Hezens* (*Comedy of the Heart*, screenplay only, directed by co-writer Rochus Gliese); *Die Finanzen des Grossherzogs* (*The Finances of the Grand Duke*); *Der letzte Mann* (*The Last Laugh*); 1925: *Tartüff* (*Tartuffe*); 1926: *Faust*.

In Hollywood: 1927: *Sunrise: A Song of Two Humans*; 1928: *4 Devils*; 1930: *City Girl*; *French Polynesia*: 1931: *Tabu: A Story of the South Seas*.

Albin Grau

Production Designer (and Co-Producer)
Born on December 22, 1884, in Schönefeld/-Leipzig; died on March 27, 1971, in Hausham.
Silents: 1921–22: *Nosferatu*; 1922: *Vorfrühling im Hochgebirge—Eine Frühlingswanderung im Dachstein- und Kaisergebirge* (High Mountain Tour in Early Spring, documentary, not released); 1923: *Schatten—Eine nächtliche Halluzination* (*Warning Shadows*); 1925: *Pietro, der Korsar* (U.S.: *The Love Pirate*); *Arme, kleine Hedwig/Das Haus der Lüge* (*The House of Lies*); 1926: *Die Abenteuer der Biene Maja* (*Adventures of Maya*).
Talkies: 1930: *Die zwölfte Stunde* (*The Twelfth Hour*, reissue of *Nosferatu*); 1936: *Skandal um die Fledermaus* (uncredited designs, art director: Erich Czerwonski).
Unrealized film scripts: ca. 1936: *Die Walzbrüder* (*The Tramps*); *Kirke—Ein besinnliches Menetekel* (*Kirke: A Thoughtful Warning*); *Johann Philipp Palm*; 1937: *Don Juans grosse Liebe* (*Don Juan's Great Love*); 1938: *Das Orchestrion* (*The Orchestrion*).

Enrico [Heinrich Otto Eduard Karl]

Co-Producer and Distributor
Born on November 13, 1897. His mother was a dancer. Adopted the name Heinrich O. Holk. Died on October 25, 1958.
Silents: 1921–22: *Nosferatu*; 1922: *Vorfrühling im Hochgebirge—Eine Frühlingswanderung im Dachstein- und Kaisergebirge* (High Mountain Tour in Early Spring, documentary, not released); 1923: *Schatten—Eine nächtliche Halluzination* (*Warning Shadows*); 1924–25: *Modernes Verkehrsflugzeugwesen* (*Modern Transport Aircraft*, short film); 1925: *Kraftvolle Schönheit* (*Vibrant Beauty*, short film).
Distributor only: 1923: *Hypnose und Suggestion* (*Hypnosis and Suggestion*); 1924: *Der Berg des Schicksals* (*The Mountain of Destiny*).

Henrik Galeen

Screenwriter
Born Heinrich Wiesenberg on January 7, 1881, in Stry, Galicia, Austria-Hungary, today Ukraine;

died on July 30, 1949, in Randolph, Vermont, United States

Silents: 1914: *Der Golem* (U.S.: *Monster of Fate*) as co-director, co-writer and actor; 1915: *Schlemihl. Ein Lebensbild* (*Schlemihl: A Portray*, as writer and actor); 1919: *Die rollende Kugel* (*The Rolling Ball*) as writer; *Die beiden Gatten der Frau Ruth* (*Ruth's Two Husbands*); 1920: *Der Golem, wie er in die Welt kam* (*The Golem: How He Came Into the World*) as co-writer; *Der verbotene Weg* (*The Forbidden Way*) as writer and director, *Judith Trachtenberg*, as director; 1921: *Die Geliebte Roswolskys* (*Roswolsky's Mistress*) as writer; **1921–22:** *Nosferatu*; 1923: *Stadt in Sicht* (*City in View*) as director; *Das Haus ohne Lachen* (*The House Without Laughter*) as director and actor; 1924: *Auf gefährlichen Spuren* (*On Dangerous Tracks*) as writer and actor; *Das Wachsfigurenkabinett* (*Waxworks*) as writer; *Die Liebesbriefe der Baronin von S...* (*The Love Letters of Baronesse S*) as writer and director; 1925: *Zigano, der Brigant vom Monte Diavolo* (*Zigano the Brigand from Monte Diavolo*) as writer and actor; *Das Fräulein vom Amt* (*The Telephone Operator*) as writer; 1926: *Harry! Augen auf!—6 Wochen unter den Apachen* (*Eyes Open, Harry!*) as writer; 1927: *Sein grösster Bluff* (*His Biggest Bluff/His Greatest Bluff*) as writer; *Alraune*, as writer and director; 1928: *Die Dame mit der Maske* (*The Lady with the Mask*) as co-writer.

Talkies: 1928: *Die singenden Marionetten* (*The Singing Marionettes*, short film) as director; 1929: *Die Siegerin* (*The Victress*) as director; *Acci-Dental Treatment* (short film) as writer and supervising director; *After the Verdict* as director; *Mr. Smith Wakes Up* as supervisor; 1931: *Schatten der Unterwelt/Ombres des bas fonds* (*Shadows of the Underworld*) as writer, 1933: *Salon Dora Green* as director; *A Daughter of Her People* as director.

Fritz Arno Wagner

First Cinematographer
Born on December 5, 1889, in Schmiedefeld am Rennsteig, Thuringia; died on August 18, 1958, in Göttingen, Lower Saxony

Silents: 1919: *Madame DuBarry*; *Vendetta*; *Der Galeerensträfling* (*The Galley Slave*); 1920: *Das Skelett des Herrn Markutius* (*The Skeleton of Mister Markutius*); *Das Martyrium* (*The Ordeal*); 1920: *Die geschlossene Kette*; 1921: *Playing with Fire*; *Nachtbesuch in der Northernbank* (*Nightly Visit at the Northernbank*); *Arme Violetta* (*Poor Violetta*), *Der müde Tod* (*Destiny*); *Schloss Vogelöd* (*The Haunted Castle*); *Pariserinnen* (*Parisiennes*); **1921–22:** *Nosferatu*; 1922: *Bardame* (*Barmaid*); *Der brennende Acker* (*The Burning Soil*, only first half); *Der Graf von Essex* (*The Earl of Essex*); *Der Ruf des Schicksals* (*The Call of Fate*); *Wem nie durch Liebe Leid geschah!*; *Lebenshunger* (*Hunger for Life*); *Das hohe Lied der Liebe* (*The Song of Love*); 1923: *Zwischen Abend und Morgen* (*Between Evening and Morning*); *Schatten—Eine nächtliche Halluzination* (*Warning Shadows*); *Die Magyarenfürstin* (*The Magyar Princess*); *Der Grossindustrielle* (*The Industrial Magnate*); 1924: *Sprung ins Leben* (*Der Roman eines Zirkuskindes*; *Leap Into Life*); 1925: *Zur Chronik von Grieshuus* (*Chronicles of the Grey House*); *Pietro der Korsar* (U.S.: *The Love Pirate*); *Das Fräulein vom Amt* (*The Telephone Operator*); 1926: *Die drei Kuckucksuhren* (*Three Cuckoo Clocks*); *Der rosa Diamant* (*The Pink Diamond*); *Vater werden ist nicht schwer...* (*It's Easy to Become a Father*); 1927: *Eine Dubarry von heute* (*A Modern Dubarry*); *Liebeshandel* (*Agentur Übersee*; Austria: *Die Mädchenfalle*; *Love Affair*); *Der Weltkrieg, 1. Teil—Des Volkes Heldengang* (*The World War, Part 1*, documentary); *Am Rande der Welt* (*At the Edge of the World*); *Die Liebe der Jeanne Ney* (*The Love of Jeanne Ney*); *Natur und Liebe* (working titles: *Von der Urzelle zum Menschen, Vom Urtier zum Menschen, Nature and Love*, documentary); 1928: *Spione* (*Spies*); *Marquis d'Eon, der Spion der Pompadour* (*The Spy of Madame Pompadour*); 1928–29: *Waterloo*; *Das letzte Fort* (*The Last Fort*); 1929: *Tagebuch einer Verlorenen* (*Diary of a Lost Girl*); *Napoleon auf St. Helena/Der gefangene Kaiser* (*Napoleon at Saint Helena*).

Talkies: 1929: *Wenn du einmal dein Herz verschenkst* (*When You One Day Give Your Heart Away*); 1930: *Westfront 1918: Vier von der Infanterie* (*Comrades of 1917/Westfront 1918*); *Die Jagd nach dem Glück* (*Chasing Fortune*, short film); *Skandal um Eva* (*Scandal About Eva*); *Dolly macht Karriere* (*Dolly Gets Ahead*; *Dolly's Way to Stardom*); *Brand in der Oper* (*La barcarolle d'amour*); *Fire in the Opera House*; *The Twelfth Hour* (reissue of *Nosferatu*); 1931: *Die 3 Groschen-Oper* (*L'opera de quat'sous/The 3 Penny Opera*); *M—Eine Stadt sucht einen Mörder* (*M Murderers*

Among Us); *Kameradschaft* (*Comradeship*); *Ronny*; 1931–33: *Das kalte Herz* (*Heart of Stone*), photographic advisor only; 1932: *Es wird schon besser* (*It's Going to Be Better*); *Das Lied einer Nacht* (*Le Chanson d'une nuit*/*The Song of a Night*); *Das schöne Abenteuer* (*La belle aventure*/*Beautiful Adventure*); *Tell Me Tonight*; *Wie sag' ich's meinem Mann?* (*How Am I Going to Tell My Husband?*); *Das Testament des Dr. Mabuse* (*Le testament du Dr. Mabuse*/*The Testament of Dr. Mabuse*); 1933: *Spione am Werk* (*Spies at Work*); *Die Nacht der großen Liebe* (*Night of the Great Love*); *Flüchtlinge* (*Refugees*); *Das Schloss im Süden* (*Château de rêve*/*Castle in the South*); 1934: *Volga en flammes*; *Au bout du monde*; *Spiel mit dem Feuer* (*Playing with Fire*); *Ein Mann will nach Deutschland* (*A Man Wants to Get to Germany*); *Turandot, Prinzessin von China* (*Turandot, Princess de Chine*/*Princess Turandot*); *Liebe, Tod und Teufel* (*Le diable en bouteille*/*Love, Death and the Devil*); 1935: *Amphitryon—Aus den Wolken kommt das Glück* (*Les dieux s'amusent*/*The Gods at Play*); *Schwarze Rosen* (*Black Roses*); *Savoy-Hotel 217*; *Unter heissem Himmel* (*Smuggled Goods*); 1937: *Glamorous Night*; *Der Mann, der Sherlock Holmes war* (*The Man Who Was Sherlock Holmes*); *Der zerbrochene Krug* (*The Broken Jug*); *Tango Notturno*; 1938: *Das Mädchen mit dem guten Ruf* (*The Girl with a Good Reputation*); *Schatten über St. Pauli* (*Shadow Over St. Pauli*); *Adrienne Lecouvreur*; 1939: *Ein hoffnungsloser Fall* (*A Hopeless Case*); *Der vierte kommt nicht* (*The Fourth Doesn't Come*); *Robert Koch, der Bekämpfer des Todes* (*Robert Koch, the Death Fighter*); 1940: *Der Fuchs von Glenarvon* (*The Fox of Glenarvon*); *Aus erster Ehe* (*Of First Marriage*); *Feinde* (*Enemies*); *Friedrich Schiller—Der Triumph eines Genies* (*Friedrich Schiller: The Triumph of a Genius*); 1941: *Ohm Krüger* (*Uncle Kruger*); *Was geschah in dieser Nacht* (*What Happened in this Night?*); 1942: *Der Fall Rainer* (*The Case of Lieutenant Rainer*); *Die Entlassung* (*The Dismissal*/*Bismarck's Dismissal*); 1942–43: *Altes Herz wird wieder jung* (*Old Heart Gets Young Again*); 1943: *Lache Bajazzo* (*Laugh Bajazzo*); *Ein glücklicher Mensch* (*A Lucky Man*); *Ich werde dich auf Händen tragen* (*I'll Carry You on My Hands*); 1944: *Herr Sanders lebt gefährlich* (*Mr. Sanders Lives Dangerously*); 1945: *Meine Herren Söhne* (*My Sons*); *Befreite Musik* (*Liberated Music*, documentary short); 1948: *Das kleine Hofkonzert* (*Palace Scandal*); 1948–49: *Die Brücke* (*The Bridge*); 1949: *Du bist nicht allein* (*You Are Not Alone*); *Mädchen hinter Gittern* (*Girls Behind Bars*); 1950: *Frauenarzt Dr. Prätorius* (*Dr. Praetorius, Gynaecologist*); *Herrliche Zeiten* (*Glorious Times*); *Das Mädchen aus der Südsee* (*The Girl from the South Seas*); 1951: *Liebestraum* (*Love Dream*); *Die Frauen des Herrn S.* (*The Women of Mr. S.*); *Die Schuld des Dr. Homma* (*The Guilt of Dr. Homma*); *Torreani*; 1952: *Mein Herz darfst du nicht fragen* (*Don't Ask My Heart*); *1. April 2000*; *Der Fürst von Pappenheim* (*The Prince of Pappenheim*); *Die leibhaftige Unschuld* (*The Innocence Personified*); 1953: *Fräulein Casanova* (*Miss Casanova*); *Die Rose von Stambul* (*The Rose of Stamboul*); *Der Vetter aus Dingsda* (*The Cousin from Batavia*); 1954: *Heideschulmeister Uwe Karsten* (*Uwe Karsten, Heath Schoolmaster*); *Die tolle Lola* (*The Great Lola*); *Aus eigener Kraft* (*By One's Own Efforts*, documentary); *Der treue Husar* (*The Faithful Hussar*); *Konsul Strotthoff*; *Clivia*; 1955: *Die Frau des Botschafters* (*The Ambassador's Wife*); *Hotel Adlon*; 1956: *Die wilde Auguste* (*The Wild Auguste*); *Meine 16 Söhne* (*My 16 Sons*); *Tausend Melodien* (*Thousand Melodies*); *Hochzeit auf Immenhof* (*Wedding on Immenhof*); *Geliebte Corinna* (*Beloved Corinna*); 1957: *Ferien auf Immenhof* (*Holidays on Immenhof*); *Das Mädchen ohne Pyjama* (*The Girl Without Pajamas*); *Kindermädchen für Papa gesucht* (*Wanted: A Nanny for Daddy*); *Liebe, Jazz und Übermut* (*Love, Jazz and High Jinks*); 1958: *Der Czardas-König* (*Die Emmerich-Kalman-Story*; *The Csardas Princess*); *Wehe, wenn sie losgelassen* (not credited); *Ohne Mutter geht es nicht* (*It Doesn't Work Without Mother*, Wagner died during production).

Günther Krampf

Second Cinematographer

Born on February 8, 1899, in Vienna; died on August 4, 1950, in London

Silents: 1916–17: *Die Lieblingsfrau des Maharadscha* (*The Favorite Wife of the Maharajah*, two parts); 1920: *Die Legende von der heiligen Simplicia* (*The Legend of Saint Simplicia*); 1921: *Die Geschichte von Barak Johnson* (*The Story of Barak Johnson*); *Die Geschichte des grauen Hauses* (*The Story of the Gray House*, Part 3 and 4); *Am roten Kliff* (*At the Red Cliff*); **1921–22: Nosferatu**; 1922: *Hochtouren im Vorfrühling—Eine Frühlingswanderung im Dachstein—und Kaisergebirge*

(*High Mountain Tour in Early Spring*, documentary, not released); *Ein Glas Wasser* (*One Glass of Water*); 1923: *Pömperly's Kampf mit dem Schneeschuh* (*Pömperly's Fight with the Snowshoe*); *Die Prinzessin Suwarin* (*Princess Suwarin*); *Der verlorene Schuh* (*The Lost Shoe*); *Erdgeist* (*Earth Spirit*); 1924: *Hotel Potemkin*; *Orlacs Hände/Die unheimlichen Hände des Doktor Orlac* (*The Hands of Orlac*); 1925: *Pension Groonen*; *Das Mädchen mit der Protektion* (*The Girl with Patronage*); 1926: *Herrn Filip Collins Abenteuer* (*The Adventure of Mr. Filip Collin*); *Der Student von Prag* (*The Student of Prague*); 1927: *Der Sohn der Hagar* (*The Son of Hagar*/U.S.: *Out of the Mist*); *Ein Mordsmädel* (*A Great Girl*); *Grand Hotel...!*; *Der König der Mittelstürmer* (*The King of the Center-forwards*); *Der Haupttreffer* (*The Jackpot*); *Sintflut* (*Deluge*); 1928: *Die von der Scholle sind*; *Schinderhannes* (*The Prince of Rogues*); *Schneeschuhbanditen* (*Snowshoe Bandits*); *Dorine und der Zufall* (*Rich, Young and Beautiful*); *Das letzte Souper* (*The Last Supper*); 1929: *Die Büchse der Pandora* (*Pandora's Box*); *Indizienbeweis* (*Vendetta*); *Narkose* (*Narcosis*); *Die Schleiertänzerin*.

Talkies: 1930: *Alraune*; *Masken* (*Masks*); *Die letzte Kompagnie* (*The Last Company*); *Cyankali*; *Königin einer Nacht* (*Queen of a Night*); *Die zwölfte Stunde* (*The Twelfth Hour*, reissue of *Nosferatu*); 1931: *Du bist meine ganze Welt* (*The Song of the Nations*); *Der brave Sünder* (*Defraudation*); *The Bells*; *Das Kind und die Welt* (*The Child and the World*, documentary); 1932: *Kuhle Wampe oder: Wem gehört die Welt?* (*To Whom Does the World Belong?*); *Rome Express*; *The Lucky Number*; 1933: *Sleeping Car*; *The Ghoul*; 1934: *Little Friend*; *Death at Broadcasting House*; *Little Stranger*; 1935: *Das Mädchen Johanna* (*Joan of Arc*); *The Tunnel*; 1936: *The Amateur Gentleman*; *Everything Is Thunder*; *His Lordship*; 1937: *Paradise for Two*; 1938: *Marigold*; 1939: *The Outsider*; *Black Eyes*; *On the Night of the Fire/The Fugitive*; 1940: *Dead Man's Shoes*; *Convoy*; *Sailors Three*; 1942: *Black Sheep of Whitehall*; *The Night Has Eyes*; *Suspected Person*; *Sabotage at Sea*; 1943: *Women Aren't Angels*; *Warn That Man*; 1944: *Aventure Malgache* (short film, not credited); *Bon Voyage* (short film, not credited); 1945: *Latin Quarter*; 1947: *Meet Me at Dawn*; *Fame Is the Spur*; 1948: *This Was a Woman*; 1950: *Portrait of Clare*; 1951: *The Franchise Affair*.

Hans Rameau

Consultant
Born Paul Hans Julius Gulder on November 28, 1901, in Berlin; died on April 9, 1980, in Gavignano near Rome

Attended Reinhardt Seminary. Acting career: 1920 Neues Schauspiel in Königsberg. 1921–24 at Kammerspiele in Munich where he was Max Schreck's partner: *Der Geizige* (*The Miser*). Rameau recommended Schreck to his friend F.W. Murnau. Murnau later cast Rameau in his *Faust* film and made him assistant director. In 1935, Rameau went to Vienna, then to Rome, 1936 to London and a year later to Hollywood where he became a screenwriter for MGM.

Silents (as writer): 1919: *Jettatore*; *Tempo! Tempo!*; 1926: *Der rosa Diamant* (*The Pink Diamond*, also acting); 1927: *Der grösste Gauner des Jahrhunderts* (*The Greatest Hustler of the Century*); *Primanerliebe* (only actor); 1928: *Am Rüdesheimer Schloss steht eine Linde*; *Die Yacht der sieben Sünden* (*Yacht of the Seven Sins*); *Der Unüberwindliche* (*The Invincible*); *Mein Freund Harry* (*My Friend Harry*); 1929: *Die Geliebte Roswolsky's* (*Roswolsky's Mistress*); *Der Zarewitsch* (*Carewitch*); *Diane—Die Geschichte einer Pariserin* (*Diane: The Story of a Parisien*); *Die Liebe der Brüder Rott* (*Will o' the Wisp*); 1929–30: *Sein bester Freund* (*His Best Friend*).

Talkies: 1930: *Die Warschauer Zitadelle* (*The Warsaw Citadel*); *Achtung! Auto-Diebe!* (*Attention! Car Thieves!*); *Nur Du* (*Only You*); *Er oder ich* (*He or I*); 1931: *Die Marquise von Pompadour* (*Un caprice de la Pompadour/Madame Pompadour*, also actor); *Die Frau, von der man spricht* (*The Woman They Talk About*); *Die Abenteurerin von Tunis* (*The Adventuress of Tunis*); *Der Schlemihl*; *Bobby geht los* (*Bobby Gets Going*); 1933: *Manolescu, der Fürst der Diebe* (*Manolescu, the Prince of Thieves*); *Sprung in den Abgrund* (*Jumping into the Abyss*); *Ein Unsichtbarer geht durch die Stadt* (*An Invisible Man Walks the City*); *Rund um eine Million* (*Around a Million*); 1934: *Die Finanzen des Grossherzogs* (*The Finances of the Grand Duke*); *Ich kenn' dich nicht und liebe dich* (*Toi que j'adore/I Don't Know You But Love You*); *Die Welt ohne Maske* (*The World Unmasked*); *Une fois dans la vie*; *...heute abend bei mir* (*...Tonight at My Place*); 1935: *Mazurka*; *Wunder des Fliegens—Der Film eines deutschen Fliegers* (*Miracle of Flying*); *Demaskierung* (*A

Night of Change); 1937: *Sein bester Freund* (*His Best Friend*, remake); *Moonlight Sonata/The Charmer* (story); *Der Mann, der nicht nein sagen konnte* (*Ma non è una cosa seria/The Man Who Couldn't Say No/But It's Nothing Serious*, not credited); *Confession* (story); *The Rat*; 1940: *Waterloo Bridge*; *The Mortal Storm*; 1942: *We Were Dancing*; *Mrs. Miniver*; 1943: *Madame Curie*; 1946: *The Yearling*; 1948: *Homecoming*.

In 1951, Rameau returned to Europe:

1951: *Maria Theresia*; 1952: *Die Spur führt nach Berlin* (*Adventure in Berlin/International Counterfeiters*); *Der keusche Lebemann* (*The Abstinent Bon Vivant*); *Der Onkel aus Amerika* (*The Uncle from America*); 1954: *Bei Dir war es immer so schön* (*It Was Always So Nice with You*); *Der Zarewitsch* (*Carewitch*); 1956: *Gaby* (early draft); *Musikparade* (*Music Parade*); *Du bist Musik* (*You Are Music*); 1957: *Die verpfuschte Hochzeitsnacht* (*The Bungled Wedding Night*); *Die Lindenwirtin vom Donaustrand*; *Wien, du Stadt meiner Träume* (*Vienna, City of My Dreams*, novella); 1958: *Münchhausen in Afrika* (*Munchausen in Africa*, story); *Scala—total verrückt* (*Scala: totally mad*); 1960: *Sabine und die 100 Männer* (*Sabine and One-Hundred Men*); 1961: *Der Transport* (*The Transport*).

German Television: 1963: *Glück zu kleinen Preisen*; 1963–64: *Menschen helfen Menschen*; 1964: *Akte Wiltau*; *Geheimbund Nächstenliebe*; *Zwei Tage von vielen*; *Mitternachtszauber*; *Wir reisen mit Musik—Ein Bummel um die Welt*; 1969: *Die Kramer* (series).

Walter Spies

Consultant

Born in Moscow in 1895, the son of a German merchant. He was inspired to try art after encounters with artists Oskar Kokoschka and Otto Dix. He never did more than five paintings a year as he had a lot of other interests: music, dancing, movies, botany, literature and foreign languages. As a painter, he was familiar with different styles: surrealism, Neue Sachlichkeit (New Objectivity), Russian folklore. After participating in the shooting of *Nosferatu*, he traveled to Java as a sailor and in 1927 to Bali where he entertained Charles Chaplin, Woolworth heiress Barbara Hutton and anthropologist Margaret Mead. A homosexual, he eventually was banished from his paradise. He spent eight months in jail and 20 months in intern camps on Java and Sumatra because he was German. When he was brought to Ceylon in 1942 on board a freighter, the ship was attacked by a Japanese plane. More than 400 German prisoners drowned, among them Walter Spies.

Dr. Phil. Hans Erdmann

Composer

Born Hans Erdmann Timotheos Guckel on November 7, 1882, in Breslau, today Wrocław, Poland; died on November 24, 1942, in Berlin

Silents: 1921–22: *Nosferatu*.

Talkies: 1930: *Zirkus "Kater Murr"*; 1930–31: *Urwaldsymphonie* (*Jungle Symphony*); 1931: *Mündiges Volk* (*Mature People*); 1931–32: *Der tolle Bomberg* (*The Mad Bomberg*); 1932–33: *Das Testament des Dr. Mabuse* (*The Testament of Dr. Mabuse*); 1935–36: *August der Starke* (*Augustus the Strong*).

For the revival of Nosferatu as *Die zwölfte Stunde* (The Twelfth Hour), they didn't use Erdmann's services but turned to a man named Georg Fiebiger. As both composers, however, were born in Breslau and both worked, at different times, with Paul Wegener, it is likely that Erdmann had recommended Fiebiger for the job, even that Fiebiger was already involved in the production of the original *Nosferatu* or participated in Erdmann's publications. Official film music credits only found for the years 1929–30, beginning with a job for a short produced by Willi Münzenberg, head of propaganda of the Comintern, and his left-wing Prometheus Film Company. Later, nothing other than credits as production manager or producer, mainly for films made at Bavaria Studios in Munich.

Georg Fiebiger

Composer and Producer

Born on June 22, 1901, in Breslau, today Wrocław, Poland; date of death unknown.

As composer: 1929–30: *Eine holländische Reise*; *Ein Filmbericht* (*A Dutch Journey*, short film); 1930: *Die zwölfte Stunde—Eine Nacht des Grauens* (*The Twelfth Hour: A Night of Horror*); *Rivalen im Weltrekord* (*Rivals in World Record*). 1930–31: *Im Banne der Berge* (*Under the Spell of the Mountains*; according to other sources, Bernhard Eichhorn did the score).

As production manager and producer: 1943: *Reise in die Vergangenheit* (*Journey to the Past*); 1944: *Der Täter ist unter uns* (*The Culprit Is Among Us*); *Spuk im Schloss* (*Ghost in the Castle*); 1945: *Münchnerinnen* (*Über alles die Liebe/Munich Women/Love Above All*, premiered in 1949); *Geld ins Haus* (*Der Millionär/The Millionaire*, premiered in 1947); 1948–49: *Der grosse Mandarin* (*The Great Mandarin*, Paul Wegener's final film appearance); *Begegnung mit Werther* (*Encounter with Werther*).

In Front of the Camera

Max Schreck

As Count Orlok
Born on September 6, 1879, in Berlin; died on February 20, 1936, in Munich
Silents: 1917: *Teufelsmädel* (*Devil Girl*); 1920: *Tanz in den Tod* (*Dance to Death*); *Der Richter von Zalamea* (*The Mayor of Zalamea*); *Der unheimliche Chinese* (*The Uncanny Chinese*); 1921: *Der Verfluchte* (*The Cursed One*); *Am Narrenseil* (part two); *Der zeugende Tod*; *Der Roman der Christine von Herre* (*The Story of Christine von Herre*); *Pique Ass*; *Der Favorit der Königin* (*The Queen's Favorite*); **1921–22:** **Nosferatu**; 1922: *Nathan der Weise* (*Nathan the Wise*); *Mysterien eines Frisiersalons* (*Mysteries of a Barber Shop*); 1923: *Die Strasse* (*The Street*); *Der Kaufmann von Venedig* (*The Merchant of Venice*); 1924: *Dudu, ein Menschenschicksal* (*Die Geschichte eines Clowns/The Story of a Clown*); *Die Finanzen des Grossherzogs* (*The Finances of the Grand Duke*); 1925: *Krieg im Frieden* (*War in Peace*); *Die gefundene Braut*; 1926: *Der rosa Diamant* (*The Pink Diamond*); 1927: *Der Sohn der Hagar* (*The Son of Hagar*/U.S.: *Out of the Mist*); *Am Rande der Welt* (*At the Edge of the World*); *Ramper der Tiermensch* (*The Strange Case of Captain Ramper*); *Die pikanten Histörchen der seligen Exzellenz*; *Dona Juana*; *Der Meister von Nürnberg* (*The Master of Nuremberg*); 1928: *Wolga Wolga, die Ballade von Stenka Rasin* (*Volga Volga: The Ballad of Stenka Rasin*); *Der alte Fritz* (*The Old Fritz*); *Luther—Ein Film der deutschen Reformation* (*Luther—a Film of the German Reformation*); *Scampolo, das Mädchen der Strasse* (*Scampolo, the Girl from the Street*); *Rasputins Liebesabenteuer* (*Rasputin's Love Adventure*); *Republik der Backfische* (*The Republic of Flippers*); *Ritter der Nacht* (*Knights of the Night*); *Moderne Piraten* (*Modern Pirates*); *Serenissimus und die letzte Jungfrau* (*Serenissimus and the Last Virgin*); *Der Kampf der Tertia* (*Fight of the Tertia*); *Ludwig der Zweite, König von Bayern* (*Ludwig II, King of Bavaria*); 1928–29: *Waterloo*.
Talkies: 1930: *Land des Lächelns* (*The Land of the Smiles*); *Die zwölfte Stunde* (*The Twelfth Hour*, reissue of **Nosferatu**); *Im Banne der Berge* (*Under the Spell of the Mountains*); *Boykott* (*Boycott*); 1931: *Die Koffer des Herrn O.F.* (*The Thirteen Trunks of Mr. O.F.*); 1932: *Peter Voss, der Millionendieb* (*Peter Voss Who Stole Millions*); *Nacht der Versuchung* (*Night of Temptation*); *Ein Mann mit Herz* (*A Man with Heart*); *Die verkaufte Braut* (*The Bartered Bride*); *Fürst Seppl* (*Prince Seppl*); 1933: *Muss man sich gleich scheiden lassen* (*Must We Get Divorced?*); *Eine Frau wie du* (*A Woman Like You*); *Fräulein Hoffmanns Erzählungen* (*Miss Hoffmann's Tales*); *Roman einer Nacht* (*Story of a Night*); 1933: *Der Tunnel* (*The Tunnel*); 1934: *Das Stahltier* (*The Steel Animal*); *Das verliebte Hotel* (*The Love Hotel*); *Klein Dorrit*; *Ein Kuss in der Sommernacht* (*A Kiss in the Summer Night*); 1933–34: *Peer Gynt*; 1935: *Der Schlafwagenkontrolleur* (*The Sleeping Coach Conductor*); *Knock Out*; *Donogoo Tonka*; 1936: *Die letzten Vier von Santa Cruz* (*The Last Four of Santa Cruz*).
Voice Artist—Dubbing: 1932: *Vampyr—Der Traum des Allan Grey* (*Vampyr—The Dream of Allan Grey*, dubbing Maurice Schutz); 1934: *Die scharlachrote Blume* (*The Scarlet Pimpernel*, dubbing Ernest Milton); 1934: *Der Graf von Monte Cristo* (*The Count of Monte Cristo*, dubbing O.P. Heggie).

Greta Schröder

As Ellen Hutter
Born Margarete Schröder on September 7, 1891, in Düsseldorf; died on June 8, 1980, in Berlin-Steglitz
Silents: 1913: *Die Insel der Seligen* (*The Island of the Blessed*); 1920: *Arme Violetta* (*Poor Violetta*); *Der Golem, wie er in die Welt kam* (*The Golem:*

How He Came Into the World); *Die geschlossene Kette*; 1921: *Der verlorene Schatten* (*The Lost Shadow*); *Zirkus des Lebens* (*Circus of Life*); *Marizza, genannt die Schmugglermadonna* (*Marizza, Called the Smuggler Madonna*); **1921–22:** ***Nosferatu***; 1922: *Es leuchtet meine Liebe* (*My Love Shines*); 1923: *Brüder* (*Brothers*); *Paganini*.

Talkies: 1930: *Die zwölfte Stunde* (*The Twelfth Hour*, reissue of *Nosferatu*); 1937: *Victoria the Great*; 1938: *Sixty Glorious Days*; 1943: *Grossstadtmelodie* (*Melody of a Great City*); *Wildvogel* (*Wild-Bird*); 1944–45: *Kolberg*; 1951: *Maria Theresia*; 1953: *Pünktchen und Anton*; 1953–54: *Die Gefangene des Maharadscha* (*Circus Girl*).

As Screenwriter: 1915: *Zucker und Zimt* (*Sugar and Cinnamon*); *Phantom der Oper* (*Phantom of the Opera*).

Gustav von Wangenheim

As Thomas Hutter
Born Ingo Clemens Adolf Freiherr von Wangenheim on February 18, 1985, in Wiesbaden; died on August 5, 1975, in East Berlin/GDR

Silents: *Passionels Tagebuch* (*Passionel's Diary*); 1916: *Das Leid der Liebe* (*The Grief of Love*); *Homunculus 3rd Part: Die Liebestragödie des Homunculus*; 1917: *Die Erzkokette* (*The Coquette*); 1918: *Ferdinand Lassalle—Des Volkstribunen Glück und Ende*; 1919: *Kitsch: Tragödie einer Intrigantin* (*Kitsch: Tragedy of an Intriguer*); 1919–20: *Romeo und Julia im Schnee* (*Romeo and Juliet in the Snow*); *Kohlhiesels Töchter* (*Kohlhiesel's Daughters*); *Der Welteroberer* (*Der Schrecken im Hause Ardon/The World Conqueror*); 1920: *Der Tempel der Liebe* (*The Temple of Love*); *Das Haus im Mond* (*The House on the Moon*); **1921–22:** ***Nosferatu***; 1922: *Das Feuerschiff* (*The Lightship*); 1922–23: *Der Liebe Pilgerfahrt* (*Pilgrimage of Love*); *Der steinerne Reiter* (*The Stone Rider*); 1923: *Schatten* (*Warning Shadows*); 1928–29: *Frau im Mond* (*Woman in the Moon*; U.S.: *By Rocket to the Moon*).

Talkies: 1930: *Die zwölfte Stunde* (*The Twelfth Hour*, reissue of *Nosferatu*); 1931: *Danton*.

As Director-Screenwriter: 1935: *Kämpfer/Bortsy* (*Fighters*); 1948: *Und wieder 48* (*1948 Once Again*); 1949: *Im Auftrag Höglers* (*At the Behest of Högler*); 1954: *Gefährliche Fracht* (*Dangerous Freight*); 1955: *Heimliche Ehen* (*Secret Matrimonies*); 1956: *Liebe über dem Tal* (*Love Above the Valley*, unfinished).

Alexander Granach

As Knock
Born Jessaja Gronach on April 18, 1890, in Werbowitz, Eastern Galicia, then Austria Hungary, today Ukraine; died on March 14, 1945, in New York City

Silents: 1919: *Das goldene Buch* (*The Golden Book*); 1920: *Die Liebe vom Zigeuner stammt...* (*Love Emanates from the Gypsy...*); 1921: *Der grosse Chef* (*The Big Big Boss*); **1921–22:** ***Nosferatu***; 1922: *Lucrezia Borgia*; *Die Tänzerin Navarro* (*Navarro the Dancing Girl*); *Mignon*; 1923: *Erdgeist* (*Earth Spirit*); *Fridericus Rex* (Parts 3 and 4); *Paganini*; *Der Mensch am Wege* (*Man by the Wayside*); *Schatten* (*Warning Shadows*); *Ein Weib, ein Tier, ein Diamant* (*A Woman, an Animal, a Diamond*); *I.N.R.I.* (as Judas); 1923–24: *Carlos und Elisabeth*; 1924: *Die Radio Heirat*; 1925: *Ein Sommernachtstraum* (*A Midsummer Night's Dream/Wood Love*); 1926: *Qualen der Nacht* (*Torments of the Night*); *Gewitter über Gottland* (*Lightning Over Gottland*, short film); 1927: *Hoppla, wir leben!*; *Svengali*; *Die berühmte Frau* (*The Famous Woman*); 1928: *Ich hatte einst ein schönes Vaterland* (*I Once Had a Beautiful Homeland*); *Polizeibericht Überfall* (*Austria: Freie Fahrt; Police Report: Assault*, short film); 1928–29: *Der Adjutant des Zaren* (*The Adjutant of the Czar*); *Das letzte Fort* (*The Last Fort*); 1929: *Grossstadtschmetterling* (*Pavement Butterfly*); *Flucht in die Fremdenlegion* (*The Legionaire*).

Talkies: 1930: *Die letzte Kompagnie* (*The Last Company*); *1914, Die letzten Tage vor dem Weltenbrand* (*1914: The Last Days Before the War*); *Die zwölfte Stunde* (*The Twelfth Hour*, reiusse of ***Nosferatu***); 1931: *Danton*; *Der Raub der Mona Lisa* (*The Theft of the Mona Lisa*); *Kameradschaft* (*Comradeship*); 1936: *Poslednîy tabor* (*Das letzte Zigeunerlager/Gypsies*); *Kämpfer/Bortsy* (*Fighters*); 1939: *Ninotchka*; *The Hunchback of Notre Dame*; 1940: *Foreign Correspondent*; 1941: *So Ends Our Night*; *A Man Betrayed*; *It Started with Eve*; *Marry the Boss's Daughter*; 1942: *Joan of Paris*; *Joan of Ozark*; *Halfway to Shanghai*; *Northwest Rangers*; *Wrecking Crew*; 1943: *Hangmen Also Die!*; *Mission to Moscow*; *For Whom the Bell Tolls*; *Three Russian Girls*; 1944: *Voice of the Wind*; *The Hitler Gang*; *The Seventh Cross*; *My Buddy*.

Georg Heinrich Schnell

As Harding
Born on April 11, 1878, in Zsifu, today Yantai, China; died on March 31, 1951, in Berlin
Silents: 1919: *Die verführte Heilige* (*The Seduced Saint*); *Ihr Sport; Die rollende Kugel* (*The Rolling Ball*); *Die Schuld* (*The Guilt*); *Die Arche* (*The Ark*, two parts, Part 2: *Die letzten Menschen/The Last Men*); *Das Werkzeug des Cosimo* (*The Tool of Cosimo*); 1919–20: *Der Welteroberer* (*Der Schrecken im Hause Ardon/The World Conqueror*); 1920: *Alkohol* (*Alcohol*); *Das rote Plakat* (*The Red Poster*); *Die Tragödie eines Großen* (*The Tragedy of a Great/Rembrandt*); *Die Stunde nach Mitternacht* (*The Hour After Midnight*); *Spuk auf Schloss Kitay* (*The Haunting of Castle Kitay*); *Moral; Die Tarantel* (*The Tarantula*); *Puppen des Todes* (*Puppets of Death*); *Der Flüchtling von Sing-Sing* (*The Fugitive from Sing Sing*); 1921: *Die Dreizehn aus Stahl* (*The Thirteen of Steel*); *Die Dame im Koffer* (*The Lady in the Trunk*); *Die Amazone* (*The Amazon*); *Das rote Plakat 2—Die eiserne Acht* (*The Red Poster*, Part 2: *The Iron Eight*); *Marodeure der Grossstadt* (*Marauders of the Big City*); *Das Geheimnis der Santa Marie* (*The Mystery of the Santa Maria*); *Narren der Liebe* (*Fools of Love*); *Die Jagd nach der Wahrheit* (*Hunt for Truth*); **1921–22: *Nosferatu*;** *Der Frauenarzt* (*The Gynecologist*, two parts); 1922: *Fräulein Julie* (*Miss Julie*); *Der Abenteurer* (*The Adventurers*); *Kinder der Zeit* (*Children of Their Time*); *Die Tochter Napoleons* (*Napoleon's Daughter*); *Marie Antoinette—Das Leben einer Königin* (*Marie Antoinette: The Life of a Queen*); *Der falsche Dimitri* (*False Dmitry*); *Nobody 25*. Episode: *Professor Lucifer* (*Lucifer*, short film); *Krawattenmacher—Der Wucherer von Berlin* (*The Shylock of Berlin*); 1923: *Fridericus Rex 3: Sanssouci; Dr. Sacrobosco, der große Unheimliche* (*Dr. Sacrobosco, the Great Uncanny*); 1924: *Um eines Weibes Ehre* (*For a Woman's Honor*); *Die Tragödie einer Liebesnacht* (*The Tragedy of a Love Night*); *Liebet das Leben* (*Love the Life*); *Der Schrecken des Meeres* (*The Terror of the Sea*); *Die blonde Hannele* (*Blonde Hannele*); 1925: *Verborgene Gluten* (*Secret Glows*); *Die suchende Seele* (*The Searching Soul*); *Dein Begehren ist Sünde…* (*Your Desire Is Sin*); *Aus der Jugendzeit klingt ein Lied* (*From the Youth Time a Song Sounds*); *In den Sternen steht es geschrieben* (*Written in the Stars*); *Venezianische Liebesabenteuer* (*Venetian Love Adventures*); *The Pleasure Garden* (*Irrgarten der Leidenschaft*, British-German co-production); *Freies Volk* (*Free People*); 1926: *Der Frauenmarder* (*The Women Marten*); *Der gute Ruf* (*The Good Name*); *Die Mühle von Sanssouci* (*The Mill of Sanssouci*); *Der Stolz der Kompanie* (*The Pearl of the Regiment*); *Wenn Menschen irren. Frauen auf Abwegen* (*Women Who Go Astray*); 1927: *Gauner im Frack* (*Hustlers in Tails*); *Die Achtzehnjährigen* (*Eighteen Years Old*); *Bigamie* (*Bigamy*); *Hast Du geliebt am schönen Rhein?* (*Did You Love at the Beautiful Rhine*); 1928: *Der alte Fritz—2. Ausklang* (*The Old Fritz Part 2: Finale*); *Hurrah! Ich lebe!* (*Hooray! I'm Living*).
Talkies: 1929–30: *Das Donkosakenlied* (*The Song of the Don Cossacks*); *Der unsterbliche Lump* (*The Immortal Rascal*); *Der Weg zur Schande* (*The Path to Shame*); 1930: *Die zwölfte Stunde* (*The Twelfth Hour*, reissue of ***Nosferatu***); 1930–31: *Ihre Majestät die Liebe* (*Her Majesty, the Love*); 1931: *Kaiserliebchen* (*The Emperor's Sweetheart*); *Danton; Schatten der Manege* (*Shadow of the Circus Ring*); *Im Geheimdienst* (*In Secret Service*); *Meine Frau, die Hochstaplerin* (*My Wife, the Confidence Trickster*); *Emil und die Detektive* (*Emil and the Detectives*); 1932: *Kampf; Tannenberg* (*Battle of Tannenberg*); 1933–34: *Wilhelm Tell—Das Freiheitsdrama eines Volkes* (*William Tell*); *Der Polizeibericht meldet* (*Police Report*); 1934: *Die bunte Platte* (short film); *Der Springer von Pontresina* (*The Champion of Pontresina; Love in St. Moritz*); *Die Insel* (*The Island*); *Strömungen und Wirbel* (short film); *Die Reiter von Deutsch-Ostafrika* (*The Riders of German East Africa*); *Ferien vom Ich* (*Holiday from Myself*); *Gorch Fock* (short film); 1934–35: *Oberwachtmeister Schwenke* (*Patrolman Schwenke*); 1935: *Strassen ohne Hindernisse—Ein Film über die Reichsautobahnen* (short film); *Stradivari; Das Mädchen vom Moorhof* (*The Girl from the Marsh Croft/The Girl of the Moors*); *Der Ammenkönig* (*Das Tal der Liebe/The Valley of Love*); *Der interessante Fall* (short film); 1936: *Schloss Vogelöd* (*The Haunted Castle*); *Heisses Blut* (*Hot Blood*); *Heiteres und Ernstes um den grossen König* (short film); *Moral; Das Schloss in Flandern* (*The Castle in Flandres*), 1937: *Es wird nicht so fein gesponnen* (short film); *Die Kronzeugin* (*The Chief Witness*); *Die gläserne Kugel* (*The Crystal Ball*); *Madame Bovary; Wenn Frauen schweigen* (*When Women Keep Silent*); *Sieben Ohrfeigen* (*Seven Slaps*); *Alarm in Peking; Heimweh* (*Home Sickness*); *Der

Mustergatte (*The Model Husband*); *Ein Volksfeind* (*An Enemy of the People*); *Die Korallenprinzessin* (*An der schönen Adria/The Coral Princess*); 1938: *Mit versiegelter Order* (*Under Sealed Orders*); *Das Mädchen von gestern Nacht* (*The Girl of Last Night*); *Der unmögliche Herr Pitt* (*Die Nacht der tausend Sensationen/The Impossible Mister Pitt*); *Die kleine und die grosse Liebe* (*Minor Love and the Real Thing*); *Stärker als die Liebe* (*Stronger Than Love*); *Am seidenen Faden* (*Ein Volk will leben/Hanging Upon a Thread*); *Sonne, Erde und Mond* (short film); *Liebe und Liebelei* (*Love and Flirt*); *Die Brücke ins Leben* (*Night of Fate*); *Pitty* (short film); 1939: *Der Polizeifunk meldet* (*Police Report*); *In letzter Minute* (*In Last Minute*); *Das Recht auf Liebe* (*The Right to Love*); *Das Gewehr über* (*Shoulder Arms*); *Die Nacht der Entscheidung* (*Night of Decision*); *Die Frau ohne Vergangenheit* (*The Woman Without Past*); 1939–40: *Ein Mann auf Abwegen* (*A Man Astray*); 1940: *Leidenschaft* (*Passion*); *Die Rothschilds*; 1941: *Carl Peters*; *Ohm Krüger* (*Uncle Kruger*); 1943: *Der ewige Klang* (*The Eternal Sound*); *Titanic*; 1943–44: *Nora*; *Die Feuerzangenbowle* (*The Brandy Punch*).

Ruth Landshoff-Yorck

As Harding's Sister
Born Ruth Levy on January 7, 1904, in Berlin; died on January 19, 1966, in New York
Silent: 1921–22: **Nosferatu**.
Talkie: 1930: *Die zwölfte Stunde* (*The Twelfth Hour*, reissue of **Nosferatu**).

John Gottowt

As Prof. Bulwer
Born Isidor Gesang on June 15, 1881, in Lemberg; murdered by an SS officer on August 29, 1942, in Wieliczka, occupied Poland
Silents: 1913: *Der Student von Prag* (*The Student of Prague*); *Das schwarze Los/Pierrots letztes Abenteuer* (*Pierrot's Final Adventure*); 1915: *Die büssende Magdalena* (*The Suffering Magdalena*); *Satan Opium*; 1917: *Die Prinzessin von Neutralien* (*The Princess of Neutralia*); 1918–19: *Peer Gynt* (two parts); 1919: *Morphium* (short film); 1919–20: *Der rote Henker* (*The Red Henchman*); 1920: *Die tote Stunde* (*The Dead Hour*); *Der Bucklige und die Tänzerin* (*The Hunchback and the Dancer*); *Der verbotene Weg* (*The Forbidden Way*); *Genuine*; *Algol—Die Tragödie der Macht* (*Algol: Tragedy of Power*); *Die Nacht der Königin Isabeau* (*The Night of Queen Isabeau*); 1921: *Brennendes Land* (*Burning Country*); *Susanne Stranzky*; *Pariserinnen/Die Lou vom Montmartre* (*Parisiennes*); **1921–22: Nosferatu**; 1922: *Menschenopfer* (*Human Sacrifice*); *Elixiere des Teufels* (*Elixirs of the Devil*); *Der schwarze Stern* (*The Black Star*); *Der falsche Dimitri* (*False Dmitry*); 1923: *Der Geldteufel* (*The Devil of Money*); *Das Wachsfigurenkabinett* (*Waxworks*); 1926: *Dürfen wir schweigen?* (*Should We Be Silent?*); *Die Flucht in die Nacht* (*The Flight in the Night*); *Prinz Louis Ferdinand*.

Talkies: 1930: *Die zwölfte Stunde* (*The Twelfth Hour*, reissue of **Nosferatu**); 1932: *Unheimliche Geschichten* (*Eerie Stories/Tales of Horror*).
As Director: 1913: *Das schwarze Los/Pierrots letztes Abenteuer* (co-directed with Emil Albes).
As Screenwriter: 1920: *Niemand weiss es* (*Nobody Knows*).

Max Nemetz

As Captain of Ship *Empusa*
Born on September 7, 1886, in Bremen; died on July 2, 1971, in Bad Herrenalb
Silents: 1921: *Der Friedhof der Lebenden* (*Graveyard of the Living*); *Marizza, genannt die Schmugglermadonna* (*Marizza, Called the Smuggler Madonna*); **1921–22: Nosferatu**; 1923: *Der Mensch am Wege* (*Man by the Wayside*).
Talkies: 1930: *Die zwölfte Stunde* (*The Twelfth Hour*, reissue of **Nosferatu**); 1954: *Rosen aus dem Süden* (*Roses from the South*).
Television: 1956: *Philemon und Baucis*; 1960: *Hexenjagd* (*Witch Hunt*); 1963: *Die Abrechnung* (*The Reckoning*); *Einsame Menschen* (*Lonely People*); *Stadtpark*; 1964: *Caesar und Cleopatra*; 1966: *Hafenpolizei*—Episode: *Taschendiebe*; *Der Fall Rouger*; *Das Missverständnis*.

Wolfgang Heinz

As Ship's Mate
Born on May 18, 1900, in Pilsen; died on October 30, 1984, in East Berlin/GDR
Silents: 1919: *Der Ritualmord* (*The Ritual Murder*); 1920: *Die entfesselte Menschheit* (*The Unleashed Mankind*); **1921–22: Nosferatu**.
Talkies: 1930: *Die zwölfte Stunde* (*The Twelfth Hour*, reissue of **Nosferatu**); 1932: *Ein blonder*

Traum (*A Blonde Dream*); 1954: *Der Komödiant von Wien* (*The Comedian from Vienna*); 1955: *Gasparone*; 1958: *Geschwader Fledermaus* (*The Bat Squadron*); 1959–63: *Das russische Wunder* (*The Russian Miracle*, second part only; narration); 1960–61: *Aktion J* (narration); *Professor Mamlock*; 1961–62: *Strimme der Wälder* (*Voice of the Woodlands*); 1966–72: *Der kleine Prinz* (*Little Prince*); 1970: *Ein Mann seltener Art: Aussagen über Hans Otto*; 1971–72: *Das goldene Ding* (*The Golden Thing*); 1973–74: *Der nackte Mann auf dem Sportplatz* (*The Naked Man on the Sports Field*); 1974: *Ich war, ich bin, ich werde sein* (*I was, I am, I will be*, narration); 1978: *Nun gut, wir wollen fechten* (*Alright, We Will Fence*); 1979: *Die Rache des Kapitäns Mitchell* (*The Revenge of Captain Mitchell*).

Albert Venohr

As Sailor
Born on September 4, 1902, in Magdeburg; died on June 22, 1979, in Berlin
Silents: 1918: *Carmen*; **1921–22: *Nosferatu***; 1927: *Gewitter über Gottland* (*Lightning Over Gottland*).
Talkies: 1930: *Die zwölfte Stunde* (*The Twelfth Hour*, reissue of ***Nosferatu***); 1935: *Das Mädchen Johanna* (*Joan of Arc*); 1936–37: *Menschen ohne Vaterland* (*Men Without a Fatherland*); 1937: *Die Warschauer Zitadelle* (*The Warsaw Citadel*); *Die gelbe Flagge* (*The Yellow Flag*); *Starke Herzen im Sturm* (*Strong Hearts in the Storm*); 1937–38: *Andalusische Nächte* (*Andalusian Nights*); *Das Geheimnis um Betty Bonn* (*The Mystery Surrounding Betty Bonn*); *Zwischen den Eltern* (*Between Parents*); 1938: *Du und ich* (*You and Me*); *Am seidenen Faden* (*Hanging Upon a Thread*); *Frauen für Golden Hill* (*Women for Golden Hill*); *Die fromme Lüge* (*The Devout Lie*); 1938–39: *Männer müssen so sein* (*Men Must Be That Way*); *Im Namen des Volkes* (*Autobanditen/In the Name of the People*); *Hochzeit mit Hindernissen* (*Wedding with Disadvantages*); 1939: *Paradies der Junggesellen* (*Paradise of Bachelors*); *Umwege zum Glück* (*The Way to Happiness*); *Irrtum des Herzens* (*Mistake of the Heart*); 1939–40: *Der Fuchs von Glenarvon* (*The Fox of Glenarvon*); *Fahrt ins Leben* (*Ride Into Life*); 1940: *Die guten Sieben* (*The Lucky Seven*); *Achtung! Feind hört mit* (*Attention! The Enemy Is Listening*); *Die drei Codonas* (*The Three Codonas*); *Das leichte Mädchen* (*The Easy Girl*); *Bismarck*; 1940–41: *Alarm*; *Mein Leben für Irland* (*My Life for Ireland*); 1941: *Das andere Ich* (*The Other Me*); 1946–47: *Kein Platz für Liebe* (*No Place for Love*); 1947–48: *Grube Morgenrot* (*Sunrise Mine*); 1948: *Affaire Blum* (*The Blum Affair*); 1948–49: *Die Brücke* (*The Bridge*); *Die Buntkarierten*; *Rotation*; 1949: *Sowjetische Zone* (*Soviet Zone*); *Und wenn's nur einer wär'* (*And even if it would be One*); *Der Kahn der fröhlichen Leute* (*The Barge of Cheerful People*); *Unser täglich Brot* (*Our Daily Bread*); 1949–50: *Bürgermeister Anna* (*Burgomaster Anna*); *Der Rat der Götter* (*The Council of Gods*); 1950: *Familie Benthin* (*Benthin Family*); *Saure Wochen—frohe Feste* (*Sore Weeks—Merry Feasts*); 1950–51: *Die Sonnenbrucks*; *Das Beil von Wandsbek* (*The Axe of Wandsbek*); 1950–52: *Strom ohne Grenzen*; 1951: *Modell Bianka* (*Model Bianca*); *Der Untertan* (*The Subject*); *Zugverkehr unregelmäßig* (*Railway Service Irregular*); 1951–52: *Karriere in Paris* (*Career in Paris*); *Das verurteilte Dorf* (*The Condemned Village*); *Sein grosser Sieg* (*His Great Victory*); 1952–53: *Die Unbesiegbaren* (*The Invincibles*); 1966–67: *The Bridge of Remagen*; 1968–69: *Todesschüsse am Broadway* (*Broadway's Deadly Gold/Dead Body on Broadway/Death Shots on Broadway*); 1969: *Pistolen-Jenny* (*Pistol Jenny*); 1978: *Die Faust in der Tasche* (*Fist in the Pocket*).
Dubbing director: *Rot und Schwarz*.
Television: 1964–65: *Der Fall Harry Domela* (*The Case of Harry Domela*); 1965: *Der Forellenhof*; 1966–67: *Ein Mann, der nichts gewinnt* (*A Man Who Doesn't Win*); 1967: *Bürgerkrieg in Russland* (*Civil War in Russia*, five parts); 1970: *Reisedienst Schwalbe*; *Tournee—Ein Ballett tanzt um die Welt*.

Gustav Botz

As Dr. Sievers, Wisborg Physician
According to the Internet Movie Database, he was born on August 4, 1883, in Bremen, and died on September 29, 1932, in Bremen
According to *Die Kinokritiker*: Born on August 4, 1883, died on September 29, 1932, in Berlin
Other sources such as Wikipedia and *filmportal.de*: Born on May 17, 1857, died on April 6, 1932, in Berlin-Charlottenburg
Silents: 1914: *Das Kriegslied der Rheinarmee* (*The War Song of the Rhine Army*); 1915: *Carlo und Carla*; 1916: *Die Entdeckung Deutschlands*

(*The Discovery of Germany*); *Das Leid der Liebe* (*The Grief of Love*); *Für den Ruhm des Geliebten* (*For the Glory of the Beloved*); *Gräfin de Castro* (*Countess de Castro*); *Der Schmuck der Herzogin* (*The Jewels of the Duchess*); 1917: *Das Wäschermädel Seiner Durchlaucht* (*The Washing Girl of His Highness*, short film); 1918: *Gänseliesel* (*Goose Girl Liesel*); *Durchlaucht Hypochonder* (*Serenity Hypochondriac*); *Der Liftjunge* (*The Lift Boy*); *Der Gezeichnete. Der Lautenspieler* (*The Marked One: The Lute Player*); *Der fremde Fürst*; *Der Teufel* (*The Devil*); 1918–19: *Ikarus, der fliegende Mensch* [*Der Adler von Flandern*] (*Icarus, the Flying Man*) [*The Eagle of Flandres*]; 1919: *Morphium* (short film); *Der Kampf um die Ehe—1. Teil: Wenn in der Ehe die Liebe stirbt, 2. Teil: Feindliche Gatten* (*Marital Quarrel 1st Part: When Love Ends in Marriage, 2nd Part: Hostile Spouses*); 1919: *Störtebeker*; *Irrwahn* (*Craze*); *Frau Hempels Tochter* (*Mrs. Hempel's Daughter*); 1919: *Der Flimmerprinz* (*The Flicker Prince*); *Das Geheimnis des Amerika-Docks* (*The Mystery of the America Dock*); 1920: *Monika Vogelsang*; *Der Kampf der Geschlechter* (*The Battle of Sexes*); *Maria Magdalene*; *Versiegelte Lippen* (*Sealed Lips*); *Der Januskopf* (*The Head of Janus*); *Katharine die Grosse* (*Catherine the Great*); *Der König von Paris—Die Geschichte des André Lifou* (*The King of Paris: The Story of André Lifou*, two parts): *Sizilianische Blutrache* (*Sicilian Vendetta*); *Mord … die Tragödie des Hauses Garrick* (*Murder … the Tragedy of the House of Garrick*); *Ede und Co.*; *Das Luxusweibchen* (*The Luxury Bitch*); 1921: *Der Mann ohne Namen* (*The Man Without Name*, seven-part serial); *Der Kurier von Lissabon* (*The Courier from Lisbon*); *Der Silberkönig* (*The Silver King*, four-part serial); *Der ewige Kampf* (*The Eternal Fight*); **1921–22: Nosferatu**; 1922: *Der brennende Acker* (*Burning Soil*); *Dr. Mabuse der Spieler* (*Dr. Mabuse the Gambler*); *Lola Montez, die Tänzerin des Königs* (*Lola Montez, the Dancer of the King*); *Wenn die Maske fällt* (*When the Mask Falls Off*); 1923: *Fridericus Rex—3: Sanssouci*; 1924: *Mein Leopold* (*My Leopold*).

Talkie: 1930: *Die zwölfte Stunde* (*The Twelfth Hour*, reissue of **Nosferatu**).

Karl Etlinger

(Not to be confused with Karl Ettlinger, writer and journalist.)

As teacher who visits Bulwer with his students

Born on October 16, 1897, in Vienna, died on May 5 (IMDb: May 8), 1946, in Berlin

Silents: 1914: *Die Bekehrung des Doktor Wundt* (*The Conversion of Dr. Wundt*); 1918: *Lenas noble Bekanntschaft* (*Lena's Noble Acquaintance*, short film); *Das Haus zum schwarzen Raben* (*The House to the Black Raven*); 1919: *Die Teufelskirche* (*The Devil's Church*); *Der Fall Popinoff* (*The Case Popinoff*, short film); *Das Hemd des Glücklichen* (*The Shirt of the Lucky*); *Karlchen wird elektrisch* (*Little Karl Gets Electrical*, short film); 1920: *Die Revolution in Krähwinkel* (*Revolution in Hick Town*, short film); *Opiumkur* (*Opium Cure*, short film); *Glanz und Elend der Kurtisanen* (*Glory and Misery of the Courtesans*); *Die rote Hexe* (*Red Witch*); 1920–21: *Die Bestie im Menschen* (*The Beast in Man*); 1921: *Die Abenteuer eines Ermordeten* (*The Adventures of a Murder Victim*, two parts); *Die Filme der Prinzessin Fantoche* (*The Films of Princess Fantoche*); *Der vergiftete Strom* (*The Poisoned Stream*); *Das Geheimnis der Santa Marie* (*The Mystery of Santa Maria*); *Der ewige Fluch* (*The Eternal Curse*); *Die Schauspielerin des Kaisers* (*The Actress of the Emperor*); *Der weisse Tod* (*The White Death*); *Das tapfere Schneiderlein* (*The Brave Little Tailor*); *Mensch—verpump deinen Frack nicht* (*Hey Man, Don't Lend Out Your Tailcoat*); **1921–22: Nosferatu**; 1922: *Das Logierhaus für Gentleman* (*The Guest House for Gentleman*); *Der böse Geist Lumpazivagabundus* (*The Evil Ghost*); *Die fünf Frankfurter* (*The Five Frankfurters*); *Phantom*; *Die Finsternis und ihr Eigentum* (*The Darkness and Its Assets*); 1924: *Soll und Haben* (*Debit and Credit*); *Gräfin Donelli* (*Countess Donelli*); 1925: *Der Mann um Mitternacht* (*The Man at Midnight*); *Die freudlose Gasse* (*The Joyless Street*); *Zigano, der Brigant vom Monte Diavolo* (*Zigano, the Brigand from Monte Diavolo*); *Das Mädchen mit der Protektion* (*The Girl with Patronage*); 1926: *Junges Blut* (*Young Blood*); *Die Abenteuer eines Zehnmarkscheines* (*Adventures of a Ten Mark Note*); *Man spielt nicht mit der Liebe* (*One Shouldn't Play with Love*); *Die lachende Grille* (*The Laughing Cricket*); *In der Heimat, da gibt's ein Wiedersehn!* (*We'll Meet Again in the Heimat*); 1927: *Das war in Heidelberg in blauer Sommernacht* (*It Happened in Heidelberg in Blue Summer Night*); *Die Frauengasse von Algier*; *Bigamie* (*Bigamy*); *Familientag im Hause Prellstein*; 1928: *Da hält die Welt den Atem an*; *Sensations-Prozess*; 1929: *That Murder in Berlin*; *Die Frau, nach der man* *sich sehnt* (*Three Loves*); *Der gefangene Kaiser* (*The Captured Emperor*); *Solang' noch untern Linden...*; *Katharina Knie*.

Talkies: 1930: *Liebeswalzer* (*Love Waltz*); *Zwei Herzen im Dreivierteltakt* (*Two Hearts in ¾ Time*); *Das lockende Ziel* (*The Alluring Goal/The Enticing Goal/The Golden Goal*/U.K.: *End of the Rainbow*); *Skandal um Eva* (*Scandal About Eva*); *Der König von Paris* (*The King of Paris*); *Olympia*; 1931: *Kismet*; *Die Maske fällt* (*The Mask Falls Off*); *Dämon des Meeres* (*Demon of the Sea*); *Der Stumme von Portici* (*The Mute Girl of Portici*); *Menschen hinter Gittern* (*Men Behind Bars*); *Bomben auf Monte Carlo* (*Bombs on Monte Carlo*); *Das Konzert* (*The Concert*); *Eine Nacht im Grandhotel* (*One Night at the Grand Hotel*); *Madame hat Ausgang* (*Madame Has a Pass*); *Die Fledermaus* (*The Bat*); 1932: *Fräulein—Falsch verbunden* (*Fräulein—I'm Sorry, You Got the Wrong Number*); *Wo wohne ich gut und billig* (short film); *Zum Goldenen Anker* (*To the Golden Anchor*); *Die Gräfin von Monte-Christo* (*The Countess of Monte Cristo*); *Melodie der Liebe* (*Melody of Love*); *Ein süsses Geheimnis* (*A Sweet Secret*); *Der Hexer* (*The Ringer*); *Das Millionentestament* (*The Million Testament*); *Wie kommen die Löcher in den Käse?* (short film); *Liebe in Uniform* (*Love in Uniform*); *Liebe auf den ersten Ton* (*Love at the First Sound*); 1934: *Kuddelmuddel* (short film); 1935: *Petersburger Nächte* (*Petersburg Nights*); *Wer wagt—gewinnt* (*Who Dares Wins*); *Varieté* (*Vaudeville*); 1935–36: *Traumulus*; 1936: *Savoy Hotel 217*; *Geheimnis eines alten Hauses* (*Secret of an Old House*); 1937: *Die gläserne Kugel* (*The Crystal Ball*); *Heiratsinstitut Ida & Co.* (*Wedding Institute Ida & Co.*); *Ein Volksfeind* (*An Enemy of the People*); 1938–39: *Hochzeit mit Hindernissen* (*Wedding with Disadvantages*); 1939: *Spassvögel* (*Funny Chaps*); *Frau am Steuer* (*Woman Driver*); *Irrtum des Herzens* (*Mistake of the Heart*); *Haydns letzter Besucher* (*Haydn's Last Visitor*); *Maria Ilona*; *Opernball* (*Opera Ball*); *Eine kleine Nachtmusik* (*A Little Night Music*); *Ein ganzer Kerl* (*A Man in Full*); *Meine Tante—deine Tante* (*My Aunt—Your Aunt*); 1940: *Leidenschaft* (*Passion*); *Polterabend* (*Eve-of-the-Wedding Party*); *Falstaff in Wien* (*Falstaff in Vienna*); *Ritorno*; *Traummusik* (*Dream Music*); *Herz—modern möbliert* (*Heart—Ready-Furnished Modern Style*); *Das leichte Mädchen* (*The Easy Girl*); *Der Kleinstadtpoet* (*The Smalltown Poet*); *Sommer, Sonne, Erika* (*Summer, Sun, Erika*); 1941: *Hochzeitsnacht* (*Wedding Night*); *Spähtrupp Hallgarten* (*Patrol Hallgarten*); *Hauptsache glücklich!* (*Happiness Is the Main Thing!*); *Der Weg ins Freie* (*The Way Out*); *Quax der Bruchpilot* (*Quax the Crash Pilot*); *Der Meineidbauer*; 1942: *Anuschka*; *Der Fall Rainer* (*The Case of Lieutenant Rainer*); *Die grosse Liebe* (*The Great Love*); *Meine Frau Teresa* (*My Wife Teresa*); *Diesel*; 1943: *Damals* (*At That Time*); *Karneval der Liebe* (*Carnival of Love*); *Der ewige Klang* (*The Eternal Sound*); *Romanze in Moll* (*Romance in a Minor Key*); *Gabriele Dambrone*; *Ein Mann mit Grundsätzen?* (*A Man with Principles?*); 1943–44: *Die Feuerzangenbowle* (*The Brandy Punch*); 1944: *Herr Sanders lebt gefährlich* (*Mister Sanders Lives Dangerously*); *Die Frau meiner Träume* (*The Woman of My Dreams*); *Philharmoniker* (*Philharmonics*); *Eine kleine Sommermelodie* (*A Little Summer Melody*); *Der verzauberte Tag* (*The Enchanted Day*); 1945: *Der Puppenspieler* (*The Puppeteer*); 1946: *Sag' die Wahrheit* (*Tell the Truth*); 1948: *Eine alltägliche Geschichte* (*An Everyday Story*); *Das kleine Hofkonzert* (*Palace Scandal*); 1949: *Der Posaunist* (*The Trombonist*); 1950: *Erzieherin gesucht* (*Governess Wanted*).

Heinrich Witte

Warden in Asylum
Born on January 8, 1888, in Berlin; died on September 10, 1933, in Berlin

Silents: 1921: *Der Richter von Zalamea* (*The Judge of Zalamea*); **1921–22: Nosferatu**; 1922: *Phantom*; *Liebes-List und-Lust* (*Love Ruse and Lust*); 1925: *Freies Volk* (*Free People*); 1927: *Maria Stuart* (two parts); *Die Geliebte auf dem Königsthron* (*Draga Maschin*; *The Concubine on the Royal Throne*).

Hardy von François

As Physician in Budapest Hospital
Born Bernhard Hermann on February 7, 1870 (according to IMDb, 1879), in Potsdam; died in 1956 in Berlin

Silents: 1921: *Der lebende Propeller* (*The Living Propeller*); *Das Geheimnis der sechs Spielkarten*, third part—*Treff As* (*The Secret of the Six Playing Cards*); **1921–22: Nosferatu**; 1922–24: *Die Nibelungen* (two parts).

Talkie: 1935: *Das Mädchen Johanna* (*Joan of Arc*).

Fanny Schreck

As Nurse in Budapest Hospital

Although Fanny Schreck is mentioned in most *Nosferatu* filmographies, Jens Geutebrück doubts that she played the part.

Born Franziska Ott on June 11 (IMDb: July 15), 1877, in Ulm; died on December 11, 1951, in Ulm-Söflingen

Occasionally credited as Fanny Schreck-Normann

Silents: 1921–22: *Nosferatu*; 1922: *Die Talfahrt des Severin Hoyey* (*The Downward Slide of Severin Hoyey*).

Talkies: 1931: *Die Koffer des Herrn O.F.* (*The Thirteen Trunks of Mr. O. F./Build and Marry*); 1935: *Das Mädchen Johanna* (*Joan of Arc*); *Das Mädchen vom Moorhof* (*The Girl of the Marsh Croft/The Girl from the Moors*); *Ehestreik* (*Matrimonial Strike*); 1936: *Der Jäger vom Fall* (*The Hunter of Fall*); 1937: *Die Nichte aus USA* (*The Granddaughter from the United States*, short film); 1939: *Sylvesternacht am Alexanderplatz* (*Night of New Year's Eve at Alexander Place*); *Die Stimme aus dem Äther* (*The Voice from the Ethers*); 1939–40: *Rote Mühle* (*Red Mill*); *Der Herr im Haus* (*A Man in the House*); *Eine Stunde* (*One Hour*, short film); 1942: *Der Seniorchef* (*The Senior Partner*); 1943: *Alles aus Liebe* (*All for Love*).

Guido Herzfeld

As innkeeper in Transylvania

Born on August 14, 1851, in Berlin; died on November 16, 1923, in Berlin

Silents: 1914: *Wollen Sie meine Tochter heiraten?* (*Do You Want to Marry My Daughter?*, short film); 1915: *Brüderherzen* (*Dear Brothers*); *Die Konservenbraut* (*The Canned Bride*); *Schlemihl. Ein Lebensbild*; *Die kinderlose Witwe* (*The Childless Widow*); *Die Abenteuer des Van Dola* (*The Adventures of Van Dola*); *Und wandern sollst du ruhelos...* (*And You Shall Wander Restlessly*); 1916: *Die Glücksschmiede* (*Luck Forge*); *Der Sekretär der Königin* (*The Queen's Secretary*); *Der Schirm mit dem Schwan* (*The Umbrella with the Swan*); *Schuhpalast Pinkus* (*Shoe Palace Pinkus*); *Theophrasius Paracelsus*; *Lehmanns Brautfahrt* (*Lehmann's Honeymoon Trip*); 1917: *Opfer der Leidenschaft* (*Victim of Fervor*); *Der standhafte Benjamin* (*The Steadfast Benjamin*); *Der Blusenkönig* (*The Blouse King*, short film); 1918: *Der Weg, der zur Verdammnis führt 1: Das Schicksal der Aenne Wolter* (*The Way That Leads to Condemnation 1st Part: The Fate of Aenne Wolter*); *Es werde Licht! Teil 3* (*Let There Be Light Part 3*); *Die seltsame Geschichte des Baron Torelli* (*The Strange Story of Baron Torelli*); *Europa postlagernd* (*Europe Poste Restante*); *Im Zeichen der Schuld* (*Under the Sign of Guilt*); *Der gelbe Schein* (*The Yellow Ticket*); *Der Teufel* (*The Devil*); 1919: *Du meine Himmelskönigin* (*You, My Queen of Heaven*); *Der junge Zar* (*The Young Czar*); *Das Gift im Weibe* (*The Poison in Woman*); *Die Sünderin* (*The Sinner*); *Nach dem Gesetz* (*By Law*); *Die Pflicht zu leben* (*The Task of Living*); *Der Weg, der zur Verdammnis führt 2: Hyänen der Lust* (*The Way that Leads to Condemnation 2nd Part: Hyenas of Lust*); *Arme Thea* (*Poor Thea*); *Die Arche* (*The Ark*); *Die letzten Menschen* (*The Last Men*, second part of *The Ark*); 1919–20: *Das Recht der freien Liebe* (*The Right to Free Love*); 1920: *Der gelbe Tod* (*The Yellow Death*, two parts); *Der Hirt von Maria Schnee* (*The Herdsman from Maria Snow*); *Der grosse Unbekannte* (*The Great Unknown*); *Der weisse Pfau* (*The White Peacock*); *Lebenshunger* (*Russalka, Hunger for Life*); *Whitechapel. Eine Kette von Perlen und Abenteuern* (*Whitechapel: A Necklace of Pearls and Adventures*); *Putschliesel*; *Bar el Manach*; *Der langsame Tod* (*The Slow Death*); *Der Sühne Sold* (*The Pay of Expiation*); 1921: *100 Millionen Volt* (*100 Million Volts*); *Exzellenz Unterrock* (*His Excellency, the Underskirt*); *Aus den Tiefen der Großstadt* (*From the Depths of the Big City*); *Der Friedhof der Lebenden* (*The Graveyard of the Living*); *Mann über Bord* (*Man Overboard*); *Die Geliebte Roswolskys* (*Roswolsky's Mistress*); *Arme Violetta* (*Poor Violet*); *Irrende Seelen* (*Wandering Souls*); *Kean*; **1921–22: *Nosferatu*;** *Das Blut* (*The Blood*); 1922: *Die fünf Frankfurter* (*The Five Frankfurters*); *Versunkene Welten* (*Sunken Worlds/Lost Worlds*); *Der bekannte Unbekannte* (*The Known Unknown*); *Tabea, stehe auf!* (*Tabea, Get Up!*); 1923: *Die Prinzessin Suwarin* (*Princess Suwarin*); *Tragödie der Liebe* (*Tragedy of Love*); *Bob und Mary* (*Bob and Mary*); *I.N.R.I.—Ein Film der Menschlichkeit*; 1924: *Die Finanzen des Grossherzogs* (*The Finances of the Grand Duke*).

Jozef Sárený

As Head Coachman
Nothing more is known about this Hungarian. He may have been a real coachman, hired for his skills with horses.

Loni Nest

As child on window in Wisborg
Although Loni Nest is mentioned in *Nosferatu* filmographies, Jens Geutebrück doesn't consider it likely that they brought a little child like Loni onto a location far from Berlin.
Born Eleonore Nest on August 4, 1915, in Berlin; died on October 2, 1990, in Nice, Alpes-Maritimes, France
Child actress. Played her first "film part" at the age of four weeks.
Silents: 1918: *Dida Ibsens Geschichte* (*The Story of Dida Ibsen*); 1919: *Harakiri*; 1919–20: *Der Golem wie er in die Welt kam* (*The Golem: How He Came Into the World*); 1920: *Kämpfende Gewalten oder Welt ohne Krieg* (*Battling Forces or, World Without War*); *Opium*; *Der Reigen—Ein Werdegang* (*The Merry-Go-Round*); *Patience*; *Seelen im Sumpf* (*Souls in the Swamp*); *Johannes Goth*; *Die Schuld der Lavinia Morland* (*The Guilt of Lavinia Morland*); 1920: *Das wandernde Bild* (*The Wandering Image*); 1921: *Schloss Vogelöd* (*The Haunted Castle*); *Ein Erpressertrick* (*A Blackmail Plot*); *Mann über Bord* (*Man Overboard*); *Sturmflut des Lebens* (*Storm Tide of Life*); *Die Perle des Orients* (*The Pearl of the Orient*); *Der Sträfling von Cayenne* (*The Prisoner from Cayenne*); *Violet*; *Pariserinnen* (*Parisiennes*); *Die Minderjährige—Zu jung furs Leben* (*The Underaged: Too Young for Life*); **1921–22: *Nosferatu***; *Der Frauenarzt* (*The Gynecologist*, two parts); 1922: *Allein im Urwald* (*Alone in the Jungle*); *Versunkene Welten* (*Sunken Worlds/Lost Worlds*); *Sterbende Völker* (*Dying Peoples*); *Tabea, steh auf!* (*Tabea, Get Up!*); 1923: *So sind die Männer* (*The Little Napoleon*); *Fräulein Raffke* (*Miss Money-Grubber*); *Tragödie der Liebe* (*Tragedy of Life*); *Die Gräfin von Paris* (*The Countess of Paris*); *Quarantäne* (*Quarantine*); *Schwarze Erde* (*Black Soil*); 1924: *Der Evangelimann* (*The Evangelist*); *Mutter und Kind* (*Mother and Child*); *Zwei Kinder* (*Two Kids*); 1925: *Aus der Jugendzeit klingt ein Lied* (*From the Youth Time a Song Sounds*); *Die Prinzessin und der Geiger* (*The Princess and the Violinist*); *Kinderfreuden* (short film); *Die freudlose Gasse* (*The Joyless Street*); *Liebesfeuer* (*Fire of Love*); 1928: *Der Sprung ins Glück* (*Jump into Luck*); *Die Heilige und ihr Narr* (*The Saint and Her Fool*).
Talkie: 1933: *Der Falschspieler* (*The Hustler/Les Amoureux*).

Eric Van Viele

Nobody had ever heard of him. Then a Wikipedia entry called him a *Nosferatu* bit player who "made numerous defamatory statements regarding the director, including calling the director a 'stupid know-nothing silly.'" The brief article seems to be a hoax.
Additional actors seen in new passage *Die zwölfte Stunde* (*The Twelfth Hour*):

Hans Behal

As the Priest in *Die Zwölfte Stunde*
Born on October 21, 1893 in Vienna; died in 1957 in Israel
Left Germany in 1933.
Talkies: 1929: *Männer ohne Beruf* (*Men Out of Job*); 1930: *Die zwölfte Stunde—Eine Nacht des Grauens* (*The Twelfth Hour*); 1931: *Schatten der Unterwelt* (*Ombres des bas fonds/Shadows of the Underworld*); *Nie wieder Liebe!* (*Love No More!*); *M*; 1932: *Wenn die Liebe Mode macht*; *Unheimliche Geschichten* (*Eerie Tales; Tales of Horror*); 1932–33: *Ich will Dich Liebe lehren* (*I Am Going to Teach You Love*); 1933: *Ganovenehre: Ein Film aus der Berliner Unterwelt* (*Crook's Honor*).

Eugen Rex

Bit part in *Die Zwölfte Stunde*
Born on July 8, 1884, in Berlin; died on February 21, 1943, in Spandau, Berlin
Silents: 1918: *Nixenzauber* (*Mermaid Magic*); *Ferdinand Lassalle*; *Der provisorische Ehemann* (*The Makeshift Husband*); *Dida Ibsens Geschichte* (*The Story of Dida Ibsen*); *Die Dame, die Probiermamsell und der Teufel* (*The Lady, the Waitress and the Devil*); 1919: *Ein sympathischer junger Mann* (*A Sympathetic Young Man*); *Die Reise um die Erde in 80 Tagen* (*The Journey Around the World in 80 Days*); *Homo sum*; *Die Frau im Käfig* (*The Woman in the Cage*); *Die gestohlene Seele* (*The Stolen Soul*); *Ut mine*

stromtid; *Der Tintenfischclub* (*The Squid Club*); *Luxuspflänzchen*; *Hannemann, ach Hannemann* (*Hannemann, oh Hannemann*); *Der Harlekin* (*The Harlequin*, also director); *Die lachende Konkurrenz* (*The Laughing Competition*, himself, documentary short); 1920: *Das einsame Wrack* (*The Lonely Wreck*); *Die Prinzessin vom Nil* (*The Princess from Nile*); *Der verbotene Weg* (*The Forbidden Way*); *Hoheit auf der Walze* (*Highness on the Road*); 1921: *Der Dummkopf* (*The Stupid*); *Susanne Stranzky*; *Das Gelübde* (*The Vow*); *Der Roman eines Dienstmädchens* (*The Story of a Maid*); *Der Schatten der Gaby Leed* (*The Shadow of Gaby Leed*); 1922: *Der brennende Acker* (*Burning Soil*); *Der Liebesroman des Cesare Ubaldi* (*The Love Story of Cesare Ubaldi*); 1923: *Der Seeteufel* (*The Sea Devil*, two parts); *Alt Heidelberg*; *Fridericus Rex* (Parts 3 and 4); *Tragödie der Liebe* (*Tragedy of Love*); *Die Gräfin von Paris* (*The Countess of Paris*); *Schatten—Eine nächtliche Halluzination* (*Warning Shadows*); *Der Puppenmacher von Kiang-Ning* (*The Puppet Maker of Kiang Ning*); *Vineta. Die versunkene Stadt* (*Vineta, the Sunken City*); *Die Magyarenfürstin* (*The Magyar Princess*); 1924: *Nanon*; *Die Todgeweihten* (*The Doomed*); *Der geheime Agent* (*The Secret Agent*); *Vitus Thavons Generalcoup/Der gestohlene Professor* (*Vitus Thavon's Big Coup/The Stolen Professor*); 1925: *Aufstieg der kleinen Lilian* (*Rise of Little Lilian*); *Sündenbabel* (*Sink of Iniquity*); *Die Puppe vom Lunapark* (*The Puppet from Luna Park*); *O alte Burschenherrlichkeit* (also writer-director); *Wenn Du eine Tante hast* (*If You Have an Aunt*); *Die Dame aus Berlin* (*The Lady from Berlin*); 1926: *Der Stolz der Kompagnie* (*The Pearl of the Regiment*); *Die Welt will belogen sein* (*The World Wants to Be Deceived*); 1927: *Die leichte Isabell*; *Die 3 Niemandskinder*; 1928: *Notschrei hinter Gittern* (*Outcry Behind Bars*); 1929: *Sündig und süss* (*Anny de Montparnasse, Sinful and Sweet/The Virgin from Paris*).

Talkies: 1930: *Die zwölfte Stunde—Eine Nacht des Grauens* (*The Twelfth Hour*); *Die Lindenwirtin*; *Die Csikosbaroness* (*The Csikos Baroness*); *Bockbierfest* (*Bock Beer Festival*); *Verklungene Träume* (*Dreams Faded Away*); *Besuch um Mitternacht: Das Nachtgespenst von Berlin* (*Visit at Midnight*, short film); 1931: *Der Weg nach Rio* (*The Way to Rio*); *Kasernenzauber* (*Barracks Magic*); *Kopfüber ins Glück* (*Head First Into Luck*); *Sonntag des Lebens* (*Sunday of Life*); *Der Liebesarzt* (*The Love Doctor*); *Tänzerinnen für Südamerika gesucht* (*Wanted: Dancing Girls for South America*); *In Wien hab' ich einmal ein Mädel geliebt* (*In Vienna I Once Loved a Girl*); *Schatten der Unterwelt* (*Ombres des bas fonds/ Shadows of the Underworld*); *Wenn die Soldaten...* (*When the Soldiers...*); *Zwischen Nacht und Morgen* (*Between Night and Morning*); *Kyritz—Pyritz*; *Der Herr Finanzdirektor* (*The Financial Manager*); *Der Kongress tanzt* (*The Congress Dances*); *Kabarett-Programm Nr. 2* (short film); *Schützenfest in Schilda/Shooting Match in Schilda*; *Der Herr Bürovorsteher* (*Chief of the Office*); *Der Hochtourist*; *Bobby geht los* (*Bobby Gets Going*); *Der Hauptmann von Köpenick* (*The Captain of Köpenick*); 1932: *Das Millionentestament* (*The Million Testament*); *Die elf Schill'schen Offiziere* (*The Eleven Schill Officers*); *Und wie kommen die Löcher in den Käse?* (short); *Liebe in Uniform* (*Love in Uniform*); *Spion im Savoy-Hotel* (*Spy at Savoy Hotel*); *Ich bei Tag und du bei Nacht* (*Me By Day and You By Night*); *An heiligen Wassern* (*Sacred Waters*); *Das Gespensterschiff* (*The Ghost Ship*); *Aufforderung zum Tanz* (*Invitation to the Dance*, short film); 1933: *Welle 4711* (short film–commercial); *Marion, das gehört sich nicht* (*Marion, That's Just Not Done*); *Ich und die Kaiserin* (*Me and the Empress*); *Die Blume von Hawaii* (*The Flower of Hawaii*); *Die Nacht im Forsthaus* (*The Night in the Forester's Lodge*); *Schüsse an der Grenze* (*Gunshots at the Border*); *Ein Unsichtbarer geht durch die Stadt* (*An Invisible Man Walks the City*); *Kleines Mädel—grosses Glück* (*Little Girl—Big Luck*); *Schwarzwaldmädel* (*Black Forest Girl*); *Die Wette* (*The Bet*, short film); *Der streitbare Herr Kickel* (*The Strident Mister Kickel*, short film); 1934: *Wenn ich König wär* (*If I Were King*); *Konjunkturritter* (*Opportunists*); *Freut Euch des Lebens* (*Enjoy the Life*); *Der Gedankenleser* (*The Mind Reader*, short film); *Selbst ist der Mann* (*Self Do, Self Have*, short film); *Ein schwerer Junge* (*A Bad Egg*, short film); 1935: *Nur nicht weich werden, Susanne!—Eine Groteske aus vergangener Zeit* (*Do Not Soften, Susanna*); *Der alte und der junge König* (*The Old and the Young King*); *Lärm um Weidemann* (*Noise About Weidemann*); *Was ist die Welt?* (narrator, documentary); *Wenn einer eine Reise tut* (short); *Das Einmaleins der Liebe* (*The 101 of Love*); *Die Frauen haben es leicht* (short); *Die selige Exzellenz* (*His Late Excellency*); 1936: *Mädchenräuber* (*Pat & Patachon als Mädchenräuber, Girlnappers*); *Die letzte Fahrt der*

Santa Margareta; Der geheimnisvolle Mister X (The Mysterious Mister X); Inkognito (Incognito); Wir gratulieren (short); *Tante Clementine (Aunt Clementine,* short film); *Klein, aber mein* (also writer, short); *Hans im Glück (Hans in Luck); Blinder Eifer (Zeal Without Knowledge,* short film); 1938: *Gute Reise, Herr Meier (Bon Voyage, Mister Meier,* short film); *Skandal um den Hahn (Scandal About the Cock); Stärker als die Liebe (Stronger Than Love); Menschen, Tiere, Sensationen (Panic in the Circus);* 1939: *Verdacht auf Ursula (Suspicion Against Ursula);* 1940: *Die Rothschilds;* 1942: *Der Hochtourist (The Summiteer);* 1943: *Maske in Blau (Mask in Blue); Fritze Bollmann wollte angeln (Fritz Bollmann Wanted to Go Fishing).*

As Director: 1919: *Der blasse Albert (Pale Albert).*

The *Nosferatu* Filmography

1921–22

Nosferatu—Eine Symphonie des Grauens

Production Company: Prana-Film G.mb.H., Berlin Moabit, Levetzowstrasse 15. (The company later occupied the offices of Filmverlag Bengen at Berlin SW 48, Ilsenhof, Friedrichstrasse 5–6.)
 Producers: Enrico Dieckmann, Albin Grau
 Director: Friedrich Wilhelm Murnau
 Screenplay: Freely adapted by Henrik Galeen (with F.W. Murnau's participation) from the novel *Dracula* by Bram Stoker
 First Cinematographer and Photographic Effects: Fritz Arno Wagner
 Second Cinematographer: Günther Krampf
 Scenic Design, Makeup, Costume Design, Insert and Intertitle Graphic Art: Albin Grau
 Nosferatu Makeup applied by Max Schreck
 Art Consultant: Walter Spies
 Casting Consultant. Paul Hans Rameau
 Musical Score: Dr. Hans Erdmann
 Cast: Max Schreck (Count Orlok, the Undead, Nosferatu), Alexander Granach (Knock, estate broker), Gustav von Wangenheim (Thomas Hutter, Knock's employee), Greta Schröder (Ellen Hutter, Thomas's wife), Georg Heinrich Schnell (Harding, ship owner and Hutter's friend), Ruth Landshoff (Ruth Harding, Harding's sister), John Gottowt (Prof. Bulwer, a Paracelsian), Gustav Botz (Dr. Sievers), Guido Herzfeld (Innkeeper in Transylvania), Max Nemetz (Captain of *Empusa*), Wolfgang Heinz (*Empusa* first mate), Albert Venohr (First sailor), Eric van Viele[1] (Second sailor), Hardy von François (Physician at Budapest hospital), Fanny Schreck[2] (Nurse at Budapest hospital), Karl Etlinger (Teacher), Heinrich Witte (Asylum guard), Jozef Sáreny (Head coachman), Loni Nest[3] (Child at window in Wisborg).
 Studio: Jofa, Johannisthaler Filmanstalt G.m.b.H., Berlin-Johannisthal, Treptow-Köpenick, Am Flughafen 6. Stage "A." *Studio Manager:* Engineer Hanns Otto.
 Locations: Wismar (Mecklenburg-Western Pomerania): Water Gate, court Holy Spirit Church, harbor; Lübeck: Salzspeicher (salt storehouses), Depenau, Aegidienhof; Lauenburg/-Elbe; Rostock; Westphalia region (North Rhine), Sylt; Heligoland; Carpathians: Arwaburg, Dolný Kubín; Koncistá in the Tatranská Polianka (High Tatras mountain range), the Granáty mountain range, Vrátna dolina ("Vrátna Valley") and Starý hrad ("Starhrad", both part of the Malá Patra mountain range, Northern Slovakia); Berlin: Tegeler Forst.
 Shooting: August until October 1921.
 35mm, black and white, tinted, silent, 1.33:1
 Sub-distributors: Excelsior-Film, Berlin SW 48, Friedrichstrasse 21 (for the territories East Germany, North Germany, Saxonia and Silesia); Süddeutsche Film-Gesellschaft, Karlsruhe i. Baden, Alderstrasse 30 (for the territories South

Count Orlok (Max Schreck) returns from the dead (from the stills collection of Deutsche Kinemathek–Museum für Film und Fernsehen, Berlin).

Germany, Rhineland and Westphalia). Contracts with these distributors were cancelled by Prana after awhile. Prana then would release the movie itself.
Length: 1967 meters. Five reels. *Running time:* 94 minutes.
Board of Censors: December 16, 1921. B 4960. Adults only.
Premiere: Marmorsaal (Marble Hall), Zoologischer Garten (Zoological Garden), Berlin, rented by the production company on March 4, 1922.
The picture was released on March 15, 1922, Berlin, Primus Palace.
In France, *Nosferatu le Vampire*: 1922, November 16–22, Paris, CinéOpéra.
French Distributor: Cosmograph. Length: 1900 meters.
On February 24, 1928, *Nosferatu le Vampire* was reissued by Ciné-latin in Paris.
In Austria: March 1923, Vienna, Gartenbau Cinema.
Special Screenings: In the Netherlands: December 10, 1927, Amsterdam, Centraal Theater, as fourth event of the Film League; in Great Britain: *Dracula*: December 16, 1928, London, New Gallery Kinema, 27th Program of the Film Society; in the United States, *Nosferatu the Vampire* (running time: 70 minutes): on May 18, 1929, and December 14, 1929, New York City, Film Guild Cinema (English intertitles by Benjamin de Casseres); in Spain: *Nosferatu—El Vampiro:* February 23, 1931, Barcelona, Avenida; November 23, 1931: Madrid, Cine de la Prensa.
Re-release 1964 (35mm, later 16mm format): Atlas Filmverleih GmbH, Duisburg and Düsseldorf. *New Musical Arrangements for Atlas Film Version:* Peter Schirmann, Berlin. *Series: Die Dämonische Leinwand (The Haunted Screen). Curated by* Erwin Leiser.
In GDR, DEFA Laboratories with the participation of Staatliches Filmarchiv (State Film Archive) released an 8mm home film version with original titles. This version was available as 120 m reel and in two parts (2 × 60 m: *Nos-*

feratu: Im Schloss der Vampire/In The Castle of the Vampires and Nosferatu: Ende des Vampirs/The Vampire's Death).

In the Federal Republic, Piccolo Film based its 120 meter Super 8 reel on the Atlas version.

Nosferatu was restored by Luciano Berritúa on behalf of Friedrich-Wilhelm-Murnau-Stiftung, Wiesbaden, in 2005–06. A 1922 tinted nitrate print with French intertitles from the Cinémathèque Française, Paris, was used as a basis for the restoration. Missing shots were completed by a safety print from 1939 from Bundesarchiv-Filmarchiv, Berlin/Koblenz, drawn from a Czech export print from the 1920s. Other shots were taken from a nitrate print of the 1930 version, distributed under the title *Die Zwölfte Stunde* (*The Twelfth Hour*), preserved at the Cinémathèque Française, Paris.

Most of the original intertitles and inserts are preserved in a safety print from 1962 by Bundesarchiv-Filmarchiv, Berlin-Koblenz, originating from a print from 1922. Missing intertitles and inserts were redesigned on the basis of the original typography by trickWilk (Thomas Wilk), Berlin. They are marked with F.W.M.S.

The lab work was carried out by L'Immagine Ritrovata, Bologna.

Digital Processing: OMNIMAGO GmbH, Ingelheim.

Hans Erdmann's original score was reconstructed and conducted by Berndt Heller, and was performed by Rundfunk Sinfonieorchester Saarbrücken. Score Production, Recording, Editing and Mixing (5.1 Surround): Klangbezirk, Andreas Radzuweit. Music Copyright-Publisher: Boosey & Hawkes Bote & Bock GmbH & Co. KG, 10787 Berlin-Tiergarten, Lützowufer 26.

Music Excerpts: Fantastisch-romantische Suite Teil 1 und Teil 2 by Hans Erdmann; Der Werwolf by T.R. Leuschner; De Profundis-Suite by Giuseppe Becce; Grande Fantasia from Un bello in Maschera (transcribed by Émile Tavan) by Giuseppe Verdi; Misterioso and Überleitung by Berndt Heller; Treachery and Vengeance by Percy E. Fletcher; Misterioso Fantastico by Giuseppe Becce; Galop (Le Bal) from Petite Suite pour orchestra after Jeu d'enfants (transcribed by Hubert Mouton) by Georges Bizet; Mefistofele (beginning of Act 3) by Arrigo Boito; Kinotheken No. 24, 36 and 51 by Giuseppe Becce; Sturm by Ernst Wiedermann.

World Sales: Transit Film GmbH, Munich. U.S. DVD release by Kino Video on November 20, 2007.

Running time: 94 minutes, 15 seconds, 1.31:1., 16 fps: 106 minutes.

Super 8 *Nosferatu* film reel released in East Germany by DEFA Laboratories (courtesy Anna Khan).

1930

Die Zwölfte Stunde. Eine Nacht des Grauens (The Twelfth Hour: A Night of Horror)

Production Co.: Deutsch-Film-Produktion (D.F.P.), Berlin SW 48, Friedrichstrasse 233.

Artistic Adaptation and Supervisor: Dr. Waldemar Ro[n]ger

Musical Score: Georg Fiebiger

Sound System: Organon G.m.b.H. (Polyphon Grammophon Concern.Trademark)

World Sales: Deutscher Tonfilm-Vertrieb G.m.b.H., Berlin

Cast: Max Schreck (Prince Wolkoff), Alexander Granach (Karsten, an estate broker), Gustav von Wangenheim (Kundberg, his employee), Greta Schröder (Margitta, his wife).

Additional Actors in new footage: Hans Behal (The Priest), Eugen Rex.

35mm, black and white.
Length: 1893 m, after cuts: 1799 m. Eight acts.
Board of Censors: November 14, 1930. B 27446. Adults only.
Screened: March 17–22, 1931, Berlin, Kamera Lichtspiele, Unter den Linden.
Note: Original *Nosferatu* version with added scenes, music and sound effects. Rumors that a version was produced but never screened that had some dialogue recorded with Max Schreck, Hans Behal, Eugen Rex, Ursula Urdang, Borwin Walth (who was in *Frau im Mond* and *M*) and Hilde Wörner are unconfirmed.

1932

Boo!

Carl Laemmle Presents "A Universal Brevity"
Production Company: Universal Pictures Corporation.
Copyright MCMXXXII by Universal Pictures Corporation—Carl Laemmle, President
  Supervision and Dialogue: Albert DeMond
  Editor: Lynn Harrison
  Sound System: Western Electric System
  Stock Music: Heinz Roemheld, James Dietrich
  Cast: Morton Lowry (Frightened man reading *Dracula*); Max Schreck, Gustav von Wangenheim, Albert Venohr, Wolfgang Heinz from *Nosferatu*; Mae Clarke, Boris Karloff, Edward Van Sloan from *Frankenstein*; Helen Twelvetrees, Lawrence Grant, Raymond Hackett, Elizabeth Patterson from *The Cat Creeps*.
  Running time: 10 minutes
  Released on December 1, 1932
  Distribution Company: Universal Pictures Corporation
Note: American comedy short about a man having nightmares. The nightmares, commented by a wisecracking narrator, consist of clips from *The Cat Creeps* with Helen Twelvetrees (apparently the only surviving footage from this film that is otherwise considered lost), *Frankenstein* with Boris Karloff and Mae Clarke. Although it was released by Universal, it opens not with scenes from the Lugosi *Dracula* but from Universal's archive print of *Nosferatu*, making a lot of fuss of Gustav von Wangenheim as a scared caretaker encountering the horror of Dracula. Albert DeMond (1901–1973) who compiled the show was the brother of Universal film editor Henry DeMond. He started writing titles for silents, then worked in short films before he became a scriptwriter for Republic Pictures. In the 1960s he was active in TV.

1978–79

Nosferatu: Phantom der Nacht/- Nosferatu, Fantôme de la Nuit (Nosferatu, the Vampyre)

Production Companies: A community production of Werner Herzog Filmproduktion, Munich; Gaumont S.A., Paris; Zweites Deutsches Fernsehen (ZDF), Mainz.
Producers: Werner Herzog, Daniel Toscan du Plantier
Presented by Michael Gruskoff
Executive Producer: Walter Saxer
Production Manager ČSSR: Rudolf Wolf
Director and Screenplay: Werner Herzog
Cinematographer: Jörg Schmidt-Reitwein
Second Camera: Michael Gast
Color by Eastmancolor. 35mm. 1.85 : 1. Mono.
Gaffer: Martin Gerbl
Lighting: Anton Urban
Still Photographer: Claude Chiarini
Production Designer: Henning von Gierke
Costume Designer: Gisela von Storch
Assistant Costume Designer: Ann Poppel
Makeup: Dominique Colladant
Nosferatu Makeup designed and applied by Reiko Kruk
Hair Stylist: Ludovic Paris
Assistant Director: Remmelt Remmelts
Czech Assistant Director: Mirko Tichacek
Script Girl: Anja Schmidt-Zähringer
Location Manager: Joschi Arpa
Special Effects: Cornelius Siegel
Consultant for Scenes involving Rats: Maarten 't Haart
Sound Mixer: Harald Maury
Sound Assistant: Jean Fontaine
Editor: Beate Mainka-Jellinghaus.
Music: Florian Fricke, Popol Vuh
Soundtrack Credits: "Rheingold" by Richard Wagner, performed by Wiener Philharmoniker, conducted by Sir Georg Solti; "Sanctus" by Charles Gounod, performed by Vokal-Ensemble

Gordela, conducted by Jean-Claude Hartemann; "Brothers of Darkness, Sons of Light": Written by Florian Fricke, performed by Popol Vuh, courtesy of Celestial Harmonies Records; "Die Nacht der Himmel": Written by Florian Fricke, performed by Popol Vuh; "Listen He Who Ventures": Written by Florian Fricke, performed by Popol Vuh; "Der Ruf der Rohrflöte": Written by Florian Fricke, performed by Popol Vuh; "Zinzkaro": Georgian folk music; performed by Vocal Ensemble Gordela

Cast: Klaus Kinski (Count Dracula), Isabelle Adjani (Lucy Harker), Bruno Ganz (Jonathan Harker), Roland Topor (Renfield), Walter Ladengast (Dr. Van Helsing), Dan van Husen (Warden), Jan Groth (Harbormaster), Lo van Hensbergen (Harbormaster's Assistant), Carsten Bodinus (Schrader), Martje Grohmann (Mina), Rijk de Gooyer (Town official), Clemens Scheitz (Clerk), John Leddy (Coachman), Margiet van Hartingsveld (Woman), Tim Beekman (Coffin-bearer), Jacques Dufilho (Captain), Michael Edols (Lord of the manor), Werner Herzog (Hand and Feet in Box with Rats), Attila Árpar (Violinist Boy), Beverly Walker (Nun), Stefan Husar, Norbert Losch, Johan te Slaa.

Shot in 1978

Locations: Delft, Zuid-Holland, Netherlands: town exteriors; Zuid-Holland; Oostvorne, Zuid-Holland: Beach. Schiedem, Zuid-Holland; Lübeck, Schleswig-Holstein, Germany: Salzspeicher (salt storehouses). Schleswig-Holstein; Guanajuato, Mexico: Museo de las Momias, opening credits footage of mummies; High Tatras, Slovakia: Carpathian Mountains; Tatra Mountains, Slovakia: Carpathian Mountains. Pernstejm, Czech Republic: Gypsy Camp; Pernsteijn Castle, Nedvedica pod Perstejne, Czech Republic: Castle Dracula; Nedvedica pod Perstejnem, Czech Republic; Telc, Czech Republic; Partnach-Klamm, Bavaria, Germany.

Studio: Bavaria Atelier, Munich Geiselgasteig.
Length: 2921 m. *Running time:* 107 minutes.
Running time U.S. theatrical version: 96 minutes.
Worldwide Distribution: Twentieth Century–Fox.
Distribution France: Gaumont S.A., Paris.
Germany FSK Freiwillige Selbstkontrolle der Filmwirtschaft: 16 years.
United Kingdom (original rating): AA.
United States certificate #25553: PG.

Released in France on January 17, 1979.
In Sweden, it was screened at the Göteborg Film Festival on February 10, 1979.
German Premiere: Berlin International Film Festival, February 25, 1970, Berlin West, Zoo Palace.
General Release in Germany: April 12, 1979 (Wiesbaden).
Released in Italy as *Nosferatu—Il Principe De La Notte* on February 15, 1979; Spain as *Nosferatu, Vampiro De La Noche* on April 14, 1979; Brazil as *Nosferatu—O Vampiro Da Noite*; Mexico on October 3, 1980, as *Nosferatu: El Vampiro*; Norway on March 2, 1979 as *Nosferatu—Nattens Vampyr*, Denmark on March 26, 1979, as *Nosferatu—Vampyren*.
In the United States, it was presented at New York Film Festival on October 1, 1979, and released in New York City on October 5, 1979.
Awards: Klaus Kinski—Deutscher Filmpreis (German Film Prize), Filmband in Gold
Production designer Henning von Gierke won a Silberner Bär (Silver Bear), International Film Festival Berlin 1979

1988

Nosferatu a Venezia (U.S. title: Vampire in Venice)

Production Company: Scena Film Production with the participation of Reteitalia S.p.A., Rome
Producer: Augusto Caminito
Executive Producer: Carlo Alberto Alfieri
Production Managers: Ennio Onorati, Angelo d'Antoni
Unit Managers: Giorgio Padoan, Silvano Zignani
Directors: Augusto Caminito, Mario Caiano
Crowd Scenes directed by Maurizio Lucidi
Original Contract Director: Pasquale Squitieri
Special Scenes directed by Klaus Kinski *and supervised by* Luigi Cozzi
Screenplay: Augusto Caminito
Preliminary Draft: Pasquale Squitieri
Story: Carlo Alberto Alfieri, Leandro Lucchetti
Director of Photography: Antonio (Tonino) Nardi
Camera Operator: Giovanni Ciarlo

Camera Assistants: Luca Alfieri, Vincenzo Carpineta
Lighting/Gaffer: Vittorio Pescetelli
Key Grip: Tarcisio Diamanti
Still Photographer: Enzo Falessi
Kodak. Color by Telecolor. 1,85:1.
Laboratory: Professional Photographic Service.
Art Directors: Joseph Teichner, Luca Antonucci
Prop Master: Claudio D'Achille
Costume Designer: Vera Cozzolino
Assistant Costumers: Francesca Carle, Raffaella Fantasia
Seamstress: Mina Tacconi
Jeweler: Nino Lembo
Stunt Coordinator: Ottaviano Dell'Acqua
Stunt Performer: Claudio Pacifico
Special Makeup Artists: Sergio Angeloni, Franco Corridoni, Luigi Rocchetti
Hair Stylists: Alberta Giuliani, Maurizio Lupi
Wigs: Rocchetti
Wig Maker: Carboni
Assistant Director and Second Unit: Andrea Prandstraller
Continuity: Annamaria Liguori
Production Office and Unit Publicist: Luigi Biamonte
Production Secretaries: Marco De Rossi, Marco Alfieri
Administration/Production Accountant: Francesco (Franco) Maia
Post-production Manager: Evandro Postorino
Sound Studio: Cinecittà S.p.A., Rome
Sound Mixing: Primiano Muratori
Boom Operator: Luciano Muratori
Re-recording Mixer: Fausto Ancillai
Sound Editor: Nick Alexander
Sound Effects: Cine Audio Effects, Fernando Caso, Alvaro Gramigna
Foley Recordist: Alvaro Gramigna
Sound Effects Editors: Fernando Caso, Edmondo Gentili, Claudio Gramigna
Editor: Claudio M. Cutry
Assistant Editors: Maria Elvira Castagnolo, Evandro Postorino
Dialogue Director: Alberto Marras
Original Score: Luigi Ceccarelli
Artem Publishing. S.r.l.
Music from album "Mask" by Vangelis
Titles: Penta Studio.

Cast: Klaus Kinski (Nosferatu the Vampire), Christopher Plummer (Prof. Paris Catalano), Donald Pleasence (Don Alvise), Barbara De Rossi (Helietta Canins), Yorgo Voyagis (Dr. Barneval), Anne Knecht (Maria Canins), Elvire Audray (Uta Barneval), Giuseppe Mannajuolo, Clara Colosimo (Medium), Maria Cumani Quasimodo (Princess), La Chuna (Woman at Gypsy Camp), Mickey Knox (Priest), Pat Starke (Helietta Canins [voice only]).
Distribution Company: Medusa Distribuzione, Via Aurelia, Rome.
German Distribution Company; Metropol Filmverleih, Munich.
Running time: 97 minutes.
Released in Germany as Nosferatu in Venedig *on September 1, 1988.*
Released in Japan on April 1, 1989, by Humax Pictures.
Italian Release: September 8, 1988.

1999–2000

Shadow of the Vampire

Working Title: Burned to Light
Presented by Saturn Film
Production Company: Long Shot Pictures in association with BBC Films, Luxembourg Film Fund and Pilgrim Films Ltd.
Producers: Nicholas Cage, Jeff Levine
Co-Producers: Jimmy de Brabant, Richard Johns
Associate Producers: Norman Golighty, Orian Williams
Executive Producer: Paul Brooks
Completion Guarantor: Michèle Grignon, James Shirras, David Wilder, Film Finances Inc.
Director: E(dmund) Elias Merhige
Screenplay: Steven Katz
Line Producer/Production Manager: Jean-Claude Schlim
Production Assistants: Nicola Altamura, David Baretti, Bob Feltgen, Kári Gylfason
Production Office Assistant: Ragna Ámy Lárusdottír
Production Secretary: Sophie Van Nest
Production Lawyer: Richard Moxon
Assistant Production Lawyer: Colleen Leader

Bookkeeper (Delux Productions): Claire P. N. Ducos
First Assistant Director: Edward Brett
First Assistant Director (first week): Lee Cleary
Second Assistant Director: Emilie Cherpitel
Third Assistant Director: Laurence Rexter-Baker
Trainie Third Assistant Director: Dominique Westaway
Script Supervisor/Continuity: Danuta Skarszweska.
Casting: Carl Proctor
Casting Assistant: Radica Jovicic (credited as Radica Vujicin)
Extra Casting Coordinator: Valérie Schiel
Casting Supervisor Luxembourg: Carrie O'Brien
Director of Photography: Lou Bogue
Camera Work: Mike Fox
Focus Puller: David Tondeur
Clapper Loader: Graham Johnston
Video Operator: Théodore (Theo) Theodorides
Director of Photography Pick-up Shots: Kenneth C. Dodds
Focus Puller Pick-up Shots: Richard Lawson
Focus Puller Second Camera: Richard Bevan
Focus Puller Second Unit: Jako Raybaut
Still Photographer: Jean-Paul Kieffer
Color. 2.35 : 1.
Equipment: Arri, Munich
Lighting/Gaffer: Glen Parsons
Generator Operator: Jack White
Key Grip: Bernard Brégier
Assistant Grips: Gérard Buffard, Pascal Delaunay, Marco Pierre Del Zotto
Additional Grip Helper: Laurent Wallerang
Grip Trainee: Carlos Ruiz
Electrician: Pierre Demience
Additional Electrician: Ernst Holtsch
Best Boy Electric Second Unit: Emmanuel Frideritzi
Electrician Pick-up Shots: Alan Ramsay
Assistant Electrician: Guillaume De Esteban
Additional Assistant Electricians: Jörg Fassl, Max Jacoby, Marco Decker
Camera Crane Supervisor: Hans Lehner
Advisor and Supplier Historical Camera Equipment: Helmut Ammon, Historical Cinematographical Museum.
Grader: John Health
Telecine Colorist: George Koran
Laboratory Liaison: David Trezise
Sales Contact: Neil Mockler
Production Designer: Assheton Gordon
Storyboard Artists: Shino Arihara, Alan Lane, W. D. Hogan
Art Director: Christopher (Chris) Bradley
Assistant Art Directors: Rosie Hardwick, Kirsten Garbade
Art Department Assistants: Colin Gilder, Christina Schaffer
Additional Art Department Assistant: Anthony Goulsbrough
Art Department Runner/Trainees: Annabelle Giorgetti, Fabrice Spelta
Assistant Carpenters: Claude Lambert, Pascale Smidt
Additional Carpenters: David Lambert, Claude Lickes, Matthieu André
Assistant Painters: Stephanie Blondel, Isabelle Brosius, Neil Hearfield, Laurent Schuster
Construction Manager: Nicholas de Maere
Construction Coordinator: Caryne Portevin
Construction Crew: Hughes de Maere, Thierry Gratien, Paddy Patterson, Marcel Barros
Construction Stand-by: Nicholas Wagner
Special Propmaker: Paul Biwer
Props Buyer: Jill Robertson Kibbey
Props Consultant-Buyer: Otfried Suppin
Dressing Props: Vincent Schilder, Tiffany Rodenfels, Dan Urbin
Dressing Prop Trainees: Oliver Möller, Özkan Arslan
Set Dresser: Véronique Souques
Trainee Set Decorators: Buchy Armand, Thiry Christophe
Scenic Painter: Edouard Pallardy
Graphic Design Assistant: Olivia Wood
Art Department Runner: Pat Berrend
Hair and Makeup Design: Ann Buchanan
Prosthetics Designer/Sculptor: Julian Murray
Prosthetics Maker/Special Makeup Design: Pauline Fowler
Prosthetics Applier: Amber Sibley
Prosthetics Assistant: Alexandra Stumm
Chief Mold Maker: Giacomo Iovino
Foam Technician: David Stoneman
Makeup–Hair Stylist: Leendert Van Nimwegen
Hair Stylist: Katja Reinert-Alexis
Additional Hair Stylist: Marliess Hupperts
Wigmaker (Mr. Malkovich): Peter Owen
Costumes Design: Caroline de Vivaise
Associate Costume Designer: Patricia Saalburg

Costume Tailor: Christopher Prins
Additional Costume Assistants: Isabelle Constantini, Stephanie Zawadzki
Wardrobe Assistants: Françoise Meyer, Aleksandra Valozic
Additional Daily Wardrobe: Christine Archer, Virginie Gutmann, Nicole Meyrat, Fa Zorgui
Laundry: Audrey Poisson, Nella Poisson
Special Effects Coordinator: Rick Wiessenhaan
Special Effects Assistants: Edward Wiessenhaan, Harry Wiessenhaan, Philippe Lebreton, Patrick Rappard
Location Manager: Claude Ludovicy
Location Assistants: Béatrice Pettovich, Frederic Roeser
Additional Location Assistants: Olivier Auclair, David Brudermann, Pascal Charlier, Richard Durand, Robert Grond, André Kamorovski, Harold Tembrink
Location Security: Abel Galiano, Ahmed Shouman, Gilles Soeder
Caretaker Studio: Jacqueline Hernandez
Caretaker Apartments: Audrey Poisson, Nella Poisson
Location Trainees: Sebastien Fernandes Tasch, Guillaume Huin
Location Cook: Diana Stiegler
Transportation Captain: Christophe Galeota
Unit Drivers: Nicola Altamura, David Baretti, Jeremy Kleinberg, Bob Feltgen, Kári Gylfason
Additional Drivers: Olivier Auclair, David Brudermann, Pascal Charlier, Robert Grond
Additional Driver Costume Department: Isabelle Constantini
Additional Unit Base Drivers: Réne Depienne, Manu Ventillard, Alphonse Weibel, Stephanie Zawadzki
Facility Driver (unit base stand-in): Jeff Edwards
Facility Driver (stand-by): Carlo Novak
Driver (Arri): Christian Kirchberger
Production Sound Recordist: Carlo Thoss
Boom Operator: Olivier Struye
Supervising Sound Editor: Nigel Heath
Assistant Sound Editor: Michael Fentum
Re-recording Mixers: Michael A. Carter, Anthony Cleal
Mix Recordist: Mark Sheffield
Foley Artists: Stan Fiferman, Diane Greaves, Ken Somerville, Jason Swanscott, Lionel Selwyn
Foley Recordist: Oliver Tharney
Foley Editor: Arthur Holland Graley
ADR Recordists: Leon Minas, Scott Jones
ADR Editor/Dialogue Editor: James Feltham
Sound Effects Editor: Julian Slater
SDDS Dolby Digital
Dolby Consultant: James Seddon
Post-Production Supervisor: Stephen Barker
Cine Image
Visual Effects Supervisors: Steven Boag, Martin Bullard, Charles Green
Digital Effects: John Goodinson
Main Title Typographer: Matthew Simonds
Editor: Chris Wyatt.
Associate Editor: Milfid (Milly) Ellis
Music: Dan Jones
Orchestration: Elizabeth Purnell
The BBC National Orchestra of Wales *Conductor:* Christopher Austin
Violinist Nicholas (Nick) Whiting
Music Mixer-Music Recordist: Martin Astle
Music Recording Assistant: Jon Trotter
Richard Wagner: "The Flying Dutchman Overture" courtesy of KPM Music Limited.
Richard Wagner: "Tristan und Isolde" courtesy of KPM Music Limited.
Main Title Design Illustrations: John Goodinson
Choreographer: Françoise Van Den Bruck
Assistant to Mr. Cage: Stephen Boures
Assistant to Mr. Malkovich: Patricia Eser
Assistant to Mr. Johns: Sharon Howat
Assistant to Mr. De Brabant: Patricia Kretschmer
Stand-in for Mr. Dafoe: Christophe Thiry
Stand-in for Mr. Malkovich: Robert Cross
Double for Mr. Kier: Thomas Kuhnen
Stand-in female: Laurence Bastien, Katina Valentina
Stand-in male: Laurence Benmakrelouf, Antonio Lima
Arm Model Pick-up Shots: Kevin Donnelly
Auditor Ivan Sopher & Co.: Liz Douglas
Pilot Albatros (plane): Jean Salis
Assistant Albatros: Daniel Koblet
Catering Supervisor: Teresa Finlay
Catering Assistants: Peta Foley, John Sanders
Catering Manager Studio: Carole Reding
Catering Chef Studio: Serge Franzen
Physicians: Dr. Adrien Kuntz, Dr. Luc Nguyen-Trong
Medical Stand-by: Carlo Novak
Unit Publicists DDA: Pete Daly, Dennis Davidson
Production Runner: Patrick Blocman

Production Trainee: Ryan Orme
Documentary Team: Reba Merrill, Jan Wlodariewicz, Warren Yeager
Animal Wrangler: Willy Loedts
Consultant on F. W. Murnau: Luciano Berriatúa
Cast: John Malkovich (Friedrich Wilhelm Murnau), Willem Dafoe (Max Schreck), Udo Kier (Albin Grau), Cary Elwes (Fritz Arno Wagner), Catherine McCormack (Greta Schröder), Eddie Izzard (Gustav von Wangenheim), Aden Gillett (Henrik Galeen), Nicholas Elliott (Paul), Ronan Vibert (Wolfgang Müller), Sophie Langevin (Elke), Myriam Müller (Maria), Milos Hlavac (Innkeeper), Marja-Lena Junker (Innkeeper's Wife), Derek Kueter (First Reporter), Norman Golighty (Second Reporter), Patrick Hastert (Third Reporter), Sascha Ley (Drunken Woman), Marie-Paule von Roesgen (Old Woman), Jean-Claude Croes, Christophe Chrompin, Graham Johnston, Orian Williams, Radica Jovicic (Members of Murnau's Crew), Ingeborga Dapkunaite (Micheline).
Archive Footage: Max Schreck (Count Orlok), Gustav von Wangenheim (Thomas Hutter).
Thanks: Jacob A. Bloom, Nancy Caldwell, Georges Calteux, Guy Daleiden, Joseph Drake, Claude Dufays, Rene Faser, Madame Frantzen, Morris Garner, Larry Greaves, Law Horwitz, Malcolm Howat, Margaret Howat, David Hutkin, Brent Jack, Christian Laboutin, Jonathan Levin, Randy Manis, Glen Meredith, Tom Ortenberg, Marie-Claude Poulin, Maurice Pujol, Jeff Sackman, Michael Schenkman, Monsieur Schub, Howard E. Smith, Art Stribley, Jean-Marie Thill, Mark Urman
Shooting: April 18, 1999–May 28, 1999
Locations: Vianden, Luxembourg: Castle interiors; Gehaansbierg, Dudelange, Luxembourg: plane and angry townfolk scene; Luxembourg.
Studio: Delux Productions, 8, rue de l'Etang, 5326 Contern, Luxembourg.
Running time: 92 minutes.
World Sales (2000–2003): Lions Gate Films.
Distribution France: Bac Films.
German Dubbing: Joachim Tennstedt (Friedrich Wilhelm Murnau), Randolf Kronberg (Max Schreck), Lutz Riedel (Albin Grau), Frank Schaff (Fritz Arno Wagner), Heike Schroetter (Greta Schröder), Jürg Löw (Henrik Galeen).
United States certificate #37595: R.
Released in Argentina as *La Sombra del Vampiro*; in Brazil as *A Sombra do Vampiro*; in China as *Xixuegui De Yingzi*; in France as *L'ombre du Vampire*; in Italy as *L'ombra del Vampiro*; in Mexico and Spain as *La Sombra del Vampiro*; in Turkey as *Vampirin Gölgesi*.
Festivals:
France, May 15, 2000, Cannes Film Festival.
June 2000, Avignon Film Festival.
Canada, September 10, 2000. Toronto International Film Festival.
Spain, October 2000, Sitges Film Festival.
USA, October 2000, Chicago International Film Festival. October 12, 2000, Austin Film Festival. Hawaii Film Festival, November 12, 2000.
Sweden, November 2000, Stockholm International Film Festival.
Argentina, 2001, March 10, Mar del Plata Film Festival.
Netherlands, April 6, 2001, Amsterdam Fantastic Film Festival. January 30, 2002.
International Film Festival Rotterdam.
Hungary, October 8, 2001, Titanic International Filmpresence Festival.
Iceland, November 9, 2001, Reykjavik Film Festival.
Poland, December 5, 2001: Camerimage Festival.
Philippines, February 13, 2003: Pelikula at Lipunan Film Festival.
Officially released in the United States on January 26, 2001, in the United Kingdom on February 2, 2001, in Italy on February 2, 2001, in Spain on March 2, 2001, in Germany on June 21, 2001, in Russia on July 26, 2001, in Hong Kong on August 2, 2001, in Japan on August 11, 2001, in Israel on November 8, 2001.
Awards:
C.I.C.A.E. Award nomination 2000, Cannes Film Festival, E. Elias Merhige, director.
Prix Tournage winner 2000, Avignon Film Festival, E. Elias Merhige, Director.
President Award winner 2000, Ft. Lauderdale International Film Festival, Willem Dafoe, Outstanding Creative Performance.
LACFA Award winner 2000, Los Angeles Film Critics Association Awards, Willem Dafoe, Best Supporting Actor.
NYFCC Award nomination 2000, New York Film Critics Circle Awards, Willem Dafoe, Best Supporting Actor.
Gran Angular Award winner 2000, Sitges—

Catalonian International Film Festival, Willem Dafoe, Best Actor—Special Mention: E. Elias Merhige.

Best Film nomination 2000, Sitges—Catalonian International Film Festival, E. Elias Merhige

Bronze Horse nomination 2000, Stockholm Film Festival, E. Elias Merhige, director.

SDFCS Award nominations 2000, San Diego Film Critics Society Award, Willem Dafoe (Best Supporting Actor), E. Elias Merhige (Best Director), Steven Katz (Best Original Screenplay).

Oscar nominations 2001, Willem Dafoe, Best Actor in Supporting Role. Ann Buchanan, Amber Sibley, Best Makeup.

Awards Circuit Community Awards nomination 2000, Willem Dafoe, Best Actor in a Supporting Role.

Golden Globes nomination 2001, Willem Dafoe, Best Performance by an Actor in a Supporting Role in a Motion Picture.

Screen Actors Guild Awards nomination, 2001, Willem Dafoe, Outstanding Performance by a Male Actor in a Supporting Role.

Saturn Award winner 2001, Academy of Science Fiction, Fantasy & Horror Films, Willem Dafoe, Best Supporting Role.

Special Award winner 2001, Academy of Science Fiction, Fantasy & Horror Films. For its behind-the-scenes take on director F.W. Murnau's classic vampire movie *Nosferatu, eine Symphonie des Grauens* (1922).

Saturn Award nomination 2001, Academy of Science Fiction, Fantasy & Horror Films, Caroline de Vivaise, Best Costume.

Saturn Award nomination 2001, Academy of Science Fiction, Fantasy & Horror Films, Ann Buchanan, Amber Sibley, Best Makeup.

Bram Stoker Award 2001 winner, Steven Katz, Screenplay.

CFCA Award nomination 2001, Chicago Critics Association Awards nomination Willem Dafoe, Best Supporting Actor.

DFWFCA nomination 2001, Dallas-Fort Worth Film Critics Association Awards Willem Dafoe, Best Supporting Actor.

Golden Frog nomination 2001, Camerimage, Lou Bogue, cinematographer.

International Fantasy Film Award winner 2001, Fantasporto, Willem Dafoe, Best Actor.

International Fantasy Film Award nomination 2001, Fantasporto, E. Elias Merhige, Best Film.

Independent Spirit Award winner 2001, Willem Dafoe, Best Supporting Male.

Independent Spirit Award nomination 2001, Lou Bogue, Best Cinematography.

IHG Award winner 2001, International Horror Guild, Best Movie.

Golden Reel Award nomination 2001, Motion Picture Sound Editors, USA, Nigel Heath, Julian Slater, Arthur Graley, James Feltham, Best Sound Editing—Foreign Feature.

NSFC Award nomination 2001, National Society of Film Critics Awards, USA, Willem Dafoe, Best Supporting Actor.

OFTA Film Award nomination 2001, Online Film & Television Association, Willem Dafoe, Best Supporting Actor.

OFTA Film Award nomination 2001, Online Film & Television Association, Best Titles Sequence.

OFTA Film Award winner 2001, Online Film & Television Association, Ann Buchanan, Pauline Fowler, Giacomo Iovino, Julian Murray, Leendert Van Nimwegen, Amber Sibley, Best Makeup and Hairstyling.

OFCS Award nomination 2001, Online Film Critics Society Awards, Willem Dafoe, Best Supporting Actor.

PFCS Award winner 2001, Phoenix Film Critics Awards, Willem Dafoe, Best Actor in a Supporting Role.

PFCS Award nomination 2001, Phoenix Film Critics Awards, Katja Reinert-Alexis, Best Makeup.

Golden Satellite Award winner 2001, Willem Dafoe, Best Performance by an Actor in a Supporting Role, Comedy or Musical.

Chlotrudis Award nomination 2002, Willem Dafoe, Best Supporting Actor.

Note: Here is a deeply bizarre black horror-comedy about the Nosferatu vampire legend, with preposterous performances from John Malkovich and Willem Dafoe which are as ripe as melting old slabs of Brie. Malkovich plays Friedrich Murnau, the great German film director and creator of the 1922 silent classic *Nosferatu, eine Symphonie des Grauens* (or *Nosferatu, A Symphony of Horror*, a pleasingly chilling subtitle sadly unmentioned in this film). Willem Dafoe is Max Schreck, the creepy, weird, bald, pallid man who played the vampire, and whose dedication to the role in this film seems to go horrifyingly beyond mere method acting.

Murnau is fastidious, demanding, cruel; he wears a white coat and goggles during filming, like a mad scientist. Malkovich's feathery voice is always threatening to snap down into his habitual basso profundo roar of rage; Dafoe is perpetually snuffling, growling, glibbering and leering like nothing so much as a rabid hamster.

The mad-visionary-director-plus-wildman-actor template is clearly inspired by the legendary relationship of Werner Herzog and Klaus Kinski, responsible for the 1979 *Nosferatu* remake. But the working dynamic between Malkovich and Dafoe is actually much more reminiscent of Gene Wilder and Marty Feldman in *Young Frankenstein*. When Dafoe suddenly grabs a bat out of the night air and crams it in his greedy gob, it's impossible not to imagine Marty munching away while Gene shrilly complains: "D-don't do that."[4]

2004

Nosferatu: The Friendly Vampire

Production Company: "Smart & Sexy!"—Films, Atlanta, *in conjunction with* GA State University.
Producer-Writer-Director-Storyboards-Makeup-Wardrobe-Editor: Karla Jean Davis
Cinematographer: Philip Gorbachov
Technical Support: Ryan Prows
Black and white. 1.33 : 1
Sound Editor: James Connelly
"The Golden Piano": *Composed by* Michael Paul (Mike) Walker
Cast: Justin Snavely (Nosferatu), Ryan Prows (German Expressionist Guy), Brian Mountain Man (Scene Kid #1), Maxine Rabren (Scene Kid #2), Travis Groo (Scene Kid #3), Chiquita (Banana).
Thanks: Jason & Eddie's Trick Shop; Oakland Cemetery; Wael Kamal; Bri Gordon & Family; F.W. Murnau; Max Shrek; Casper; Cesare, Crispin Glover, and the bassist from Interpol (all of whom may or may not be the same person).
Shooting: March 2004
Location: Atlanta, Georgia, USA
VHS: Troma Entertainment
Running time: ca. 5 minutes
Note: He may be "Lord of the Undead," but that doesn't mean poor Nosferatu has an easy time making friends. Student film.

2007

The Language of Shadows: Friedrich Wilhelm Murnau and His Films

Documentary on the Making of *Nosferatu*
A film by Luciano Berriatúa
Produced by Manuel Cerejo (tve)
In Association with Filmoteca Madrid
Voice of Albin Grau: David Howard
English edition produced by Bret Wood
Narrated by Brad Brooks
Wiesbaden: Friedrich Wilhelm Murnau Stiftung, 2007

2012

Nosferatu Over the Cuckoo's Nest

Directors-Animators: Joe Bichard, Chryso Haralambous, Rachel Lillie
Running time: 1 minute 19 seconds
Note: A UPA-style students' animation from Kingston University's Illustration Animation BA (Hons) course.

Nosferatu, a Symphony of Claymation

Running time: 26 seconds
Note: Amateur Claymation recreation of Murnau's final scene: Nosferatu puppet sucking Ellen's blood and vaporizing in the sunlight.

2013

Nosferatu

Note: Cut-out animated German *Nosferatu* short made by children in a workshop with narration in rhymes.

2014

Nosferatu vs. Father Pipecock & Sister Funk (Tony Watt's Secret Vampire Movie)

Working title: The Horny Wives of Nosferatu

Production and Distribution Companies: Slum Goddess Inc. and Tony Watt, Inc., Canada
Executive Producers: Vivita, Tony Watt
Director, Story and Screenplay: Tony "Tex" Watt
Co-Director: Vivita
Opening title sequence created by John Migliore
Cinematographer: Slurpy Goodwill [Tony Watts]
Color and black and white. "Watt-a-Rama"
Makeup Supervisors: Vivita, Tony Watt
Makeup: Tegan Ridge
Special Effects Supervisor: Elvis Parsley
Special Effects: Pepe Chingadero, Vivita
Art Director: Clarence Trigonometry [*sic*!]
Prop Makers: Tegan Ridge, Tony Watt
Editors: Vivita, Tony Watt
Cast in new footage: Vivita (Sister Funk), Trenchmouth Colitis [Tony Watt] (Father Dingus Q. Pipecock), Kelly Mari (Ariana, Bride of Orlock), John Migliore (Johnny Goulash), Sara Dagoda (Fräulein Wassermann, Mistress of Count Orlock), Sophia the Cat, Kim Sonderholm (narration).
Seen in footage from the 1922 movie: Max Schreck, Greta Schröder, Gustav von Wangenheim, Alexander Granach, John Gottowt, Georg Heinrich Schnell, Ruth Landshoff, Max Nemetz, Wolfgang Heinz, Albert Venohr, Guido Herzfeld, Fanny Schreck, Gustav Botz, Karl Etlinger, Loni Nest.
Running time: 134 minutes
Canadian Release: March 9, 2014.
Note: Incorporates the original footage of *Nosferatu* into a new movie.

Nosferatu in Love

British TV movie
Presented by Playhouse, *Season 3, Episode 2*
Production Company: Bonafide Films in association with Czech Anglo Productions
Producer: Margery Bone
Co-Producer: Denis Wray
Production Manager: Zuzana Mesticová
Writer-Director: Peter Straughan
Cinematography: Ole Bratt Birkeland
VT Operator: Will Akbar
Still Photographer: Dusan Martincek
Costume Design: Simona Rybáková
Costume Supervisor: Iveta Trmalova
Set Costumer: Jana Milerová
Prosthetic Makeup Designer: Jen Cardno
Special Effects Teeth: Chris Lyons
Stand-by Props: Karel Krejnik, Cloud Razali
Casting: Jina Jay, Maya Kvetny
Assistant Director: Geoff Dibben
Unit Manager: Klára Botliková
Location Manager: Kristyna Hanusova
Production Accountant: Lanny Nenicka
Post-Production Manager: Todd Kleparski
Post Production: Molinare Studio
Sound Mixer: Igor Pokorný
Boom Operator: Jan Blazek
ADR Mixer: Stefano Marchetti
Sound Effects Editor: Tony Gibson
Editor: Barney Pilling
Cast: Mark Strong (Actor playing Nosferatu), Petr Vanek (Fonso), Klára Issová (Luna), Thiana Valent (Dooriya), Zdenek Maryska (Director), Jakub Kohák (Ondrej), Vojta Vomacka (Noli), Adam Kyznar (Onas), Dagmar Spain (Woman in Bar), Damian Odess-Gillett (First AD), Tomás Lagierski (Prisoner), Martin Hub (Viktor), Bruce Davidson (Security Guard), Petr Nacovsky (Barman), Jakub Vindis (Runner), Daniel Peterka (Tough Boy), Christophe Gilland (Bike Sitter).
Filmed in the Czech Republic
World Sales: Sky Vision
Running time: 24 minutes
Episode aired on May 8, 2014.
Note: On location for a remake of *Nosferatu* in the Czech Republic, an actor has arguments with his wife. In a fit of rebellion, he runs away and meets pretty crook Fonso, who mistakes him for the lead singer of a heavy metal band, and releases the 12,000 rats which have been brought in for the film. They end up in prison with the actor's wife suing for divorce.

2015–2017

NYsferatu: A Symphony of a Century

Production Company: More Art
Director-Animator: Andrea Mastrovito
Original Score: Simone Giuliani.
Note: NYsferatu is a rotoscope recreation of Murnau's seminal vampire film. Each background scene has been entirely redrawn to set the film in present day New York City. Taking the first step in a three-year process, Italian-born

multimedia artist Andrea Mastrovito and a team of 12 colleagues drew each background three times to replicate the beautifully eerie flickering shutter process of early cinema. Her film questions the classical interpretation of the vampire, seen here as the prototypical outsider, while it addresses the countless obstacles encountered by immigrants who often escape war and hardships at home only to face challenges such as economic exploitation, discrimination and xenophobia in their new country.

2016–2018

Nosferatu

Production Company: BeamScreen Productions
Producers: Jenna Ceddici, Christopher Duddy, Paula Elins, Johnny Steverson, Derek Zemrak
Associate Producer: Mindy Zemrak
Executive Producer: Leonard Pirkle
Production Supervisor: Jane Stupp O'Neil
Production Assistants: Maria Carey-Walton, Melissa Cheng, Peter Horgan, Chris Hudson, Dan Shea
Director and VFX Supervisor: David Lee Fisher
Color
Cinematographer: Christopher Duddy
First Assistant Camera: David E. Thomas Jr.
Second Assistant Camera: Brian Austin, Alejandro Echevarria, Nate Garcia, Nicholas Piatnik
Digital Imaging Technician: Clifford Corigliano
Lighting/Gaffer: Jeff Billings
Key Grip: King J. Greenspon
Best Boy Grip: Richard J. Perez
Grips: Sean Emer, Pilar Troncoso
Electricians: Sebastian Johnson, Anderson Ko, Taylor Leach, Evan Ostrovsky, Tylor Rousseau, Eric Valencia-Hughes, Ted von Beyern
Casting: James Levine
First Assistant Director: Michael Thompson
Second Assistant Director: Thealonious Dickerson
Script Supervisors: Christopher Adam Hruby, Alyssa Lana, Jillian Terwedo
Script Supervisor: Dayplayer: Rhona Rubio
Production Designer: Calder Greenwood
Construction Coordinator: Donald Biggs
Art Department Production Assistants: Tony Denman, Blake Heron, Kota Hidaka, Ronnie Lovette, Ryan Martin, Patrick Nugent, Tessa Philbrick, Hakim Selby, Hill Vinot
Set Dresser: Stephanie Serra
Property Masters: Wixon Greenwood, Grahm Petersen
Costume Design: Lisa Anne Fullerton
Assistant Costume Designer: Danielle Schuck
Costume Department Head: Paula Elins
Makeup Department Head: Mo (Melissa) Meinhart
Special Makeup: Benjamin D. Ploughman
Key Makeup Artist: Erica Preus
Sound Mixers: Nick Campbell, Stacy Hill, Saif Parker
Boom Operator–Production Sound Mixer: David Cook
Editor: Clifford Corigliono, Jr.
Additional Editor: Marvin Nuecklaus
Social Media Coordinator: Denea Buckingham
Cast: Doug Jones (Count Orlok), Sarah Carter (Ellen), Joely Fisher (Ruth), Jack Turner (Wolfram), Time Winters (Prof. Sievers), Eddie Allen (Knock), Sarah Montez (Florica), Emrhys Cooper (Thomas Hutter), Corey Allen Kotler (Innkeeper), Cinda Adams (Nurse), Samuel Parker (Young Boy), Joseph Michael Harris (The Attendant), George Maguire (Bulwer), Rhoda Pell (Flower woman), Brian Hanford (Grunewald), David W. Ross (Sailor Two), Karen Teliha (Hilde), Drew Leger (Policeman), Travis Stevens (Policeman 2), Christian Prentice (Nik), Ron E. Dickinson (The Butcher), Greg Lawrence (Town Mayor).
Special thanks: Joy Costanza.
Note: The Vampire Lives. A young woman's quest to save her true love's soul, and the entire world from the shadow of infernal darkness. A digital remix of new performances with images from the 1922 film.

2018

Nosferatu's Secret Love Child!

Production Companies: Crabs You Can Eat Productions, Scranton Films

Producer-Director-Cinematographer-Editor: Luz Cabrales
Co-Directors: Felipe Arias, Tony Susi
Screenplay: Julian Santos
Co-Cinematographers: Felipe Arias, Michael Patti
Still Photographers: Autumn Granza, Theresa Wilusz
Art Director: Tony Susi
Makeup: Gina Calavano
Boom Operator: Felipe Arias
Location Manager: Teresa Muto

Cast: Lloyd Kaufman (Uncle Lloyd), Eric Wilusz (Nosferatu), Gina Calavano (Girl), Tyler Bruno (Man).
Thanks: John P. Brennan, Carissima Hodovanec, Troma Studios, Tony Susi
Location: Throop, Pennsylvania, USA
Black and white. 16 : 9 HD
Note: A short film within a longer movie, *Edgar and Annabel*: Uncle Lloyd shows a horror flick starring Nosferatu as he slurps blood from the neck of a woman.

Filmography II: The Silent Era of German Expressionist, Fantasy and Alchemical Films

The following list is far from complete. The bulk of silent film history is lost, as are many documents. We know of titles that sound like fantastical entries but maybe are not. Anyway, this is the most complete list of German fantasy, speculative and science fiction silent films so far. Not included in this list are fairy tales made for children's matinees.

1912–13

Der Andere (The Other)

Production Company: Deutsche Vitascope G.m.b.H., Berlin. *Producers*: Hermann Fellner, Jules Greenbaum. *Director:* Max Mack. *Screenplay*: Paul Lindau adapted from his play. *Cinematographer*: Hermann Böttger. *Conductor (Premiere)*: Capellmeister Altmann-Nemo.
Cast: Albert Bassermann (Dr. Hallers, attorney), Emmerich Hanus (Counsel Arnoldy), Nelly Ridon (Agnes, Arnoldy's sister), Hanni Weisse (Amalie, maid), Léon Resemann (Dickert, burglar, Hallers's accomplice), Otto Collot (Dr. Feldmann, Sanitätsrat/Medical Consultant), Willi Lengling (Weigert, detective superintendent), Paul Passarge (Kleinchen, Hallers's secretary).
Studio: Vitascope, Lindenstrasse 32–34, Berlin
Length: 1766 m. Five acts. *Running time*: 65 minutes.
Board of Censors: February 12, 1913. Adults only.

Premiere: January 31, 1913, Berlin, Mozartsaal Nollendorfplatz (preview: January 21, 1913)
Following a riding accident, Dr. Hallers develops a split personality and joins a criminal breaking into his own house.

1913

Der Student von Prag (The Student of Prague)

A romantic drama in four acts by Hanns Heinz Ewers. Staged by the Author.
Production Company: Deutsche Bioscop Gesellschaft m.b.H., Berlin. *Director*: Stellan Rye in cooperation with Paul Wegener. *Screenplay and Artistic Supervisor*: Hanns Heinz Ewers. Loosely based on *Faust* by Johann Wolfgang von Goethe, *"Peter Schlemihls wundersame Geschichte"* by Adelbert von Chamisso and *"William Wilson"* by Edgar Allan Poe. *Cinematographer and Photographic Effects:* Guido Seeber. *Scenic and Costume Designs*: Klaus Dietrich, Rochus Gliese. *Set

Decorator: Robert A. Dietrich. *Costumes:* Max Tilke. *Original Score:* Josef Weiss.

Cast: Paul Wegener (Balduin, a student), Lyda Salmonova (Lyduschka, a gypsy woman), Grete Berger (Countess Margit von Schwarzenberg), Lothar Körner (Count Schwarzenberg, her father), Fritz Weidemann (Baron Waldis-Schwarzenberg, her cousin und fiancé), John Gottowt (Scapinelli, an old adventurer).

Studio: Bioscop Glass House, Neubabelsberg
Locations: Prague (Prague Castle), Belvedere Castle, Palais Fürstenberg, Lobkoviczký palác.
Length: 1548 m. *Running time:* 85 minutes.
Board of Censors: August 26, 1913. Adults only.
Premiere: August 22, 1913, Mozartsaal Nollendorfplatz, Berlin
Reissue of the digitally restored version: Berlin International Film Festival, February 15, 2013, Volksbühne, Berlin

A student needs money to impress a countess he loves, and makes a bargain with the Devil. He sells his mirror-image to a Jewish profiteer and becomes a victim of his own self. The Jew is portrayed by John Gottowt, who played Bulwer the Paracelsian in *Nosferatu*.

Die Insel der Seligen (The Island of Bliss/The Island of the Blessed)

A buoyant film play in four acts by Arthur Kahane. Staged by Max Reinhardt
Production Company: Projektions-AG Union (PAGU), Berlin. *Producer:* Paul Davidson. *Director:* Max Reinhardt. *Screenplay:* Arthur Kahane. *Cinematographer*: Friedrich Weinmann (according to other sources: Karl Freund).

Cast: Wilhelm Diegelmann (The Indulgent/A Sea God), Willy Prager (The Fierce One/Triton, another Sea God), Gertrud Hackelberg (Cheer-

Paul Wegener in a dual role in *The Student of Prague* (author's collection/Deutsche Kinemathek–Museum für Film and Fernsehen, Berlin).

ful Girl, the daughter of the indulgent father), Lore Wagner (Shy Girl, the daughter of the fierce father), Werner Lotz (Audacious Lad), Ernst Hofmann (Bemused Lad), Friedrich Kühne (Grumpy Bachelor/Water Devil), Ernst Mátray (Scattered Bachelor/Faun), Greta Schröder (Psyche), Mary Dietrich (Galathea, Mistress of the Floods), Erila de Planque (Amor), Leopoldine Konstantin (Circe, the Nymph).

Locations: Marina di Massa near Carrara, Gulf of Spezia

Distribution Company: Projektions-AG »Union« (PAGU), Berlin

Length: 1888 m. *Running time:* 75 minutes.

Board of Censors: September 29, 1913

Premiere: October 3, 1913, Berlin, Union Palace

The ancient fantasy world of Greek gods on the Island of Happiness and Sensual Fulfilment is populated by nymphs and fauns. Two young bachelors go there with their girls. The girls' fathers follow them anxiously but Circe transforms them into pigs. Finally the mortals decide that it is better to leave the isle to the immortals. Greta Schröder of *Nosferatu* fame is seen as Psyche, the Greek goddess of the soul (and wife of Eros, the god of love). It is not true that Max Reinhardt had his actors appear nude in front of the camera. Nudity wouldn't have passed the Board of Censors in those days. Circe is played by Austrian actress Leopoldine Konstantin. Her last screen role was as Claude Rains's possessive mother in Alfred Hitchcock's *Notorious* in 1946. After that, she made guest appearances on forgotten American TV shows.

1913–14

Der andere Student von Prag (The Other Student of Prague)

Production Company: Deutsche Bioscop Gesellschaft m.b.H., Berlin. *Director:* Emil Albes. *Cinematographer:* Kurt Hasselmann.

Cast: Hugo Fink, Emil Albes.

Length: 340 m. *Running time:* 13 minutes.

Board of Censors: February 2, 1914

Premiere: April 3, 1914

A parody of Wegener's *Student* produced by the same film company. Between 1910 and his untimely death in 1923, Emil Albes, the son of an opera singer, starred in and directed numerous films.

Ein Sommernachtstraum in unserer Zeit (A Summernight Dream in Our Time)

Production Company: Deutsche Bioscop Gesellschaft m.b.H., Berlin. *Director:* Stellan Rye. *Screenplay and Artistic Supervisor:* Hanns Heinz Ewers. Based on the play by William Shakespeare. *Cinematographer:* Guido Seeber.

Cast: Grete Berger (Puck), Carl Clewing (Lysander), Jean Ducret, Anni Mewes, Ida Winter, Hanni and Otto Reinwald (Children).

Studio: Bioscop Glass House, Neubabelsberg

Board of Censors: October 23, 1913

Grete Berger, then married to Bioscop dramaturge Hanns Heinz Ewers, played Puck in her husband's modern-day adaptation of Shakespeare's play.

Die Augen des Ole Brandis (The Eyes of Ole Brandis)

Production Company: Deutsche Bioscop Gesellschaft m.b.H., Berlin. *Director:* Stellan Rye. *Screenplay and Artistic Supervisor:* Hanns Heinz Ewers. *Cinematographer:* Guido Seeber.

Cast: Alexander Moissi (Ole Brandis, painter), Grete Berger (Marga Hendrich), Lothar Körner (Coppilander, antiques dealer), Jean Ducret (Smirnoff), Eva Holländer (Ulla, an artist's model), Maria Carlotta (Lady Clara Vere de Vere), Emil Albes (Dr. Petersen, art historian).

Studio: Bioscop Glass House, Neubabelsberg

Length: 1412 m. *Running time:* 52 minutes.

Board of Censors: November 6, 1913

Trieste-born Alexander Moissi (1879–1935), one of Germany's most prominent stage actors, played the title character, a painter: Thanks to some mysterious gift of a crippled Jewish antiques dealer, he has the ability to recognize man's true nature. Hanns Heinz Ewers, who concocted the story, was not pleased with Moissi's play: "Moissi set his mind on doing pantomime; all my begging and pleading was useless—he was downright goofy."[1]

1914

Das Geheimnis der M-Strahlen (The Secret of the M Rays)

Production Company: Treumann-Larsen Film Vertriebs Gesellschaft m.b.H., Berlin SW 48, Friedrichstr. 16. *Producers:* Wanda Treumann, Viggo Larsen. *Director:* Viggo Larsen.

Cast: Wanda Treumann (Bella Mira, tightrope artist), Viggo Larsen (Dr. Ernst Buchmann, a scientist).

Three acts

Board of Censors: April 1914

Not to be confused with a movie of the same title made in 1923 by Hermann Grau.

Dr. Buchmann's special research topic is the secret of the M rays which have an enormous healing power, but after awhile the effect is deadly. Bella Mira, a tightrope artist he has fallen in love with, sacrifices herself in a self-experiment, a martyr of love and science. The shocked scientist commits suicide.

Erlkönigs Tochter (Erl-King's Daughter)

Production Company: Deutsche Bioscop Gesellschaft m.b.H., Berlin. *Writer-Director:* Stellan Rye. *Cinematographer:* Guido Seeber.

Cast: Grete Wiesenthal (Erl-King's Daughter), Carl Ebert (Baron Paul Bille), Grete Berger (Countesse Ebba), Siddie Sinnen.

Studio: Bioscop Glass House, Neubabelsberg

Length: 845 m. *Running time:* 46 minutes. Three acts.

Board of Censors: June 18, 1914

A dancing fantasy: A young nobleman is possessed by a fay, who finally destroys him. Based on a legend published in a collection of *Volkslieder* (folk songs) edited by Johann Gottfried Herder in 1778–79. Grete Wiesenthal (1885–1970), who danced the part of the elf, was a member of the corps de ballet of the Hofoper in Vienna.

Ein seltsamer Fall (A Strange Case)

Production Company: Vitascope G.m.b.H. merged with Projektions-AG Union (PAGU), Berlin. *Producers:* Paul Davidson, Jules Greenbaum. *Director:* Max Mack. *Screenplay:* Richard Oswald. Based on the novel *The Strange Case of Dr. Jekyll and Mr. Hyde* (1886) by Robert Louis Stevenson.

Board of Censors: November 1914

Premiere: December 6, 1914

An early screen adaptation of *Dr. Jekyll and Mr. Hyde*.

1914–15

Der Golem (The Golem/Monster of Fate)

Production Company: Deutsche Bioscop Gesellschaft m.b.H., Berlin. *Directors and Screenplay:* Paul Wegener, Henrik Galeen. *Cinematographer:* Guido Seeber. *Golem Mask from a sculpt by* Rudolf Belling. *Set Decorator:* Rochus Gliese.

Cast: Paul Wegener (The Golem), Lyda Salmonova (Jessica), Henrik Galeen (Junk dealer), Carl Ebert (The Count), Rudolf Blümner (A Starving Scholar), Jabob Tiedtke. (According to other sources, the count was portrayed by Henrik Galeen.)

Studio: Bioscop Glass House, Neubabelsberg

Location: Hildesheim

Length: 1250 m. *Running time:* 60 minutes. Five acts.

Board of Censors: December 22, 1914. Adults only.

Premiere: January 15, 1915, Berlin, U.T. Cinema Kurfürstendamm

The Golem is revived in modern-day Prague and starts a new rampage.

Seven years after making this movie, Wegener's partner (and Hanns Heinz Ewers's former assistant) Henrik Galeen wrote the script for *Nosferatu*.

1915

Und wandern sollst Du ruhelos... (And You Shall Wander Restlessly...)

Working title: Die schöne Sünderin (The Lovely Sinner)

Production Company: Lothar Stark Film, Berlin. *Producer, Director and Screenplay:* Richard Oswald. *Cinematographer:* Carl Hoffmann.
Cast: Tatjana Irrah (The Unfaithful Wife of the Knight), Erich Kaiser-Titz (The Junker/Nobleman?), Guido Herzfeld (Jester, Junk dealer, Scholar, Landlord, Pharmacist), Lupu Pick (The Count's antiques collector), Emil Lind (The Knight?), Käte Oswald.
Running time: 62 minutes. Three acts.
Board of Censors: September 1915
Premiere: September 29, 1915, Berlin, Tauentzien Varieté
Special Screening: November 19, 1915, Berlin, Admiralstheater
The appearance of a female ghost, wife of a medieval knight, is part of a curse that has to be broken.

Die Toten erwachen (The Dead Awake)

Production Company: Stuart Webbs Film Company Reicher and Reicher, Berlin. *Producer:* Ernst Reicher. *Director:* Adolf Gärtner. *Cinematographer:* Max Fassbender.
Cast: Ernst Reicher (Stuart Webbs), Stefanie Hantsch, Hans Stock, Fritz Richard, Arthur Ullmann.
Studio: Stuart Webbs Film-Atelier, Berlin-Weissensee, Franz-Josef-Strasse 9. *Location:* Bad Saarow-Peskow.
Length: 1342 m. *Running time:* 73 minutes. Four acts.
Board of Censors: October 9, 1915
Premiere: October 1915, Berlin, Marmorhaus
An episode of the Stuart Webbs series (a poor man's Sherlock Holmes) initiated by Ernst Reicher (1885–1936). Reicher was the half-brother of Frank Reicher, who made a career as supporting actor in Hollywood and played Capt. Englehorn in the original *King Kong*.

Der Vampyr des Schlosses (The Vampire of the Castle)

Production Company: DMB Deutsche Mutoskop und Biograph G.m.b.H., Berlin.
Board of Censors: November 1915.
Nothing is known about this lost film, not even if it's a real vampire movie.

1915–16

Die grosse Wette (The Great Bet, aka The Electro Man: A Fantastic Adventure of the Year 2000)

Production Company: Bayerische Film Vertriebs G.m.b.H. Fett & Wiesel. *Producers:* Isidor Fett, Karl Wiesel. *Director and Screenplay:* Harry Piel. *Musical Director (Premiere):* Siegbert Goldschmidt.
Cast: Ludwig Trautmann (George Fogg), Victor [Viktor] Janson (Ardan, his friend), Mizzi Wirth (Lee Kennedy), Harry Piel (The Electro Man), Adolf Suchanek, Rudolf Hilberg.
Running time: 61 minutes
Board of Censors: December 1915
Premiere: January 11, 1916, or February 12, 1916, Berlin, Marmorhaus
The first robot of the German film was created by Harry Piel, a director and stunt actor, Germany's proverbial "man without nerves." Piel was quite interested in animal and action films as well as pulp stories and futuristic novels. He knew the works of Jules Verne and H.G. Wells (one of his early sound films, 1933's *Ein Unsichtbarer geht durch die Stadt*, was inspired by Wells's *The Invisible Man*). And of course he knew the German writers working in this field, foremost Robert Kraft (who died in 1916) and Hans Dominik (1872–1945).

Hubert August (Harry) Piel, the German Douglas Fairbanks, was born on July 12, 1892, in Düsseldorf. After finishing secondary school, he enlisted for seven years as a cadet on the sailing ship *Grossherzogin Elisabeth*, and at the age of 19 he went to Paris to become a stunt pilot. There he met film director Léonce Perret, who arranged for him to work at Gaumont. Piel wrote his first script, and the idea of embarking on a future career in films captivated him. In 1912, on his return to Germany, he founded his own company, the Art Film Publishing House [Kunst-Film Verlags-Gesellschaft]. *Schwarzes Blut* (*Black Blood*) was the film that started his career as "Dynamite Director." Exploding bridges and houses became Piel's trademark. These explosions were often real, since he was friendly with a demolition expert who let him know when buildings were about to be blown up. Although Piel's first movie was a success, his company went bankrupt. But Piel had tasted blood and made movie after movie.

In 1933, he joined the NSDAP and became a patron member of the SS. Following World War II he was sentenced to six months in prison and prohibited from working until 1949. Eventually he gave up his company and quit the movie business. Harry Piel died on March 27, 1963, in Munich.

Hoffmanns Erzählungen (The Tales of Hoffmann)

Production Company: Lothar Stark Film, Berlin. *Producer-Director:* Richard Oswald. *Screenplay:* Fritz Friedmann-Frederich, Richard Oswald based on *The Tales of Hoffmann*, opéra fantastique by Jacques Offenbach and the life story of E.T.A. Hoffmann. *Cinematographer:* Ernst Krohn. *Art Director:* Manfred Noa. *Artifacts and Interior Decoration:* Hohenzollern Kunstgewerbe

Cast: Erich Kaiser-Titz (E.T.A. Hoffmann), Kurt Wolowsky [Kurt von Wolowski], *Lessing Theater* (Young Hoffmann), Max Ruhbeck, *Kleines Theater* (Hoffmann's Uncle), Paula Ronay, *Deutsches Theater* (Hoffmann's Aunt), Werner Krauss, *Deutsches Theater* (Count Dapertutto), Friedrich Kühne (Coppelius), Lupu Pick, *Kleines Theater* (Spalanzani, conservator), Alice Scheel-Hechy (Olympia, the mechanical puppet), Thea Sandten (Giulietta), Louis Neher, *Komödienhaus* (Schlemihl), Ernst Ludwig, *Kleines Theater* (Crespel, councilor), Nelly Ridon (Angela Crespel, his wife), Ressel Orla (Antonia, Crespel's daughter), Ruth Oswald (Little Antonia), Andreas von Horn (Dr. Mirakel), Ferdinand Bonn, *Deutsches Theater* (Lindorf, city councilor), Käthe Oswald (Stella, an actress), Richard Oswald (Man at the gravesite of German poet Friedrich Schiller).

Shot in February 1916
Length: 1585 m. *Running time:* 67 minutes. Three acts.
Board of Censors: February 1916. Adults only.
Premiere: February 25, 1916, Berlin, Marmorhaus
Reissue: May 26, 1921, Berlin, Richard Oswald Cinema

Episodes from the life story of Ernst Theodor Wilhelm (later changed to Amadeus) Hoffmann (1776–1822): E.T.A. Hoffmann, a true representative of Dark Romanticism, was Germany's premier creator of spooky Gothic, supernatural and fantastical stories that gave him the nickname Ghosts-Hoffmann and inspired Jacques Offenbach's operetta *The Tales of Hoffmann*. Hoffmann was born in Königsberg, Prussia, today Kaliningrad. Following the family tradition, he became a lawyer but was more interested in music, literature and the arts and started a new career as music critic and author. One might call him a European predecessor of Edgar Allan Poe. He died on June 25, 1822, in Berlin.

Das Phantom der Oper (The Phantom of the Opera)

Production Company: Greenbaum Film G.m.b.H., Berlin. *Producer:* Jules Greenbaum. *Director:* Ernst Mátray. *Screenplay:* Greta Schröder, based on the novel *Le Fantôme de l'Opéra* by Gaston Leroux. *Cinematographer:* Mutz Greenbaum.

Cast: Aud Egede-Nissen (Christine Daaé), Nils Chrisander (Erik the Phantom), Ernst Mátray.
Board of Censors: March 1916

The first film version of Gaston Leroux's novel was written by Greta Schröder (later to star as Ellen in *Nosferatu*), ten years before Universal produced it in Hollywood with Lon Chaney in the title role. Swedish actor Nils Olaf Chrisander played Erik opposite Norwegian actress Aud Egede-Nissen.

Die Wunderlampe des Hradschin (The Magic Lamp of the Prague Castle)

Production Company: Deutsche Bioscop Gesellschaft m.b.H., Berlin *Director:* Walter Schmidthässler. *Screenplay:* Robert Reinert.

Cast: Emil Albes (Nathan, an old Jew), Miss Roscher (Rahel, Nathan's daughter), Joseph Klein (The Nobleman), Arthur Bergen (The Rabbi), Vera Häberlin.

Distribution Company: Deutsche Bioscop Gesellschaft m.b.H., Berlin
Length: 1428 m. *Running time:* 53 minutes.
Premiere: June 10, 1916, Berlin, Tauentzien Palace

The plot combines the Arabian Nights fable of Aladdin's Magic Lamp with the Jewish mysticism of Old Prague

1916

Dr. Satansohn A Fantastic Play

Production Company: Projektions-AG »Union« (PAGU), Berlin. *Producer:* Paul Davidson. *Director and Screenplay:* Edmund Edel. *Cinematographer:* Ernst Krohn.
Cast: Ernst Lubitsch (Dr. Satansohn), Hans Felix (Prof. Waldow), Yo Larte (Meta Waldow, his wife), Marga Köhler (Ilona Werner, her mother), Erich Schönfelder (Nepomuk).
Studio: Union Film Studio, Berlin-Tempelhof
Running time: 44 minutes. Three acts.
Board of Censors: March 1916. Adults only.
Premiere: June 19, 1916, Vienna, Filmhaus Polo
Ernst Lubitsch stars as the Devil who operates a beauty parlor. At the end, all is a dream.

Das lebende Rätsel (The Living Enigma)

Production Company: Bayerische Film Vetriebs G.m.b.H. Fett & Wiesel. *Producers:* Isidor Fett, Karl Wiesel. *Writer-Director:* Harry Piel.
Cast: Ludwig Trautmann (Olaf Peer), Hermann Vallentin (Prof. Mikett), Leontine Kühnberg (Melya, Mikett's daughter), Julius Markow, Victor [Viktor] Janson.
Original length: 1400 m. *Length of released version:* 1129 m. Four acts.
Board of Censors: July 1916. Adults only.
In H.G. Wells's novel *When The Sleeper Wakes* (1899), the protagonist sleeps for 203 years. Harry Piel is content with 100 years. Prof. Mikett is able to revive Olaf Peer, a millionaire, after a hundred years of deep sleep. Peer is not only staggered by the progress but also falls in love with Mikett's daughter. Marston, Mikett's assistant, gets jealous and kills Peer with deadly Mars Rays developed by the professor.

Homunculus

Production Company: Deutsche Bioscop Gesellschaft m.b.H., Berlin. *Producer:* Hanns Lippmann. *Director:* Otto Rippert. *Screenplay:* Robert Reinert, based on his novel. *Cinematographer:* Carl Hoffmann. *Art Director:* Robert A. Dietrich. *Musical Score:* Siegbert Goldschmidt.
Cast: Olaf Fønss (Richard Ortmann, the Homunculus), Ernst Ludwig (Prof. Ortmann), Albert Paul (Dr. Hansen), Lore Rückert (Margarete Hansen, his daughter), Max Ruhbeck (General Procurator Steffens), Lia Borré (Daughter of General Procurator Steffens), Friedrich Kühne (Famulus Edgar Rodin), Theodor Loos (Sven Fredland), Mechthildis Thein (Margot), Thea Sandten (Magda), Ernst Benzinger (Prince Delasagra), Margarete Ferida (The Princess), Mely Lagarst (Stepdaughter Eleonore), Einar Bruun (Eleonore's fiancé), Erna Thiele (Anna), Walter Wolffgram (The Baron), Gustav von Wangenheim (Heinrich), Ilse Lersen (Luise), Hedwig Wiese (Luise's mother), Maria Immhofen (Maria), Fritz Steidel (Rudolf), Aud Egede-Nissen, Maria Carmi, Josef Bunzl, Lupu Pick, Robert Reinert, Jr.
Studio: Bioscop Glass House, Neubabelsberg
Shooting began in May 1916
Distribution Company: Deutsche Bioscop Gesellschaft m.b.H., Berlin
Complete Length: 9163 m. *Complete running time:* 360 minutes.
Part 1 Board of Censors: June 22, 1916. Adults only.
Part 2 Board of Censors: September 1916. Adults only.
Part 3 Board of Censors: October 1916. Adults only.
Part 4 Board of Censors: November 1916. Adults only.
Part 5 Board of Censors: November 1916. Adults only.
Part 6 Board of Censors: January 1917. Adults only.
Part 1 Premiere: August 18, 1916, Berlin, Marmorhaus
Part 2 Premiere: October 13, 1916, Düsseldorf, Residenz
Part 3 Premiere: October 27, 1916, Hamburg, Lessing Theater
Part 4 Premiere: December 1, 1916, Berlin, Marmorhaus
Part 5 Premiere: December 1, 1916, Hamburg, Lessing Theater
Part 6 Premiere: January 1917, Berlin, Marmorhaus

A six-part science fiction serial with a Homunculus, an artificially created human being, who is going to avenge himself on mankind: elements of Mary W. Shelley's *Frankenstein* story in a modern-day setting. Episode titles: 1. The Birth of Homunculus; 2. The Mysterious Book; 3. The Love Tragedy of Homunculus; 4. The Revenge of Homunculus; 5. The Extermination of Mankind; 6. The End of Homunculus.

Homunkulieschen (Parodistic Farce in 2 Acts)

Production Company: Christoph Mülleneisen Berlin-Charlottenburg and Cologne. *Producer:* Christoph Mülleneisen, Sr. *Writer-Director:* Franz Schmelter.
Cast: Lo Vallis (Lieschen), Manny Ziener (Dr. Girlande Klagenfurt), Johanna Ewald (Famula Euphemia), Franz Schmelter (Knötschke, fruit dealer), Emmy Wyda (His wife).
Length: ca. 840 m. Two acts.
Board of Censors: October 1916. Adults only.
Premiere: November 3, 1916, Berlin, Tauentzien Palace

Homunkulieschen is no real Homunculus but an interchanged twin who plays the artificially inseminated girl just for the sake of science. There was a sequel: *Homunkulieschen wird Filmdiva* (*Homunkulieschen Becomes a Screen Goddess*).

Der Yoghi (The Yogi)

Production Company: Projektions-AG »Union« (PAGU), Berlin. *Producer:* Paul Davidson. *Writer-Director:* Paul Wegener. *Assistant and Art Director:* Rochus Gliese. *Cinematographer:* Mads Anton Madsen.
Cast: Paul Wegener (The Yogi/Rasmus), Fritz Huf (God Shiva), Lyda Salmonova (Myra).
Distribution Company: Nordische Films Co. G.m.b.H., Berlin
Board of Censors: September 1916
Premiere: October 1916, Berlin, Cinema U.T. Kurfürstendamm

Paul Wegener in a dual role: as Rasmus, a natural scientist, and a Yogi, who lives in a remote village where he hides Myra, a beauty from India. The Yogi is able to render himself invisible.

Rübezahls Hochzeit (Rübezahl's Wedding)

Production Company: Projektions-AG »Union« (PAGU), Berlin. *Producer:* Paul Davidson. *Writer-Director:* Paul Wegener. *Assistant and Art Director:* Rochus Gliese. *Cinematographer:* Mads Anton Madsen. *Title Silhouettes:* Lotte Reiniger.
Cast: Paul Wegener (Rübezahl/The Storyteller), Lyda Salmonova (The Little Fairy), Ernst Waldow (Home Tutor), Emilie Kurz (Governess), Georg Jacoby (Forester), Arthur Ehrens (The Count), Rochus Gliese (Haircutter), Marianne Niemeyer (Grandmother).
Studio: Union Studios, Berlin-Tempelhof
Location Shooting: Giant Mountains/German Riesengebirge: Schreiberhau, Moritzburg manor
Distribution Company: Nordische Films Co. G.m.b.H., Berlin
Length: 1264 m. Five acts.
Board of Censors: October 1916. Adults only.
Premiere: 1916, Berlin, UFA Theater

As early as 1662, a mountain ghost, Rübezahl, has found his way out of the secret mutterings of spinning rooms and long winter nights into printed literature—to which he was introduced by Johannes Praetorius under the Latin title "Daemonologia Ruebenzalia Silesii" solemnly as well as awkwardly—living his double existence in the mind of the people:

To big and small children he is known as well as to those who did not get tired of doing research about his nature and his origin. The cornerstone to this work was laid in 1782 by a former Pagenhof master and later professor at Weimar gymnasium, Karl August Musaeus.[2]

Wegener's film is the first to bring the character on the screen showing the towering ghost that has fallen in love with a fairy (Lyda Salmonova). At that time he was really in love with his fellow performer and soon would marry her.

Das unheimliche Haus (The Haunted House)

Production Company: Richard Oswald Film G.m.b.H., Berlin. *Producer-Writer-Director:* Richard Oswald. *Cinematographer:* Max Fassbender. *Art Director:* Manfred Noa.
Cast: Werner Krauss (Albert von Sievers), Lupu Pick (Arthur Wüllner), Alfred Breiderhoff (Matthias, valet), Käte Oswald (Lily, chamber-

maid), Rita Clermont (Juliette, the woman in the mirror), Heinz Sarnow (Fritz Bodmer), Max Bing (Martin Wist, detective), Dr. Arnold Czempin, Ernst Ludwig.

Shooting: July 1916

Length: 1539 m [1478 m after reviewed again by the Censors on March 10, 1921]. Four acts.

Board of Censors: August 1916. Adults only.

Premiere: September 1916, Cologne, Scala Theater; September 22, 1916, Berlin, Mozartsaal Nollendorfplatz

An unemployed young man is hired to work as secretary in a house which turns out to be haunted. Out of a mirror, a woman appears and asks him for help. A detective is consulted and solves the case. More parts of Richard Oswald's *Haunted House* detective series to follow.

Das unheimliche Haus, 2. Teil [The Haunted House, Part 2] aka *Freitag, Der 13. (Friday The 13th/Black Friday)*

Production Company: Richard Oswald Film G.m.b.H., Berlin. *Producer-Writer-Director:* Richard Oswald, based on story ideas by Edgar Allan Poe. *Cinematographer:* Max Fassbender. *Art Director:* Manfred Noa. *Set Construction:* Alfred Dahlheim.

Cast: Reinhold Schünzel (Engelbert Fox), Max Gülstorff (Fix, his friend), Ernst Ludwig (Herbert von Eulenstein), Hans Marton (Marcell, his son), Franz Ramharter (Dr. Schmidt), Werner Krauss (Prof. Cardallhan), Rosa Liechtenstein (Leonie, his sister), Emil Rameau (Eibner), Kissa von Sievers (Mary Seeber), Lupu Pick.

Shot in September 1916.

Length: 1505 m. Four acts.

Board of Censors: October 1916. Adults only.

Premiere: November 10, 1916, Berlin, Kammerlichtspiele

Superstition has it that the heads of the Eulenstein family will die on Friday the 13th. Detective Engelbert Fox and his friend Fix are chosen to protect the new lord of the manor.

Das unheimliche Haus, 3. Teil (The Haunted House, Part 3) aka *Der chinesische Götze (The Chinese Idol)*

Production Company: Richard Oswald Film G.m.b.H., Berlin. *Producer-Writer-Director:* Richard Oswald. *Cinematographer:* Max Fassbender. *Art Director:* Manfred Noa. *Set Construction:* Alfred Dahlheim.

Cast: Werner Krauss (Franz Mollheim, a millionaire), Käte Oswald (Else Mollheim, his daughter), Arthur Wellin (Dick Gröhner), Reinhold Schünzel (Ralph Robin, private eye), Max Gülstorff (Hans Osten, commissioner), Lupu Pick (Wu, a Chinese servant).

Length: 1445 m. Four acts.

Board of Censors: October 1916. Adults only.

Premiere: October 27, 1916, Berlin

A Chinese idol puts detective Reinhold Schünzel on the track of Chinese fanatics, who form a plot in a secret temple hidden in a scary house. The basic idea is similar to the hidden temple in Steven Spielberg's *Young Sherlock Holmes* (1985).

Das wandernde Licht (The Wandering Light)

Production Company: Messter Film G.m.b.H., Berlin. *Producer:* Oskar Messter. *Director:* Dr. Robert Wiene. *Screenplay:* Irene Daland, based on a novel by Ernst von Wildenbruch. *Cinematographer:* Karl Freund. *Musical Score (Premiere):* Dr. Giuseppe Becce.

Cast: Henny Porten (Anna von Glassner), Bruno Decarli (Count von Fahrenwald), Theodor Becker (The Count's valet), Emil Rameau (Major von Glassner, Anna's uncle), Elsa Wagner (Frau von Glassner, Anna's aunt).

Shot in July 1916.

Premiere: September 1, 1916, Berlin, Mozartsaal Nollendorfplatz

Anna, the bride of Count von Fahrenwald, is warned that the bridegroom is mentally disordered. Actually, the count is not mad, but his valet is.

1916–17

Die Gespensterstunde (The Witching Hour)

Production Company: Saturn Film A.G., Berlin. *Writer-Director:* Urban Gad.

Cast: Maria Widal (Agga), Nils Chrisander (Magnus Berten), Carl Zickner (Old Count de la Porte), Victor Senger (August, his elder son), Hans Adalbert Schlettow (Johann, his younger son), Senta Eichstaedt (Luise-Marie, Johann's wife), Olga Engl (Countess Herrn, Luise-Marie's mother), Carl Dibbern (Tobias, valet).
Length: ca. 1400 m. *Running time:* 56 minutes. Three acts.
Board of Censors: September 1916
Premiere: May 1917, Berlin, Passage Theater
A family drama with spooky elements that include a hunchback creature.

Nächte des Grauens aka Nächte des Schreckens (Nights of Terror)

Production Company: Lloyd Film, Berlin. *Producer:* Lu Synd. *Director and Screenplay:* Arthur Robison.
Cast: Lu Synd (The Woman, a circus artist), Werner Krauss (Her Husband, circus artist), Emil Jannings (The Banker), Hans Mierendorff (Judicial officer), Lupu Pick, Lorenz Köhler.
Length: 1120 m. *Running time:* 56 minutes. Four acts.
Board of Censors: December 1916. Adults only.
Premiere: February 7 or 9, 1917, Berlin, Motivhaus
An artist (Werner Krauss) disguises himself in an ape suit and murders everybody who comes near his wife. The film's star Lu Synd aka Pauline Müller was also its producer.

Die Entdeckung Deutschlands (The Discovery of Germany)

Production Company: Mars Film G.m.b.H., Berlin. *Directors:* Georg Jacoby, Richard Otto Frankfurter. *Screenplay:* Richard Otto Frankfurter.
Cast: Gustav Botz (Marsilius, a scholar from Mars), Edith Meller (Masilietta, his daughter), Paul Heidemann (Mavortin, editor of Martian paper *Der Sonnensee/The Sunsea*), Karl Roos (A Soldier in Field-gray), Kapitänleutnant Paul König (Submarine Commander).
Location Shooting: Munich, Berlin, Kiel, Cologne
Distribution Company: Werners Filmverleih, H. Werner, Berlin SW 68, Kochstrasse 6–7.

Six acts.
Board of Censors: February 1917. Adults only. Later G-rated.
Premiere: December 12, 1916, Berlin, Union Palace
German wartime propaganda: Martians land in Germany and, after seeing everything, declare the country fit for winning the war.

1917

Der Golem und die Tänzerin (The Golem and the Dancer)

Production Company: Projektions-AG »Union« (PAGU), Berlin. *Producers:* Paul Davidson, Siegmund Jacob, Hanns Lippmann. *Writer-Director:* Paul Wegener. *Cinematographer:* Mads Anton Madsen. *Art Director:* Rochus Gliese.
Cast: Paul Wegener (Himself/The Golem), Lyda Salmonova (Jela Olschevska, the dancer), Rochus Gliese, Emilie Kurz, Erich Schönfelder, Wilhelm Diegelmann, Ernst Waldow, Friedrich Feilchenfeld [Fritz Feld] (Page Boy).
Board of Censors: April 1917
Wegener falls in love with a young dancer who has seen him as the Golem on screen. But Jela is not interested in the actor, only in the clay figure which she wants to purchase. Instead of the figure, Wegener has himself delivered in full Golem outfit.

Das Bildnis des Dorian Gray (The Picture of Dorian Gray)

Production Company: Richard Oswald Film G.m.b.H., Berlin. *Producer-Writer-Director:* Richard Oswald, based on the novel *The Picture of Dorian Gray* (1890–91) by Oscar Wilde. *Cinematographer:* Max Fassbender. *Art Director:* Manfred Noa.
Cast: Bernd Aldor (Dorian Gray), Ernst Pittschau (Duke Henry Wotton), Ernst Ludwig (Basil Hallward, artist), Andreas von Horn (Alan Campbell, chemist), Lea Lara (Sibyl Vane), Sophie Pagay (Sibyl's mother), Arthur Wellin (James Vane, Sibyl's brother), Lupu Pick (Dorian Gray's valet).
Finished in June 1917
Length: 1766 m. Three acts.

Board of Censors: July 1917. Adults only.
Premiere: July 1917, Berlin

In July 1938, Constantinople-born Bernd Aldor was expelled from the Nazi *Reichsfilmkammer*, the statutory corporation controlled by the Ministry of Enlightenment and Propaganda, for being "non–Aryan" He died in 1950 in Vienna.

Hilde Warren und der Tod (Hilde Warren and Death)

Production Company: May Film G.m.b.H., Berlin. *Producer-Director:* Joe May. *Screenplay:* Fritz Lang. *Cinematographer:* Curt Courant. *Art Director:* Siegfried Wroblewsky.

Cast: Mia May (Hilde Warren), Bruno Kastner (Hector Roger), Hans Mierendorff (Hans von Wengraf, intendant), Ernst Mátray (Egon Warren, Hilde's son), Georg John (Death), Hermann Picha (Hotel physician), Fritz Lang (Old Priest/Young Messenger).

Shot in June 1917

Length: 1497 m. Four acts.

Board of Censors: 1917. Not suited for children. Adults only.

Premiere: August 31, 1917, Berlin, Tauentzien Palace

Hilde Warren, an actress, doesn't understand how somebody could possibly yearn for death, but finally she learns to suffer the hard way. Actor Georg John, who played Death, became a favorite of Fritz Lang. In the autumn of 1941, he was deported to the Łódź Ghetto where he died on November 18, 1941, at the age of 62.

Furcht (Fear)

Production Company: Messter Film G.m.b.H., Berlin. *Producer:* Oskar Messter. *Writer-Director:* Dr. Robert Wiene. *Art Director:* Ludwig Kainer.

Cast: Bruno Decarli (Count Greven), Conrad Veidt (Priest from India), Mechthildis Thein, Bernhard Goetzke, Hermann Picha.

Studio: Messter Film Studio, Berlin

Distribution Company: Hansa Film Verleih G.m.b.H., Berlin

Length: 1496 m. Four acts.

Board of Censors: September 1917. Adults only.

Premiere: September 21, 1917, Berlin, Mozartsaal Nollendorfplatz

Count Greven, who took a Buddha figure from India, feels haunted by an Indian priest and fears for his life.

Ahasver, Part 1
Part 2: Die Tragödie der Eifersucht (The Tragedy of Jealousy)
Part 3: Das Gespenst der Vergangenheit (The Ghost from the Past)

Production Company: Deutsche Bioscop G.m.b.H., Berlin. *Writer-Director:* Robert Reinert. *Cinematographer:* Helmar Lerski. *Art Directors:* Robert A. Dietrich, Artur Günther.

Cast: Carl de Vogt (Ahasver), Johannes Riemann (Janson, a young doctor), Toni Zimmermann, Dora Schlüter, Sybille Binder, Helene Brahms.

Studio: Bioscop Glass House, Neubabelsberg

Shot from May until June 1917

Length of Part 1: 1729 m. *Part 2:* 1526 m. *Part 3:* 1526 m. Four acts each part. *Running time Part 1:* ca. 63 minutes. *Part 2:* ca. 56 minutes. *Part 3:* ca. 56 minutes.

Board of Censors: August 1917.

Premiere Part 1: September 21, 1917, Berlin, Union Palace, Kurfürstendamm

Premiere Part 2 and 3: October 1917

Length Re-release: 1637 m. Five acts.

Board of Censors Re-release: September 10, 1921

The tale of Ahasver, who insulted Christ on his way to Calvary crucifixion and was condemned to wander restlessly through the ages, was created in medieval times. Following the success of *Homunculus*, Deutsche Bioscop released the three-part serial in 1917: In each episode, the "Eternal Jew" gets enmeshed in a tragic love story that ends badly.

In 1921, the three parts were re-released in a single condensed version.

Hans Trutz im Schlaraffenland (Hans Trutz in Schlauraffenland)

Production Company: Projektions-A.G. »Union« (PAGU), Berlin. *Producer:* Paul Davidson. *Writer-Director:* Paul Wegener. *Cinematographer:* Frederik Fuglsang. *Art Director:* Rochus Gliese.

Cast: Paul Wegener (Hans Trutz), Lyda Salmonova (Märte, Trutz's wife). Ernst Lubitsch (Satan), Wilhelm Diegelmann, Rochus Gliese, Gertrud Welcker, Fritz Rasp (Schlauraffenland Creature).

Location: the area surrounding Bautzen
Distribution Company: Zadek Film, Berlin
Board of Censors: October 1917

Hans Trutz (Paul Wegener), a poor peasant, encounters Satan (Ernst Lubitsch), who offers him a chance to live on the fat of the land of the Schlauraffen in exchange for his soul. The film was made during the Turnip Winter, a period of profound civilian hardship in Germany due to World War I.

Dornröschen (Sleeping Beauty)

Production Company: Projektions-AG »Union« (PAGU), Berlin. *Producer:* Paul Davidson. *Director, Art Director and Costume Design:* Paul Leni. *Screenplay:* Paul Leni, Rudolf Presbar, based on a fairy tale recorded by the Brothers Grimm.

Intertitles: Rudolf Presbar. *Cinematographer:* Alfred Hansen. *Sets:* Kurt Richter.

Cast: Mabel Kaul (Dornröschen/Sleeping Beauty), Harry Liedtke (The Prince), Käthe Dorsch (The Queen), Georg Kaiser (The King), Hermann Picha (The Old Witch), Victor Janson (Court Marshal), Paul Biensfeldt, Maria Grimm-Einödshofer.

Studio: Union Studio, Berlin-Tempelhof, Oberlandstrasse

Distribution Company: Nordische Films Co. G.m.b.H., Berlin

Length: 1381 m. *Running time:* 67 minutes. Four acts.

Premiere: December 20, 1917, Berlin, U.T. Alexanderplatz

Director Paul Leni began his career as a stage designer for Max Reinhardt.

1917–18

Die Memoiren des Satans (Satan's Memoirs/Memoirs of Beelzebub)

Part 1: Dr. Mors
Part 2: Fanatiker des Lebens (Fanatics of Life)
Part 3: Der Fluchbeladene (The Cursed One)
Part 4: Der Sturz der Menschheit (The Downfall of Mankind)

Production Company: Luna Film, Berlin. *Writer-Director:* Robert Heymann, based on a novel by Wilhelm Hauff. *Cinematographer:* Ernst Plhak.

Cast: Friedrich Kühne, Käthe Dorsch, Paul Brenkendorf, Ernst Hofmann, Michael Rainer, Paul Passarge, Ilse Oeser, Ingeborg Gleiche, Cläre Bauer, Jutta von Matuszkiewicz, Grete Weixler, Valy Arnheim, Ernst A. Becker, John Rappeport, Herbert Kieper, Max Köhler, Victor Senger, Arthur Schröder, Harry Wendlandt.

Studio: Luna Film Studio, Berlin, Friedrichstrasse 224

Length Part 1: 1527 m. Five acts. Part 2: 1681 m. Five acts. *Running time* Part 1: ca. 74 minutes. Part 2: ca. 81 minutes.

Board of Censors: Part 1: October 1917. Part 2: November 1917. Part 3: February 1918. Part 4: March 1918.

Four episodes based on the work of Stuttgart-born poet Wilhelm Hauff (1802–1827), who had collected since his studies enough material to record the memoirs of Satan in eternal search of human souls. At the end, self-sacrificing love overcomes the intrigues and scheme of Mephistopheles. Next to *Homunculus*, this was the most expensive German film project of World War I. Writer-director Robert Heymann (1879–1946) published novels and dramas, worked for theaters as dramaturge and wrote and directed films between 1916 and 1924.

1918

Der Ring der drei Wünsche (The Ring of the Three Wishes)

Production Company: Amboss Film Dworsky & Co., Berlin. *Producer and Technical Supervisor:* Rudolf Dworsky. *Director:* Arthur Wellin.

Screenplay: Hans Lund [Hugo Landsberger], Emil Rameau.

Cast: Alexander Moissi (The Hunchback), Ria Jende, Eduard von Winterstein, Paul Passarge.

Board of Censors: July 1918

A hunchback (Alexander Moissi) obtains a wishing ring that grants youth, beauty and health.

Der fliegende Holländer (The Flying Dutchman)

Production Company: Naturfilm Friedrich Müller G.m.b.H., Berlin. *Producers:* Heinrich Nebenzal, Friedrich Müller. *Director:* Hans Neumann. Based on an old Frisian legend and motifs from the opera by Richard Wagner. *Cinematographers:* Guido Seeber, Edgar S. Ziesemer. *Art Director:* Artur Günther.

Cast: Guido Schützendorf (Jan van der Straaten), Olga Desmond (Senta Daland), Josef Basch (Daland, her father, a merchant), Fritz Clemens (The Young Steersman), M.L. Rohde (His Mother), Ernst Benzinger (The Capitular), Fritz Steinhofer (The Priest), Willy Schweissguth (The Municipality Servant), Bernhard Croé (The Sacristan), Jeanette Bethge (Daland's Housekeeper), Hildegard Bork (Daland's maiden and a baggage train woman), Leonhard Haskel (Innkeeper of Rathskeller), Grete Blaha (Publican), Herbert Kieper (Tailor), Marga Vilany (Spanish Noblewoman), Walter Ebert (Town Clerk, her cavalier), Robert Fuchs (Old Steersman), Fritz Henkels (Young Sailor), A. von Poblotzka (Ship's Boy), Walter Neumann (Epiphany of Archangel), Gustav Rodegg (Figure of Jesus Christ), Eugenie Schulz (Young Witch), Walter Mey (First Juryman), Ernst Eger (Second Juryman), Ilse Schemonn (Baggage train woman).

Studio: Bioscop Glass House, Neubabelsberg

Location Shooting: Stettin Lagoon, Baltic Sea

Length: 1147 m. *Running time:* ca. 55 minutes. Five acts.

Board of Censors: August 1918. *Post-Censorship:* 1921, G-rated.

The legend of Captain Jan van der Straaten, whose ghost ship can never make port and is doomed to sail the oceans until he finds a woman who will break the curse. Young Senta redeems him by her death.

Die Augen der Mumie Ma (The Eyes of the Mummy)

Production Company: Projektions-AG »Union« (PAGU)/Universum Film Aktiengesellschaft (UFA), Berlin. *Producer:* Paul Davidson. *Director:* Ernst Lubitsch. *Screenplay:* Hanns Kräly, Emil Rameau. *First Cinematographer:* Theodor Sparkuhl. *Second Cinematographer:* Alfred Hansen. *Art Director:* Kurt Richter.

Cast: Pola Negri (Ma), Emil Jannings (Radu, the Guardian), Harry Liedtke (Alfred Wendland, an artist), Max Laurence (Prince Hohenfels), Margarete Kupfer.

Studio: Backlot Berlin-Tempelhof. *Location Shooting:* Limestone Mountains Rüdersdorf.

Distribution Company: Universum Filmverleih G.m.b.H. (UFA), Berlin.

Length: 1193 m. *Running time:* 63 minutes.

Board of Censors: August 13, 1918. Adults only.

Premiere: October 3, 1918, Berlin

Pola Negri as a kidnapped Oriental dancer held captive in an Egyptian temple. After she is freed, her guardian (Emil Jannings) pursues her to England.

Der Rattenfänger (The Pied Piper)

Production Company: Projektions-AG »Union« (PAGU)/Universum Film Aktiengesellschaft (UFA), Berlin. *Producer:* Paul Davidson. *Writer-Director:* Paul Wegener. Based on the fairy tale "The Pied Piper of Hamelin" recorded by Johann Wolfgang von Goethe in a poem (1803) and by Jacob and Wilhelm Grimm in their collection *Deutsche Sagen* (1816). *Cinematographer:* Frederik Fluglsang. *Art Director:* Rochus Gliese. *Title Silhouettes and assisting with the stop-motion animation of wooden rat models:* Lotte Reiniger.

Cast: Paul Wegener (The Strange Musician), Wilhelm Diegelmann (The Mayor), Elsa Wagner (The Mayor's Wife), Lyda Salmonova (Ursula, the Mayor's daughter), Märte Rassow (Märte), Jakob Tiedtke (The Pharmacist), Armin Schweizer (Skinny City Councilman), Clemens Kaufung (Farm Servant), Hans Sturm (Henchman).

Location: Bautzen and surrounding area, Hildesheim

Shooting: summer 1918 (?)

Distribution Company: Universum Filmverleih (G.m.b.H. UFA), Berlin.

Premiere: December 19, 1918, Berlin, U.T. Nollendorfplatz

The story of a rat-catching pied piper, called in by Hamelin councilmen to get rid of the rats that plague the town.

Aladdins Wunderlampe (Aladdin's Wonderful Lamp)

Production Company: Harmonie Film G.m.b.H., Berlin. *Director:* Hans Neumann.
Premiere: January 1919
A tale of the Arabian Nights.

1918–19

Alraune, die Henkerstochter, genannt die Rote Hanne (Alraune, the Henchman's Daughter Called the Red Hanne)

Production Company: Neutral Film G.m.b.H., Berlin. *Producer:* Josef Rideg. *Director-Cinematographer:* Eugen Illés. *Screenplay:* Carl Froelich, Georg Tatzelt. *Art Director:* Artur Günther.
Cast: Hilde Wolter (Alraune), Joseph Klein, Friedrich Kühne, Ernst Rennspies, Tatjana Sand, Gustav Adolf Semler, Max Auzinger.
Running time: 88 minutes
Board of Censors: December 1918
Premiere: February 28, 1919, Düsseldorf, Asta Nielsen Theater

A childless duchess has recourse to the magic of a mandrake root, with fatal results for the whole family.

Die Dame, der Teufel und die Probiermamsell (The Lady, the Devil and the Waitress)

Production Company: Messter Film G.m.b.H./Universum Film Aktiengesellschaft (UFA), Berlin. *Director:* Rudolf Biebrach. *Screenplay:* Dr. Robert Wiene. *Cinematographer:* Karl Freund. *Art Director:* Kurt Richter. *Music Director (Premiere):* Dr. Giuseppe Becce.
Cast: Henny Porten (The Waitress), Ida Perry (A Woman of Fashion), Alfred Babel (Baron/Devil), Eugen Rex (Fritz), Rudolf Biebrach.
Shot in December 1918
Distribution Company: Hansa Film Verleih G.m.b.H., Berlin
Premiere: January 17, 1919, Berlin, Mozartsaal Nollendorfplatz

A food taster (Henny Porten) is so fascinated by an ermine coat she saw in a shop window that the customer who bought it appears in her dream. He looks like the Devil, takes her to Hell and offers her the coat provided she accept his conditions.

Ikarus, der fliegende Mensch (Ikarus, the Flying Man)

Working title: Der Adler von Flandern (The Eagle of Flandres)
Production Company: Neutral Film G.m.b.H., Berlin. *Producer:* K.J. Fritzsche. *Director:* Carl Froelich. *Co-Director:* Eugen Illés (?). *Screenplay:* Herr Breitner, with a prologue by Leo Heller. *Cinematographer:* Hermann Böttger. *Art Director:* Artur Günther.
Cast: Ernst Hofmann (Günther Ellinghaus, engineer), Esther Carena (Clemence de Montignon, French spy), Gustav Botz (Privy Councilor Ellinghaus, President of Orient Bank, Günther's father), Olga Engl (Frau Ellinghaus, Günther's mother), Edith Sorel (Erika, Günther's cousin), Heinz Sarnow (Baron d'Aubigny, French spy), Ernst Rennspies (A Political Agent).
Studio: Literaria Film, Berlin, Oberlandstrasse
Length: 2000 m. *Running time:* 135 minutes. Six acts.
Board of Censors (Post-Censorship): June 1, 1921
Press Screening: October 27, 1918, Berlin, Mozartsaal
Premiere: July 4, 1919, Berlin, Marmorhaus

Two French spies blackmail German engineer Günther Ellinghaus into handing over the construction plans for the new Ikarus engine. Desperate, Ellinghaus flees to New York where he works as a waiter. But at the outbreak of World War I he returns to Germany. He enlists as a fighter pilot to fight the two spies. All three of them survive.

Ikarus was the final German war film, finished right before the defeat of the German armies but released after the surrender. At the end of the film, the former enemies join hands.

1919

Cagliostros Totenhand (Cagliostro's Death Hand)

Production Company: Deutsche Bioscop Gesellschaft m.b.H., Berlin. *Director:* Nils Chrisander. Based on a literary source by Ernst Rennspies. *Cinematographer:* Kurt Hasselmann. *Art Director:* Gustav A. Knauer.

Cast: Martha Novelly (Lorenza Hofer), Eugen Klöpfer, Eduard Eysenck, Helga Molander.

Studio: Bioscop Glass House, Neubabelsberg
Distribution Company Rheinlicht-Bioscop
Length: 1050 m. *Running time:* ca. 51 minutes. Four acts.
Released in Austria-Hungary on September 19, 1919

Considered a talisman, the death hand of Cagliostro causes bad luck until the ghost of the dead magician returns and reclaims the relic.

Alraune und der Golem (Alraune and the Golem)

Production Company: Deutsche Bioscop Gesellschaft m.b.H., Berlin. *Director:* Nils Chrisander. *Screenplay:* Richard Kühle, based on *Isabella von Ägypten* by Achim von Arnim. *Cinematographer:* Guido Seeber.

Cast: Uschi Elleot, Ilse Wilke.

Distribution Company: Rheinlicht-Bioscop
Poster Art by Jupp Wiertz, Aachen

Paul Wegener was no longer with Deutsche Bioscop, but the company still tried to capitalize on *The Golem*, teaming the colossus of clay with the equally successful female magic of *Alraune*: maybe the first "monster rally." There is some speculation if the movie was made at all, which is unlikely. The movie itself is lost but Richard Kühle's novelization, published in 1920, survives.

Die Arche (The Ark), Part 1
Die letzten Menschen (The Last Men), Part 2

Production Company: Richard Oswald Film G.m.b.H., Berlin. *Producer-Director:* Richard Oswald. *Screenplay:* Robert Liebmann, Richard Oswald, based on the novel *Die letzten Menschen* by Werner Scheff. *Cinematographer:* Karl Freund. *Art Director:* Julius Hahlo.

Cast: Leo Connard (Ernst Pogge, ship owner), Eva Speyer (Helga, his daughter), Georg Heinrich Schnell (Klaus Donken, captain), Oevid Molander (Walter Fahr, engineer), Eugen Klöpfer (Volkert, steersman), Guido Herzfeld (Dr. Milius, physician), Kissa von Sievers (Helga's Maid), Emil Lind (Prof. Keigo Sotuma, a Japanese astronomer), Max Gülstorff (Prince Kunibert), Felix Hecht, W. Arnoldi.

Length Part 1: 2184 m (censorship 1920). Seven acts.
Length Part 2: 2164 m (censorship 1920: 2161 m). Six acts.
Board of Censors: July 9, 1920. Adults only.
Premiere Part 1: September 16, 1919, Berlin, Richard Oswald Cinema, Kantstrasse 163
Premiere Part 2: October 1919, Berlin, Kant Cinema, Kantstrasse

The devastating effects of a comet wipe out mankind except for those who were diving in a submarine.

Die Pest in Florenz (Plague in Florence)

Production Company: Decla Film Gesellschaft Holz & Co., Berlin. *Producer:* Erich Pommer. *Director:* Otto Rippert. *Screenplay:* Fritz Lang. *Cinematographer:* Willy Hameister. *Additional Location Shooting:* Emil Schünemann. *Art Directors:* Hermann Warm, Franz Jaffé, Walter Reimann, Walter Röhrig. *Costumes Supplied by* F. & A. Diringer, Munich. *Musical Score:* Bruno Gellert.

Cast: Theodor Becker (Franciscus, hermit), Marga Kienska (Julia, courtesan), Julietta Brandt (The Plague), Otto Mannstaedt (Cesare, the Ruler of Florence), Anders Wikmann (Lorenzo, Cesare's son), Karl Bernhard (Lorenzo's Confidant), Franz Knaak (The Cardinal), Erner Hübsch (Monk), Auguste Prasch-Grevenberg (Julia's First Waitress), Hans Walter (Julia's Confidant), Erich Bartels.

Studio: Lixie Glass House and backlot, Berlin-Weissensee
Shot between June until the end of September 1919

Length: 1979 m. Seven acts.
Distribution Company: Decla Film Verleih G.m.b.H., Decla House, Berlin SW 48, Friedrichstrasse 22
Head of Distribution: Hermann Saklikower
Board of Censors: October 1919. Not suitable for children.
Premiere: October 23, 1919, Berlin, Marmorhaus

A production intended by Decla for international release, classified Decla World-Class: Due to the activities of an evil courtesan named Julia, Florence transforms into a cesspool of iniquity and is punished by the plague. Fritz Lang, the author of the screenplay, seems to have used plot elements from Poe's "The Masque of the Red Death."

Wahnsinn (Madness)

Production Company: Veidt Film, Berlin. *Producers:* Conrad Veidt, Richard Oswald. *Director:* Conrad Veidt. *Screenplay:* Margarete Lindau-Schulz, Hermann Fellner, based on a novel by Karl Münzer. *Cinematographer:* Carl Hoffmann. *Art Director:* Willi A. Herrmann.
Cast: Conrad Veidt (Friedrich Lorenzen, a banker), Gussy Holl (A Girl), Reinhold Schünzel (Jörges, proxy), Grit Hegesa (Marion Cavello, dancer).
Length: 1662 m. Five acts.
Board of Censors: October 1919
Premiere: October 15, 1919, Berlin

An insanely jealous banker learns that his mistress and his proxy betrayed him. He approaches a gypsy fortuneteller for advice. She predicts that he will find rest in a trunk that will bring fortune as well as death. Eventually he suffocates, caged in a trunk by the proxy, who has forced the girl into prostitution.

Unheimliche Geschichten (Eerie Tales/Tales of Horror)

Production Company: Richard Oswald Film G.m.b.H., Berlin. *Producer-Director:* Richard Oswald. *Screenplay:* Robert Liebmann, Richard Oswald, based on tales written by Anselma Heine ("*Die Erscheinung,*" 1912), Robert Liebmann ("*Die Hand,*" original story), Edgar Allan Poe ("*The Black Cat,*" 1843), Robert Louis Stevenson ("*The Suicide Club,*" 1848) and Richard Oswald ("*Der Spuk,*" original story). *Cinematographer:* Carl Hoffmann. *Set Decorator:* Julius Hahlo.
Cast: Reinhold Schünzel (The Devil in frame story; Dr. Riedmann, ex-husband: Episode 1; Murderer: Episode 2; Drunk: Episode 3; Artur Silas, police detective: Episode 4; Baron: Episode 5), Conrad Veidt (Death in frame story; Stranger: Episode 1; Murderer: Episode 2; Traveler: Episode 3; President of Suicide Club: Episode 4; Husband: Episode 5); Anita Berber (The Prostitute in frame story; Woman: Episode 1; Girlfriend: Episode 2; The Drunk's Wife: Episode 3; The President's Sister: Episode 4; Wife: Episode 5), Bernhard Goetzke (A Friend at table séance), Hans Heinrich von Twardowski (Restaurant waiter), Hugo Döblin, Paul Morgan, Georg John, Richard Oswald (Himself in prologue).
Length: 2318 m (Censorship 1920). *Running time:* 112 minutes.
Board of Censors: July 16, 1920. Adults only.
Premiere: November 6, 1919, Berlin, UFA Theater and Richard Oswald Cinema

A veritable *Trio infernal*—Death, Devil and a prostitute—meets at midnight to tell spooky tales and act them out for fun. The episodes consist of three published stories (Poe, Stevenson, Anselma Heine) and two originals (by director Richard Oswald and by Robert Liebmann, who became one of Germany's most prominent screenwriters—*The Blue Angel* made Marlene Dietrich a star). Liebmann was murdered in Auschwitz.

Die Puppe (The Doll)

Production Company: Projektions-AG »Union« (PAGU), Berlin. *Producer:* Paul Davidson. *Production Manager and Technical Supervisor:* Kurt Waschneck. *Director:* Ernst Lubitsch. *Screenplay:* Hanns Kräly, Ernst Lubitsch, inspired by the operetta *La poupée (Eine lustige Geschichte aus einer Spielzeugschachtel)* by Edmond Audran, translated by Alfred Maria Wilners and motifs of the tale *Der Sandmann* by E.T.A. Hoffmann. *Cinematographer:* Theodor Sparkuhl. *Art Director and Costume Designer:* Kurt Richter.

Cast: Ossi Oswaldi (Ossi Hilarius), Hermann Thimig (Lancelot), Victor [Viktor] Janson (Hilarius, puppet maker), Marga Köhler (Mrs. Hilarius), Jakob Tiedtke (Prior), Gerhard Ritterband (Apprentice of Hilarius), Max Kronert (Baron von Chanterelle), Josefine Dora (Lancelot's Foster mother), Ernst Lubitsch (Prop Master in opening scene), Paul Morgan (Hippolyt, the Baron's valet), Arthur Weinschenk, Herr Lapitski.
Studio: Union Film Studio, Berlin-Tempelhof
Distribution Company: Universum Film Verleih G.m.b.H. (UFA), Berlin
Running time: 66 minutes
Premiere: December 5, 1919, UFA Palace at Berlin Zoo

Ernst Lubitsch considered this wonderful little film one of his most inventive, particularly the beginning when he himself appears on screen arranging the scenery like a puppet theater out of a toy box.

Prinz Keo. Der Raub der Mumie (Prince Keo: The Rape of the Mummy)

Production Company: Union-Film Co. m.b.H., Munich. *Screenplay:* Franz Seitz.
Cast: Albert Steinrück (Prof. Skrupello), Hugo Schneider, Carla Ferra.
Board of Censors: October 30, 1920. Adults only.
Length: 1470 m. Four acts.

Albert Steinrück as Prof. Skrupello, an excavator, is asked to steal a mummy, but he refuses as the mummy has appeared in his dreams and he fears the curse.

1919–20

Hypnose (Hypnosis) aka Sklaven fremden Willens (Slaves of a Foreign Will)

Production Company: Eichberg Film G.m.b.H., Berlin. *Producer-Director:* Richard Eichberg. *Screenplay:* Carl Schneider. *Cinematographer:* Joe Rive. *Art Director:* Willi A. Herrmann.

Cast: Gertrud de Lalsky (Kommerzienrätin Raven), Lee Parry (Claire, her daughter), Karl Halden (Wolf Woerner, factory owner), Bela Lugosi (Prof. Mors), Jenny Höhne (Mrs. Mors), Rudolf Klein-Rhoden (Jack Weller), Marga Köhler (Mrs. Steffens, a mother), Emil Rameau (Peter Hain), Violetta Napierska (Eva Hain, Peter's daughter), Gustav Birkholz (Senator Holbein).
Length: 1945 m. *Running time:* ca. 94 minutes. Six acts.
Distribution Company: Central Film Vertriebs G.m.b.H., Berlin; in Austria: Singer Film Gesellschaft, Vienna.
Board of Censors: December 1919. Adults only.
Premiere: January 3, 1920, Berlin, Schauburg

Professor Mors has gained a reputation as a hypnotist. When doctors fail to cure Claire Raven, a girl who comes from a good home, he is called in for help and puts her under his hypnotic spell. The Svengali-type professor seems to be a loan from George du Maurier's novel *Trilby* that was serialized in 1894 and published in book form in 1895. In this lost film, Bela Lugosi as a hypnotist performed the hypnotic gestures and mannerism he used later in *Dracula*. Such cinematic portrayals, of course, had next to nothing to do with the reality of hypnosis.

Nachtgestalten (Night Creatures)

Production Company: Richard Oswald Film/Deutsche Bioscop Aktiengesellschaft, Berlin. *Producer-Writer-Director:* Richard Oswald, based on the novel *Eleagabal Kuperus* (1910) by Karl Hans Strobl. *Cinematographer:* Carl Hoffmann. *Art Director:* Hans Dreier. *Technician:* Ernst Kunstmann (?).
Cast: Paul Wegener (Thomas Bezug, billionaire), Reinhold Schünzel (His Secretary), Erna Morena (Elisabeth, his daughter), Erik Charell (Arnold, his son, "ape"), Conrad Veidt (Clown), Anita Berber (Dancer), Paul Bildt (Inventor), Theodor Loos, Willi Allen.
Length: 2192 m. Six acts.
Board of Censors: July 16, 1920 (post censorship). Adults only.
Premiere: January 9, 1920, Berlin, Richard Oswald Cinema

A screwy billionaire (Paul Wegener) is the

richest man in the world and father to a son more like an ape than a boy. He surrounds himself with musclemen and dwarfs and has set his mind on buying all the countries in the world.

Gustav Meyrink, Hanns Heinz Ewers and Austrian-born Karl Hans Strobl (1877–1946), the author of this picture's literary source, were the Great Three of German Speculative Fiction after 1900. Strobl edited, in collaboration with Alfons von Czibulka, a magazine for speculative fiction and erotic literature called *Der Orchideengarten*. During Austrofascism, he campaigned for Hitler and the NSDAP. After the annexation of Austria, he became NS country director of *Reichsschrifttumskammer* in Vienna. In 1945, he was temporarily arrested by the Red Army. He died penniless in an old folks' home after a series of strokes.

Die Herrin der Welt (The Mistress of the World)

Serial:
Part 1: *Die Freundin des gelben Mannes* (*The Girlfriend of the Yellow Man*)
Part 2: *Die Geschichte der Maud Gregaards* (*The Story of Maud Gregaards/The Race for Life*)
Part 3: *Der Rabbi von Kuan-Fu* (*The Rabbi of Kuan-Fu/The City of Gold*)
Part 4: *König Makombe* (*King Macombe*)
Part 5: *Ophir, die Stadt der Vergangenheit* (*Ophir, City of the Past*)
Part 6: *Die Frau mit den Milliarden* (*The Woman with the Billions*)
Part 7: *Die Wohltäterin der Menschheit* (*The Benefactress of Mankind*)
Part 8: *Die Rache der Maud Fergusson* (*The Revenge of Maud Fergusson*)

Production Company: May Film G.m.b.H., Berlin. *Producer:* Joe May. *Production Manager:* Hermann Fellner. *Directors:* Joe May (parts 2, 3 and 8); Josef Klein (parts 1 and 4); Uwe Jens Krafft (parts 4, 5 and 6); Karl Gerhardt (part 7). *Screenplay:* Joe May, Richard Hutter, Ruth Goetz, Wilhelm Roellinghoff, Fritz Lang. *Cinematographer:* Werner Brandes. *Set Designer:* Martin Jacoby-Boy. *Art Directors:* Otto Hunte, Karl Vollbrecht, Erich Kettelhut. *Costumes and Props:* Company Leopold Verch, Berlin-Charlottenburg. *Musical Score:* Ferdinand Hummel.

Cast: Mia May (Maud Gregaards), Michael Bohnen (Consul Madsen), Henry Sze (Dr. Kien-Lung), Hans Mierendorff (Baron Murphy), Paul Hansen (Allan Stanley, engineer), Ernst Hofmann (Credo Merville), Rudolf Lettinger (Hunt, detective), Paul Morgan (Pius Gotthilf Karpeter, theatrical agent), Victor Janson (Bullbox, newspaper reporter), Hermann Picha (Jonathan Fletcher), Wilhelm Diegelmann (Hannibal Harrison), Louis (Lewis) Brody (Simba), Bamboula (King Makombe), Henry Bender (Stockbroker), Eduard Rothauser, Hedwig Bleibtreu, Bruno Decarli, Hedy Searle, Hans Pagay, Alexander Ekert, Nien Son Ling.

Production started on June 24, 1919.
Total budget: ca. 8 million Reichsmark
Studio: Greenbaum, Berlin-Weissensee
Backlot: May Film, Berlin-Woltersdorf
Distribution Company: Universum-Film Verleih G.m.b.H. (UFA), Berlin
Board of Censors: December 1919. Adults only.
Premieres of individual episodes between December 5, 1919 and January 30, 1920, Berlin, Tauentzien Palace
All eight parts opened on February 6, 1920, Berlin, Kammerlichtspiele

The incredible adventures of a young, independently rich Danish woman named Maud Gregaards on her trip round the world, trying to locate the treasure of the Queen of Sheba. Star Mia May was the director's wife. Born Hermine Pfleger in Vienna, she died in 1980 in Hollywood at the age of 96.

Die Spinnen (The Spiders)
Part 1: Der goldene See (The Golden Lake)
Part 2: Das Brillantenschiff (The Brilliant Ship)

Production Company: Decla Film Gesellschaft Holz & Co., Berlin. *Executive Producer:* Erich Pommer. *Production Manager:* Rudolf Meinert. *Writer-Director:* Fritz Lang. *Cinematographers:* Carl Hoffmann, Emil Schünemann (Part 1); Carl Hoffmann, Karl Freund (Part 2). *Camera Assistant to Mr. Freund:* Robert Baberske (Part 2). *Art Directors:* Hermann Warm, Otto Hunte, Carl Ludwig Kirmse. *Set Decoration:* Völkerkundliches Museum [Ethnological Museum] Heinrich Umlauff, Hamburg. *Musical Director [Premiere]:* Max Josef Bojakowski.

Cast: Carl de Vogt (Kay Hoog), Lil Dagover (Naela, Priestess of the Sun), Ressel Orla (Lio Sha), Georg John (Dr. Telphas), Rudolf Lettinger (John Terry, the Diamond King), Edgar Pauly (Four Finger-John), Paul Morgan (Diamond Expert), Meinhardt Maur (Bookworm/Chinese), Friedrich Kühne (Yogi All-Hab-Mah), Reiner Steiner (Captain of the Brilliant Ship), Thea Zander (Ellen Terry), Paul Biensfeldt, Karl A. Römer, Gilda Langer.

Shooting: from June until August 1919 (Part 1); from October until December 1919 (Part 2).

Location Shooting: Hamburg, Tierpark Hagenbeck (Hagenbeck Zoo)

Distribution Company: Decla-Bioscop Verleih G.m.b.H, Decla House, Berlin SW 48, Friedrichstrasse 22.

Head of Distribution: Hermann Saklikower
Length Part 1: 1951 m. Five acts. *Length Part 2:* 2815 m. Six acts.

Board of Censors Part 1: October 1919.

Board of Censors Part 2: January 2, 1920. Adults only.

Premiere Part 1: October 3, 1919, Berlin, Richard Oswald Cinema

Premiere Part 2: February 5, 1920, Berlin, Theater at Moritzplatz

Kay Hoog, an ancestor of James Bond, fights the crime syndicate of *The Spiders*.

Satanas

Production Company: Viktoria Film Co m.b.H., Berlin. *Producer:* Ernst Hofmann. *Director:* Friedrich Wilhelm Murnau. *Artistic Supervision, Screenplay and Costume Design:* Dr. Robert Wiene. *Cinematographer:* Karl Freund. *Art Director:* Ernst Stern.

Cast: Episode 1: Fritz Kortner (Pharao Amenhotep), Sadjah Gezza (Nouri, the stranger), Ernst Hofmann (Jorab, the shepherd), Margit Barnay (Phahi, the Pharao's wife), Conrad Veidt (The Wise Man of Elu).

Episode 2: Conrad Veidt (Gubetta, a Spanish adventurer), Elsa Berna (Lucrezia Borgia), Curt Ehrle (Gennaro, her son), Marcella Gremo (Seven-year-old dancer), Jaro Fürth (Rustinghella), Ernst Stahl-Nachbaur (Prince Alfonso d'Este).

Episode 3: Conrad Veidt (Dr. Ivan Vladimir Grodski), Martin Wolfgang (Hans Conrad, a revolutionary student), Marija Leiko (Irene, his mistress), Elsa Wagner (Mother Conrad), Max Kronert (Father Conrad).

Studio: Bioscop Glass House, Neubabelsberg
Shooting time: from August until September 1919
Length: 2561 m. Six acts.
Board of Censors: January 1920
Premiere: January 30, 1920, Berlin, Richard Oswald Cinema

Satanas (Conrad Veidt) works his way through episodes of world history: from Ancient Egypt to Renaissance to the present age.

Das Cabinet des Dr. Caligari (The Cabinet of Dr. Caligari)

Production Company: Decla Film Gesellschaft Holz & Co., Berlin. *Administration:* Erich Pommer. *Production Manager:* Rudolf Meinert. *Director:* Dr. Robert Wiene. *Screenplay:* Carl Mayer, Hans Janowitz. *Cinematographer:* Willy Hameister. *Sets Designed and Painted by* Hermann Warm, Walter Reimann, Walter Röhrig. *Technicians:* Ernst Kunstmann(?) and others. *Musical Score:* Dr. Giuseppe Becce. *Promotional Campaign*: Rudolf Meinert, Dr. Robert Wiene, Julius Sternheim.

Cast: Werner Krauss (Dr. Caligari), Conrad Veidt (Cesare), Friedrich Fehér (Francis), Lil Dagover (Jane), Hans Heinrich von Twardowski (Alan), Rudolf Lettinger (Dr. Olsen, Medical Officer of Health), Hans Lanser-Rudolff [aka Hans Lanser-Ludolf] (Old Man), Henri Peters-Arnolds (Young Doctor), Ludwig Rex (Murderer), Elsa Wagner (Landlady).

Shooting time (estimated): from September until October 1919

Studio: Lixie Glass House, Berlin-Weissensee, Franz Josef Strasse 9–12

Distribution Company: Decla-Bioscop Verleih G.m.b.H., Decla House, Berlin SW 48, Friedrichstrasse 22

Head of Distribution: Hermann Saklikower
Released in the United States by Goldwyn Distribution Company

Length: 1780 m. *Running time:* 76 minutes. Six acts.

Board of Censors: March 1920. [Post-Censorship] Adults only.

Premiere: February 26, 1920, Berlin, Marmorhaus
Reissue Distributor in 1964: Atlas Filmverleih GmbH, Duisburg and Düsseldorf. *Music Score of Atlas Version*: Peter Schirmann. Atlas Retro Series: *Die dämonische Leinwand* (*The Haunted Screen*). *Curator:* Erwin Leiser.
Premiere of Digitally Restored Version: February 9, 2014, Berlin International Film Festival, Philharmonie Berlin. *Musical Director:* John Zorn.

The peak of Expressionist cinema in Germany: The director of an asylum convinces a somnambulist to kill people who attend a fair in Holstenwall. There is a rumor that Rudolf Klein-Rogge played the killer. This might have been an original casting idea but he wasn't in the final cast.

Der schwarze Meister (The Black Master)

Production Company: Münchner Lichtspielkunst Aktiengesellschaft (Emelka), Munich. *Director:* Ottmar Ostermayr. *Screenplay:* Gustav Meyrink.
Board of Censors: February 1920

Based on one of two original screenplays that Gustav Meyrink, the author of the *Golem* novel, wrote.

1920

Kurfürstendamm: Ein Höllenspuk in 6 Akten (A Hell Spook in 6 Acts)

Production Company: Richard Oswald Film G.m.b.H., Berlin. *Producer-Writer-Director:* Richard Oswald. *First Cinematographer:* Carl Hoffmann. *Second Cinematographer:* Axel Graatkjaer. *Art Director:* Hans Dreier.
Cast: Conrad Veidt (The Devil), Asta Nielsen (Lissy/Mulatta/Film Star/Marie, the cook), Erna Morena (Frau von Alady), Henry Sze (Dr. Li from Peking), Rosa Valetti (Frau Lesser, owner of Pension Elvira), Paul Morgan (Fritz, her son), Rudolf Forster (Ernst Duffer), Theodor Loos (Raoul Haselzwing).

Length: 2424 m. Six acts.
Board of Censors: July 12, 1920. Adults only.
Premiere: July 30, 1920, Berlin, special screening at Richard Oswald Cinema

Out of boredom, the Devil takes a trip to Berlin. But the Kurfürstendamm, the famous avenue, is even too much for him.

Der Bucklige und die Tänzerin (The Hunchback and the Dancer)

Production Company: Helios Film Erwin Rosner, Berlin. *Producer:* Erwin Rosner. *Director:* Friedrich Wilhelm Murnau. *Screenplay:* Carl Mayer, from his own script *Der grüne Kuss* (*The Green Kiss*). *Cinematographer:* Karl Freund. *Art Director:* Robert Neppach.
Cast: Sascha Gura (Gina, the dancer), John Gottowt (James Wilton, the hunchback), Paul Biensfeldt (Smith, a rich bachelor), Anna von Pahlen (His Mother), Henri Peters-Arnolds (Percy, a young rich Baron), Bella Polini (A Dancer).
Length: 1540 m.
Board of Censors: December 15, 1920 [post censorship]. Adults only.
Premiere: July 8, 1920, Berlin, Marmorhaus

Using a mysterious elixir, a wealthy hunchback kills the men who dare to kiss a beautiful dancer: first her fiancé, then her lover.

Der Januskopf: Eine Tragödie am Rande der Wirklichkeit (The Head of Janus/Love's Mockery: A Tragedy on the Border of Reality)

Production Company: Lipow Film/Decla-Bioscop Aktiengesellschaft, Berlin. *Producers:* Jean Lipowetzki, Erich Pommer. *Director:* Friedrich Wilhelm Murnau. *Screenplay:* Hans Janowitz, freely adapted from the novel *The Strange Case of Dr. Jekyll and Mr. Hyde* (1886) by Robert Louis Stevenson. *Cinematographers:* Karl Freund, Carl Hoffmann, Carl Weiss. *Camera Assistant to Mr. Freund:* Robert Baberske. *Art Director:* Heinrich Richter.

Cast: Conrad Veidt (Dr. Warren/Mr. O'Connor), Magnus Stifter (Dr. Warren's Friend), Margarete Schlegel (Grace/Jane Lanyon), Bela Lugosi (Dr. Warren's Butler), Margarete Kupfer, Willy Kaiser-Heyl, Danny Guertler, Gustav Botz, Jaro Fürth, Hans Lanser-Rudolf, Marga Reuter, Lanja Rudolph.
Studio: Cserépy Studio, Berlin
Distribution Company: Decla-Bioscop Verleih G.m.b.H., Decla House, Berlin SW 48, Friedrichstrasse 22
Head of Distribution: Hermann Saklikower
Length: 2222 m. *Running time:* 107 minutes. Six acts.
Board of Censors: August 21, 1920. Adults only.
Premiere: August 26, 1920, Berlin, Marmorhaus

F.W. Murnau's film adaptation of a case of split personality. Reviewers wrote that Conrad Veidt gave a great performance. Bela Lugosi has a supporting part as Veidt's butler.

Die Luftpiraten (The Air Pirates)

Production Company: Metro Film G.m.b.H., Berlin. *Producer:* Harry Piel. *Production Manager:* Wilhelm Zeiske. *Director:* Harry Piel. *Screenplay:* Max Bauer, Harry Piel. *Cinematographer:* Gustave Preiss. *Art Director:* Albert Korell. *Makeup:* Paul Thürnagel. *Stunts:* Hermann Stetza.
Cast: Friedrich Berger, Albert Collani, Paula Cora, Mary Marion, Harry Piel, Margot Thisset.
Board of Censors: July 6, 1920
Premiere: July 16, 1920, Leipzig; August 27, 1920, Berlin

This movie was most likely inspired by a pulp series called *Der Luftpirat und sein lenkbares Luftschiff,* also known as *Captain Mors The Air Pirate,* modeled after Jules Verne's Robur and Captain Nemo. Between 1908 and 1912, 165 issues appeared.

Das fliegende Auto (The Flying Car)
Part 1: *Das Blumenmädchen von der Rialto Brücke (The Flower Girl from the Rialto Bridge)*
Part 2: *Der Klub der Teufelsbrüder (The Club of the Devil Brothers)*

Production Company: Metro Film G.m.b.H., Berlin. *Producer-Director:* Harry Piel. *Screenplay:* Max Bauer, Harry Piel. *Cinematographer:* Georg Muschner. *Special Designs:* Albert Korell. *Makeup:* Paul Thürnagel. *Stunts:* Hermann Stetza.
Cast: Harry Piel (Harry Peel), Max Laurence (The Inventor of the Flying Car), Fritz Schroeter (Gusson), Tilly Thönnessen, Margot Thisset, Richard Georg, Adolf Wenter, Friedrich Berger, William Zeiske.
Length (2 parts): 2503 m. *Running time* (2 parts): ca. 122 minutes. Six acts.
Board of Censors: September 7, 1920. Adults only.
Premiere: September 10, 1920, Berlin, Schauburg

A criminal named Gusson steals the construction plans and prototype of a flying car. Another entry in Harry Piel's sensational detective series. A contemporary reviewer wrote:

> Harry Piel works the American way: five somehow connected acts but each with a stunning sensation. Brilliant climbing tours, jewel thefts, man-trained police dogs, breathless chases and original jiu-jitsu, death falls from the roof down to the pavement, jump into the water from the fourth floor and last not least stunt car driving... [I]n addition to that: horse races, women wrestling ... a tiny bit undressing and nudity—and speed—one enjoys it without overworking the brain.

Genuine

Production Company: Decla-Bioscop Aktiengesellschaft, Berlin. *Executive Producer:* Erich Pommer. *Production Manager:* Rudolf Meinert. *Director:* Dr. Robert Wiene. *Screenplay:* Carl Mayer. *Cinematographer:* Willy Hameister. *Art Director and Costume Designer:* César Klein. *Assistant Art Directors:* Bernhard Klein, Kurt Hermann. *Associate Art Director:* Walter Reimann.
Cast: Fern Andra (Genuine), Hans Heinrich von Twardowski (Florian, hair cutter apprentice), Ernst Gronau (Lord Melo, an eccentric), Harald Paulsen (Percy), John Gottowt (Guyard, haircutter), Albert Bennefeld (Lord Curzon), Lewis [Louis] Brody (Lord Melo's Valet).
Distribution: Decla-Bioscop Verleih G.m.b.H., Decla House, Berlin SW 48, Friedrichstrasse 22

Head of Distribution: Hermann Saklikower
Board of Censors: August 1920. Adults only.
Premiere: September 2, 1920, Berlin, Marmorhaus

Despite the Decla board of directors' doubts, Robert Wiene and producer Rudolf Meinert tried a second Expressionist story following their triumph of *Dr. Caligari*, but this time they failed: A barber shop apprentice falls in love with a slave girl who thirsts for male blood. According to Rudolf Kurtz:

> *Genuine* is an Expressionist film because Expressionism was a success. But rather than a method of composition, it became the content of the film, so to speak. With this paradoxical discrepancy, the expressionist film faded. *Genuine* was the official proof that these films do not constitute a business. The "boom" was over.[3]

Star Fern Andra was born Fern Andra Andrews in Natzeka, Illinois, in 1894 and became famous on the German silent screen. She passed away in 1974 in Aiken, South Carolina.

Algol: Eine Tragödie der Macht (Tragedy of Power)

Production Company: Deutsche Lichtbild Gesellschaft e.V. (DLG), Berlin. *Director:* Hans Werckmeister. *Screenplay:* Hans Brennert, Friedel Köhne. *Cinematographer:* Axel Graakjaer. *Cinematographer during final shooting days:* Hermann Kricheldorff. *Art Director:* Walter Reimann.

Cast: Emil Jannings (Robert Herne, miner), Ernst Hofmann (Reginald Herne, his son), Käte [Käthe] Haack (Magda Herne, his daughter), Gertrud Welcker (Leonore Nissen), Hans Adalbert Schlettow (Peter, dual role: father and son), Hanna Ralph (Maria Obal), Erna Morena (Yella Ward), John Gottowt (Alien from Planet Algol), Sebastian Droste.

Location Shooting: Potsdam (Orangerie, Park Sanssouci), North Sea, Hamburg
Shooting time: June 1920: exteriors; from July until August 1920: interiors, studio
Distribution Company: Deulig-Film G.m.b.H., Berlin
Length: 2144 m. *Running time:* 81 minutes. Five acts.
Board of Censors: August 25, 1920. Adults only.
Premiere: September 3, 1920, Berlin, U.T. Kurfürstendamm

An evil alien from Planet Algol (a star called Demon), 93 light years from Earth, gives an ordinary miner a gift of mysterious power that makes him rich but also destroys his family. Paul Scheerbart isn't mentioned in the credits, but certain futuristic design ideas in this film seem to refer to his work.

Die Tarantel (The Tarantula)

Production Company: Messter Film G.m.b.H., Berlin. *Director:* Rudolf Biebrach. *Screenplay:* Karl Figdor. *Cinematographer:* Willy Gaebel. *Art Director:* Jack Winter.

Cast: Georg Heinrich Schnell (Frank Davis, the detective of the millionaires), Magnus Stifter (Fernando), Franz von Egenieff (Jackson, magnate of a trust), Marion Regler (Inez Rodino), Max Laurence (Old Rodino, Inez's father), Lothar Müthel (Johannes, private scholar), Boris Michailow (Bu Mohammed, an Arabian fisherman).

Length: 1895 m. *Running time:* 70 minutes.
Premiere: September 17, 1920

An American-style crime story concerning a world-shaking invention, a radium motor.

Die Legende von der Heiligen Simplicia (The Legend of Saint Simplicia)

Production Company: May Film G.m.b.H., Berlin. *Producer-Director:* Joe May. *Assistant Director and Location Manager:* Robert Wuellner. *Screenplay:* Thea von Harbou. *First Cinematographer:* Werner Brandes. *Second Cinematographer:* Günther Krampf. *Art Director:* Martin Jacoby-Boy. *Associate Art Director:* Erich Kettelhut. *Music Score:* Alexander Schirmann.

Cast: Eva May (Saint Simplicia), Alfred Gerasch (Rochus the Knight), Wilhelm Diegelmann (Warden), Elisabeth Wilke (Mother Superior of Monastery), Georg John (Blind Beggar), Max Gülstorff (Wanderer), Lia Eibenschütz (Maiden of the Dragon Castle), Martha Rema, Rudolf Biebrach.

Shot in August 1920.
Backlot: May Film backlot, Woltersdorf near Berlin
Length: 2310 m. Six acts.

Board of Censors: September 30, 1920. Adults only.
Premiere: October 8, 1920, Berlin, Tauentzien Palace

Rochus, a knight, tries to seduce a young nun. Under his spell, Simplicia commits mortal sins, but the deeds always turn to good account. Finally, Simplicia stabs herself. The knight regrets what he has done. At the end, both are united in death.

Eva May, the erratic female star, did commit suicide in real life after a tragic love affair. Her mother Mia, Joe May's superstar, withdrew from filmmaking after her daughter's death.

Der Golem, wie er in die Welt kam (The Golem: How He Came Into the World)

Production Company: Projektions-AG »Union« (PAGU)/Universum Film Aktiengesellschaft (UFA), Berlin. *Producer:* Paul Davidson. *Director and Story:* Paul Wegener. *Co-Director:* Carl Boese. *Screenplay:* Paul Wegener, Henrik Galeen. *Cinematographer:* Karl Freund. *Camera Assistant:* Robert Baberske. *Art Director:* Hans Poelzig. *Associate Art Director:* Kurt Richter. *Costumes:* Rochus Gliese. *Music Score:* Hans Landsberger.

Cast: Paul Wegener (The Golem), Albert Steinrück (Rabbi Loew), Lyda Salmonova (Mirjam, Rabbi's daughter), Ernst Deutsch (Famulus), Lothar Müthel (Junker Florian, a Christian nobleman), Otto Gebühr (Emperor), Doris Paetzold (The Emperor's Mistress), Loni Nest, Ursula Nest (Little Girls), Hans Sturm (Rabbi Jehuda), Max Kronert (First Temple Servant), Carl Ebert (Second Temple Servant), Greta Schröder (Maiden holding a rose), Fritz Feilchenfeld [Fritz Feld] (Court Jester).

Studio: UFA Union Studio, Berlin-Tempelhof, Oberlandstrasse. The ghetto was built on the backlot.

Shooting: from May until June 1920.

Length: 1922 m. *Running time:* 101 minutes. Five acts.

Distribution Company: Universum-Film Verleih G.m.b.H. (UFA), Berlin

Released in the United States by Famous Players Lasky Corporation/Paramount Pictures Corporation, New York City

Board of Censors: October 21, 1920. Adults only.
Premiere: October 29, 1920, UFA Palace, Berlin Zoo

In 16th-century Prague, Rabbi Loew brings to life a man of clay to protect his people from persecution but finally has to stop the creature.

Guido Seeber, who is credited on several prints as second cinematographer, wasn't involved in this production.

American distributors called it *Titan of the Screen*: **A Paramount Super Special That Strides Among Ordinary Film Dramas Like a Giant Among Pygmies!** »*The Golem*«

Now terrible as all the passions of earth let loose. Now tender as a child's caress. Sweeping into its mighty scenes whole multitudes of living men and women. The most compelling figure in screen history. Not merely a photoplay; an EVENT in the life of the city. A strange, inspiring, beautiful thing! Resembling nothing you've ever seen before. See it![4]

Das Gefängnis auf dem Meeresgrunde (The Prison on the Ocean Floor)

Production Company: Metro Film G.m.b.H., Berlin. *Producer-Director:* Harry Piel. *Screenplay:* Max Bauer, Harry Piel. *Cinematographer:* Georg Muschner. *Art Director:* Hans Neirath. *Special Designs:* Albert Korell. *Makeup:* Paul Thürnagel. *Stunts:* Hermann Stetza. *Location Manager:* Walter Zeiske.

Cast: Harry Piel, Fritz Schroeter, Tilly Thönnessen, Richard Georg, Margot Thisset, Bella Polini, Friedrich Berger.

Length: 2354 m. Six acts.

Board of Censors: December 4, 1920. Adults only.

Premiere: December 3, 1920, Berlin, Schauburg

Judging from the stills, this movie seems to have featured an underwater laboratory.

Der Graf von Cagliostro (The Count of Cagliostro)

Production Company: Lichtbild Fabrikation Schünzel Film, Berlin/Vereinigte Filmindustrie Micheluzzi & Co. (Micco-Film), Vienna. *Pro-*

ducers: Victor Micheluzzi, Reinhold Schünzel. *Director:* Reinhold Schünzel. *Screenplay:* Robert Liebmann. *Cinematographer:* Carl Hoffmann. *Camera Assistant:* Kurt Lande. *Art Director and Costume Designer:* Oskar Friedrich Werndorff.

Cast: Reinhold Schünzel (Alessandro Cagliostro/Count Phoenix), Anita Berber (Lorenza, Cagliostro's slave girl), Conrad Veidt (The Minister), Carl Goetz (The Prince), Hugo Werner-Kahle (Cagliostro's Servant), Hanni Weisse (Favorite of the Prince), Hilde Wörner (The Chambermaid of the Favorite), Armin Seydelmann, Walter Huber, Heinrich Jensen, Wilhelm Sichra.

Locations: Castle Schönbrunn et al.
Sales: Wörner Film, Berlin W, Kurfürstendamm 16
Length: 2158 m. Six acts.
Post Censorship: January 7, 1921. Adults only.
Premiere Austria: December 21, 1920, Vienna, Busch Cinema
Premiere Germany: February 10, 1921, Berlin, Marmorhaus

A German-Austrian "biopic" depicting stages of the life of Giuseppe Balsamo, who called himself Cagliostro.

1920–21

Die schwarze Spinne (The Black Spider)

Production Company: Turma Film G.m.b.H., Berlin. *Writer-Director:* Siegfried Philippi. *Cinematographer:* Heinrich Gärtner. *Art Director:* Edmund Heuberger.

Cast: Lissy Lind, Olga Engl, Max Ruhbeck, Josef Roemer, Hugo Flink, Ortrud Wagner, Charles Willy Kayser, Marga Köhler, Rudolf Klein-Rohden.

Board of Censors: January 20, 1921. Adults only.
Premiere: August 8, 1921, Berlin, Passage Theater

An adaptation of a novel with a supernatural background, written by Jeremias Gotthelf in 1842.

Von morgens bis mitternachts (From Morn to Midnight)

Production Company: Ilag Film (Isenthal and Juttke), Berlin. *Director:* Karlheinz Martin. *Screenplay:* Karlheinz Martin, Herbert Juttke, based on the drama by Georg Kaiser. *Cinematographer:* Carl Hoffmann. *Art Director-Costume Designer:* Robert Neppach.

Cast: Ernst Deutsch (Cashier), Erna Morena (Lady), Hans Heinrich von Twardowski (Young Gentleman), Eberhard Wrede (Bank director), Roma Bahn (Daughter/Beggar/Salvation Army member/Girl/Prostitute), Frida Richard (Grandmother), Adolf Edgar Licho (Fat Gentleman), Hugo Döblin (Broker), Lotte Stein (Woman), Elsa Wagner, Lo Heym.

Running time: 73 minutes
Board of Censors: August 15, 1921
Special Screening for Members of the Press: mid–1922, Munich, Regina Cinema.
Premiere: December 3, 1923, Tokyo (titled *Hongo-za*)

Japan was the only country where they seemed to understand and appreciate this largely experimental drama: A bank cashier (Ernst Deutsch) has embezzled a large sum of money, goes to the graveyard to discuss the case with a skeleton, and shoots himself as police are coming to arrest him.

Das Haus zum Mond (The House to the Moon)

Production Company: Neos Film G.m.b.H., Berlin. *Director:* Karlheinz Martin. *Screenplay:* Rudolf Leonhard, Karlheinz Martin. *Cinematographers:* Carl Hoffmann, Gotthardt Wolf. *Art Director and Costume Designer:* Robert Neppach.

Cast: Erich Pabst (Nathanael, astronomer), Leontine Kühnberg (Bettina, his wife/Luna, his daughter), Fritz Kortner (Jan van Haag, wax figure trader), Paul Graetz (Kornill, actor), Hans Schweikart (Fabian, his son), Käthe Burg (Pirzel, waitress), Max Gülstorff (Just, Actuarius), Frida Richard (Julchen, his wife), Annemarie Mörike (Minchen, his daughter), Leopold von Ledebur (Peter Pohl, coal dealer), Sophie Pagay (Babett, his wife), Gustav von Wangenheim (Andreas, his son), Hugo Döblin (Schlinge, court officer), Max Adalbert.

Length: 2232 m. Six acts.
Board of Censors: January 13, 1921. Adults only.
Premiere: January 28, 1921, Berlin, Richard Oswald Cinema

An astronomer owns an old house, called the

Moon. Strange figures lurk throughout the house's floors, from the scholar with his observatory on the roof, to an old actor and a waxworks maker à la E.T.A. Hoffmann, on down to the coal cellar and the bordello. The waxwork maker shapes a figure that resembles the astronomer's wife, which he embraces. This arouses the suspicion of unfaithfulness in the husband, who perceives only vague outlines at a window. The wife bears a daughter, Luna, who has a mysterious relationship to the moon, and sleepwalks. Conflict unfolds around her, causing the old man's ruin, death, insanity, and the destruction of the house. And above it all, the moon shines softly, mysteriously, as though it channeled destiny; its beams have infused the blood of all the inhabitants of the house with otherworldliness.[5]

Karlheinz Martin (born Karl Joseph Gottfried Martin on May 6, 1886, in Freiburg) was a stage director whose career started in 1904 in Kassel. In 1919 Berlin, he co-founded the avant-garde theater Die Tribüne. With the advent of sound films, he co-wrote the screen version of Alfred Döblin's *Berlin—Alexanderplatz* and made a handful of entertainment films. In 1940, the Nazis banned him from the profession. On August 15, 1945, after the fall of the Nazi capital, he re-opened Hebbel Theater with Brecht's *Threepenny Opera*. He died on January 13, 1948, in Berlin.

Der müde Tod: Ein deutsches Volkslied in sechs Versen (The Weary Death aka *Destiny: A German Folksong in Six Verses)*

Production Company: Decla-Bioscop Aktiengesellschaft/Universum Film Aktiengesellschaft (UFA), Berlin. *Producer:* Erich Pommer. *Director, Script and Editorial Supervisor:* Fritz Lang. *Screenplay:* Thea von Harbou. *Cinematographers:* Erich Nitzschmann; Hermann Saalfrank (Old German frame story); Fritz Arno Wagner (Venetian, Oriental, Chinese episodes); Bruno Mondi; Bruno Timm. *Gaffer:* Robert Hegewald. *Technical Assistant on scenes that show Death appearing and vanishing:* Ernst Kunstmann. *Art Directors:* Robert Herlth (Chinese episode); Walter Röhrig (Old German frame story); Hermann Warm (Venetian, Oriental, Chinese episodes, willow hill of frame story). *Artifacts and Costumes:* Völkerkundliches Museum [Ethnological Museum] Heinrich Umlauff, Hamburg. *Sculptor:* Walter Schulze-Mittendorf. *Musical Score:* Dr. Giuseppe Becce.

Cast: Lil Dagover (The Young Woman/Zobeide, the Caliph's sister/Mona Fiametta/Tiao Tsien), Walter Janssen (The Young Woman's Lover/The Franconian/Francesco/Liang), Bernhard Goetzke (The Death/El Mot, gardener/Bowman of the emperor of China), Hans Sternberg (The Mayor), Ernst Rückert (Parson), Max Adalbert (The Notary), Erich Pabst (The Teacher), Paul Rehkopf (The Gravedigger), Edgar Klitzsch (The Physician), Hermann Picha (The Tailor), Georg John (The Beggar), Grete Berger (The Mother), Rudolf Klein-Rogge (The Dervish/Girolamo), Edgar Pauly (The confidant of the Dervish), Paul Biensfeldt (A Hi, the magician), Karl Huszár-Puffy (The Emperor of China), Lydia Potechina (The Landlady), Eduard von Winterstein (The Caliph), Erika Unruh (Ayesha, confidant of Zobeide), Lothar Müthel (Emissary/Confidant), Paul Neumann (The Henchman), Karl Harbacher (The Traveling Journeyman), Edgar Pauly (First Confidant of Girolamo), Hellmuth Hiemstra (Second Confidant of Girolamo), Aloisia Lehnert (A Mother), Marie Wismar (An Old Woman), Louis [Lewis] Brody (Moor), Erner Hübsch (First Eunuch), Victor Hartberg (Second Eunuch), Lina Paulsen (Foster Mother), Max Pfeiffer (Night Watchman), Hermann Vallentin.

Studio and Backlot: Decla-Bioscop, Neubabelsberg

Distribution Company: Universum-Film Verleih G.m.b.H. (UFA), Berlin

Length: 2307 m. *Running time:* 105 minutes. Six acts.

Board of Censors: October 4, 1921. Adults only.

Premiere: October 6, 1921, Berlin, U.T. Kurfürstendamm, Mozartsaal Nollendorfplatz

Distribution Company Reissue 1964: Atlas Filmverleih GmbH, Duisburg and Düsseldorf. *Musical Director of Atlas version:* Peter Schirmann. *Series: Die dämonische Leinwand (The Haunted Screen). Curator:* Erwin Leiser.

Musical Adaptation ZDF version (1983): Wilfried Schröpfer.

Reissue: Berlinale Classics, February 12, 2016. *Orchestra conducted by:* Frank Strobel.

In postwar Germany, the question of whether

Death had become weary certainly suggested itself since he'd had so much to do on the battlefields: A young, grief-stricken woman's desperate attempts to bring her dead lover back to life are contrasted with episodes of tragic love that happened in the caliph's city, during Carnival in Venice and in the Middle Kingdom of China. For Fritz Lang, the movie marked a personal loss too: His mother died while he prepared it. Like many great storytellers, Lang had an attitude of inventing and exaggerating personal stories that later would become the salt in the soup prepared by his biographers such as the following childhood tale when he was ill in bed with fever, delivered to posterity by Patrick McGilligan:

> He recalled envisioning the approach of "the dark stranger" in a wide-brimmed hat, illumined by the moonlight streaming in through a half-open window. "I slept and dreamed—or was I awake?" He glimpsed "the tear-stained face of my adored mother," as she slipped from the view. He raised himself up weakly, to be led away by Death. Helping hands grabbed him, pushed him down, saved him. The horror of the dream-experience combined with "a kind of mystical ecstasy which gave me, boy though I still was, the complete understanding of the ecstasy which made martyrs and saints embrace Death." Lang recovered, "but the love of Death, compounded of horror and affection, stayed with me and became a part of my films."[6]

Der verlorene Schatten (The Lost Shadow)

Production Company: Projektions-A.G. »Union« (PAGU). Berlin, *Producers:* Paul Davidson, Paul Wegener. *Director–Costume Designer:* Rochus Gliese. *Screenplay:* Paul Wegener, Rochus Gliese, based on the novel *Peter Schlemihls wundersame Geschichte* (1813) by Adelbert von Chamisso. *First Cinematographer:* Karl Freund. *Second Cinematographer, Technical and Photographic Supervisor:* Kurt Waschneck. *Camera Assistant to Mr. Freund:* Robert Baberske. *Art Director:* Kurt Richter. *Silhouette Artist:* Lotte Reiniger.

Cast: Paul Wegener (Sebaldus, town musician), Greta Schröder (Countess Dorothea Durande), Werner Schott (Count Durande), Lyda Salmonova (Barbara, Dorothea's foster sister), Wilhelm Bendow (Cousin Theobald), Adele Sandrock (Mother Superior), Leonhard Haskel (Mayor), Hedwig Gutzeit (The Mayor's Wife), Hans Sturm (Dapertutto the magician).

Shot in summer 1920.
Location: Wachau (Castle Schönbühel, Dürnstein)
Distribution Company: Universum-Film Verleih G.m.b.H. (UFA), Berlin
Length: 1629 m. *Running time:* 60 minutes. Five acts.
Board of Censors: December 1, 1920
Premiere: February 3, 1921, Berlin, U.T. Kurfürstendamm

Paul Wegener plays a role similar to his *Student of Prague*. This time, he doesn't sell his mirror image but his shadow.

1921

Der Gespenster-Klub (The Ghost Club)

Production Company: Cabinetfilm Toni Attenberger, Munich and Berlin. *Producer:* Toni Attenberger.
Length: 1639 m. Five acts.
Board of Censors: June 21, 1921. Adults only.

This may be a story woven around a ghost club and ghost hunters.

Das Abenteuer des Dr. Kircheisen (The Adventure of Dr. Kircheisen)

Production Company: Maxim Film Gesellschaft Ebner & Co., Berlin. *Director:* Rudolf Biebrach. *Screenplay:* Dr. Robert Wiene. Based on the novel *Mangobaumwunder* by Paul Frank and Leo Perutz. *Art Director:* Hans Sohnle.

Cast: Hermann Thimig (Dr. Theophil Kircheisen, a chemist), Hans Marr (Baron Bogh), Lotte Neumann (Gretl), Mabel May-Young (Ilsa Ziegler), Leopold von Ledebur (Ulam Singh), Albert Kunze (Old David).

Length: 1453 m. *Running time:* 54 minutes. Five acts.
Board of Censors: August 31, 1921. Adults only.
Premiere: September 23, 1921, Berlin, U.T. Kurfürstendamm

Hermann Thimig has invented a serum and proves its strange effects on the human body right before death in a dream.

Die goldene Pest (The Golden Plague)

Production Company: Richard Oswald Film Aktiengesellschaft, Berlin. *Producer:* Richard Oswald. *Director:* Louis Ralph. *Screenplay:* Paul Merzbach, based on the novel by Gjert Øvre Richter Frich. *Cinematographer:* Willy Goldberger. *Art Director:* Stefan Lhotka.

Cast: Louis Ralph (Jacques Delma), Anita Berber (Natasha), Paul Bildt (John Marker, student of chemistry), Hans Adalbert von Schlettow (Dr. Jonas Fjeld), Emil Wittig (Brocke), Felix Norfolk (Bradley), Arthur Bergen (Okine), Hans Wallner (Croft), Rudolf Klein-Rhoden (Faber), Michael Rainer-Steiner (Lord Cavendish, president of the Bank of England), Karl Martell (Patrick Murphy, his secretary), Friedrich Berger (James Clifford, first detective), Emil Stammer (Hansen, second detective), Hermann Picha (Ohlsen, third detective), Conrad Curt Cappi (Binet, fourth detective).

Distribution Company: National Film, Berlin
Length: 2085 (2073) m. Six acts.
Board of censors: November 11, 1921. Adults only.
Premiere: November 18, 1921, Berlin, Richard Oswald Cinema

One of the silent screen's alchemist tales: A student of chemistry has found the Philosopher's stone and makes gold from natrium.

Das indische Grabmal (The Indian Tomb)
Part 1: Die Sendung des Yoghi (The Mission of the Yogi)
Part 2: Der Tiger von Eschnapur (The Tiger of Bengal)

Production Company: May-Film G.m.b.H., Berlin. *Producer-Director:* Joe May. *Screenplay:* Thea von Harbou in collaboration with Fritz Lang. *Cinematographer:* Werner Brandes. *Assistant Camera:* Karl Puth. *Art Directors and Set Decoration Supervisors:* Martin Jacoby-Boy, Erich Kettelhut, Karl Vollbrecht, Otto Hunte. *Costume Designer:* Martin Jacoby-Boy. *Location Manager:* Robert Wuellner. *Musical Director (Premiere):* Wilhelm Löwitt.

Cast: Olaf Fønss (Herbert Rowland, architect), Mia May (Irene, Rowland's bride), Conrad Veidt (Ayan, Maharaja of Eshnapur/Bengal), Erna Morena (Maharani Savitri), Bernhard Goetzke (Yogi Ramigani), Lya de Putti (Myrrha, dancer), Paul Richter (Mac Allan, a British officer), Karl Platen (Rowland's valet), Hermann Picha (Prof. Leyden, an Orientalist), Wilhelm Diegelmann (Captain), Georg John (Penitent), Louis [Lewis] Brody (Black Servant), Wolfgang Ritter von Schwind, Max Adalbert, Maria Forescu.

Studio: May Film backlot, Woltersdorf near Berlin
Distribution Company: E.F.A., Berlin
Released in the United States in 1922 by: Famous Players Lasky Corporation/Paramount Pictures Corp., New York City
Length: 2967 m. *Running time Part 1:* 120 minutes. *Running time Part 2:* 100 minutes. Six acts.
Board of Censors: October 20, 1921. Adults only.
Premiere: October 22, 1921, UFA Palace at Berlin Zoo
Running time of the restored version: 212 minutes.

A story of Indian love and obsession: Ayan, the maharajah of Bengal, awakens Yogi Ramigani from his holy sleep. The yogi has the power to transcend space and time, read people's minds and grant their wishes. Asked by the maharajah to fetch a renowned English architect, the yogi rematerializes the maharajah in Herbert Rowland's living room in England. Rowland offers to build the most lavish and beautiful tomb in the world for the maharajah's wife. But Princess Savitri, the wife, is still alive and has no intention to die for the sake of the building.

1921–22

Dr. Mabuse, der Spieler (Dr. Mabuse the Gambler)
Part 1: Der grosse Spieler—Ein Bild der Zeit (The Great Gambler: A Picture of the Time)
Part 2: Inferno—Ein Spiel von Menschen unserer Zeit (Inferno: A Game of the People of Our Age)

Production Company: Uco Film G.m.b.H./Decla-Bioscop Aktiengesellschaft/Universum

Film Aktiengesellschaft (UFA), Berlin. *Producer:* Erich Pommer. *Director:* Fritz Lang. *Screenplay:* Thea von Harbou, in collaboration with Fritz Lang. Based on the 1921 novel by Norbert Jacques. *First Cinematographer:* Carl Hoffmann. *Second Cinematographer:* Erich Nitzschmann. *Assistant Camera:* Bruno Timm. *Camera Effects:* Ernst Kunstmann. *Art Directors:* Carl Stahl-Urach, Otto Hunte, Erich Kettelhut, Karl Vollbrecht. *Costumes:* Vally Reinecke.

Cast: Rudolf Klein-Rogge (Dr. Mabuse), Aud Egede-Nissen (Cara Carozza), Gertrude Welcker (Countess Dusy Told), Alfred Abel (Count Told), Bernhard Goetzke (Von Wenk, prosecutor), Paul Richter (Edgar Hull), Robert Forster-Larrinaga (Spoerri), Hans Adalbert Schlettow (Georg), Georg John (Pesch), Julius Falkenstein (Karsten), Grete Berger (Fine, Mabuse's servant), Anita Berber (Dancer in tailcoat), Edgar Pauly (Fat Spectator), Lydia Potechina (The Russian), Karl Huszár-Puffy (Hawasch), Julius E. Hermann (Schramm), Karl Platen (Told's Valet), Paul Biensfeldt (Man with pistol), Julie (Julietta) Brandt, Adele Sandrock, Max Adalbert, Gustav Botz, Heinrich Gotho, Hans Junkermann, Olaf Storm, Erich Pabst, Hans Sternberg, Leonhard Haskel, Erner Hübsch, Gottfried Huppertz, Adolf Klein, Erich Walter, Ilse Arkow.

Studios: Decla-Bioscop Studios, Neubabelsberg; Jofa Studios, Berlin-Johannisthal

Shot from November 1921 until March 1922

Distribution Company: Universum-Film Verleih G.m.b.H. (UFA), Berlin

Length (part 1) 3496 m. Six acts. (part 2). 2531 m. Six acts.

Board of Censors: April 25, 1922 (part 1); May 20, 1922 (part 2). Adults only.

Premiere: April 27, 1922 (part 1); May 26, 1922 (part 2), UFA Palace at Berlin Zoo

Distribution Company Reissue 1964: Atlas Filmverleih GmbH, Duisburg and Düsseldorf. *Musical Score of Atlas version*: Konrad Elfers. Series: *Die dämonische Leinwand* (*The Haunted Screen*). *Curator:* Erwin Leiser.

The DEFA Laboratories in German Democratic Republic released an 8mm version (5 × 66 m). In 1972, it also became available in Super 8.

Musical Score restored version: Osmán Pérez Freire, Michael Obst.

Running time of restored version (part 1): 155 minutes, (part 2): 115 minutes, complete: 270 minutes.

In his 1921 novel, Luxembourgist novelist Norbert Jacques (1880–1954) invented a master criminal, a clever hypnotist and gambler with many faces and disguises, just like his French counterpart Fantomas.

1922

Lucifer

Production Company: Promo Film Aktiengesellschaft, Berlin. *Director:* Josef Stein. *Writer:* Peter Heuser. *Cinematographers:* Ewald Daub, Adolf Otto Weitzenberg. *Art Director:* Edmund Heuberger.

Cast: Sylvester Schäffer, Jr. (Detective Nobody), Lili Dominici (Gabriele, his wife), Paul Hansen (Flederwisch, his best friend), Georg Heinrich Schnell (Lucifer), Walter Doerry (Vouk), Leonhard Haskel (Schimek, notary), Grete Hollmann (Olga, dancer), Edmund Löwe (Ralph), Ernst Pittschau (Baron Wennendorf), Ludwig Rex (Friesholm, banker), Mara Marlice (Sieglinde, Friesholm's daughter).

Board of Censors: June, 9, 1922

Short film episode of *Nobody* detective series started in 1921 starring Berlin-born artist-magician-juggler Sylvester Schäffer, Jr. He later refused to entertain Hitler in a private show and to separate from his Jewish agent. He died in Hollywood exile in 1949. In the 25th entry of the *Nobody* series, G. H. Schnell, the ship owner in *Nosferatu*, co-starred as a criminal who called himself Lucifer.

Teufelssymphonie (Devil's Symphony)

Production Company: Inpro Film G.m.b.H., Munich. *Director*: Josef Firmans.

Cast: Erna Morena (Countess Kings-Hall), Fritz Greiner.

Length: 2131 m. Six acts.

Sportsman Fred Kelly marries a countess and rescues her from the grip of an alleged fakir who murdered her father (using snake venom) and her two former husbands. The criminal, Electric Bill, tries to get the couple into a cage and sink them into a burning shaft but Kelly frees them and pursues the murderer up the castle tower.

The latter falls to his death. The synopsis sounds like early Jess Franco. The picture was approved by the censors in 1922 but banned in 1924 for reasons of crime, violence and atrociousness.

Phantom

Production Company: Uco Film G.m.b.H./Decla-Bioscop Aktiengesellschaft Berlin. *Producer:* Erich Pommer. *Director:* Friedrich Wilhelm Murnau. *Screenplay:* Thea von Harbou, based on the novel *Phantom. Aufzeichnungen eines ehemaligen Sträflings* written between 1915 and 1921 by Gerhart Hauptmann. *First Cinematographer:* Axel Graatkjaer. *Second Cinematographer:* Theophan Ouchakoff. *Set Designer:* Hermann Warm. *Art Director:* Erich Czerwonski. *Costumes:* Vally Reinecke. *Music Score:* Leo Spieß.

Cast; Alfred Abel (Lorenz Luboda), Frida Richard (Mother Luboda), Aud Egede Nissen (Melanie Luboda), Hans Heinrich von Twardowski (Hugo Luboda), Karl Etlinger (Starke, master bookbinder), Lil Dagover (Marie Starke), Grete Berger (Mrs. Schwabe, pawnbroker), Anton Edthofer (Wigottschinski), Ilka Grüning (The Baroness), Lya de Putti (Melitta, daughter of the Baroness/Veronika Harlan), Adolf Klein (Emmo Harlan, hardwareman), Olga Engl (Mrs. Harlan), Heinrich Witte (Usher), Wilhelm Diegelmann, Eduard von Winterstein, Arnold Korff.

Shot from May to October 1922
Studio: Decla-Bioscop and backlot, Neubabelsberg
Distribution Company: Decla-Bioscop Verleih G.m.b.H./Universum-Film Verleih G.m.b.H. (UFA), Berlin
Head of Distribution: Hermann Saklikower
Length: 2905 m. *Running time:* 117 minutes. Six acts.
Board of Censors: November 3, 1922. Adults only.
Premiere: November 10, 1922, Düsseldorf, Decla Cinema; November 13, 1922, UFA Palace at Berlin Zoo

Lorenz Lubota (Alfred Abel), a clerk in a minor government office, longs to be a poet. He becomes obsessed with the vision of a mysterious woman in a carriage. He ends up in prison. Abel (1879–1937) was to become Fritz Lang's master of *Metropolis*.

1922–23

Mysterien eines Frisiersalons (Mysteries of a Barbershop/The Mysteries of a Hairdresser's Shop)

Production Company: Kurpo Film Dr. Koch, Munich. *Director:* Erich Engel, supported by Bertolt Brecht. *Script:* Bertolt Brecht, Erich Engel, Karl Valentin.

Cast: Karl Valentin (Barbershop Apprentice), Blandine Ebinger (Barbershop Waitress), Erwin Faber (Prof. Moras), Annemarie Hase (Moras's Mistress), Kurt Horwitz (Moras's Antagonist, the Beheaded), Liesl Karlstadt (Customer with Wart), Otto Wernicke (Owner of the Barbershop), Carola Neher (Moras's Friend at the Café), Max Schreck (Customer with Big Bushy Beard), Hans Leibelt (Second Customer), Josef Eichheim (Customer with sideburns).

Filmed in the attic of a house in Munich, Tengstrasse
Running time: 32 (25) minutes. Two acts.
Distribution Company: FLAG Filmindustrie und Lichtspiel Aktiengesellschaft, Berlin
Board of Censors: July 14, 1923. Adults only.
Reissued in 16mm by Atlas Film + AV, Duisburg

As a joke, Bertolt Brecht wrote a short scenario for what was to become an absurd slapstick film, while he began rehearsals for his drama *In The Jungle of Cities* at the Munich National Theater in February 1923. Max Schreck is briefly seen as a customer of comedian Karl Valentin's barbershop. Rediscovered in the 1970s in the Moscow Film Archive.

Der steinerne Reiter (The Stone Rider)

Production Company: Decla-Bioscop Aktiengesellschaft/Universum Film Aktiengesellschaft (UFA), Berlin. *Producer:* Erich Pommer. *Writer-Director:* Fritz Wendhausen. *Original Idea:* Thea von Harbou. *Director of Photography:* Carl Hoffmann. *Cinematographers:* Günther Rittau, Karl Becker. *Art Director-Costume Designer:* Heinrich Heuser. *Set Construction:* Heinrich Heuser, Karl Vollbrecht. *Musical Score:* Dr. Giuseppe Becce.

Cast: Rudolf Klein-Rogge (Master of the Mountain), Fritz Kampers (First Companion of the Master of the Mountain), Otto Framer (Second Companion of the Master of the Mountain), Georg John (Gatekeeper), Emilie Unda (Steward of the Estate), Emil Heyse (Lord of the Castle), Paul Biensfeldt (Gatekeeper of the Lord of the Castle), Hans Sternberg (Cellarar of the Lord of the Castle), Lucie Mannheim (Shepherd), Grete Berger (The Shepherd's Mother), Anni Mewes (Bride), Martin Lübbert (Bridegroom), Gustav von Wangenheim (The Huntsman), Wilhelm Diegelmann (The Bard), Erika von Thellmann.

Studio: Decla Bioscop Studio and backlot, Neubabelsberg

Shot from May to August 1922

Distribution Companies: Decla Bioscop Verleih G.m.b.H./Universum-Film Verleih G.m.b.H. (UFA), Berlin

Length: 1978 m. *Running time*: 73 minutes.

Premiere: January 23, 1923, Berlin, U.T. Kurfürstendamm

The ballad of a sinister Master of the Mountain, who is struck by lightning and petrified at the end of the picture.

1922–24

Die Nibelungen
Part 1: Siegfried
Part 2: Kriemhilds Rache
(Kriemhild's Revenge)

Production Company: Decla-Bioscop Aktiengesellschaft/Universum Film Aktiengesellschaft (UFA), Berlin. *Producer*: Erich Pommer. *Director*: Fritz Lang. *Screenplay*: Thea von Harbou based on *Nibelungenlied*. *First Cinematographer*: Carl Hoffmann. *Second Cinematographer and Camera Effects*: Günther Rittau. *Art Directors*: Otto Hunte, Erich Kettelhut. *Construction of the Dragon*: Karl Vollbrecht. *Costumes*: Paul Gerd Guderian, Änne Willkomm. *Costumes of the Huns, armor and arms*: Völkerkundliches Musem [Ethnological Museum] Heinrich Umlauff, Hamburg. *Makeup*: Otto Genath. *Schüfftan Photography*: Eugen Schüfftan, Ernst Kunstmann. *Falcon Dream animated by* Walter Ruttmann. *Location Managers*: Rudi George, Gustav Püttjer. *Editorial Assistant*: Paul Falkenberg (?). *Musical Score*: Gottfried Huppertz.

Cast: Paul Richter (Siegfried the Dragonslayer), Margarethe Schön (Kriemhild of Burgund), Hanna Ralph (Queen Brunhild of Isenland), Theodor Loos (King Gunther of Burgund), Hans Adalbert Schlettow (Hagen von Tronje), Bernhard Goetzke (Volker von Alzey the bard), Hardy von François (Dankwart), Rudolf Klein-Rogge (Etzel, King of the Huns), Georg John (Mime the Smith/Alberich the Nibelung/Blaodel, Etzel's brother), Rudolf Rittner (Margrave Rüdiger of Bechlarn), Gertrude Arnold (Queen Ute), Hans Carl Müller (Gerenot of Burgund), Erwin Biswanger (Giselher of Burgund), Frida Richard (The Runes Maid), Georg [Juri] Jurowski (The Priest), Iris Roberts (Childe), Fritz Alberti (Dietrich of Bern), Hubert Heinrich (Werbel the Minstrel), Georg August Koch (Hildebrandt), Annie Röttgen (Dietlind of Bechlam), Gerhard Bienert, Ernst Legal, Rosa Liechtenstein.

Studio and Backlot: UFA, Neubabelsberg

Preparation and shooting time: from 1921 until November 1923

Distribution Company: Universum-Film Verleih G.m.b.H. (UFA), Berlin

Length (Part 1): 3210 m. *Running time*: 143 minutes. *Length* (Part 2): 3358 m. *Running time*: 144 minutes.

Premiere: February 14, 1924 (Part 1); May 10, 1924 (Part 2), Berlin UFA Palace at Zoo

Released in the United States on August 23, 1925, *in the short-lived* DeForest Phonofilm *sound-on-film process (conductor: Hugo Riesenfeld)*: New York City, Century Theater.

Reissue of Part 1 on May 29, 1933, as sound film version *Siegfrieds Tod* (*Siegfried's Death*), curated by Franz B. Biermann and narrated by Theodor Loos.

Distribution Company of West-German reissue (Part 1: *Siegfrieds Tod/Siegfried's Death*): NWDF Nordwestdeutscher Filmverleih Erich J. A. Pietrek (35mm), Ing. Ewald Paikert (16mm), Düsseldorf. (Part 2: *Kriemhilds Rache/Kriemhild's Revenge*): Atlas Film, Duisburg (16mm). *Musical Score Atlas version* Part 2: Konrad Elfers.

Premiere of the digitally restored version: April 27, 2010, Berlin, Deutsche Oper. Symphony Orchestra conducted by Frank Strobel.

Fritz Lang's nationalistic, pathetic film adaptation of the Germanic epic poem written around

AD 1200, a mythical mix of folklore, magic and treason. One of Hitler's favorite movies. Costumer Paul Gerd Guderian, who died during production, was the brother of Hitler's tank expert Heinz Guderian.

1923

Schatten: Die Nacht der Erkenntnis/- Eine nächtliche Halluzination (Warning Shadows: A Nocturnal Hallucination)

Production Company: Pan Film G.m.b.H., Berlin SW. 48, Friedrichstrasse 5–6. *Producers:* Enrico Dieckmann, Willy Seibold. *Director:* Arthur Robison. *Screenplay:* Rudolf Schneider, Arthur Robison. *Original story:* Albin Grau. *Cinematographer:* Fritz Arno Wagner. *Art Director:* Albin Grau. *Shadow Play:* Ernst Moritz Engert. *Musical Score:* Ernst Riege.

Cast: Fritz Kortner (The Jealous Husband), Ruth Weyher (His Wife), Gustav von Wangenheim (The Wife's Lover), Alexander Granach (The Traveling Performer), Eugen Rex (First Cavalier), Max Gülstorff (Second Cavalier), Ferdinand von Alten (Third Cavalier), Fritz Rasp (First Servant), Karl Platen (Second Servant), Lilli Herder (Chambermaid), Heinrich Gotho (A Musician).

World Sales: Deutsch-Amerikanische Film-Union Aktiengesellschaft (Dafu), Berlin SW. 48, Friedrichstrasse 5–6

Distribution Company (Berlin-Eastern territories-Middle Germany-South Germany): Dafu Filmverleih G.m.b.H., Berlin SW. 48, Friedrichstrasse 5–6

Distribution Company (Rhineland-Westphalia): Metropol Film Verleih Rhenania G.m.b.H., Düsseldorf, Worringerstrasse 115

Distribution Company (North Germany): Niedersächsische Film G.m.b.H., Hanover, Handelshof.

Length: 2002 m. *Running time:* ca. 90 minutes.
Press Screening: July 26, 1923, Berlin, Primus Palace
Premiere: October 16, 1923, Berlin, U.T. Nollendorfplatz

Albin Grau's "sequel" to *Nosferatu* is a shadow play about love and jealousy.

Der Puppenmacher von Kiang-Ning (The Puppet Maker of Kiang Ning)

Production Company: Lionardo Film, Berlin. *Producer-Director:* Dr. Robert Wiene. *Screenplay:* Carl Mayer. *Cinematographer:* Willy Hameister. *Art Directors:* César Klein, Walter Reger.

Cast: Werner Krauss (The Puppet Maker), Lia Eibenschütz, Ossip Runitsch, Lucie Mannheim, Julius Falkenstein, Fritz Achterberg, Hans Schweikart, Georg Jurowski, Eugen Rex, Alexander Alexandrowski.

Distribution Company: Internationaler Filmvertrieb Dietz & Co., Berlin
Board of Censors: May 29, 1923
Premiere: November 1923, Berlin

A mad Chinese puppet maker is going to kidnap a woman, because he has lost his face: She is more beautiful than the best of his works. The woman is rescued, and the puppet maker falls to death.

Der Geisterseher (The Apparationist)

Production Company: Spezial Film Aktiengesellschaft, Berlin. *Director:* Heinrich Brandt. *Screenplay:* Maurice Krol, Ruth Goetz, based on the novel fragment by Friedrich von Schiller and a novel by Hanns Heinz Ewers. *Cinematographer:* Adolf Otto Weitzenberg. *Art Director:* Robert A. Dietrich.

Cast: Suzanne Marville, Ferdinand von Alten, Georg Heinrich Schnell, Kurt Vespermann, Grete Berger, Hugo Flink, Ernst Laskowski, Ilse Götzen, Alfred Haase, Eduard Rothauser, Anna von Palen, Ferdinand Robert.

Board of Censors: July 27, 1923
Premiere: September 1923, Berlin, Primus Palace

Although unfinished, *The Apparitionist* was highly popular with readers who longed for the ingredients of Gothic fiction such as spiritualism, necromancy and conspiracies. When Hanns Heinz Ewers ventured to finish it his way in 1922, critics were not enthusiastic but at least Ewers could sell it to the movies.

Dr. Sacrobosco, der grosse Unheimliche (Dr. Sacrobosco, the Great Uncanny)

Production Company: FLAG Film Industrie (Filmindustrie und Lichtspiel Aktiengesellschaft), Berlin and Leipzig. *Director:* Josef Firmans. *Screenplay:* Gustav Meyrink. *Cinematographer:* Arthur von Schwertführer. *Art Director:* Robert Georg Wiesengrund. *Location Manager:* Ernst Gethke.

Cast: Adolf Böckl, Margit Piller, Käte Robert-Wenk, Wilhelm Diegelmann, Victor Colani, Georg Heinrich Schnell, Hans Lanser-Rudolff, Fritz Greiner, Annie Gräsenau.

Distribution Company: FLAG Filmindustrie und Lichtspiel Aktiengesellschaft, Berlin

Board of Censors: November 29, 1923

Premiere: December 1923, Munich

Original screenplay by the author of the *Golem* novel: Unlike his colleagues Strobl and Ewers, Gustav Meyrink was an enemy of excessive German nationalism. Albert Zimmermann, a *"völkisch"* journalist, called him "one of the cleverest and most dangerous opponents of the German nationalist ideal. He will influence—and corrupt—thousands upon thousands, just as [Heinrich] Heine did." Meyrink died on December 4, 1932, about two months before the Nazis came to power.

The film was directed by Josef Firmans (1884–1957). He mainly worked for the theater and directed movies only between 1920 and 1923, including the banned *Teufelssymphonie*.

I.N.R.I. *(Crown of Thorne)*

Production Company: Neumann Film Produktion G.m.b.H., Berlin. *Producers:* Hans Neumann, Hans von Wolzogen. Based on a 1905 novel by Peter Rosegger. *Writer-Director-Editor:* Dr. Robert Wiene. *Cinematographers:* Axel Graatkjaer, Ludwig Lippert, Reimar Kuntze. *Art Director-Costume Designer:* Ernö Metzner. *Music Director (Premiere):* Willy Schmidt-Gentner.

Cast: Grigori Chmara (Jesus Christ), Henny Porten (Mary), Asta Nielsen (Mary Magdalene), Werner Krauss (Pontius Pilatus, Roman Proconsul), Emanuel Reicher (High Priest Kaiphas), Alexander Granach (Judas Iscariot), Theodor Becker (Roman Officer), Robert Taube (High Priest Annas), Bruno Ziener (Simon Petrus), Hans Heinrich von Twardowski (Johannes), Emil Lind (Thomas), Max Kronert (Jacobus the Elder), Max Magnus (Jacobus the Younger), Walter Neumann (Matthew), Guido Herzfeld (Simon), Wilhelm Nagel (Philippus), Lionel Royce (Bartholomew), Eduard Kandl (Andreas), Walter Werner (Judas Lebbaeus), Paul Graetz (Jairus), Maria Kryschanowskaja (Jairus's Little Daughter), Mathilde Sussin (Paralyzed Woman), Erik Ode (Jesus as Child), Erwin Kaiser (Man in Prison), Elsa Wagner (Mother), Erich Walter (Monk), Ernst Dernburg (The Presiding Judge), Gustav Oberg (Prosecutor), Jaro Fürth (Criminal Defender), Pawel Pawlow (Warden), Rose Veldtkirch, Paul Henckels.

Studio: Filmwerke Staaken, Berlin

Shot between May and September 1923

Distribution Company: Bayerische Film G.m.b.H. (Emelka), Munich

Length: 3444 m. Seven acts.

Board of Censors: November 19, 1923. G-rated.

Premiere: December 25, 1923, Berlin, Mozartsaal Nollendorfplatz; Schauburg; Marmorhaus

The story of Jesus Christ: Judas is portrayed by Alexander Granach (Knock in *Nosferatu*) as a social revolutionary who wants Jesus to lead an uprising against the Roman occupation forces.

Der verlorene Schuh (The Lost Shoe)

Production Company: Decla-Bioscop Aktiengesellschaft./Universum Film Aktiengesellschaft (UFA), Berlin. *Producer:* Erich Pommer. *Writer-Director:* Dr. Ludwig Berger, based on the fairy tale *"Cinderella."* *Cinematographers:* Günther Krampf, Otto Baecker. *Art Directors:* Rudolf Bamberger, Heinrich Heuser. *Costumes:* Maria Willenz. *Location Managers:* Erich Kubat, Max Wogritsch. *Musical Director (Premiere):* Guido Bagier.

Cast: Helga Thomas (Marie von Cucoli), Paul Hartmann (Prince Anselm Franz, heir to the throne), Lucie Höflich (Countess Benrat, Marie's stepmother), Mady Christians (Daughter Violante Benrat), Olga Tschechowa (Daughter Stella Benrat), Max Gülstorff (Von Cucoli), Frida Richard (Marie's Godmother), Hermann Thimig (Adjutant Baron Steiss-Steißling), Leonhard Haskel (Prince Habakuk XXVI), Emilie Kurz (Princess Aloysia), Werner Hollmann (Court Marshall Count Ekelmann), Gertrud Eysoldt (Rauerin, an evil woman), Georg John (Jon, valet), Paula Conrad-Schlenther (Princess

Anastasia), Karl Eichholz (Franz, the old valet), Edith Edwards.

Studio: Decla-Bioscop backlot, Neubabelsberg

Shooting from April to October 1923

Distribution Companies: Decla-Bioscop Verleih G.m.b.H./Universum-Film Verleih G.m.b.H. (UFA), Berlin

Head of Distribution: Hermann Saklikower
Premiere: December 5, 1923, Berlin UFA Palace at Zoo

Ludwig Berger's charming interpretation of *Cinderella*.

1923–24

Das kalte Herz (The Heart of Stone)

Production Company: Hermes Film G.m.b.H., Berlin. *Director:* Fred Sauer. *Screenplay:* Walter Wassermann, Fred Sauer, based on the fairy tale by Wilhelm Hauff. *Cinematographer:* Heinrich Gärtner. *Art Director:* Siegfried Wroblewsky. *Location Manager:* Paul Goergens.

Cast: Fritz Schulz (Kohlenmunk Peter), Grete Reinwald, Frida Richard, Heinrich Peer, Dr. Philipp Manning, Paul Walker (The Glass Manikin?), Victor Costa, Gustav Trautschold, Edith Penner, Harry Berber.

Board of Censors: December 19, 1923

From the well-known German fairy tale: A Black Forest charburner sells his heart to an evil ghost of the forest and in return receives a heart of stone that kills any empathy. This story was filmed repeatedly; the best version was a 1950 DEFA production in Agfacolor.

Das Wachsfigurenkabinett (Waxworks)

Production Company: Neptun Film Aktiengesellschaft, Berlin. *Production Manager:* Alexander Kwartiroff. *Director–Production Designer:* Paul Leni. *Co-Director and Dramaturge:* Leo Birinski. *Assistant Director:* Wilhelm [William] Dieterle. *Screenplay:* Henrik Galeen. *Cinematographer:* Helmar Lerski. *Still Photographer:* Hans Lechner. *Set Construction:* Fritz Maurischat, Alfred Junge. *Props:* Paul Dannenberg. *Costumes:* Ernst Stern. *Location Manager:* Arthur Kiekebusch.

Cast: Emil Jannings (Harun al-Rashid), Conrad Veidt (Czar Ivan the Terrible), Werner Krauss (Jack the Ripper), Wilhelm Dieterle (The Poet/Assad the baker/A Russian Prince/Rinaldo Rinaldini), Olga Belajeff (Eva/Maimune/A Boyar), John Gottowt (Owner of the Wax Museum), Paul Biensfeldt (Grand Vizier), Ernst Legal (Poison-maker of the Czar), Georg John (Prisoner).

Studio: May Film, Berlin Weissensee

Shot from June to September 1923

Distribution Company: Universum-Film Verleih G.m.b.H. (UFA), Berlin

Released in the United States in 1926 by Film Arts Guild

Board of Censors: February 14, 1924. Adults only.

Premiere: October 6, 1924, Vienna; November 13, 1924, Berlin

Max Reinhardt student Wilhelm Dieterle, who later went to the United States where he co-directed *A Midsummer Night's Dream* and directed the Charles Laughton version of *The Hunchback of Notre Dame*, plays a young poet who is hired by the proprietor of a wax museum to concoct stories around the eerie wax personifications of Harun al-Rashid, Ivan the Terrible and Jack the Ripper. He dreams himself and the proprietor's daughter in the stories. A fourth episode woven around Rinaldo Rinaldini was planned but not shot.

Rudolf Kurtz wrote in his book *Expressionism and Film* that director Paul Leni showed an instinctive feeling for the kinetic energy, the tensile strength, of the expressionist scenery. To him the appearance of Werner Krauss as the Ripper who haunts a pair of lovers was particularly remarkable:

His mask a spellbinding gaze; slow, deliberate steps; austere grandeur; all are aimed by actor Werner Krauss at pure expression. The brief, frantic chase, with Krauss' calm yet rigid face always behind two fearful, fleeing young people, ensues amidst a catastrophe of space—under walls that bend over, split up and crack; under lights that seem to pound the set into lurid pieces. Natural shape is recklessly abandoned; the bound and released mass of spaces and lines, walls and bodies, crossbeams and projections, is represented most expressionistically. It is always full of energy that must explode, animated sets leaving themselves into space, voracious openings, and the dizzying ascent of stairs.

Leni has decorated this clearly composed set with light, as it were. This light, distilled from a thousand sources, creates feverish dreams in the space, underscores every curve, careers along broken lines, creates depths without background: it conjures up blackness on the slanting ruins that seem to stretch up out of it. He makes use of the technical possibilities of the apparatus, filming things into and over one another. This frees the motions of forms in space from their conventional ties, allowing them to ascend to a metaphysical sphere. And so confidently are means and material subordinated to the strong decorative resolve that the audience greeted these very abstract, subtle scenes with great applause.[7]

1923–26

Die Abenteuer des Prinzen Achmed (The Adventures of Prince Achmed)

Production Company: Comenius Film G.m.b.H. *Producer:* Louis Hagen. *Writer-Director and Animation:* Lotte Reiniger. *Technical Assistant and Stop Frame Cinematographer:* Carl Koch. *Art Effects:* Walter Ruttmann, Berthold Bartosch, Alexander Kardan, Walter C. Türck, Lore Leudesdorff. *Musical Score:* Wolfgang Zeller. *Conductor (German Premiere, Gloria Palace Berlin):* Max Roth.

Distribution Company: Universum-Film Verleih G.m.b.H. (UFA), Berlin

World Sales: Lothar Stark Film G.m.b.H., Berlin

Length: 1811 m. *Running time:* 81 minutes. Five acts.

Board of Censors: January 15, 1926. G-rated.

Regular German release: September 3, 1926, Berlin, Gloria Palace

During Germany's financial crisis, Louis Hagen, a banker, invested in a large quantity of raw film stock as a shelter from inflation, but the gamble hadn't paid off—and so Lotte Reiniger was allowed to use it to make her animated *Adventures of Prince Achmed*, a *Thousand and One Night* fantasy, in the magnificent tradition of the Shadow Theatre that originated from Asia, from China, India and Indonesia, which in fact is one of the founding stones of intercultural synergy between East and West.

Shadow puppetry may be as old as the discovery of shadows themselves. Folk tales, fables and legends are favorite topics on the shadow screen in any culture and time period.

The technique of shadow or silhouette film is quite simple. As with cartoon drawings, the silhouette films are photographed movement by movement. But instead of using drawings, silhouette marionettes are used. These marionettes are cut out of black cardboard and thin lead, every limb being cut separately and jointed with wire hinges. A study of natural movement is very important, so that the little figures appear to move just as men and women and animals do. But this is not a technical problem. The backgrounds for the characters are cut out with scissors as well, and designed to give a unified style to the whole picture.

Describing the process of animation, Lotte Reiniger explained that before any acting there is a lot of technique involved to move the flat silhouette puppets around:

> When you are going to play with your figure seriously, make sure that you are seated comfortably. The shooting will take up a long time and you will have to keep yourself as alert as possible. Don't wear any bulgy sleeves; they might touch your figure unexpectedly and disturb its position. If possible, arrange to place an iron or wooden bar five inches above the set along your field of action and let your arms rest on it, so that you touch your figure only with the fingertips, or with your scissors. [...]
>
> The most cautiously executed movements must be the slow ones, where you have to alter the position only the fraction of an inch. A steady, slow walk is one of the most tricky movements to execute. Here the most frequent mistake at the beginning is to let the body lag behind the legs, so that they seem be running away from under the body. If you touch the center of the body first and move it forward, holding the legs in the initial position, you will notice that they fall into the next position almost by themselves.
>
> Tall, lean figures are more prone to these errors than round, short ones, which roll along easily, whilst the balance of the long ones is more difficult to establish. [...]
>
> If a figure is to turn round it had best to do so in a quick motion. If you want the movement

Artist Lotte Reiniger and assistants animating silhouette figures (courtesy Caroline Hagen Hall, Primrose Film Productions Ltd.).

slower you might partly hide it in a convenient piece of the setting.[8]

For a long time, Reiniger's animated silhouette fairy tale of the Arabian Nights was considered the first feature-length animation film until Giannalberto Bendazzi found out that the honor belongs to a filmmaker from Argentine, Quirino Cristiani.

1924–25

Lebende Buddhas (Living Buddhas)

Production Company: Paul Wegener Film Aktiengesellschaft, Berlin. *Production Manager:*

Berthold Held. *Producer-Director:* Paul Wegener. *Screenplay:* Paul Wegener, Hans Sturm. *Cinematographers:* Guido Seeber, Reimar Kuntze, Joseph Rona. *Special Photographic Effects:* Guido Seeber. *Animation and Form Plays:* Walter Ruttmann. *Art Directors:* Hans Poelzig, Botho Höfer. *Sculptures:* Christiane Naubereit. *Costumes:* Berti Rosenberg, *Musical Score:* Willy Schmidt-Gentner.

Cast: Paul Wegener (The Great Lama), Asta Nielsen (Tibetan Girl), Heinrich Schroth (Dr. Smith), Hans Sturm (Prof. Campbel), Käthe Haack (Mrs. Campbel), Carl Ebert (Prof. Smith), Gregori Chmara (Young Lama Jeb-sun), Friedrich Kühne (First Lama), Max Pohl (Second Lama), Eduard Rothauser.

Distribution Company: Terra Filmverleih G.m.b.H., Berlin

Length: 2382 m. *Running time:* 93 minutes Five acts. [*Censored version*]: 87 minutes.

Board of Censors: February 9, 1925. Adults only.

Premiere: May 12, 1925, Berlin, Theater Nollendorfplatz

Paul Wegener who was a Buddhist, founded his own production company, asked Hans Poelzig to build a Tibetan landscape in the studio, complete with temple and village, and cast Asta Nielsen as a beautiful Tibetan human sacrifice. Englishmen disturb the monks' ceremony and bring the girl abroad, but they cannot escape the power of the Great Lama. The production proved a disaster and almost ruined Wegener.

Orlacs Hände (The Hands of Orlac)

Production Company: Pan Film Aktiengesellschaft, Vienna, in association with Berolina Film G.m.b.H., Berlin. *Director:* Dr. Robert Wiene. *Screenplay:* Louis Nerz, based on the 1920 novel *Les Mains d'Orlac* by Maurice Renard. *Cinematographers:* Günther Krampf, Hans Androschin. *Art Director:* Stefan Wessely in collaboration with Hans Rouc and Karl Exner, *Musical Score*: Pierre Oser.

Cast: Conrad Veidt (Paul Orlac), Alexandra Sorina (Yvonne Orlac), Fritz Kortner (Nera), Carmen Cartellieri (Regine), Fritz Strassny (Paul's Father), Paul Askonas (Valet).

Studio: Listo Film, Vienna

Shot in the late summer of 1924

German Distribution Company: Berolina Film G.m.b.H., Berlin

Length: 2507 (2357) m. *Running time:* 92 minutes. Seven acts.

German Board of Censors: September 25, 1924; February 5, 1925. Adults only.

German Premiere: September 24, 1924, Berlin, Haydn Cinema

German Release: January 30, 1925, Berlin, U.T. Nollendorfplatz

Austrian Release: March 6, 1925, Vienna

Released in the United States in 1928 by: Aywon Film.

In an accident, a famous pianist loses his hands. New hands are grafted on but these are the hands of a murderer.

Ein Sommernachtstraum (A Midsummer Night's Dream)

Production Company: Neumann Film Produktion G.m.b.H., Berlin. *Producer-Director:* Hans Neumann. *Screenplay:* Hans Behrendt, Hans Neumann, based on the play *A Midsummer Night's Dream* by William Shakespeare. *Intertitles:* Alfred Henschke. *Cinematographer:* Guido Seeber. *Camera Assistant:* Reimar Kuntze. *Art Director-Costume Designer*: Ernö Metzner. *Musical Score:* Hans May.

Cast: Theodor Becker (Theseus, Duke of Athens), Paul Günther (Egeus, Father to Hermia), Charlotte Ander (Hermia), André Mattoni (Lysander), Barbara von Annenkoff (Helena), Hans Albers (Demetrius), Werner Krauss (Niklaus Zettel/Nick Bottom), Lori Leux (Titania, Queen of the Fairies), Valeska Gert (Puck), Tamara Geva (Oberon, King of the Fairies), Wilhelm Bendow (Franz Flaut/Francis Flute), Fritz Rasp (Schnauz/Tom Snout), Alexander Granach (A Sprite), Walter Brandt (Schnock/Snug), Armand Guerra (Wenzel), Martin Jacob (Schlucker/-Robin Starveling), Ernst Gronau (Peter Squenz/-Peter Quince), Ruth Weyher (Hippolyta), Bruno Ziener (Milon, General of the Greeks), Hans Behrendt, Paul Biensfeldt, Adolf Klein, Rose Veldtkirch.

Running time: 80 minutes.

Board of Censors: February 27, 1925

Premiere: March 10, 1925

Having filmed the Gospels and I.N.R.I., Hans Neumann this time tried Shakespeare.

Die Biene Maja und ihre Abenteuer (Adventures of Maya)

Production Company: Kulturfilm Aktiengesellschaft, Berlin. *Director*: Wolfram Junghans. *Screenplay*: Curt Thomalla. *Script Supervisor, Intertitles and Co-Director* (*Fairy Scene*): Waldemar Bonsels, based on his book. *Cinematographer*: Adolf Otto Weitzenberg. *Production Designer*: Svend Noldan. *Designer of hornet castle*: Albin Grau.

Board of Censors: January 12, 1925
Premiere: March 3, 1925, Dresden, Capitol
Waldemar Bonsels's 1915 book about the adventures of a honey bee fighting the evil hornets, all portrayed by real bees and insects.

Wunder der Schöpfung (In the World of the Stars aka Our Heavenly Bodies)

Production Company: Colonna Film G.m.b.H./UFA Kulturfilm Division, Berlin. *Director*: Hanns Walter Kornblum. *Assistant Directors*: Johannes Meyer, Rudolf Biebrach. *Screenplay*: Hanns Walter Kornblum, Ernst Krieger. *Cinematographers*: Hermann Boehlen, Max Rinck, Wera Cleve, Bodo Kuntze, Hans Scholz, Friedrich Paulmann, Ewald-Matthias Schuhmacher, Friedrich Weinmann. *Special Photographic Effects*: Otto von Bothmer. *Animation Camera*: Major Hans Ewald, Sr., Bodo Kuntze, Wera Cleve, Hermann Boehlen. *Schüfftan Photography*: Eugen Schüfftan, Helmar Lerski, Ernst Kunstmann. *Art Directors*: Carl Stahl-Urach, Gustav Hennig, Walter Reimann, Hans Minzloff, Otto Moldenhauer. *Title Artist*: Dassel-Weil. *Musical Score*: Ignatz Waghalter.

Cast: Margarete Schön, Theodor Loos, Paul Bildt, Margarethe Schlegel, Oscar Marion, Willy Kaiser-Heyl.

Premiere: September 14, 1925, Berlin
Distribution Company: Universum-Film Verleih G.m.b.H. (UFA), Berlin
Prints: tinted
Length: 1714 m. *Running time*: 75 minutes (20 fps).
Restoration and Print: Film Museum Munich. *Supervisor*: Stefan Drössler

Semi-documentary with feature film scenes showing mankind's way to the stars and the end of the world. According to John Kindberg,

> Fifteen special effects experts and nine cameramen were involved in the production of this film which combines documentary scenes, historical documents, fiction elements, animation scenes and educational impact. It is beautifully colored, using tinting and toning in a very elaborated way. Some visual ideas in the sequences with a space shuttle visiting different planets in the universe seem to have to be the inspiration for Stanley Kubrick's *2001: A Space Odyssey*.[9]

In the context of Germany's Kulturfilm phenomenon, *Wunder der Schöpfung* was among the greatest achievements of the 1920s. The production was constructed, rehearsed and shot over a period of two and a half years, under the supervision of Hanns Walter Kornblum. The idea to describe the universe and man's place in it suited UFA's Grossfilm mentality, one year before the *Metropolis* catastrophe. Hundreds of skilled craftsmen participated in the project, building props and constructing scale models drawn by 15 special effects draughtsmen, while nine cameramen in separate units worked on the historical, documentary, fiction, animation and science-fiction sequences. […]

The film's symbol to progress and the new scientific era is a spacecraft, traveling through the Milky Way, making all the planets and their inspiring worlds familiar to us, with the extravaganza of their distinctive features. The film's educational intentions, however, become steadily more obscure, humorous or even campy as this popularization project proceeds. With the excuse of presenting the end of the world, a not-so-new concept, as a new, undeniably scientific truth, the film veers happily along a new path, displaying detailed apocalyptic scenes of the end of mankind.[10]

1925

Aus der Urzeit der Erde (From Primordial Times)

Production Company: Ewald Film G.m.b.H., Berlin *Producer and Animation Supervisor*: Major Hans Ewald, Sr.

This short film, made by a Berlin animation studio, follows the popular production of Conan Doyle's *The Lost World* using the technique of

1925–26

Geheimnisse einer Seele (Secrets of a Soul)

Production Company: Neumann Film Produktion G.m.b.H./UFA Kulturfilm Division, Berlin. *Producer:* Hans Neumann. *Director:* G.W. Pabst. *Assistant Director:* Mark Sorkin. *Screenplay:* Colin Ross, Hans Neumann. *Cinematographers:* Guido Seeber, Curt Oertel, Robert Lach. *Special Photographic Effects:* Guido Seeber. *Set Designer:* Ernö Mezner. *Scientific Consultants:* Dr. Karl Abraham, Hanns Sachs. *Location Manager:* Richard Ortlieb. *Musical Director (Premiere):* Dr. Giuseppe Becce.

Cast: Werner Krauss (Martin Fellmann/The Man), Ruth Weyher (His Wife/The Woman), Jack Trevor (Erich/The Cousin), Pawel Pawlow (Dr. Orth/The Physician), Hertha von Walther (Fellmann's Assistant), Ilka Grüning (The Mother), Renate Brausewetter (The Maid), Colin Ross (Detective Superintendent), Lili Damita.

Shot between September and November 1925.

Running time: 97 minutes

Distribution Company: Universum-Film Verleih G.m.b.H. (UFA), Berlin

Rating: Volksbildend (for national education)

Premiere: March 24, 1926, Berlin, Gloria Palace

Psychoanalysis had established a stronghold in 1920s Berlin: Werner Krauss is tormented by an irrational fear of knives and the compulsion to murder his wife. The film includes a fantasy dream sequence full of tricks and visual effects.

Faust: Eine deutsche Volkssage (Faust: A German Folk Legend)

Production Company: Universum Film Aktiengesellschaft (UFA), Berlin. *Producer:* Erich Pommer. *Director:* F.W. Murnau. *Screenplay:* Hans Kyser, based on the plays by Johann Wolfgang von Goethe and Christopher Marlowe and a script by Dr. Ludwig Berger titled *Das verlorene Paradies* (*The Lost Paradise*). *Cinematographer:* Carl Hoffmann. *Camera Assistant:* Erich Grohmann. *Art Directors, Landscapes, Costumes:* Robert Herlth, Walter Röhrig. *Assistant Art Directors:* Arno Richter, Georges Annenkov. *Makeup:* Waldemar Jabs. *Musical Director (Premiere):* Werner Richard Heymann using motifs from works by Richard Wagner and Richard Strauss.

Cast: Gösta Ekman (Faust), Emil Jannings (Mephistopheles), Camilla Horn (Gretchen), Frieda Richard (Gretchen's Mother), Wilhelm Dieterle (Valentin), Yvette Guilbert (Marthe Schwerdtlein, Gretchen's aunt), Eric Barclay (Duke of Parma), Hanna Ralph (Duchess of Parma), Werner Fuetterer (Arch Angel Gabriel), Hans Brausewetter (A Swain), Lothar Müthel (The Monk), Hans Rameau, Hertha von Walther, Emmy Wyda.

Studio: UFA Studios, Berlin-Tempelhof (and Neubabelsberg)

Shot from September 1925 until mid–1926

Distribution Company: Universum-Film Verleih GmbH (UFA)/Parufamet (Paramount-UFA-Metro-Verleihbetriebe G.m.b.H.), Berlin

Length: 2484 m. *Running time:* 106 minutes. Seven acts.

Board of Censors: August 17, 1926. Adults only.

Premiere: October 14, 1926, Berlin, UFA Palace at Zoo. (Press screening on August 25, 1926, at UFA Theater Nollendorfplatz.)

Released in the United States on December 5, 1926, *by* Metro-Goldwyn-Mayer in New York City.

1995 *restored version:* "Project Lumière," Luciano Berriatúa (Filmoteca Espanola, Madrid) in cooperation with the Friedrich Wilhelm Murnau Foundation, German Film Institute and Det Danske Filmmuseum.

The granddaddy of Teutonic fantasy and speculative fiction: Faust the alchemist makes a pact with the Devil in exchange for his soul. Emil Jannings dominates the picture as Mephistopheles while Swedish actor Gösta Ekman as Faust remains weak.

1925–27

Metropolis

This film was commissioned by UFA and is released by Parufamet. *Production Company:* Universum Film Aktiengesesllschaft (UFA), Berlin. *Producer:* Erich Pommer. *Director:* Fritz Lang. *Screenplay:* Thea von Harbou in collaboration with Fritz Lang. *Metropolis,* novel by Thea von Harbou, was published as preprint: Illustriertes Blatt, Frankfurt, as book: August Scherl Verlag G.m.b.H. *First Cinematographer:* Karl Freund. *Camera Assistant to Mr. Freund:* Robert Baberske. *Second Cinematographer and Special Photographic Effects:* Günther Rittau. *Camera Assistant to Mr. Rittau:* H.O. [Hugo Otto] Schulze. *Special Photography:* Konstantin Tschet [Tschetwerikoff]. *Still Photographer:* Horst von Harbou. *Art Directors:* Otto Hunte, Erich Kettelhut, Karl Vollbrecht. *Assistant:* Willy Müller. *Special Art Effects:* Erich Kettelhut. *Costumes:* Änne Willkomm. *Costumes manufactured by* UFA workshops and Theaterkunst Hermann J. Kaufmann, Berlin. *Completion of the Costumes for the Men in the "Eternal Gardens":* Fashion Shop Knize, Berlin. *Completion of the Shoes for the Women in the "Eternal Gardens":* Footwear Store Reiss, Berlin. *Completion of the Shoes for the Men in the "Eternal Gardens":* Footwear Store Breitspecher, Berlin. *Sculptor* (Machine Man, Seven Deadly Sins and other sculptures): Walter Schulze-Mittendorf. *Schüfftan Photography*: Eugen Schüfftan, Helmar Lerski, Ernst Kunstmann, Heinrich Weidemann. *Miniature Supervisor:* Edmund Ziehfuss. *Consultant on Miniatures:* Konrad Wachsmann. *Location Manager:* Rudi George. *Production Assistants*: Heinz Blanke, Erich Holder, Gustav Püttjer, Hans Taussig. *Directorial Trainee:* Slatan Dudow. *Musical Score:* Gottfried Huppertz. *Orchestra* (*Premiere*): UFA Symphony Orchestra conducted by Otto Härzer.

Cast: Alfred Abel (Joh Fredersen), Gustav Fröhlich (Freder, Joh Fredersen's son), Brigitte Helm (Maria/the Machine Maria), Rudolf Klein-Rogge (C.A. Rotwang, the inventor), Heinrich George (Grot, Guardian of the Heart Machine), Theodor Loos (Josaphat/Joseph), Fritz Rasp (The Slim One/The Thin Man), Erwin Biswanger (Georgy, worker no. 11811), Olaf Storm (Jan), Hanns Leo Reich (Marinus), Heinrich Gotho (Master of Ceremonies), Margarete Lanner (Woman in Car/Woman in "Eternal Gardens"), Max Dietze, Georg John, Walter Kurt Kühle, Arthur Reinhardt, Erwin Vater (Male Workers), Grete Berger, Olly Böheim, Ellen Frey, Lisa Gray, Rose Liechtenstein, Helene Weigel (Female Workers), Beatrice Garga, Anni Hintze, Helen von Münchhofen, Hilde Woitscheff (Women in "Eternal Gardens"), Fritz Alberti (The Creative Man), Lewis [Louis] Brody (Carrier of Incense Burner), Ilse Davidsohn.

Studio: UFA Studios, Neubabelsberg; Filmwerke Staaken

Shot from May 22, 1925, until October 30, 1926

Distribution Company: Parufamet (Paramount-UFA-Metro-Verleihbetriebe G.m.b.H.), Berlin

Length: 4174 (Original: 4189) m. *Running time:* 153 minutes. Nine acts.

Board of Censors: November 13, 1926. Adults only.

Premiere: January 10, 1927, Berlin, UFA Palace at Zoo

Released in the United States by: Famous Players Lasky Corporation/Paramount Pictures, New York City

Released in Japan by Shochikuza; Towa Shoji Bunka Eiga-bu

Distributor of German Reissue in 1962: NWDF-Unitas Filmverleih GmbH Erich J. A. Pietrek, Düsseldorf. 16mm: Ing. Ewald Paikert, Düsseldorf. 8mm: Atlas Film/Piccolo.

International Reissue with Music by Giorgio Moroder.

Colors and Opticals—Moroder version: Ray Mercer & Company

World Sales of Complete Version: Transit Film GmbH on behalf of Friedrich Wilhelm Murnau Foundation.

Declared World document heritage of UNESCO.

A revolution, evoked by a machine woman created by a vengeful alchemist-inventor, is stopped by the love of a pure worker girl and the son of an industrialist.

1926

Der Student von Prag (The Student of Prague)

Production Company: H. R. Sokal Film G.m.b.H., Berlin. *Producer:* Harry R. Sokal. *Writer-Director:* Henrik Galeen, based on an original idea by Hanns Heinz Ewers. *Assistant Director:* Erich Kober. *First Cinematographer and Photographic Effects:* Günther Krampf. *Second Cinematographer:* Erich Nitzschmann. *Art Director* Hermann Warm. *Art Titles:* Rafaello Busoni. *Location Manager:* Max Maximilian. *Musical Score:* Willy Schmidt-Gentner.

Cast: Conrad Veidt (Balduin, student), Werner Krauss (Scapinelli, usurer), Elizza La Porta (Lyduschka, flower vendor), Fritz Alberti (Count von Schwarzenberg), Agnes Esterhazy (Margit, his daughter), Ferdinand von Alten (Baron von Waldis-Schwarzenberg, Margit's fiancé), Erich Kober (Student), Max Maximilian (Student), Horst Wessel (Extra/Corps Student), Sylvia Torf, Marian Alma.
Studio: Filmwerke Staaken, Berlin
Shot from July to September 1926
Length: 3173 m. Seven acts.
Board of Censors: October 19, 1926. Adults only.
Rating: Volksbildend, Künstlerisch (for national education, artistical)
Premiere: October 25, 1926, Berlin, Capitol
In 1930, a sound version with musical score and sound effects was released.
Musical Director–Adaptation: Willy Schmidt-Gentner. *Musical Director–Conductor:* Philipp de la Cerda. *Sound Recordist* (Selenophon): Aurel Nowotny, Hans Bucek, Othmar Hampel.
Length: 2778 m. *Running time:* 101 minutes.
Premiere of the sound version: July 25, 1930, Vienna
A remake of Paul Wegener's 1913 film about a student who sells his shadow to an evil magician.

1927

Svengali

Production Company: Terra Filmkunst G.m.b.H., Berlin. *Producer:* Max Glass. *Production Manager and Location Manager:* Hermann Grund. *Director:* Gennaro Righelli. *Screenplay:* Max Glass, based on the novel *Trilby* (1895) by George L. Du Maurier. *Cinematographer:* Arpad Viragh. *Art Director:* Hans Jacoby. *Set Designer:* Fritz Maurischat. *Musical Score:* Walter Ulfig.
Cast: Paul Wegener (Svengali), Anita Dorris (Trilby), Paul Biensfeldt (Martine, a model), Teddy Bill (Leard, artist), Hans Brausewetter (Taffy, artist), Alexander Granach (Gecko, violinist), Irma Green (Student), André Mattoni (Billy, artist), Hermann Picha (Landlord of Coffee House), Alice Torning (Martine's Wife), Hertha von Walther (Sascha, a dancer), Emil Heyse.
Studio: Terra Glass Stage, Berlin-Marienfelde
Shot in May 1927.
Distribution Company: Terra Filmverleih G.m.b.H., Berlin
Seven acts
Board of Censors: August 4, 1927. Adults only.
Premiere: September 7, 1927, Berlin, Beba Palace Atrium
Paul Wegener in the title role as the hypnotist and music lover who transforms Trilby into a diva. When DuMaurier's novel was published, the portrayal of Svengali was highly criticized for anti–Semitism.

Ramper, der Tiermensch (The Strange Case of Captain Ramper)

Production Company: Deutsche Film-Union AG (Defu), Berlin. *Production Manager:* Eugen Thiele. *Director:* Max Reichmann. *Screenplay:* Curt J. Braun. *First Cinematographer:* Friedrich Weinmann. *Second Cinematographer:* Herbert Körner. *Art Director:* Leopold Blonder. *Musical Score:* Walter Ulfig,
Cast: Paul Wegener (Ramper), Camillo Kossuth (Ipling), Kurt Gerron (Chocolat), Georg D. Gürtler (Fredy), Mary Johnson (Zizi/Tony), Hermann Vallentin (Barbazin), Hugo Döblin (The "Doctor"), Raimondo van Riel (Captain), Max Schreck (Tall Crew Member).
Distribution Company: Deutsche Film Union AG (Defu)/Deutsche First National Pictures G.m.b.H. (Defina), Berlin
Board of Censors: September 19, 1927
Released in the United States on June 3, 1928, by First National Pictures
Premiere: October 21, 1927, Berlin
Captain Ramper, an aviator, makes a pioneering flight across the Arctic. Near the North Pole, the engine fails and the plane crashes in the wastes. Ramper finds a supply base containing food left behind by a previous expedition. After 15 years he is found: mutated, half-human, half-animal.

1927–28

Alraune

Production Company: Ama Film G.m.b.H., Berlin. *Director and Screenplay:* Henrik Galeen, based on the 1911 novel by Hanns Heinz Ewers. *Cinematographer:* Franz Planer. *Still Photographer:* Walter Lichtenstein. *Art Directors:* Walter Reimann, Max Heilbronner. *Location Manager:* Helmuth Schreiber. *Musical Score:* Willy Schmidt-Gentner.

Cast: Brigitte Helm (The Girl Alraune), Paul Wegener (Prof. Jakob ten Brinken), Ivan Petrovich (Franz Braun, his nephew), Mia Pankau (The Prostitute), Valeska Gert (A Streetwalking Girl), Georg John (The Murderer), Wolfgang Zilzer (Wölfchen/Little Wolf), Louis Ralph (The Magician), Hans Trautner (The Animal Tamer). John Loder (The Vicomte), Heinrich Schroth (A Gentleman in the Bar), Alexander Sascha (A Gentleman in the Coupé).

Distribution Company: Ama Film G.m.b.H., Berlin, and district distributors

Length: 3346 m (3390 m before censorship). Seven acts.

Board of Censors: January 28, 1928. Adults only.

Rating: Künstlerisch wertvoll (artistically valuable)

Premiere: January 25, 1928, Berlin, Capitol

Hanns Heinz Ewers's decadent and blackly humorous tale of an artificially birthed *femme fatale.* Ewers's friend Paul Wegener plays the role of Prof. ten Brinken, a veritable alchemist who has impregnated a prostitute with the semen of a hanged murderer. Romanticism would lead Ewers (and Wegener) to join the most deadly cult of German exceptionalism, the Nazis.

Geheimnisse des Orients (Secrets of the Orient)

Production Company: Universum-Film Aktiengesellschaft (UFA), Berlin/Ciné-Alliance, Paris. *Production Managers:* Noé Bloch, Gregor Rabinowitsch. *Director:* Alexander Wolkoff. *Assistant Director:* Anatole Litvak. *Screenplay:* Norbert Falk, Robert Liebmann, Alexander Wolkoff. *First Cinematographer:* Curt Courant. *Second Cinematographer:* Nikolai Toporkoff. *Third Cinematographer:* Fedor Bourgassoff. *Art Directors:* Alexander Loschakoff, Wladimir von Meinhardt. *Musical Director (German Premiere):* Willy Schmidt-Gentner.

Cast: Nikolaj Kolin (Ali, a cobbler), Nina Koschitz (Fatme, his wife), Iván Petrovich (Prince Achmed), D. Dimitrieff (Sultan Schariah), Marcella Albani (Sobeide, Sultan Schariah's Mistress), Agnes Petersen (Princess Gylnare), Gaston Modot (Prince Hussein), Julius Falkenstein (Astrologer at the Sultan's Court), Hermann Picha (The Sultan's Jester), Alexandre Vertinsky (Vizier), Dita Parlo (Slave Girl of the Princess), Steffi Vida.

Studio: Backlot of Franco Films, Nice. *Location Shooting*: Gabez (near Tunis).

Shooting: from November 1927 until April 1928.

Distribution Company for Germany: Universum-Film Verleih G.m.b.H. (UFA), Berlin

Distribution Company for France: Alliance Cinématographique Européenne (A.C.E.), Paris

Length: 2500 m. *Running time:* 114 minutes.

Premiere in Germany: October 19, 1928, Berlin

Premiere in France: August 30, 1929

Released in New York City on December 30, 1931 by Kolb

Made by Russian expatriates as a French-German co-production: Ali, a cobbler out of the Arabian Nights, gets hold of a magic pipe. Watch for the stunning hanging miniatures, similar to those in Douglas Fairbanks's 1924 *Thief of Bagdad.*

Der geheimnisvolle Spiegel (The Mysterious Mirror)

Production Company: Universum-Film Aktiengesellschaft (UFA), Berlin. *Directors:* Carl Hoffmann, Richard Teschner, Robert Reinert. *Cinematographer:* Carl Hoffmann. *Art Director:* Carl Böhm. *Musical Score:* Walter Winnig.

Cast: Felicitas [Fee] Malten (Anna, the granddaughter of the castle castellan), Dante Capelli (The Castle Castellan), Eduard von Winterstein (The Castle Caretaker), Fritz Rasp (The Rich Man), Rina de Liguoro (The Girlfriend of the Rich Man), Wolf-Albach Retty (The Sculptor), Max Magnus (The Friend of the Sculptor), Heinrich Gretler (The Chief Farm Hand), Alice Kempen (The Chief Maid).

Distribution Company: Universum-Film Verleih G.m.b.H. (UFA), Berlin

Length: 2496 m. *Running time*: 92 minutes.

Board of Censors: January 2, 1928

Premiere: March 21, 1928

During a full moon, a magic mirror found in

a castle foretells the future. The new lord of the castle (Fritz Rasp) is a brute. When he looks into the mirror, he sees how he is being murdered. Rasp once claimed that for a brief time, they had him in mind for becoming the successor of Lon Chaney.

1928

Vormittags-Spuk (Ghosts Before Breakfast)

Production Company: Hans Richter-Gesellschaft Neuer Film, Berlin. *Producer-Director:* Hans Richter. *Script:* Werner Graeff, Hans Richter. *Cinematographer:* Reimar Kuntze. *Musical Score:* Paul Hindemith.

Cast: Willi Pferdekamp, Hans Richter, Werner Graeff, Paul Hindemith, Darius Milhaud, Madeleine Milhaud, Hans Oser, Walter Gronostay.

Length: 170 m. *Running time:* ca. 9 minutes. 1 Act.

Board of Censors: July 11, 1928. G-rated.

Premiere: August 1928, Baden-Baden, Kurtheater (as part of the *Kammer Musikfest*)

Sound System: Tobis-Industrie G.m.b.H. (Tiges), Berlin

Premiere of the Sound Version: Baden-Baden, Film Palace (*Kammer Musikfest*).

Music (1983): Fernando Lafferière.

A Dadaist experimental film made by famed avant-gardist Hans Richter (1888–1976)

1928–29

Frau im Mond (Woman in the Moon aka By Rocket to the Moon)

Production Company: Fritz Lang Film G.m.b.H. in association with Universum Film Aktiengesellschaft (UFA), Berlin. *Producer-Director:* Fritz Lang. *Screenplay:* Thea von Harbou. *Cinematographers:* Curt Courant, Otto Kanturek. *Special Photography and Animation Effects:* Oskar Fischinger. *Miniature Photography* (*Launch of Space Rocket*): Konstantin Tschetwerikoff [Tschetwerikoff], Ernst Kunstmann. *Still Photographer:* Horst von Harbou. *Art Associate:* Gustav Wolff. *Scientific Consultants:* Josef Danilowatz, Hermann Oberth, Rudolf Nebel, Willy Ley. *Location Manager:* Eduard Kubat. *Musical Score:* Willy Schmidt-Gentner. *Lyrics*: Fritz Rotter.

Cast: Willy Fritsch (Wolf Helius), Gerda Maurus (Friede Velten), Gustav von Wangenheim (Hans Windegger, engineer), Klaus Pohl (Prof. Georg Manfeldt), Fritz Rasp (The Man Who Calls Himself Walter Turner), Gustl Stark-Gstettenbaur (Gustav, the boy), Tilla Durieux, Mahmud Terja Bey, Hermann Vallentin, Borwin Walth, Max Zilzer ("Brains and Chequebooks"), Margarete Kupfer (Frau Hippolt, Helius's housekeeper), Max Maximilian (Grotjan, Helius's chauffeur), Alexa von Porembsky (Violet Vendor), Karl Platen (Man at the Microphone), Gerhard Dammann (Master Workman at Helius Airfield), Heinrich Gotho (Lodger at first floor), Edgar Pauly, Alfred Loretto (Obvious Characters), Julius E. Herrmann, Josephine the Mouse.

Studio: UFA Studios, Neubabelsberg

Shot from October 1928 until June 1929

Distribution Company: Universum-Film Verleih G.m.b.H. (UFA), Berlin

Length: 4365 m. *Running time:* 156 minutes. 11 acts.

Board of Censors: September 25, 1929. G-rated.

Premiere: October 15, 1929, Berlin UFA Palace at Zoo

The first rocket to the moon, a triangular love story and a conspiracy thriller all in one. A ruthless American con man (Fritz Rasp) and his backers are after the gold that Prof. Manfeldt believes is to be found on the moon.

Timeworn melodrama blended with Aaron's rod and state-of-the-art science. Among Lang's consultants was Hermann Oberth, one of the founding fathers of German rocketry and mentor of Wernher von Braun. Oberth was supposed to launch a modest rocket at the time of the premiere but failed to do so.

Chapter Notes

Paul Wegener and Hanns Heinz Ewers

1. Paul Wegener, *Sein Leben und seine Rollen. Ein Buch von ihm und über ihn*, Arranged by Kai Möller, Hamburg, 1954.
2. *Ibid.*
3. *Erzählungen eines Skandalautors: Von blutgierigem Liebestaumel.* Deutschlandfunk, April 20, 2015.
4. *Peter Schlemihls wundersame Geschichte* was written in 1813.
5. Allegedly the name was an homage to Ewers's friend, the novelist Balduin Möllhausen, who had passed away in 1905. Kracauer spells his name Baldwin.
6. Guido Seeber, "Vom Film meines Lebens," in *Taschenbuch des Kameramannes für Lehr- und Nachschlagezwecke* (Berlin, 1928), 289.
7. Helmut Herbst, "1913 oder die Verbrechen der Phantasie und ihre Maschinisten," in *Special Effects*, Rolf Giesen (Ebersberg, 1985), 56.
8. Wolfgang Noa, *Paul Wegener* (Berlin: GDR, 1964).
9. Siegfried Kracauer, *From Caligari to Hitler: A Psychological History of the German Film* (Princeton, NJ: Princeton University Press, 1947), 36.
10. Kraft Wetzel, *Liebe, Tod und Technik. Utopie und NS-Ideologie im Phantastischen Kino des Dritten Reiches* (Berlin: Verlag Volker Spiess, 1977), 17.
11. Between 1967 and 1969 he edited a filmography of *German Silents* in 9 volumes.
12. Hanns Heinz Ewers, *Der Student von Prag* (Berlin, 1930), 12–14.
13. See *Künstliche Menschen: Dichtungen und Dokumente über Golems, Homunculi, Androiden und liebende Statuen*, edited by Klaus Völker (Munich: Hanser, 1971).
14. Friedrich Korn, *Herausgegeben und mit Anmerkungen begleitet von einem Unbefangenen* (Leipzig: Robert Friese, 1834).
15. "The real **new** earliest known source in print for the Golem of Prague?," Friday March 04, 2011: onthemainline.blogspot.com/.../real-new-earliest-known-source-i...
16. *The Miraculous Deeds of the MaHaRal of Prague.*
17. Chajim Bloch, *Der Prager Golem, von seiner "Geburt" bis zu seinem "Tod,"* preface by Hans Ludwig Held, 2nd edition (Berlin: Verlag Benjamin Harz, 1920), 12–13.
18. These extracts were taken from the only surviving original film script *Der Golem. Phantastisches Filmspiel in vier Akten* by Paul Wegener and Henrik Galeen. The title page is labeled Lyda Salmonova—Praha—Berlin and was given to Wegener's biographer Kai Möller by Mrs. Salmonova-Wegener in December 1949.
19. Meyrink's novel was filmed only once faithfully by Piotr Szulkin, a Polish film director, in 1979. In our filmography, however, you will find two original screenplays written by Meyrink.
20. *Der Golem*, original edition Kurt Wolff Verlag (Leipzig 1915/16).
21. Kay Weniger, *Das grosse Personenlexikon des Film*, Volume 3: F-H (Berlin: Schwarzkopf & Schwarzkopf Verlag, 2001), 170.
22. See Hans-Michael Bock, *Henrik Galeen* (Berlin, 1992).
23. Ilona Brennicke and Joe Hembus, ed., *Klassiker des deutschen Stummfilms* (Munich: Goldmann, 1983), 67.
24. *Golem and Mirjam*, Jewish Museum Berlin: https://www.jmberlin.de/.../online-catalog-golem-goldem-and-mirjam
25. Rolf Giesen, "Der Trickfilm: A Survey of German Special Effects," *Cinefex* number 25, February 1986.

Conrad Veidt and The Cabinet of Dr. Caligari

1. In 1917, on the Neubabelsberg Bioscop Studio lot, Reinert wrote and directed a 3-part mystery play about the "Eternal Jew" starring Carl de Vogt in the title part.
2. Claus Groth, "Du musst Caligari werden," *Illustrierter Film-Kurier*, No. 6, 1920.
3. *Caligari und Caligarismus* (Berlin: Deutsche Kinemathek, 1970), 11–16.
4. Collection of Deutsche Kinemathek Berlin.
5. Curt Siodmak quoted in Rolf Giesen, *Lexikon des phantastischen Films. Horror—Science Fiction—Fantasy*, Volume 1 (Berlin; Vienna; Frankfurt: Ullstein, 1984), 8.
6. *Der Caligari-Komplex* (Munich: Belleville, 2012).
7. Siegfried Kracauer, *From Caligari to Hitler: A Psychological History of the German Film.* (Princeton, NJ: Princeton University Press, 1947), 61.

8. Interview with Olaf Brill re: *Der Caligari-Komplex, Filmgeschichte jenseits der Legenden.*
9. Olaf Brill, *Der Caligari-Komplex* (Munich: Belleville, 2012), 222.
10. Graeme Gilloch, *Siegfried Kracauer: Our Companion in Misfortune.* (Polity Press: Cambridge, UK, 2015).
11. Marcel Reich-Ranicki, *Mein Leben* (Munich, 1999).

Dr. Jekyll, Murnau and Dracula

1. Lotte H. Eisner, *Murnau* (Frankfurt am Main: Deutsches Filmmuseum, 1986), 186.
2. *Film-Kurier*, July 9, 1920.
3. *Strange Case of Dr. Jekyll and Mr. Hyde*, 1886.
4. 1967 published by Friedrich Verlag in Velber/Hanover.
5. A Paramount picture directed by John S. Robertson. Both Veidt and Barrymore starred in United Artists' *Beloved Rogue* in 1927.
6. Walter Kaul, "Pikant pointiert," *Internationale Filmfestspiele Berlin*, July 7, 1975, 8.

Dracula in Germany

1. Albin Grau, *Bühne und Film,* 1921.
2. Philipp Stiasny, "Zwischen den Welten: Die lebenden Toten, Verlorenen und Heimkehrer des Weimarer Kinos," in *Weimarer Kino—neu gesehen.* (Berlin: Bertz + Fischer, 2018), 53.
3. The story goes that it was Grau's poster for *Mountain of Destiny* that caught Leni Riefenstahl's attention at Nollendorfplatz in Berlin and made her want to see the picture. She was so excited that she decided "on the spot" to meet the film's director, Dr. Arnold Fanck and enter into a liaison with him (and his male star, Luis Trenker).
4. German pamphlet published in 1488 in Nuremberg.
5. Nicholas Dima, *Journey to Freedom* (Washington, DC: Selous Foundation for Public Policy Research, 1990), p. 352.
6. Bram Stoker, *Dracula* (London: Archibald Constable and Company, 1897).
7. Jennifer Latson, "What made the Spanish Flu so Deadly?," Mar 11, 2015: www.time.com.
8. Edinburgh and New York, 1888.
9. Emily Gerard, *Transylvanian Superstitions: The Nineteenth Century (London: Henry S. King,* 1885), 128–144.
10. Wilhelm Schmidt, *Das Jahr und seine Tage in Meinung und Brauch der Rumänen Siebenbürgens. Ein Beitrag zur Kenntnis des Volksmythus* (Hermannstadt, Austria-Hungary: A Schmiedicke, 1866), 34.

Casting a Man Named "Shock"

1. *Der Tag*, Vienna, March 9 1923.
2. David Pirie, *Vampir-Filmkult* (Gütersloh: Prisma Verlag, 1977).
3. Ado Kyrou, *Le Surréalisme au cinema* (Paris: Arcanes, 1953).
4. We have mentioned that there is some speculation if Nosferatu was played in some shots by a different actor. Jens Geutebrück and others are convinced that the vampire aboard the ship was not Max Schreck. Maybe it was Hans Rameau who stalked the deck in disguise.
5. Hanns-Georg Rodek, *Die Welt*, Berlin, April 22, 2008.
6. Hanns Braun, *Münchener Zeitung*, November 15, 1921.
7. https://sites.google.com/site/grabsteinfuermaxschreck/
8. Chaney played a monstrous "semi-vampire" with top hat in Tod Browning's lost MGM production *London After Midnight* in 1927.
9. *Völkischer Beobachter*, December 24, 1930.
10. *Film-Kurier*, October 12, 1921.
11. *Costuming & Makeup: Nosferatu.* Rachelsfeaturepresentations.blogspot.com
12. Ibid.
13. *Berliner Lokal-Anzeiger*, October 17, 1921.
14. Barry McLoughlin and Kevin McDermott (ed.), *Stalin's Terror: High Politics and Mass Repression in the Soviet Union* (New York: Palgrave Macmillan, 2003), 185.
15. Irena R. Makaryk and Joseph G. Price, *Shakespeare in the Worlds of Communism and Socialism* (Toronto: University of Toronto Press, 2006), 180.
16. See also *Gustav von Wangenheim Tribute Page.* www.henrybwalthall.com/Wangenheim.html
17. Wilhelm von Kaulbach was a German painter who died in 1874 in Munich.
18. Sabine Rohlf, *"Zeig' ihm lieber deine Tennismuskeln. Ruth Landshoff-Yorck war gutgelaunt, stilsicher und emanzipiert. Ein Leben lang," Berliner Zeitung* No. 296, December 18/19, 2015.

Shooting Nosferatu *in Kafka's Castle*

1. Basil Copper, *The Vampire in Legend, Fact and Art* (London: Corgi, 1975), 129.
2. Peter-André Alt, "Die Burg des Grauens," *Süddeutsche Zeitung*, May 10, 2010.
3. Today Děčín.
4. Albin Grau, "Filmreise zur Hohen Tatra," *Film-Tribüne* No. 34/36, 1921, 33.
5. Albin Grau, "Licht-Regie im Film," *Film-B.Z. (Berliner Zeitung)*, March 5, 1922.
6. Albin Grau, "Über das Wesen der künstlerischen Filmausstattung," *Gebrauchsgraphik* No. 6, 1924/25.
7. *Film-Kurier*, May 11, 1920.
8. *Der Film*, No. 43, October 23, 1921. At that time the budget was already tight. Ruth Landshoff-Yorck recalled that she was asked to bring her own nightgown because the production had to save money on the costumes.

Premiere and Contemporary Reviews

1. *Lichtbild-Bühne Berlin* No. 11, March 11, 1922, 49.
2. Berndt Heller quoted from *F. W. Murnau Nosferatu* (Munich 1987), 30.
3. Stefan Eickhoff, *Max Schreck: Gespenstertheater* (Munich 2009), 138/140.

4. Hans Wollenberg, *Licht-Bild-Bühne* No. 11, March 11, 1922, 49.

Frater Pacitius, Aleister Crowley's Berlin Disciple

1. Sylvain Exertier, *Positif* No. 228, March 1980, In: *F. W. Murnau Nosferatu*. A publication of Kulturreferat Munich 1987. Editor: Fritz Göttler, pp. 38ff.
2. Albin Grau, "Wie Nosferatu entstand," *Film-Kurier* No. 289, December 12, 1921.
3. Albin Grau, *Der Film der Intellektuellen*, 1921.
4. Joris-Karl Huysmans, *Lust for the Devil: The Erotic-Satanic Art of Felicien Rops* (Wet Angels Books, 2013).
5. W. Somerset, Maugham, *A Fragment of Autobiography*, reprinted as the Preface to *The Magician*, Vintage Classics (Penguin Random House, 2000).
6. John T. Soister, *Of Gods and Monsters: A Critical Guide to Universal Studios' Science Fiction, Horror and Mystery Films, 1929–1939* (Jefferson, NC: McFarland, 1999).

Great Plans and Nightly Hallucinations

1. Big budget film.
2. Letter *Prana* to F. W. Murnau, dated December 21, 1921, *Deutsche Kinemathek*, Schriftgutarchiv.
3. Lawrence Poston, III, *Beyond the Occult: The Godwinian Nexus of Bulwer's Zanoni*. www.thevictorianweb.org/authors/bulwer/zanoni.poston.html
4. R. W., *Berliner Börsen-Courier*, No. 110, March 6, 1922.
5. E. J., *Vossische Zeitung*, No. 111, March 7, 1922.
6. H. W., [Hans Wollenberg] *Lichtbild-Bühne*, No. 11, March 11, 1922, 49.
7. *Film-Kurier*, August 10, 1922.
8. Lotte Reiniger, *Shadow Theatres and Shadow Films* (London and New York: B. T. Batsford Ltd. and Watson-Guptill, 1970), 11.
9. Kantonsbibliothek [Canton library] Appenzell Ausserrhoden, Switzerland. KBAR, CMO.

Fritz Lang Hits It Big— And Murnau Carries On

1. Patrick McGilligan, *Fritz Lang: The Nature of the Beast* (New York: St. Martin's Press, 1997), 63.
2. Fritz Olimsky, *Der Kinematograph* No. 794, May 7, 1922.
3. *Die Filmwoche* No. 7, 1924, Special issue: *Die Nibelungen*.
4. Original slogans, Metropolis Press and Propaganda Bulletin (Berlin: Parufamet, 1927).
5. H. G. Wells, *The New York Times*, April 17, 1927.
6. Patrick McGilligan, *Fritz Lang: The Nature of the Beast* (New York: St. Martin's Press, 1997).
7. David Desser, "Race, Space, and Class: The Politics of Cityscapes in Science-Fiction Films," in *Alien Zone II: The Spaces of Science-Fiction Cinema*, Annette Kuhn, ed. (London and New York: Verso, 1999), 82–83.
8. Sydney newspaper advertisement announcing the screening of *Metropolis* in April 1928.
9. Herbert Moulton, "Magical Effects Brought to Screen by Unique Process," *Los Angeles Times*, April 18, 1926.
10. Note by Walter Schulze-Mittendorf, *Der Maschinenmensch: Seine Entstehung [The Machine Man: Its Creation]*.
11. H. G. Wells, *The New York Times*, April 17, 1927.
12. Klaus Kreimeier, *The Ufa Story: A History of Germany's Greatest Film Company 1918–1945* (Berkeley/Los Angeles/London: University of California Press, 1999), 251.
13. Barry Keith Grant (ed.), *Fritz Lang Interviews* (Jackson: University Press of Mississippi, 2003), 69.
14. *Berliner Lokal-Anzeiger* No. 487, October 15, 1926.
15. Carl Zuckmayer, *Geheimreport* (Göttingen: Wallstein Verlag, 2002).
16. Deutsche Kinemathek Berlin, Marlene Dietrich Collection.

The Vampire Jew and the Curse of Anti-Semitism

1. Lotte H. Eisner, *Murnau* (Berkeley & Los Angeles: University of California Press, 1973), 110.
2. *Ibid.*, 115.
3. Kim Newman, *Vampyr* and the Vampire: https://www.criterion.com/current/.../560-vampyr-and-the-vampi...
4. Cited in Erwin Leiser, *"Deutschland erwache!" Propaganda im Film des Dritten Reiches* (Reinbek/Hamburg: Rowohlt, 1968), 30.
5. Obviously Kracauer had seen a print of *Nosferatu* that put back Stoker's role names.
6. Siegfried Kracauer, *From Caligari to Hitler: A Psychological History of the German Film* (Princeton, NJ: Princeton University Press, 1947).
7. *Nosferatu at 90: The Jew as Vampire*: https://www.Thevaultofhorror.blogspot.com/.../nosferatu-at-90-jew-as-vampir...
8. The cynicism of the Adenauer era allowed the same Giese to voice the commentary for the West German release trailer of Ernst Lubitsch's *To Be or Not to Be*.
9. *Nosferatu at 90: The Jew as a Vampire*: thevaultofhorror.blogspot.com/2012/07/nosferatu-at-90-jew-as-vampire.html.
10. *Ibid.*
11. See: Marie Mulvey-Roberts, *Dangerous Bodies: Historicising the Gothic Corporeal*, published on University Press Scholarship Online, September 2016: *In chapter 4, the vampire theme continues with a discussion of Dracula, Jewishness and blood. It will be argued that the early film version of Stoker's novel, Nosferatu, encrypts the ostensibly dangerous vampire body as metaphor for the crypto-Jew.*
12. Charlotte Hansen, "Anti-Semitism in Bram Stoker's Dracula," Georgetown University, *Methods of Literary and Cultural Studies*, February 25, 2015.
13. *Nosferatu*, Independent Study in World Cinema, The Unaffiliated Critic, January 20, 2013: https://unaffiliatedcritic.com/2013/01/nosferatu-1922/
14. Ushi Derman, *The Myth of the Vampire Jew and Blood Libels*, translation to English: Danna Paz Prins.

Beit Hatfutsot The Museum of the Jewish People. https://www.bh.org.il/blog-items/myth-vampire-jew-blood-libels/**

The Revival of Nosferatu

1. Announced in the publishing program of Belleville Verlag Michael Farin, Munich.
2. George Pendle, *The Occult Rocket Scientist Who Conjured Spirits with L. Ron Hubbard*, Jan 2, 2015: https://motherboard.vice.com/en_us/the-last-of-the-magicians
3. *Ibid.*
4. *New York Film Society,* January 1960.
5. January 14, 2014.
6. Same is true for the 8mm versions of *Dr. Mabuse, der Spieler* printed by *DEFA Laboratories.*

Christopher Lee vs. Klaus Kinski

1. "Lugosi at Emotional Pitch in Dracula Role," Universal Publicity Release, circa 1931.
2. "Bela Lugosi Haunted by Role He Made Famous in Dracula," Universal Publicity Release, circa 1931.
3. *L.A. Record,* June 7, 1931.
4. "Horror is my Business," *Films and Filming,* 1963.
5. "An Exclusive Interview with Christopher 'Dracula' Lee," *Nightmare Magazine,* 1974. The interview was taped the 21st of July, 1973, in Madrid.
6. *Ibid.*
7. Lars-Olav Beier, "Werner Herzog's German Comeback: Cinema Legend Heads Berlinale Jury," *Der Spiegel,* February 11, 2010.
8. Werner Herzog, *The Making of* Nosferatu, documentary, 1979.
9. *'Fascist, Psychopath, Genius, Madman': Klaus Kinski, as Jesus Christ, Loses his Shit Onstage.* https://dangerousminds.net/comments/fascist_psychopath_genius_madman_klaus_kinski_as_jesus-christ.
10. TV interview given during the shooting of the film.
11. www.guido-boehm.info
12. Reiko Kruk lived in France. Herzog's *Nosferatu* was her first film work.
13. Patrick Maxwell, "Nosferatu Reawakens: An Evening with Werner Herzog and a New 35mm Print of Nosferatu the Vampyre," May 21, 2014: www.moviemaker.com
14. Michael Atkinson, "A Bloody Disgrace," *The Guardian,* January 25, 2001.
15. Patrick Maxwell, "Nosferatu Reawakens," www.moviemaker.com
16. Interview with Luigi Cozzi, Offscreen Festival 2011, Reel News.
17. Robert Simonson/Christine Ehren, *Nikolai Kinski Follows in Dad's Footsteps in* Nosferatu. Playbill, *May 25–June 22.* May 25, 2000.

Shadow of the Vampire

1. Michael Atkinson, "A Bloody Disgrace," *The Guardian,* January 25, 2001.
2. E. Elias Merhige on *Shadow of the Vampire,* December 23, 2000:www.oneguysopinion.com
3. John Lees Comics: Stories, Reviews and Commentary, February 2, 2001.
4. Reviewed by Simon Hill, *End Evil Games,* July 23, 2014.
5. MORIA, Science Fiction, Horror and Fantasy Film Review:moria.co.nz/…/nosferatu-vs-father-pipe-cock-and-sister-funk-2014.
6. Mark Olsen, "Re-release of Werner Herzog's 'Nosferatu': 'It's not a remake,'" *Los Angeles Times,* May 16, 2014.
7. Perri Nemiroff, www.collider.com, February 18, 2016.
8. Zack Sharf, *'The Witch' Breakouts Robert Eggers and Anya Taylor-Joy Reuniting for 'Nosferatu' Remake:* www.indiewire.com
9. Emily Kubincaner, "*Nosferatu* and the Challenges of a Horror Remake," August 17, 2017: https://filmschoolrejects.com/nosferatu-challenges-horror.remake/
10. Pamela Hutchinson, "Nosferaaarghtu: why they shouldn't remake Dracula's best film outing," *The Guardian,* July 29, 2015.

The Nosferatu *Filmography*

1. Not confirmed and rather unlikely.
2. Fanny Schreck's appearance is not confirmed.
3. It is rather unlikely that the little girl at the window really was Loni Nest.
4. Peter Bradshaw, *"Shadow of the Vampire,"* The *Guardian,* February 2, 2001.

Filmography II

1. Hanns Heinz Ewers, *Anfänge des Films.* Typescript.
2. Frank Maraun, *Der Deutsche Film*: Special Issue 1940/41.
3. Rudolf Kurtz, *Expressionism and Film* (New Barnet, Herts: John Libbey Publishing Ltd., 2016), 75.
4. Film advertisement of the American distributor.
5. *Ibid.*, p. 76.
6. Patrick McGilligan, *Fritz Lang: The Nature of the Beast* (New York: St. Martin's Press, 1997), 70–88.
7. Rudolf Kurtz, *Expressionism and Film* (New Barnet, Herts: John Libbey Publishing Ltd., 2016), 81–82.
8. Lotte Reiniger, *Shadow Theatres and Shadow Films* (London and New York: B. T. Batsford Ltd. and Watson-Guptill, 1970) p. 105–108.
9. Film Museum Munich.
10. Juha Kindberg, Helsinki 2002.

Bibliography

Andriopoulos, Stefan. *Ghostly Apparitions: German Idealism, the Gothic Novel, and Optical Media*. New York: Zone Books, 2013.
Berriatúa, Luciano. *Los proverbios chinos de F. W. Murnau*. Madrid: Filmoteca Espanola, Instituto de las Artes, 1990–92.
Blettenberg, Detlef. *Murnaus Vermächtnis*. Cologne: DuMont, 2010.
Bock, Hans-Michael (ed.). *CineGraph: Lexikon zum deutschsprachigen Film*. Munich: text + kritik, 1984.
_____ [compilation]. *Paul Leni. Grafik Theater Film*. Exhibition Catalogue. Frankfurt am Main: Deutsches Filmmuseum, 1986.
_____, and Wolfgang Jacobsen (ed.). *Henrik Galeen*. Film-Materialien 2. A publication supported by the initiative KOMMUNALES KINO Hamburg e.V. (METROPOLIS). Hamburg-Berlin: May 1992.
Bozza, Mike and Michael Herrmann (ed.). *Schattenbilder—Lichtgestalten: Das Kino von Fritz Lang und F. W. Murnau*. Filmstudien. Bielefeld: transcript Verlag, 2009.
Brill, Olaf. *Der Caligari-Komplex*. Munich: Belleville, 2012.
Copper, Basil. *The Vampire in Legend, Fact and Art*. London: Corgi, 1975.
Courtade, Pierre. *Cinéma Expressioniste*. Paris: Henri Veyrier, 1984.
Cronin, Paul (ed.). *Herzog on Herzog*. London: Faber & Faber, 2002.
Dahlke, Günther, and Günter Karl (ed.). *Deutsche Spielfilme von den Anfängen bis 1933. Ein Filmführer*. Berlin/GDR: Henschel, 1988.
David, Christian. *Kinski. Die Biographie*. Berlin: Aufbau-Verlag, 2008.
Davidowicz, Klaus S. *Film als Midrasch: der Golem, Dybbuks und andere kabbalistische Elemente im populären Kino*. Göttingen: V&R unipress, 2017.
Eickhoff, Stefan. *Max Schreck. Gespenstertheater*. Munich. Belleville, 2009.
Eisner, Lotte H. *The Haunted Screen: Expressionism in the German Cinema and the Influence of Max Reinhardt*. Oakland: University of California Press, 2008.
_____. *Murnau*. University of California Press, 1973. Frankfurt am Main: Deutsches Filmmuseum, 1979.
Elsaesser, Thomas. *Das Weimarer Kino—aufgeklärt und doppelbödig*. Berlin: Vorwerk 8, 1999.
Erdmann, Hans, Giuseppe Becce and Ludwig Brav. *Allgemeines Handbuch der Film-Musik*. 2 volumes. Berlin-Lichterfelde: Schlesinger'sche Buchhandlung, 1927.
Farin, Michael, and Hans Schmid (ed.). *Nosferatu: Eine Symphonie des Grauens*. Revised edition. Munich: Belleville, 2018.
Friedrich Wilhelm Murnau. Die privaten Fotografien 1926–1931. Berlin, Amerika, Südsee. Catalogue. Berlin: Schwulenmuseum, 2013.
Fritz Langs Metropolis. Edited by Deutsche Kinemathek–Museum für Film und Fernsehen. Munich: Belleville, 2010.
F. W. Murnau Nosferatu. Eine Publikation des Kulturreferates der Landeshauptstadt München 1987. Redaktion: Fritz Göttler.
Gehler, Fred, und Ulrich Kasten. *Friedrich Wilhelm Murnau*. Berlin: Henschel, 1990.
Gerard, Emily. *Transylvanian Superstitions*. London: Henry S. King, 1885.
Geser, Guntram. *Fritz Lang, Metropolis und die Frau im Mond. Zukunftsfilm und Zukunftstechnik in der Stabilisierungszeit der Weimarer Republik*. Meitingen: Corian, 1999.
Geyer, Peter. *Klaus Kinski: Leben, Werk, Wirkung*. Frankfurt am Main: Suhrkamp Verlag, 2006.
Giesen, Rolf. *Lexikon des phantastischen Films. Horror—Science Fiction—Fantasy*. 2 volumes. Berlin; Frankfurt/M; Wien: Ullstein, 1984. [Reprint: Munich: Apex Verlag, 2018.]
_____. *Nazi Propaganda Films: A History and Filmography*. Jefferson, North Carolina: McFarland, 2003.
Gilloch, Graeme. *Siegfried Kracauer: Our Companion in Misfortune*. Cambridge, UK/Malden, MA, USA: Polity Press, 2015.
Grafe, Frieda, and Enno Patalas (ed.). *Licht aus Berlin. Lang Lubitsch Murnau*. Berlin: Brinkmann & Bose, 2003.
Granach, Alexander. *There Goes an Actor*. Garden City: Doubleday, Dorian and Co., Inc., 1945.
Grant, Barry Keith (ed.). *Fritz Lang Interviews*. Jackson: University of Mississippi Press, 2003.
Grob, Norbert. *Fritz Lang: "Ich bin ein Augenmensch."* Berlin: Propyläen Verlag, 2014.
Herzog, Werner. *Vom Gehen im Eis: München-Paris 23.11. bis 14. 12. 1974*. Fischer, 2009.
Hollfelder, Moritz. *Werner Herzog. Die Biografie: "Jeder Film ist eine Eintrittskarte zur Welt."* Munich: Langen-Müller, 2012.
Jackson, Kevin. *Nosferatu—Eine Symphonie des Grauens*. A BFI book. London: Palgrave Macmillan on behalf of the British Film Institute, 2013.
Kaes, Anton. *Shell Shock Cinema: Weimar Culture and*

the Wounds of War. Princeton and Oxford: Princeton University Press, 2009.
Kagelmann, André. *Der Krieg und die Frau. Thea von Harbous Erzählwerk zum Ersten Weltkrieg*. Kassel: Media Net, 2009.
Kalbus, Oskar. *Vom Werden deutscher Filmkunst. 1: Der stumme Film*. Altona-Bahrenfeld: Cigaretten-Bilderdienst, 1935.
Keiner, Reinhold. *Hanns Heinz Ewers und der Phantastische Film*. Studien zur Filmgeschichte 4. Hildesheim: Olms, 1988. [2nd edition E-Book: Kassel 2012.]
_____. *Thea von Harbou und der deutsche Film bis 1933*. Hildesheim/Zurich/New York: 1984.
Kinski, Klaus. *All I Need Is Love*. New York: Random House, 1988.
Kornberger, Silvia. *Vampire, Monster, irre Wissenschaftler: So viel Europa steckt in Hollywoods goldener Horrorfilmära*. Hamburg: disserta Verlag, 2014.
Kracauer, Siegfried. *From Caligari to Hitler: A Psychological History of the German Film*. Princeton, New Jersey: Princeton University Press, 1947.
Kreimeier, Klaus. *The Ufa Story: A History of Germany's Greatest Film Company*. Translated by Robert and Rita Kimber. Berkeley/Los Angeles/London: University of California Press, 1999.
Kugel, Wilfried. *Der Unverantwortliche. Das Leben des Hanns Heinz Ewers*. Düsseldorf: Grupello, 1992.
Kuhn, Annette (ed.). *Alien Zone II: The Spaces of Science-Fiction Cinema*. London and New York: Verso, 1999.
Kurtz, Rudolf. *Expressionism and Film*. New Barnet, Herts: John Libbey Publishing Ltd., 2016. English translation of German original: *Expressionismus und Film*. Berlin: Verlag der Lichtbildbühne, 1926. [Reprint: Zurich 2007.]
Kyrou, Ado. *Le Surréalisme au cinema*. Paris: Arcanes, 1953.
Lamprecht, Gerhard. *Deutsche Stummfilme*. 9 volumes: 1903–1912; 1913–1914; 1915–1916; 1917–1918; 1919; 1920; 1921–1922; 1923–1926; 1927–1931. Berlin: Deutsche Kinemathek e.V., 1967–69.
Leiser, Erwin. *"Deutschland erwache!" Propaganda im Film des Dritten Reiches*. Reinbek/Hamburg: Rowohlt, 1968.
Mack, Max. *Die zappelnde Leinwand*. Berlin: Dr. Ensler & Co., 1916.
McGilligan, Patrick. *Fritz Lang: The Nature of the Beast*. New York: St. Martin's Press, 1997.
McNally, Raymond T. and Radu Florescu. *In Search of Dracula: A true history of Dracula and vampire legends*. New York: Warner Paperback Library, 1973.
Möller, Kai. *Paul Wegener. Sein Leben und seine Rollen. Ein Buch von ihm und über ihn*. Hamburg 1954.
Mulvey-Roberts, Mary. *Dangerous Bodies: Historicising the Gothic Corporeal*. Published to University Press Scholarship Online: September 2016.

Nagl, Tobias. *Die unheimliche Maschine. Rasse und Repräsentation im Weimarer Kino*. Munich: edition text + kritik, 2009.
Noa, Wolfgang. *Paul Wegener*. Berlin/GDR 1964.
Nosferatu: A Symphony of Horror—A Film by F. W. Murnau: A Shot-by-Shot Presentation by Roy A. Sites M.L.A. CreateSpace Independent Publishing Platform, 2014.
Parrill, William B. *European Silent Film on Video: A Critical Guide*. Jefferson, NC: McFarland, 2006.
Pirie, David. *Vampir-Filmkult*. Gütersloh: Prisma Verlag, 1977.
Prinzler, Hans Helmut (ed.). *Friedrich Wilhelm Murnau—Ein Melancholiker des Films*. Berlin: Bertz, 2003.
Prager, Brad (ed.). *A Companion to Werner Herzog*. Chichester et al: Wiley-Blackwell, 2012.
Rodek, Hanns-Georg, and Rolf Giesen. *Nosferatu lebt*. In: Welt am Sonntag, May 21, 2017.
Rops, Félicien, Candice Black, and J.-K. Huysmans. *Lust for the Devil: The Erotic-Satanic Art of Félicien Rops*. [England?]: Wet Angel, 2013
Schoenemann, Heide. *Paul Wegener. Frühe Moderne im Film*. Stuttgart/London 2003.
Seesslen Georg, and Claudius Weil. *Kino des Phantastischen*. Reinbek bei Hamburg: Rowohlt, 1980.
Skal, David J. *Hollywood Gothic: The Tangled Web of Dracula from Novel to Stage to Screen*. Revised ed. Faber & Faber, Inc., 2004.
_____. *Something in the Blood: The Untold Story of Bram Stoker, the Man Who Wrote Dracula*. New York/London: Liveright Publishing Corporation. A Division of W. W. Norton & Company, 2016.
Soister, John T. *Conrad Veidt on Screen. A Comprehensive Illustrated Filmography*. Jefferson, NC: McFarland, 2002.
_____. *Of Gods and Monsters: A Critical Guide to Universal Studios' Science Fiction, Horror and Mystery Films, 1929-1939*. Jefferson, NC: McFarland, 1999.
Stiasny, Philipp. *Zwischen den Welten: Die lebenden Toten, Verlorenen und Heimkehrer des Weimarer Kinos*. In: *Weimarer Kino—neu gesehen*. Berlin: Bertz + Fischer, 2018.
Strauss, Stefan. *Albin Grau—Biografie und Œuvre*. 22 December 2010. Inaugural Dissertation. Ruhr Universität Bochum, Fakultät füt Philologie. First referee: Prof. Dr. Wolfgang Beidenhoff. Second referee: Prof. Dr. Peter M. Spangenberg.
Strzelczyk, Florentine. *Motors and Machines, Robots and Rockets: Harry Piel and Sci-Fi Film in the Third Reich*. In: German Studies Review Vol. 27, No. 3. Published by The John Hopkins University Press, October 2004.
Wahl, Chris (ed.). *Lektionen in Herzog. Neues über Deutschlands verlorenen Filmautor Werner Herzog und sein Werk*. Munich: edition text+kritik, 2011.
Zuckmayer, Carl. *Geheimreport*. Göttingen: Wallstein Verlag, 2002.

Index

Abbott, Bud 4, 120
Abbott & Costello Meet Dr. Jekyll & Mr. Hyde 4
Abbott & Costello Meet Frankenstein 4
Abbott & Costello Meet the Invisible Man 4
Abbott & Costello Meet the Mummy 4
Abel, Alfred 6, 37, 75, 86, 197
Das Abenteuer des Dr. Kircheisen 194
Die Abenteuer des Prinzen Achmed 202–203
Ackerman, Forrest J 2, 33, 126, 130
Ackerman, Wendayne 33
Aden, John 1
The Adventures of Prince Achmed see *Die Abenteuer des Prinzen Achmed*
The Adventures of the Brave Soldier Sveijk [play] 66
Aguirre, der Zorn Gottes 124
Ahasver 179
Aladdins Wunderlampe 182
Albes, Emil 171
Aldor, Bernd 179
Alexander, Kurt 77, 79
Algol 190
All Quiet on the Western Front 64
Almodóvar, Pedro 133
Alphaville 63
Alraune [movie, 1927] 105, 208–209
Alraune [movie, 1930] 86, 105
Alraune [novel, 1911] 105, 183
Alraune, die Henkerstochter, genannt die Rote Hanne 182
Alraune und der Golem 183
Alt, Peter-André 72
Der Alte und der junge König 90
Altes Herz wird wieder jung 86
Altmann, Max 37

Les Amours de la Reine 5
Amphitryon 86
Am Rande der Welt 67, 86
Der Andere 10, 169
Der Andere Student von Prag 171
Andersen, Hans Christian 18
Andra, Fern 190
Angelus Silesius 17
Anger, Kenneth 2, 101
Antonioni, Michelangelo 133
The Apparitionist see *Der Geisterseher*
Die Arche 183
Argento, Dario 129
The Ark see *Die Arche*
Arnim, Achim von 14
As You Like It [play] 66
Ashby, Hal 133
Askonas, Paul 38
At the Edge of the World see *Am Rande der Welt*
Atlantis 22
Die Augen der Mumie Ma 181
Die Augen des Ole Brandis 171
August der Starke 77, 137
Aus den Akten einer anständigen Frau 87
Aus den Geheimnissen eines Frauenarztes 87
Aus der Urzeit der Erde 205–206
Aventure Malgache 86

Baberske, Robert 97
Balázs, Béla 62
Balderston, John L. 119
Balsamo, Giuseppe 192
Balser, Ewald 87, 116
Bamberger, Ludwig see Berger, Dr. Ludwig
Barnum, P.T. 82
Barrymore, John 34, 106
The Bartered Bride see *Die Verkaufte Braut*
Bassermann, Albert 10, 86

Báthory, Elizabeth 37
Batman Returns 63
Baudelaire, Charles 81
Becce, Giuseppe 76
Behal, Hans 104, 151
Behrenbaum, Hans 32
Belling, Rudolf 19
Bendazzi, Giannalberto 203
Bengen, Alex 36, 87
Bennett, Joan 102
Berber, Anita 29, 90
Der Berg des Schicksals 36
Berger, Grete 11, 171
Berger, Dr. Ludwig 29, 85, 89, 100, 101, 201
Berger, Senta 6
Bergman, Ingmar 116, 133
Bergman, Ingrid 70
Bergner, Elisabeth 6
Berlin—Alexanderplatz 193
Bernhardt, Curtis (Kurt) 67
Bernhardt, Sarah 5
Berriatúa, Luciano 117
Die Biene Maja und ihre Abenteuer 88, 205
Biensfeldt, Paul 11
Das Bildnis von Dorian Gray 178–179
Bildt, Paul 86
Birgel, Willy 86
The Black Cat [movie, 1934] 82
The Black Indies [novel] 92
Blackwood, Algernon 39
Blade af Satans Bog 31, 104
The Blade Runner 14, 63
Blanc, Mel 133
Blaskó, Béla see Lugosi, Béla
Der Blaue Engel 101, 184
Bloch, Chajim 15
Bloch, Robert 29
The Blue Angel see *Der Blaue Engel*
Blue Öyster 132
Blumenberg, Hans 71
Bock, Hans-Michael 37
Böcklin, Arnold 20

Bon Voyage 86
Bonney, Graham 116
Bonsels, Waldemar 88, 205
Boo! 158
Borland, Carroll 120
Bormann, Martin A. 11
Bosch, Hieronymus 39
Botz, Gustav 75, 147–148
Boulanger 87
Boykott 67
Bracht, Eugen 35
Brahm, Otto 5
Brakhage, Stan 114
Brandis, Helmut 69
Brandt, Willy 71
The Brandy Punch see *Die Feuerzangenbowle*
Braun, Wernher von 210
Brauner, Artur 86, 102
Brav, Ludwig 77
Brecht, Bertolt 70, 86, 116, 193, 197
Der Brennende Acker 75
The Bride of Frankenstein 67
Brill, Olaf 27, 28
Browning, Tod 104, 120, 124, 133
Der Bucklige und die Tänzerin 32–33, 34, 39, 188
Buffy the Vampire Slayer 110, 136
Bulwer-Lytton, Edward 39, 84
Bunuel, Luis 104, 133
The Burning Soil see *Der Brennende Acker*
Burton, Tim 120
By Rocket to the Moon see *Frau im Mond*

Das Cabinet des Dr. Caligari (1920) 2, 3, 21, 22–30, 31, 32, 39, 84, 85, 106, 116, 124, 136, 187–188
The Cabinet of Dr. Caligari (1920) see *The Cabinet des Dr. Caligari*
Cage, Nicholas 1
Cagliostros Totenhand 183
Caiano, Mario 129
Calmet, Augustin 115
Caminito, Augusto 129
Čapek, Karel 92
Carmilla [novel] 37, 104
Carreras, James 120
Casablanca 30, 38
The Castle [novel] 72–73
The Cat Creeps 158
Ceaușescu, Nicolae 37–38
Chabrol, Claude 133
Chamisso, Adelbert von 8
Chaney, Lon 63, 64, 105, 174, 210
Chaney, Lon, Jr. 19
Chaplin, Charles 5, 70, 116
Charell, Erik 66

Der Chinesische Götze see *Das Unheimliche Haus, 3. Teil*
Chomón, Segundo de 7
Chrisander, Nils Olaf 69, 174
Christians, Mady 37
Clarke, Mae 158
Claudius, Erich 118
Clewing, Carl 11
Clift, Denison 28
Cobra Verde 124
Cocteau, Jean 28
The Coming Race [novel] 39, 84
Conan Doyle, Arthur 15, 206
El Conde Dracula 123, 124
Cooper, Gary 70, 116
Cooper, James Fenimore 33
Corbucci, Sergio 124
Corda, Maria see Korda, Maria
Corelli, Marie 31
Costello, Lou 4, 120
Count Dracula see *El Conde Dracula*
The Count of Monte Cristo 67
Courths-Mahler, Hedwig 33
Cozzi, Luigi 2, 129
Cristiani, Quirino 203
Cromwell [play] 66
Cronenberg, David 22
Crowley, Aleister 8, 13, 81–82, 84, 85, 101, 113
Cruise, Tom 114
The Curse of Frankenstein 120, 121
Curtiz, Michael 38
Cushing, Peter 3, 63, 120, 121
Der Czardas-König 86
Czibulka, Alfons von 186

Dafoe, Willem 1, 131, 164
Daghofer, Fritz 29
Dagover, Lil 23, 29, 124
Dahlke, Paul 86
D'Amato, Joe 121
Die Dame, der Teufel und die Probiermamsell 182
Dämon Blut 36
Dance of the Vampires 2
Danton 74
Davidson, Paul 5, 6, 11, 19
Dean, James 113
Deane, Hamilton 119
De Palma, Brian 133
De Putti, Lya 75
de Vogt, Carl 89
Delfs, Holger 2, 135
Deltgen, René 86
Del Toro, Benicio 1
del Toro, Guillermo 29
Destiny see *Der Müde Tod*
Deutsch, Ernst 29, 192
Dick, Philip K. 16
Dieb und Weib 36
Dieckmann, Enrico [Heinrich] 36, 83, 85, 87, 88, 118, 138

Dieterle, William [Wilhelm] 6, 201
Dietrich, Marlene 70, 86, 101, 102, 184
The Discovery of Germany see *Die Entdeckung Deutschlands*
Dix, Otto 142
Döblin, Alfred 193
Dr. Jekyll and Mr. Hyde (1920) 33
Dr. Jekyll and Mr. Hyde (1931) 120
Dr. Mabuse the Gambler see *Doktor Mabuse, der Spieler*
Doctor Zhivago 124
The Doctor's Dilemma [play] 66
Dohm, Will 67
Doktor Mabuse, der Spieler 90, 116, 195–196
Doktor Sacrobosco, der grosse Unheimliche 199–200
Doktor Satansohn 175
Dokumentendiebstahl 87
The Doll see *Die Puppe*
Dominik, Hans 173
Don Carlos [play] 67
Don't Look Now 124
Dornröschen 180
Dracula [movie, 1931] 3, 33, 88, 104, 119, 121, 124, 185
Dracula [movie, 1958] 120–121
Dracula [novel, 1897] 36, 37, 40, 80, 109, 133
Dracula, Prince of Darkness 122
Dracula's Death see *Drakula Halála*
Drakula Halála 38
Die 3 Groschen-Oper [play] 193
Die 3 Groschen-Oper [movie] 86
Dreyer, Carl Theodor 31, 67, 104
Drössler, Stefan 117
Droste-Hülshoff, Annette von 14
Du bist die Richtige 69
Eine Dubarry von heute 86
Dudow, Slatan 86
Dumas, Alexandre 66
DuMaurier, George 185, 208
Der Dummkopf 87
Durieux, Tilla 11

Eaten Alive! 121
Ebert, Roger 3
Eckelkamp, Hanns, Jr. 2, 116, 123, 133–134
Eckelkamp, Hanns, Sr. 116
Ed Wood 120
Eerie Tales see *Unheimliche Geschichten*
Egede-Nissen, Aud 69, 174
Eggers, Robert 134–135
Die Ehe der Maria Braun 68, 116

Eickhoff, Stefan 63
Eisenstein, Sergej M. 116
Eiserne Acht 87
Eisner, Lotte H. 3, 31, 33, 39, 103, 116, 123
Ekman, Gösta 206
Elfers, Konrad 116
Elwes, Cary 1
Embrace of the Vampire 130
Die Entdeckung Deutschlands 75, 178
Erdmann, Dr. Hans 76–77, 84, 85, 137, 142
Erlkönigs Tochter 172
Erster April 2000 86
The Eternal Jew see *Der Ewige Jude*
Etlinger, Karl 148–149
Ewers, Hanns Heinz 7, 8, 10, 11, 18, 37, 39, 78, 105, 106, 171, 172, 186, 199, 209
Der Ewige Jude 106–107
Ewiger Strom 36
The Excursion to Tilsit [novel] 101
Exertier, Sylvain 80
The Exorcist 125
The Eyes of the Mummy see *Die Augen der Mumie Ma*

Fairbanks, Douglas 209
Falckenberg, Otto 67
Falkenberg, Paul 111
Der Falschspieler 36
Fanny [play] 66
Fantomas 21
Fassbinder, Rainer Werner 68, 116, 133
Faust [movie, 1926] 6, 100–101, 206
Faust [play] 66, 78
Der Favorit der Königin 66
Fehér, Friedrich 23
Feld, Hans 27
Feldman, Marty 165
Ferrera, Abel 133
Feuchtwanger, Lion 30, 70
Die Feuerzangenbowle 70
Feuillade, Louis 21
Fiebiger, Georg 142–143
Fighters see *Kämpfer*
Finances of the Grand Duke see *Die Finanzen des Grossherzogs*
Die Finanzen des Grossherzogs 67
Fincher, David Lee 29
Firmans, Josef 200
Fischer, Samuel 70
Fischer, O.W. 6
Fisher, Terence 120
Fitzcarraldo 124
Flaherty, Robert J. 101
Das Fliegende Auto 189
Der Fliegende Holländer 181

The Flying Car see *Das Fliegende Auto*
The Flying Dutchman see *Der Fliegende Holländer*
Fonda, Henry 102
Fønss, Olaf 22, 36
For a Few Dollars More 124
For Whom the Bell Tolls 70
Ford, John 88, 116
4 Devils 63
Fox, William 101
Franco, Jess 33, 123, 197
François, Hardy von 149–150
Franken, Gisbert 127
Frankenpimp 132
Frankenstein [movie, 1910] 15
Frankenstein [movie, 1931] 3, 16, 19, 120
Frankenstein Meets the Wolf Man 26, 120
Frankenstein, or The Modern Prometheus [novel] 14, 176
Franz Ferdinand of Austria, Archduke 18
Frau im Mond 99, 210
Fräulein Hoffmanns Erzählungen 67
Freeland, John 101
Freitag, der 13. see *Das Unheimliche Haus, 2. Teil*
Freund, Karl 6, 34, 75, 97, 100
Frey, A.M. 87
Fridericus Rex 74
Friedrich, Caspar David 80
Fritsch, Willy 99
Fröhlich, Gustav 83
From Morn to Midnight see *Von morgens bis mitternachts*
Frye, Dwight 124
Fulci, Lucio 121
Fundvogel 105
Furcht 179

Gabin, Jean 102
Gad, Urban 9
Galeen, Henrik 1, 2, 4, 6, 12, 18, 34, 35, 37, 38, 39, 40, 62, 64, 81, 84, 86, 105, 113, 133, 134, 137, 138–139, 172
Game of Thrones 90
Der Gang in die Nacht 36
Ganz, Bruno 126
Garbo, Greta 70
Das Gasthaus an der Themse 124
Gaynor, Janet 101
Gebühr, Otto 74
Gefährliche Fracht 69
Das Gefängnis auf dem Meeresgrunde 191
Das Geheimnis der Gelben Narzissen 124
Das Geheimnis der M-Strahlen 172

Geheimnisse des Orients 209
Geheimnisse einer Seele 206
Der Geheimnisvolle Spiegel 209–210
Der Geisterseher 199
Gelbin, Cathy S. 19
The General 116
Genschow, Fritz 86
Genuine 39, 189–190
George, Heinrich 6, 99
Gerard, Emily 39
Gérard, Henriette 104, 105
Gernsback, Hugo 92
Gesang, Isidor see Gottowt, John
Gesek, Ludwig 10
Das Gesicht im Mondschein 36
Der Gespenster-Klub 194
Die Gespensterstunde 177–178
Geutebrück, Jens 2, 64, 65, 117–118
The Ghost of Frankenstein 19
The Ghoul 86
Gide, André 114
Giehse, Therese 67
Giese, Harry 107–108
Gioia, Dana 132
Das Glas Wasser 85, 89
Gliese, Rochus 19
Glombeck, Robert 10
Gnass, Friedrich 86
Godard, Jean-Luc 63, 133
Goebbels, Dr. Joseph 86, 90, 100, 105, 107
Goethe, Johann Wolfgang von 7, 66, 78, 79, 100
Gogol, Nikolai 66
Gold [project] 83
Goldberg, Heinz 83
Die Goldene Pest 195
Der Golem [movie] 2, 15–17, 18, 37. 172, 183
Der Golem [novel] 15, 17–18, 80
Der Golem und die Tänzerin 178
Der Golem—wie er in die Welt kam 19, 29, 191
Golling, Alexander 86
Gordon, Richard 120
Goritzke, Paul W. 85
Gorki, Maxim 69
Goron, Sascha 75
Gotthelf, Jeremias 192
Gottowt, John 4, 6, 12, 34, 39, 137, 170
Der Graf von Cagliostro 191–192
Granach, Alexander 4, 6, 30, 43, 70, 83, 85, 86, 88, 109, 110, 137, 144, 200
Granach, Gad 30
The Grand Duke's Finances see *Die Finanzen des Grossherzogs*
Grau, Albin 4, 34, 35, 36, 37, 64, 71, 73, 74, 75, 79, 80–82,

85, 86, 87, 88, 100, 104, 113, 116, 119, 133, 138, 199
Grau, Annamaria 113
Grau, Gustav Alwin [father] 35
Grau, Hermann 172
Grau, Laurence [Laura] 113
Great Catherine [play] 66
The Great God Pan [novel] 87
The Great Silence 124
Gregorius, Gregor A. *see* Grosche, Eugen
Griffith, David Wark 31
Grimm, Jacob 7, 14, 32, 78
Grimm, Wilhelm 7, 32, 78
Gronach, Jessaja *see* Granach, Alexander
Grosche, Eugen 82
Die grosse Wette 92, 173
Grube, Elisabeth 77
Die Gruft mit dem Rätselschloss 124
Grünau, Curt von 36, 37
Gründgens, Gustaf 6, 67, 69
Grune, Karl 67, 86
Guckel, Hans Erdmann Timotheos *see* Erdmann, Dr. Hans
Guderian, Heinz 199
Guderian, Paul Albert 199
Gulliver's Travels [project] 96–97
Gunzburg, Nicolas Louis Alexandre, Baron de 104

Haas, Willy 75
Hackenberger, engineer 74
Hagen, Louis 202
Halbblut 89
Halm, Peter 18
Hameister, Willy 26
Hamilton, Margaret 65
Hamlet [movie, 1921] 76
Hamlet [play] 69
The Hands of Orlac see Orlacs Hände
Hanfstaengl, Ernst 8
Hangmen Also Die! 70
Hanneles Himmelfahrt [play] 66
Hans Trutz im Schlaraffenland 179–180
Hans Westmar Einer von vielen 105
Harbou, Thea von 75, 85, 89–90, 99, 100
Hardwicke, Cedric 86
Hardy, Oliver 116
Harlan, Veit 30, 69, 70, 86, 90, 106
Harryhausen, Ray 20
Hartmann, Dr. Franz 81
Hartmann, Paul 37
Hasselmann, Karl 11
Hauff, Wilhelm 31, 180
The Haunted Castle (1921) *see Schloss Vogelöd*

The Haunted Castle (1960) *see Das Spukschloss im Spessart*
Hauptmann, Gerhart 22, 66, 100
Das Haus zum Mond 192–193
The Head of Janus see Der Januskopf
Heggie, O.P. 67
Heideschulmeister Uwe Karsten 86
Heine, Anselma 184
Heinz, Wolfgang 55, 56, 146–147
Heller, Berndt 77, 116
Helm, Brigitte 67, 86, 97, 105
Hemingway, Ernest 70
Henderson, Alva 132
Henning, Magnus 67
Herakles 123
Herbst, Helmut 9
Herder, Johann Gottfried 172
Die Herrin der Welt 89, 186
Der Herrscher 90
Herzfeld, Guido 150
Herzog, Werner 2, 123–127, 133, 134, 135, 165
Heymann, Robert 31, 33, 180
High Noon 116
Hilde Warren and Death see Hilde Warren und der Tod
Hilde Warren und der Tod 179
Hippler, Dr. Fritz 106, 108
Hirschfeld, Magnus 8
Hitchcock, Alfred 68, 70, 86, 116, 171
Hitler, Adolf 7, 8, 64, 67, 85, 86, 99, 100, 105, 106, 127, 199
Hochtouren im Vorfrühling 85
Hoffmann, E.T.A. 8, 10, 14, 18, 78, 81, 92, 106, 174
Hoffmanns Erzählungen [movie, 1916] 174
Höflich, Lucie 11
Hofmann, Ernst 31
Hohenheim, Philip von *see* Paracelsus
Holk, Heinrich O. *see* Dieckmann, Enrico
Höllenträume [project] 83
Homunculus 21, 36, 81, 175–176, 179
Homunkulieschen 176
Homunkulieschen wird Filmdiva 176
Horror of Dracula see Dracula [movie, 1958]
Horst Wessel [novel] 105
The House of Frankenstein 26
Hubbard, L. Ron 84, 113, 114
Hubschmid, Paul Christian 2, 6, 102
Hugo, Victor 32
The Hunchback and the Dancer see Der Bucklige und die Tänzerin

The Hunchback of Notre Dame (1923) 64
The Hunchback of Notre Dame (1939) 201
Hunte, Otto 90, 95, 99
Huppertz, Gottfried 116
The Hustler 95
Hutchinson, Pamela 135
Huth, Dr. Walther 74
Hutton, Barbara 142
Huysmans, Joris Karl 82
Hypnose 185
Hypnose und Suggestion 36

Ibsen, Henrik 32, 66
The Idiot 125
Ikarus, der fliegende Mensch 182
Ikarus, the Flying Man see Ikarus, der fliegende Mensch
In Nacht und Eis 21
In the Jungle of the Cities [play] 197
The Indian Tomb see Das Indische Grabmal
Das Indische Grabmal (1921) 22, 63, 89, 195
Das Indische Grabmal (1959) 102
Das Indische Tuch 124
The Informer [movie, 1929] 88
The Informer [movie, 1935] 88
Ingram, Rex 13
I.N.R.I. 200
Die Insel der Seligen 5–6, 31, 170–171
Interview with the Vampire: The Vampire Chronicles 114
Intolerance 31
Invasion of the Body Snatchers 108
The Invisible Man 173
Irving, Henry 38
The Island of the Blessed see Die Insel der Seligen
It Came from Outer Space 108
Ivan Grosny 75
Ivan the Terrible see Ivan Grosny
Ivens, Joris 69

Jackson, Michael 130
Jackson, Peter 122, 134
Jacques, Norbert 196
Die Jagd nach dem Dollar 36
Jannings, Emil 6, 74, 86, 90, 100, 101, 181, 206
Janowitz, Hans 25, 27, 28, 33, 39
Der Januskopf 33, 34, 188–189
Jesserer, Gertraud 6
Jessner, Leopold 70
Jew Suss [movie, 1934] 30
Jew Suss [movie, 1940] *see Jud Süss* [movie, 1940]
Joan of Arc see Das Mädchen Johanna

John, Georg 179
Jones, Doug 29
Jones, Terry 133
Jud Süss [movie, 1940] 20, 29, 30, 90, 106
Jud Süss [novel] 30
Judex 21
Junge, Alfred 30
Jürgens, Udo 116

Kafka, Franz 72–73
Kaiser, Roland 116
The Kaiser, the Beast of Berlin 64
Das Kalte Herz [movie, 1924] 201
Das Kalte Herz [movie, 1950] 201
Kameradschaft 86
Der Kampf der Tertia 67
Kämpfer 69, 70
Kan, Erwin van 132
Karloff, Boris 6, 19, 63, 82, 86, 120
Kasten, Ulrich 23
Katz, Steven A. 1, 131
Der Kaufmann von Venedig 66–67
Kaul, Walter 33
Kaulbach, Wilhelm von 70
Keaton, Buster 116
Kellner, Carl 81
Kermbach, Otto 77
Kerouac, Jack 115
Kertész, Mihály *see* Curtiz, Michael
Kettelhut, Erich 90–91, 95, 97, 99
Kieling, Wolfgang 68
Kier, Udo 1
King, Stephen 65
King Kong (1933) 106, 134, 173
King Kong (2005) 134
Kinski, Klaus 2, 84, 119, 123–127, 129–130, 133, 134, 136, 165
Kinski, Nikolai 125, 130
Kinski Paganini 84
Klabund [Alfred Georg Hermann Henschke] 66
Klaue, Wolfgang 2, 117
Klein, Heinrich 81
Klein-Rogge, Rudolf 88, 89, 90, 91, 98, 99, 188
Klingler, Werner 67
Klöpfer, Eugen 75
Der Knabe in Blau 31
Knecht, Anne 130
The Knight [project] 134
Knudsen, Lars 135
Kohn, Joseph Seligmann 14
Kokoschka, Oskar 70, 142
Kolberg 69, 90
Konstantin, Leopoldine 171
Koppenhöfer, Maria 86

Korda, Alexander 29, 86
Korda, Maria 86
Kornblum, Hans Walter 205
Kortner, Fritz 32, 88
Kracauer, Siegfried 3, 7, 27, 28, 30, 105, 106, 113
Kraft, Robert 173
Kräly, Hanns 76
Krampf, Günther 4, 85–86, 140–141
Krauss, Werner 6, 20, 23, 29, 30, 74, 75, 88, 178, 201, 206
Der Krieg und die Frau [novel] 89–90
Kruk, Reiko 125
Kubin, Alfred 25, 80
Kubrick, Stanley 205
Kugel, Wilfried 10
Kuhle Wampe 86
Kun, Béla 33
Kunstmann, Ernst 96
Kurfürstendamm: Ein Höllenspuk in 6 Akten 188
Kurosawa, Akira 116, 133
Kurtz, Rudolf 190, 201
Kyrou, Ado 63
Kyser, Hans 100, 106

Ladengast, Walter 126
Laemmle, Carl, Jr. [Julius] 119
Laemmle, Carl, Sr. 29, 64, 65, 96
Lajthay, Károly 38
Lamprecht, Gerhard 11, 103
Landau, Martin 120
Landshoff, Ruth 70, 146
Landshoff-Yorck, Ruth *see* Landshoff, Ruth
Lang, Anton 89
Lang, Fritz 27, 70, 75, 84, 86, 88, 89–95, 99, 100, 101, 102, 179, 184, 194, 197, 198, 210
Lang, Pauline 89, 100
Langer, Gilda 19
Langlois, Henri 115
The Language of Shadows: Friedrich Wilhelm Murnau and His Films 165
The Last Company see *Die Last Kompagnie*
The Last Days of Pompeii [novel] 39
The Last Laugh see *Der Letzte Mann*
The Last Waltz see *Der Letzte Walzer*
Latté, Lily 100
Laughton, Charles 201
Laurel, Stan 116
Lean, David 124
Leatherstocking: The Deerslayer see *Lederstrumpf: Der Wildtöter*
Lebende Buddhas 12, 13, 203–204

Das Lebende Rätsel 175
Lederer, Hugo 28
Lederstrumpf: Der Wildtöter [movie] 33
Lee, Christopher 2, 3, 63, 119, 121–123, 124
LeFanu, Joseph Sheridan 37, 104
Die Legende von der heiligen Simplicia 85, 190–191
Der Leidensweg der Blanche Gordon 36
Leiser, Erwin 116
Leni, Paul 6, 29, 180, 201, 202
Lenin, Vladimir 137
Lenzi, Umberto 121
Leone, Sergio 124
Leroux, Gaston 174
Lessing, Gotthold Ephraim 66
Die Letzte Kompagnie 86
Der Letzte Mann 34, 100, 116
Der Letzte Walzer 88
Die Letzten Vier von Santa Cruz 67
Levine, Jeff 1
Die Liebe der Jeanne Ney 86
Liebeneiner, Wolfgang 86
Liebesleben der Natur 36
Die Lieblingsfrau des Maharadscha 85
Liebmann, Robert 184
Lied über dem Tal 69
Lipowetzki [producer] 34
Lippert, Robert L. 28
Liszt, Franz 83
Litauische Nacht 36
Living Buddhas see *Lebende Buddhas*
Loanic, Minhoi Geneviève 125
Löb, Karl 86
Loew, Rabbi Judah 14, 15, 18, 94, 191
The Love Pirate see *Pietro der Korsar*
Lommel, Michael 11
London After Midnight 105
Loos, Theodor 86, 99
Lord of the Rings 122
Lorey, Guillarmo 87
Lorre, Peter 100, 127
The Lost Shadow see *Der Verlorene Schatten*
The Lost Shoe see *Der Verlorene Schuh*
The Lost World 206
The Love Pirate see *Pietro der Korsar*
Löwitsch, Klaus 6
Lubitsch, Ernst 6, 33, 69, 76, 101, 175, 180, 185
Lucas, George 122
Lucidi, Maurizio 129
Lucifer 196
Lucifer Rising 2

Lucrezia Borgia [novel] 32
Ludendorff, Erich 79
Luftpirat und sein lenkbares Luftschiff, Der [pulp series] 189
Die Luftpiraten 189
Lugosi, Béla 3, 6, 28, 33, 63, 82, 104, 119–120, 124, 185, 189
Lugosi, Hope 33
Lumet, Sidney 133
Ly, Grete 36

M 86, 100
Macbeth [play] 69
Machen, Arthur 87
Mack, Max 67, 85
The Mad Ghoul 76
Das Mädchen Johanna 86
Madness see *Wahnsinn*
Maffay, Peter 116
The Magician [movie] 82
The Magician [novel] 13, 82
Malkovich, John 1, 131, 164, 165
Man Eater 121
The Man Who Laughs 29
Mandel, Rena 104
Mann, Erika 67
Mann, Heinrich 71
Mann, Thomas 67, 70, 71
Mann für Mann 68
Ein Mann will nach Deutschland 137
March, Fredric 120
Marian, Ferdinand 87
Mark of the Vampire 120
Markus, Winnie 6
Marschner, Heinrich 79
Martin, George R.R. 90
Martin, Karlheinz 193
The Masque of the Red Death [short story] 184
Mastrovito, Andrea 167
Matkowsky, Adalbert 66
Mátray, Ernst 69
Maugham, W. Somerset 13, 82
Maurischat, Fritz 2
Maurus, Gerda 99
May, Eva 85, 191
May, Joe 22, 63, 85, 89, 191
May, Karl 33
May, Mia 89, 191
Mayer, Carl 25, 28, 29, 36, 100, 101
Mayne, Ferdy 2
McGilligan, Patrick 194
Mead, Margaret 142
Meinert, Rudolf 23, 25, 26, 190
Mein Kampf [documentary] 116
Méliès, Georges 7, 20
Die Memoiren des Satans 31, 33, 180
The Memoirs of Beelzebub see *Die Memoiren des Satans*
Mendes, Lothar 30

Mengers, Minna 69
Menschen 36
The Merchant of Venice see *Der Kaufmann von Venedig*
Merhige, E. Elias 1, 131
The Merry Wives of Windsor [play] 66
Mesina, Ines 77
Metropolis 6, 67, 84, 92–95, 99, 100, 101, 116, 197, 206–207
Metzger, Radley 133
Meyerink, Hubert von 87
Meyrink, Gustav 15, 17–18, 39, 80, 186, 188
Midnight City of the Deathbird [radio play] 132
A Midsummer Night's Dream [play] 66, 69
A Midsummer Night's Dream [movie] 6, 201
Mikels, Ted V. 133
Milland, Ray 102
Milton, Ernest 67
Minetti, Bernhard 86
Minna von Barnhelm [play] 66
The Miser [play] 64
The Mistress of the World see *Die Herrin der Welt*
Moissi, Alexander 11, 171, 181
Molière 63
Monk, Egon 116
Monteverdi, Claudio 77
Morena, Erna 36
Morgan, Jack 3
Mountain of Destiny see *Der Berg des Schicksals*
Der Müde Tod 86, 116, 193–194
Müller, Pauline see Synd, Lu
The Mummy 6
Münzenberg, Willi 142
Murnau, Friedrich Wilhelm 1, 2, 3, 4, 6, 19, 31, 32, 33, 34, 36, 37, 38, 39, 62, 63, 64, 65, 67, 89, 70, 71, 72, 73, 74, 75, 77, 81, 82, 83, 86, 100, 101, 103, 104, 114, 115, 119, 131, 136, 138, 164, 165, 189
Musaeus, Karl August 176
Mutter Krausens Fahrt ins Glück 74
Mutter Krause's Journey to Happiness see *Mutter Krausens Fahrt ins Glück*
Mysterien eines Frisiersalons 197
The Mystery of the Marie Celeste 28
Mystery Science Theater 3000 133

Nächte des Grauens 88, 177
Nächte des Schreckens see *Nächte des Grauens*
Nachtgestalten 185–186
Nalder, Reggie 65

Nathan der Weise 66
Negri, Pola 181
Nemetz, Max 4, 55, 146
Nest, Loni 19, 151
Neues vom Hexer 124
Neumann, Hans 204
Newman, Kim 104
Newman, Paul 95
Die Nibelungen [movie, 1924] 88, 90–92, 99, 100, 102, 198–199
Die Nibelungen [movie, 1966] 102
Die Nibelungen [play, 1861] 66
Niccolo Paganini [project] 83
Nielsen, Asta 8, 12, 76, 204
Nietzsche, Friedrich 32
Night Creatures see *Nachtgestalten*
Ninotchka 70
Noa, Wolfgang 10
Non Mortuus [project] 84
Normann, Fanny see Schreck, Fanny
Nosferatu [comic book] 132
Nosferatu [English Gothic band] 132
Nosferatu [opera, 2005] 132
Nosferatu [2013, cut-out animation] 165
Nosferatu (2018) 167
Nosferatu [Robert Eggers's film project] 134–135
Nosferatu, a Symphony of Claymation 165
Nosferatu a Venezia 129–130, 159–160
Nosferatu—Eine Symphonie des Grauens 1, 2, 4, 6, 12, 13, 18, 30, 35, 38, 39, 41–61, 62, 63, 64, 65, 69, 70, 71–79, 80, 83, 84, 85, 86, 87, 88, 99, 101, 103–104, 105, 106, 108, 109, 113, 114–118, 119, 120, 123, 131, 132, 133, 134, 135, 136, 155–157, 164, 165, 166, 170, 171, 199, 200
Nosferatu in Love 166
Nosferatu Over the Cuckoo's Nest 165
Nosferatu—Phantom der Nacht 2, 124–127, 133, 136, 158–159, 165
Nosferatu: The Friendly Vampire 165
Nosferatu the Vampire [musical] 132
Nosferatu: The Wrath of Malachi [game] 132
Nosferatu—Vampirische Leidenschaft see *Embrace of the Vampire*
Nosferatu vs. Father Pipecock & Sister Funk 132–133, 165–166

Nosferatu's Secret Love Child!
 167–168
Notorious 171
NYsferatu: Symphony of a Century 166–167

Obal, Max 11
Oberth, Hermann 210
O'Brien, George 101
Offenbach, Jacques 174
O'Flaherty, Liam 88
Ogle, Charles 16
Ohm Krüger 68, 86
Ohne Mutter geht es nicht 86
Ondra, Anny 67
One Glass of Water see *Das Glas Wasser*
Orlacs Hände 29, 38, 86, 204
Oswald, Richard 29, 83, 105, 177, 184
The Other see *Der Andere*
Otto, Hanns 74
Our Heavenly Bodies see *Wunder der Schöpfung*

Pabst, Georg Wilhelm 86
Paganini [movie] 83, 85
Paganini, Niccolò 83–84
Paget, Debra 102
Pagnol, Marcel 66
Pal, George 98
Pan's Labyrinth 29
Paracelsus 22
Patalas, Enno 116
The Patriot 76
Paul, Jean 10
Peckinpah, Sam 133
Peer Gynt 67
Pericles, Prince of Tyre [play] 66
Perret, Léonce 173
Die Pest in Florenz 27, 183–184
Pfleger, Hermine see May, Mia
Phantom 197
Das Phantom der Oper (1915) 69, 174
The Phantom of the Opera (1925) 64, 174
Phantom Ship see *The Mystery of the Marie Celeste*
The Picture of Dorian Gray see *Das Bildnis des Dorian Gray*
Piel, Harry 92, 173–174, 175, 189
Pierrot [monodrama] 77
Pietro der Korsar 86, 88
Pirie, David 62
Piscator, Erwin 66, 70, 137
Pitt, Brad 114
Plague in Florence see *Die Pest in Florenz*
Plan 9 from Outer Space 120
Platen, Karl 88
The Pleasure Garden 70
Plummer, Christopher 130
Plumpe, Bernhard 32

Plumpe, Friedrich Wilhelm see Murnau, Friedrich Wilhelm
Plumpe, Robert 32
Poe, Edgar Allan 8, 33, 78, 81, 174, 184
Poelzig, Hans 12, 19
Pohl, Gerd Josef 2, 126–129, 130
Polanski, Roman 2, 116
Pommer, Erich 25, 26, 89
Ponto, Erich 86, 87
Popol Vuh 127
Poppe, Rosa 66
Porten, Henny 182
Post, Don 126
Powell, Michael 13, 29
Power, Tyrone 102
Praetorius, Johannes 176
Preminger, Otto 6
Preuschhoff, Heinz J. 101
Price, Vincent 63
Primanerehre see *Boykott*
Prinz Keo. Der Raub der Mumie 185
Psycho 29
Pulver, Liselotte 29
Die Puppe 184–185
Der Puppenmacher von Kiang-Ning 199

Der Rächer 124
Raeburn, Malcolm 132
Rains, Claude 171
Rameau, Hans 63, 64, 141–142
Ramper der Tiermensch 12, 63, 208
Ranft, Michael 115
Rasp, Fritz 88, 210
Rasputin [miniseries project] 134
Rasputin [play] 137
Rathenau, Walther 8
Der Rattenfänger 181–182
Ray, Nicholas 133
Reicher, Ernst 173
Reicher, Frank 173
Reif, Fritz 67
Reimann, Walter 23, 26
Reinert, Robert 22
Reinhardt, Max 5, 6, 12, 18, 19, 29, 31, 32, 39, 66, 69, 70, 171, 180, 201
Reiniger, Lotte 202, 203
Reinl, Dr. Harald 102
Die Reiter von Deutsch-Ostafrika 70
Rembrandt [movie, 1942] 116
Reschke, Ernst 84
Reuss, Theodor 81
Rex, Eugen 104, 151–153
Richter, Hans 210
Richter, Paul 88, 91
Der Richter von Zalamea 66
The Riders of German East Africa see *Die Reiter von Deutsch-Ostafrika*

Rieber-Zimmemann, Maria 87
Riefenstahl, Leni 102
Riemann, Johannes 76
Der Ring der drei Wünsche 180–181
Rippert, Otto 21, 27
Rittau, Günther 97, 98
Robert Koch, der Bekämpfer des Todes 86
Robinov, Jeffrey 135
Robinson, Edward G. 102
Robison, Arthur 88, 106
Rodek, Hanns-Georg 2, 63
Roeg, Nicolas 124
Roger, Waldemar see Ronger, Waldemar
Rohlf, Sabine 70
Rohmer, Sax 39
Röhrig, Walter 23, 26
Rohwer, Elisabeth 69
Romero, George A. 133
Ronger, Waldemar 104, 117
Rops, Félicien 81
Rosemary's Baby 126
Rosen, Arthur 75
Rosenberg, Jehuda Judel 14, 15
Rosenberg, Marianne 116
Rosher, Charles 101
Das Rote Plakat 36
Die Rote Redoute 36
Die Rothschilds 68
Rübezahls Hochzeit 176
Rühmann, Heinz 70
The Ruler see *Der Herrscher*
R.U.R. [play] 92
Rye, Stellan 10, 11

Sadoul, Georges 114
Salem's Lot 65
Salloker, Angela 86
Salmonova, Lyda 18–19, 176
Salon Dora Green 37
Sandrelli, Amanda 130
Saptaparna [project] 83
Sárený, Jozef 151
Satanas 31–32, 187
Sauerbruch, Ferdinand 35
Sauerländer, Paul 17
Scanners 22
The Scarlet Pimpernel 67
Schäfer, Horst 2
Schäffer, Sylvester, Jr. 196
Schall, Heinz 76
Schatten 86, 87–88, 100, 199
Scheerbart, Paul 93–94, 190
Schenk, Ilse von 105
Schildkraut, Rudolf 12
Schinderhannes 74
Schirmann, Peter 116
Schlettow, Hans Adalbert 99
Schloss, Sybille 67
Schloss Vogelöd 86
Schmeling, Max 67
Schmidt, Wilhelm 40

Schmitz, Sybille 104
Schnell, Georg Heinrich 4, 70, 145–146, 196
Schnieber, Christina 117
Schoedsack, Ernest B. 133
Schopenhauer, Arthur 32
Schreck, Augustin 68
Schreck, Fanny 66, 86, 150
Schreck, Gisela *see* Uhlen, Gisela
Schreck, Gustav Ferdinand 65
Schreck, Max 1, 3, 4, 6, 12, 13, 45, 48, 49, 51, 56, 63–68, 72, 78, 81, 84, 85, 105, 117, 119, 120, 124, 125, 131, 136, 137, 143, 164, 197
Schreck, Pauline 65, 66, 68
Schröder, Greta 4, 6, 12, 42, 69–70, 83, 84, 85, 143–144, 171, 174
Schröder-Wegener, Margarete *see* Schröder, Greta
Schrutz, Demetrius 66
Schüfftan, Eugen 95–96
Schulze, H[ugo] O[tto] 2, 98
Schulze-Mittendorf, Walter 97–98
Schünzel, Reinhold 29, 177
Schutz, Maurice 67
Schwabach, Erik-Ernst 18
Der Schwarze Abt 124
Der Schwarze Meister 188
Die Schwarze Spinne 192
Schwarzes Blut 173
Secrets of a Soul see Geheimnisse einer Seele
Secrets of the Orient see Geheimnisse des Orients
Seeber, Guido 9, 11, 12, 17, 20, 191
Seghers, Anna 70
Seibold, Willy 87, 88
Selpin, Herbert 70
Die Seltsame Gräfin 124
Ein Seltsamer Fall 172
Sennett, Mack 72
Seubert, Martha *see* Dagover, Lil
The Seventh Cross 70
Shadow of the Vampire 1, 131–132, 160–165
Shakespeare, William 5, 32, 66, 76, 124, 171, 204
The Shape of Water 29
Shaw, George Bernard 66
Shelley, Mary W. 14, 16, 176
Shrek 63, 136
Siefert, Gertrud 27
The Silence 116
Siodmak, Curt 2, 26
Sixty Glorious Years 69
Sklaven fremden Willens see Hypnose
The Sleeper Wakes [novel] 175

Sodom und Gomorrha 38
Ein Sommernachtstraum 204
Ein Sommernachtstraum in unserer Zeit 171
The Sorrows of Satan [movie] 31
The Sorrows of Satan [novel] 31
S.O.S. Die Insel der Tränen 18
The Spiders see Die Spinnen
Spielberg, Steven 177
Spies, Walter 72, 142
Die Spinnen 89, 186–187
Spione 86
Spongebob Squarepants 136
Das Spukschloss im Spessart 29
Squitieri, Pasquale 129
Das Stahltier 67
Stanislavski, Konstantin Sergeevich 3
Star Wars 122, 132
Staudte, Wolfgang 75
Steiner, Berta 18
Steiner, Hermann 18
Steiner, Rudolf 37
Steiner-Prag, Hugo 18, 80
Das Steinerne Phantom [project] 37
Der Steinerne Reiter 197–198
Steinhoff, Hans 105
Steinrück, Albert 19, 185
Stern, Ernst 19
Sternheim, Julius 23
Stevenson, Garcia 101
Stevenson, Robert Louis 33, 39, 184
Stiasny, Philipp 2, 35, 36
Stoker, Bram 37, 38, 39, 40, 62, 80, 88, 104, 109, 133
Stoker, Florence 88, 104
Störtebeker, Klaus 71
The Strange Case of Captain Ramper see Ramper der Tiermensch
Strange Case of Dr. Jekyll and Mr. Hyde [novella] 33, 172
Stranz, Fred 66
Die Strasse 67
Straus, Oscar 88
Strauss, Stefan 2, 113
The Street see Die Strasse
Streicher, Julius 109–110
Strindberg, August 5
Strobl, Karl Hans 186
Struss, Karl 101
Stuck, Franz von 18
The Student of Prague see Der Student von Prag
Der Student von Prag (1913) 7, 8, 9, 10, 20, 34, 169–170, 194, 208
Der Student von Prag (1926) 10, 86, 105, 207–208
Der Student von Prag (1935) 88, 106
Sturges, Preston 133

Sturm 36
Sturm, Hans 12
Suchland, Otto 77
Sudermann, Hermann 101
Der Sumpfteufel [project] 83
Sumurun 33
Sunrise 19, 63, 101
Švankmajer, Jan 133
Svengali (1927) 137, 208
Svengali (1931) 106
Synd, Lu 178

Tabu 72, 101
The Tales of Hoffmann [operetta] 174
Tales of Horror see Unheimliche Geschichten
Der Tanz in den Tod 66
Die Tänzerin [dancing pantomime] 77
Die Tarantel 190
Tartuffe [Tartüff] 100
Taschendiebe 87
Tati, Jacques 116
Taubert, Dr. Eberhard 107
Taylor, Bernard J. 132
Taylor-Joy, Anna 135
Das Testament des Dr. Mabuse 77
Teufelssymphonie 196–197, 200
The Thief of Bagdad (1924) 209
The Thief of Bagdad (1940) 29
Thimig, Hermann 194
The Third Man 29
The Thousand Eyes of Dr. Mabuse 102
The Three Musketeers 66
The Threepenny Opera see Die 3-Groschen Oper
Thring, George Herbert 88
Tietze, Conrad 36
Tiller, Nadja 6
The Time Machine [novel] 92
Tolkien, J.R.R. 122
Der Tolle Bomberg 77
Torn Curtain 68
Die Toten Augen von London 124
Die Toten erwachen 173
Der Totentanz 8–9
Towers, Harry Alan 123
Tracy, Spencer 102
Trissenaar, Elisabeth 6
True Blood 110
Truffaut, François 116
Der Tunnel 67
Die Tür mit den sieben Schlössern 124
The Twelfth Hour see Die Zwölfte Stunde
Twelvetrees, Helen 158
Twilight 110
2001: A Spce Odyssey 205
Tykwer, Tom 133

Index

Ucicky, Gustav 86
Uhlen, Gisela 68
Uhlen, Susanne 68
Ulmer, Edgar G. 63, 82
Das Unbewohnte Haus [novel] 87
Und wandern sollst Du ruhelos... 172–173
Und wieder 48 69
Der Unheimliche Chinese 66
Unheimliche Geschichten 29, 184
Das Unheimliche Haus 176–177
Das Unheimliche Haus, 2. Teil 177
Das Unheimliche Haus, 3. Teil 177
Ein Unsichtbarer geht durch die Stadt 173
Urwaldsymphonie 77

Vadim, Roger 133
Valentin, Karl 197
Valentino, Rudolph 119
Vampire in Venice see *Nosferatu a Venezia*
Vampyr 67, 104–105
Der Vampyr [opera] 79
Der Vampyr des Schlosses 173
Van Hoy, Jay 135
Van Sloan, Edward 121
"Van Viele, Eric" (?) 151
Veidt, Conrad 3, 10, 21, 23, 29–30, 33, 34, 36, 38, 62, 63, 83, 86, 100, 105, 187, 189
Eine Venezianische Nacht 5–6
Venohr, Albert 55, 86, 147
Der Verführte 11
Die Verkaufte Braut 67
Der Verlorene 127
Der Verlorene Schatten 194
Der Verlorene Schuh 85, 89, 200–201
Verne, Jules 173, 189
Vernon, Howard 63
Das Verrätertor 124
Victoria the Great 69
Villon, François 124
Vlad III. Dräculea 38
Vollbrecht, Karl 90–91, 95, 99
Vollmoeller, Karl Gustav 70
Von morgens bis mitternachts 192
Vormittags-Spuk 210
Voyagis, Yorgo 130

Das Wachsfigurenkabinett 29, 201
Wagner, Fritz Arno 1, 4, 75, 86, 88, 103, 139–140
Wagner, Richard 118
Wahnsinn 184
Walbrook, Anton see Wohlbrück, Adolf
The Walk Into the Night see *Der Gang in die Nacht*
Walken, Christopher 63
Wallace, Edgar 68, 124
Waltz, Christoph 6
Das Wandernde Licht 177
Wangel, Hedwig 67
Wangenheim, Eduard Clemens Franz Freiherr von see Winterstein, Eduard von
Wangenheim, Gustav von 3, 4, 6, 42, 45, 48, 49, 51, 68–69, 70, 75, 84, 88, 99, 144
Warm, Hermann 23, 25, 26–27
Warner, Jack L. 6
Warning Shadows see *Schatten*
Wäscher, Aribert 86, 87
Waterloo 67
Watt, Tony 132–133
Waxworks see *Das Wachsfigurenkabinett*
Way Out West 116
Wayne, Justin 132
Wegener, Paul 7, 8, 9, 11, 12, 13, 15, 18, 19, 20, 29, 34, 37, 39, 63, 69, 77, 82, 85, 89, 105, 137–138, 172, 176, 178, 180, 183, 194, 204, 208, 209
Weir, Peter 133
Weiss, Helmut 70
Weiss, Josef 10
Wellin, Arthur 33
Wells, H.G. 92, 98–99, 173, 175
Wendlandt, Horst 124
Wessel, Horst 105
West, Julian see Gunzburg, Baron de
Westfront 1918 86
Weyher, Ruth 88
Whale, James 67
Whelan, Tim 29
Whitehill, Clarence 118
Whiteside Parsons, John 113–114
Whitlock, Albert 29

Wicki, Bernhard 6
Widtmann, Heinz 37
Wiene, Dr. Robert 22, 23, 25, 26, 27, 28, 29, 31, 32, 38, 39, 86, 190
Wiesenberg, Heinrich see Galeen, Henrik
Wiesenthal, Grete 11, 172
Wilcox, Herbert 69
The Wild Duck [play] 66
Wilde, Oscar 124
Wilder, Billy 105
Wilder, Gene 165
Winehouse, Amy 133
Winter, Max 66
Winterstein, Eduard von 69, 75
The Witch 134, 135
Witt, Georg 29
Witte, Heinrich 149
The Wizard of Oz 65
Wohlbrück, Adolf 88
Wolf, Christopher Howard 132
The Wolf Man 26
Wolff, Kurt 17
Wood, Ed 133
Wood, Sam 70
Wronker-Flatow, Dr. 88
Wunder der Schöpfung 205
Die Wunderlampe des Hradschin 174–175

Der Yoghi 176
York von Wartenberg, Friedrich Heinrich 70
Young, Jack H. 65
Young Frankenstein 165
Young Sherlock Holmes 177

Zanoni [movie project] 84
Zanoni [novel] 39, 84
Zeiske, Erich 11
Der Zerbrochene Krug 86
Ziehfuss, Edmund 95
Zimmermann, Albert 200
Zimmermann, Franz 87
Der Zinker 124
Zinnemann, Fred 70
Zombi 2 121
Zucker und Zimt 69
Zuckmayer, Carl 101
Zukor, Adolph 5
Die Zwölfte Stunde 103–104, 117, 157–158

www.ingramcontent.com/pod-product-compliance
Ingram Content Group UK Ltd.
Pitfield, Milton Keynes, MK11 3LW, UK
UKHW051652180426
11947UKWH00021B/1924